ADVANCE PRAISE

"Alex Tapscott takes us to the frontiers of finance, where digital assets are transforming money, reimagining financial markets, and disrupting leading institutions, including central banks. *Digital Asset Revolution* is a wake-up call for financial and business leaders everywhere."

—*Hon. J. Christopher Giancarlo, Former Chairman, US Commodity Futures Trading Commission; Co-founder, Digital Dollar Project*

"This is an important book for enterprise leaders to better understand blockchain and how digital assets will change the future of business."

—*Tyler Winklevoss, Co-founder and Chief Executive Officer, Gemini Trust Company LLC*

"To succeed as a trader in the markets, you need to do your own research—especially in the fast paced and constantly evolving world of digital assets. Whether you're starting your journey or you're a seasoned market participant, *Digital Asset Revolution* should be on your reading list. Alex Tapscott's latest is brimming with original insights on the digital asset ecosystem, with some far-sighted predictions on where we are headed."

—*Scott Melker, Host, The Wolf of All Streets Podcast*

"*Digital Asset Revolution* demonstrates the tremendous potential of Web3 and digital assets by describing their roles in powering this new era of technology innovation and economic progress. Specifically, the categorization of digital assets turns this fast-moving and rapidly evolving industry into a clear and understandable framework without losing any of the nuance or significance of what is occurring. A must-read!"

—*Sandeep Nailwal, Co-founder, Polygon Technology*

"Alex Tapscott is a leading voice in the digital asset world. His latest book, *Digital Asset Revolution*, is required reading for investors, executives, and anyone else trying to understand how to capitalize on the next big thing."

—*Daniela Cambone, Editor-at-Large and Chief Anchor, Stansberry Research*

"Alex Tapscott has been ahead of the curve on digital assets since the beginning. In *Digital Asset Revolution*, he offers the clearest picture yet of where we are headed. This book is required reading for investors, executives, hobbyists, and anyone trying to understand the future."

—*John Wu, President, Ava Labs Inc.*

"To grasp the fundamentals and intricacies of the most revolutionary financial innovations of our time, there is no better guide than Alex Tapscott's *Digital Asset Revolution*— as insightful and instructive for those looking to understand the future of personal and global finance as it is for those investing in it."

—*Perianne Boring, Founder and President, Chamber of Digital Commerce*

"As distrust in our institutions hits new lows, the digital asset revolution that began with bitcoin lights a different path, one where we have greater agency over our assets and ourselves. How far can this go? *Digital Asset Revolution* explores the far-reaching consequences of this revolution, from money and banking to art and real estate and even our identities online."

—*Bill Barhydt, Founder and Chief Executive Officer, Abra*

"Every technological shift needs that one book that centers the conversation. Read and absorb."

—*Matthew Roszak, Co-founder and Chairman, Bloq Inc.*

"This book has plenty to chew on for the business reader but also contains insights into how we forge that new path in practical ways."

—*Ethan Buchman, Chief Executive Officer, Informal Systems; Co-founder, Cosmos Network*

DIGITAL ASSET
REVOLUTION

BLOCKCHAIN RESEARCH INSTITUTE
ENTERPRISE SERIES

*Digital Asset Revolution: How Blockchain Is
Decentralizing Finance and Disrupting Wall Street*
Edited with a preface by Alex Tapscott

*Financial Services Revolution: How Blockchain Is
Transforming Money, Markets, and Banking*
Edited with a preface by Alex Tapscott

*Platform Revolution: Blockchain Technology
as the Operating System of the Digital Age*
Edited with a preface by Don Tapscott

*Supply Chain Revolution: How Blockchain
Technology Is Transforming the Global Flow of Assets*
Edited with a foreword by Don Tapscott

ALSO BY
ALEX TAPSCOTT

Blockchain Revolution: How the Technology
Behind Bitcoin Is Changing Money, Business, and the World,
Penguin Portfolio, 2018
Co-author, Don Tapscott

Blockchain Revolution for the Enterprise Specialization
INSEAD and Coursera, 2019
Co-instructor, Don Tapscott

DIGITAL ASSET REVOLUTION

How **BLOCKCHAIN** Is
Decentralizing Finance and Disrupting Wall Street

Edited with a preface by
ALEX TAPSCOTT
Co-Founder, Blockchain Research Institute

BARLOW BOOKS
fine books for enterprising authors

111 Peter Street, Suite 708, Toronto, ON M5V 2G9 Canada

Copyright © 2022 Blockchain Research Institute

To refer to this book, we suggest the following citation:

> *Digital Asset Revolution: How Blockchain Is Decentralizing Finance and Disrupting Wall Street*, edited with a preface by Alex Tapscott (Toronto: Barlow Books, 2022).

ISBN: 978-1-988025-74-2

Printed in Canada

1 3 5 7 9 10 8 6 4 2

Publisher: Sarah Scott/Barlow Books
Book producer: Tracy Bordian/At Large Editorial Services
Book design (cover and interior) and layout: Ruth Dwight

For more information, visit www.barlowbooks.com.

Barlow Book Publishing Inc.,
96 Elm Avenue, Toronto, ON
M4W 1P2 Canada

CONTENTS

LIST OF CONTRIBUTORS

Mohamed El-Masri is the founder and CEO of PermianChain Technologies Inc. and director and CEO of Brox Equity Ltd. He holds securities qualifications from the Canadian Securities Institute and the Capital Market Authority of Riyadh, KSA.

The **Honorable J. Christopher Giancarlo** served as thirteenth chairman of the US Commodity Futures Trading Commission. He is senior counsel to the international law firm, Willkie Farr & Gallagher, and co-founder of the Digital Dollar Project.

Alan Majer is the founder of Good Robot, exploring the potential of artificial intelligence, robotics, blockchain, and the metaverse. A member of the local "maker" scene, he frequents spaces like HackLab. TO and InterAccess. He holds an MBA from McGill University.

Massimo Morini is chief economist of the Algorand Foundation. He is a professor of fixed income at Bocconi University and teaches blockchain and financial markets at universities in Italy, Switzerland, and the United Kingdom.

Alyze Sam is a blockchain strategist, a novel educator, and a vehemently driven advocate. She is founder and community director of Women in Blockchain International and co-author of *Stablecoin Economy* as well as *Stablecoin Evolution.*

Alex Tapscott is managing director of the Digital Asset Group, a division of Ninepoint Partners LP, an investment firm with $8 billion in assets under management and institutional contracts. Ninepoint's Bitcoin ETF was the first carbon-neutral spot Bitcoin ETF in the world.

Don Tapscott is CEO of the Tapscott Group, executive chairman of the Blockchain Research Institute, an author of 15+ books, an adjunct professor at INSEAD, and former two-term chancellor of Trent University in Ontario.

Anthony D. Williams is co-founder and president of the Digital Entrepreneurship and Economic Performance Centre and co-author (with Don Tapscott) of the groundbreaking best seller, *Wikinomics: How Mass Collaboration Changes Everything*.

Andrew Fennell Young is CEO of Layer2 Blockchain and a co-founder of SX Network (SportX), a DeFi prediction market and blockchain. Andrew specializes in the analysis of economic incentives and tokenomics of new DeFi projects.

PREFACE

Alex Tapscott

Business leaders who are new to blockchain can quickly find themselves overwhelmed or bewildered by the innovative digital assets, peer-to-peer marketplaces, and open economic systems that blockchain pioneers are creating. As a result, they tend to focus on a handful of important blockchain use cases, such as the substitution of bitcoin (BTC) for gold in investor portfolios or government exploration of so-called *central bank digital currencies* (CBDCs).

To these newcomers, acronyms like DeFi and NFTs (for *decentralized finance* and *non-fungible tokens*) are as cryptic as the code underlying them. In this book, we intend to remedy that. In each chapter, we ask executives and investors to step back and witness the grand transformation underway. Financial services, foundational to all industries and economic activity, is undergoing a big shake-up. Every aspect of the sector is changing, from how we move and store value to how we access credit, invest, trade, transact, and insure against risk.

But this upheaval is about more than disrupting existing services like banking or insurance. It's about realizing new business strategies and organizational capabilities that will transform existing industries and redefine the architecture of the firm and other institutions. At the root of this upheaval are blockchains—in essence, software protocols—with which we can create new asset classes, business models, and governance systems for the digital age. In this new age, we can transfer, store, manage, organize, govern, create, fragment, and direct anything and everything of value to whatever purpose we desire peer to peer.

Because of this capability, digital assets have played a high-profile role in funding the Ukrainian war effort against Russia. Twelve days into the conflict, thousands of anonymous individuals (as well as a few companies and public figures) had raised more than $50 million in crypto donations to fight off the invasion and aid those under siege. The anti-Putin art collective Pussy Riot helped coordinate the UkraineDAO, for *decentralized autonomous organization*, a new type of virtual organization enabled by blockchain, which raised over $6.5 million. But this was not just a grass-roots effort. The government of Ukraine's official Twitter account tweeted "stand with the people of Ukraine. Now accepting cryptocurrency donations. Bitcoin, Ethereum, USDT" (for USD Tether, a stablecoin). Within a week, more than $30 million in donations had flooded in.

These new digital assets are also changing every market. In chapter 1, I set the stage for the disruptive effects of DeFi applications on the nine functions that Wall Street currently performs. I explore Web 3 innovations, with Layer 1 and Layer 2 solutions to such implementation challenges as scalability, interoperability, and ease of use. I also expand upon my taxonomy of nine cryptoassets—such as CBDCs, stablecoins, DeFi index funds, synthetic securities, and NFTs—with many examples. Each asset type has different properties, functions, and behaviors. If bitcoin was the spark for the financial services revolution, then DeFi and digital assets are the accelerant.

Chapter 2 covers one of the most critical implementation challenges of blockchain technologies: *interoperability*. Enterprise users are reluctant to tokenize their assets or invest seriously in DeFi and digital asset management capabilities without assurances that they will be able to move these assets across blockchain platforms. What if chosen platforms fail? What if better platforms emerge? Some of the best minds in the space are addressing these issues head-on with a range of innovative solutions. This chapter features two of them: Cosmos and Polkadot. It looks at their origins and ethos, architecture and core technology components (including the role of their native tokens ATOM and DOT), consensus and governance, and the applications already using them. Finally, the author reviews what enterprise decision-makers need to know as they weigh their options. Tech investor Kevin Rooke initiated this project for us. He conducted interviews and mapped out relevant distinctions, and we thank him for this critical legwork. Anthony Williams of DEEP Centre fleshed it out by addressing the interests and concerns of our enterprise stakeholders. They want to understand these interoperability projects from an enterprise perspective, and Anthony did a fine job.

In chapter 3, Andrew Fennell Young of Layer2 and SX Networks discusses the promise of community-owned prediction markets. He argues that decentralized crypto networks are inevitable and important to society. Today, sports and political betting are the most popular genres of prediction markets. Global prediction market protocols allow anyone to create a community-owned-and-operated marketplace to bet on the outcomes of future events, such as whether countries will fulfill their climate change commitments on time. The next multi-billion-dollar prediction market will be a smart contract protocol deployed as a public utility on the Ethereum blockchain, where user ownership will intensify network loyalty and engagement. A *smart contract* is a set of promises, specified in digital form—as a *decentralized application* (dapp)—that includes protocols within which the parties execute these promises.[1] Implementation challenges include voter apathy, stakeholder alignment, ongoing funding, and upgradability because of their decentralized and open-source nature. Predictions markets will become an important tool in leveraging the wisdom of crowds in policy decisions.

In chapter 4, Chris Giancarlo, also known as "CryptoDad" and former chair of US Commodity Futures Trading Commission (CFTC), presents his vision of the digital dollar amid economic disruptions and global turbulence. In conversation with me and Don Tapscott, Giancarlo distinguishes among three types of cryptocurrencies—*distributed* (Bitcoin), *central bank* (US digital dollar), and *corporate* (Facebook's Libra, then Diem, and now Meta's use of the Paxos stablecoin). Giancarlo explains how blockchain technology opens up new policy options and how digital currencies differ from other financial assets. He argues for modernization of our financial infrastructure and regulation, with a US digital dollar as the global reserve currency. Diversity in cryptocurrencies make for a healthy marketplace. Distributed ledgers and smart contracts will eventually transform other financial instruments and unleash the next wave of economic innovation.

In chapter 5, Alyze Sam takes a closer look at distinct kinds of stablecoins and how they provide price stability in DeFi systems. The author achieves three goals. First, she examines different ways to stabilize the price of a cryptocurrency. Some are backed by assets with stable value such as US dollars or gold, others are stabilized by algorithms, and some combine those two approaches. Second, she surveys the landscape of stablecoins and analyzes the top stablecoins by market capitalization. Finally, she suggests ways to use stablecoins in protecting the value of cryptoasset portfolios. Her presentation is by no means dry; she sprinkles in the motivations of several stable-coin entrepreneurs.

Chapter 6 focuses on the creation and use of financial derivatives with smart contracts on blockchain. Its author, Massimo Morini, is a veteran banking professional, a blockchain and financial technology (fintech) expert, and a finance and economics professor. He understands both theory and practice. Featuring Barclays, Nivaura, and MakerDAO, his chapter underscores the importance of financial derivative contracts as use cases for blockchain technology in general and for smart contracts in particular. Blockchain and dapps can increase transparency, automate the movement of collateral, reduce the need for reconciliation, and automate the management of covenants against counterparty default. We include an excerpt of Anthony Williams's case study on Nivaura for greater detail.

Chapter 7 looks at how blockchain creates value through *natural asset tokens* (NATs) in oil and natural gas. Its author Mohamed El-Masri, explains the technology behind the start-up PermianChain. Its use of blockchain is changing how exploration and production companies raise capital and how investors and consumers participate in energy markets. PermianChain's solution consists of a Hyperledger Fabric blockchain explorer, decentralized cloud storage, and an Ethereum-based platform that supports two ERC-20 tokens—one a security token and the other a utility token—plus an idea for powering bitcoin mining rigs that could provide an upstream source of revenue for oil and gas operators. It's the kind of fresh thinking that this industry needs!

The book's final chapter takes an enterprise view of NFTs, those programmable digital assets that spiked again in popularity in 2021, reaching a new level of maturity in tools, infrastructure, and proven use cases. These advances have catalyzed the interest of enterprise leaders seeking to understand the value of NFTs in their businesses. This chapter focuses on what companies should know about this fledgling industry for unique digital assets, from brands and franchises to farming and manufacturing. It is the second piece of research on NFTs by Alan Majer. In his view, NFTs present opportunities to tokenize intellectual property (IP), reputation, conversations, and tangible assets, and new ways to engage fans, customers, employees, and communities. From social media and online gaming to enterprise software and physical goods, organizations should find use cases worth pursuing.

In summary, this is an eminently practical book for professionals responsible for sizing up the potential of blockchain-based digital assets in their businesses, supply chains, and government sectors. It is a must-read for leaders who want to understand how DeFi and these digital assets will transform every aspect of the global economy. Disrupters and incumbents alike will find this compilation of research clear, focused, and directed with a comprehensive framework for understanding the transformation underway.

CHAPTER 1

DIGITAL ASSET REVOLUTION
The Rise of DeFi and the Reinvention of Financial Services
Alex Tapscott

INTRODUCTION: THE BUILDING BLOCKS OF DISRUPTION

Financial services, foundational to all industry and economic activity, is going through the greatest upheaval since the invention of double-entry bookkeeping in the Middle Ages. Every aspect of the industry is about to change, from how we move and store value to how we access credit, invest, trade, transact, and insure against risk. But this upheaval is about more than changes to existing industries like banking or insurance. It's about enabling new business models and organizational capabilities that will not only transform existing industries but also redefine the architecture of the firm and other institutions, change profoundly how we interact online with companies and with each other, alter the fabric of daily life, reimagine the nature of work, and more.

THE RISE OF DIGITAL ASSETS AND THE FUTURE OF FINANCIAL SERVICES

At the root of this upheaval are blockchains, which allow us to create new asset classes, business models, and governance systems for the digital age. The industrial-age solution of companies and vast government bureaucracies coordinating human activity and the movement of value in the economy and in society is coming to an end. Blockchain enables new decentralized governance systems that are more inclusive, participatory, transparent, and trustworthy.

Blockchains are tamper-resistant ledgers of transactions distributed across a network maintained by many parties. These shared ledgers serve as common sources of the truth. In effect, they supplant the records of banks, governments, corporations, and the large technology companies that intermediate much of the digital economy. Blockchains are the first digital medium for value, just as the Internet was the first digital medium for information.

In this brave new world, we can move, store, manage, organize, govern, create, fragment, and direct anything and everything of value to whatever end we desire peer to peer. Financial services are no longer centralized within an industry; they are decentralized across blockchain networks such as Bitcoin, Ethereum, Solana, Terra Luna, Avalanche, and Cosmos. DeFi is shaking the windows and rattling the walls of Wall Street banks, government agencies, and global institutions. Call it the DeFi Revolution. Like many revolutions, it holds great promise and great peril. Critics malign its chaotic and seemingly uncoordinated growth as well as its potential to displace jobs and accuse it of undermining the monetary sovereignty of governments, exacerbating inequality, and warming the planet.

The revolution began in 2008 with the launch of the Bitcoin blockchain. Its creator Satoshi Nakamoto once quipped, "I'm better with code than words."[2] But his brilliant white paper, "Bitcoin: A Peer-to-Peer Electronic Cash System," introduced a radical new concept: cash for the Internet and a means of minting, moving, and storing value without intermediaries such as banks and governments.[3] What's more, bitcoin worked. It set the wheels in motion for changes we see now.

DeFi extends Satoshi's concept of peer-to-peer (P2P) electronic cash to lending, trading, investing, managing risk, and more, all of which are built on top of distributed networks, not corporations. These innovations are possible thanks to a breakthrough called a *smart contract,* an immutable self-executing dapp settled on a blockchain such as Ethereum. Contracts are the foundation of every asset class, every corporation, and all economic activity. Yet, most of today's contracts are quite dumb. The changes wrought by dapps in general and smart contracts in particular will be cataclysmic. Every industry will feel DeFi's impact, because finance is the cardiovascular system of the global economy, the lifeline of all other industries.

WEB 3 AND THE NEW INTERNET OF VALUE

In *Blockchain Revolution,* we predicted that blockchains would usher in a new era of the Internet that we dubbed "the Internet of value," where individuals could transact, do business, and create value in a trustless and P2P way without the need for traditional intermediaries and gatekeepers. This was a radical idea and a big departure from the old ways of doing things. The first era of the Internet—the Internet of *information*—was more limited. In Web 1, the Internet was mainly a broadcast medium for publishing information, mostly text but also some images and video. In Web 2, the Internet evolved into a collaborative communication medium: a platform for mass organizing online (e.g., Wikipedia, GitHub), building communities (as on Reddit and Slack), engaging on social media (e.g., TikTok, YouTube), and hosting web apps (e.g., Dropbox, Google Analytics) that have become critical to the fabric of daily life.[4]

With Web 2, we rely on intermediaries—not only banks, but also social media giants and digital conglomerates—to perform many essential functions, from moving and storing value to verifying identities and performing such basic business logic as record keeping, contracting, and so forth, all to establish trust in online transactions. This reliance is problematic for several reasons. For one, such intermediaries are centralized, which makes them vulnerable to cyberattack and corruption. Financial intermediaries also add friction to transactions online, adding delays of days or weeks, charging fees as high as

20 percent for international money transfers, and engaging in other rent-seeking behavior.

Banks as well as social media companies and Internet service providers are gatekeepers that exclude many people. In banking, over a billion people lack access to financial services. These gatekeepers also capture all the data and much of the value created online—the largest companies in the world are digital conglomerates like Apple and social media companies like Facebook, which have built their empires in part or in whole on user data. But they don't protect our privacy—think of the breaches of Facebook, Nintendo, Twitter, Zoom, and even Whisper in 2020.[5] Those in control often misalign the incentives of management, shareholders, and deposit holders (known as *moral hazard*) so that managers act in the short term for their own sake at the expense of everyone else. We saw this misalignment in the actions of the big banks during the financial crisis of 2008, when managers took on outsized risks to earn handsome bonuses at the expense of clients, shareholders, and ultimately taxpayers.

Chris Dixon, general partner at the venture capital firm Andreessen Horowitz, captured the central limitation of Web 2: "Web 2 left out digital property rights. When you use a site (or app), it would only let you borrow or rent things. Imagine if in the real world you had to buy everything from scratch every time you went to a new place. That's Web 2."[6] Consider videogames, where every time we download a new game, we must buy that game's digital goods. We can't take them with us and, if the game developer goes belly up or changes the code, then we may lose them forever. We rent our identities because every time we log onto a new service, we share personal information about ourselves. Our identities are not owned by us but by the digital conglomerates and other third parties who have access to it. They monetize it, reaping vast rewards, while we get bread crumbs.

Blockchain gives us a way to digitize and manage our property rights online peer to peer. Digital bearer assets, commonly referred to as *tokens*, enable us to hold and port valuable digital goods from platform to platform online. These goods can be currencies, securities, and other financial assets as well as collectibles, IP, identities, and the as-yet unimagined. Dixon explained how this new Internet of value, commonly referred to as *Web 3*, will reshape our global economy:

> Like websites, tokens are digital primitives that can be generalized to represent almost anything—money, art, photo, music, text, code, game items, control, access, and whatever people dream up in the future. Users can now have a persistent inventory of objects in their wallet that they take from one app to another. If their objects increase in value, the user gets the upside. This is a big change from Web 2 where the upside was mostly captured by tech companies.[7]

Web 3 will be built on top of blockchain networks. But just what networks exactly? At the bottom of Web 3 are the platforms like Ethereum and Solana that enable us to create, move, and manage digital goods, and interact with them via dapps. On top of these so-called "Layer 1" platforms can be additional blockchains that help to scale the Layer 1s so they're more useful. These "Layer 2" platforms like Polygon help to reduce the cost and increase the metabolism of protocols like Ethereum by moving some transactions off the main chain, where the network can become congested due to DeFi's surging popularity.

Connecting the various Layer 1s with each other (so we can move assets seamlessly between different platforms) are interoperability protocols such as Cosmos and Polkadot. Cosmos supports an "Internet of blockchains" known as IBC (the inter-blockchain communication protocol) that allows many other chains to connect with one another so that assets and applications can interoperate across different chains. More than $125 billion worth of assets are connected through IBC. Finally, on top of this stack are the dapps in DeFi, NFTs, and beyond. We will discuss these different kinds of networks and corresponding cryptoassets and their impact on finance and more in this chapter.

THE GOLDEN NINE: ESSENTIAL FUNCTIONS OF THE FINANCIAL INDUSTRY

DeFi is already disrupting capital markets. In one year, the DeFi industry's market capitalization has ballooned 30 times to $150 billion.[8] The total value of user deposits (known in the industry as *total value locked* or TVL) has surged 100 times to nearly $200 billion.[9] What's driving this unprecedented growth?

Sandeep Nailwal, co-founder of multibillion-dollar blockchain protocol Polygon explained, "DeFi solves five key problems inherent in the current system of finance—centralized control, limited accessibility, inefficiency, lack of interoperability, and lack of transparency—by transforming legacy financial products into trustless and transparent protocols that run without intermediaries."[10] Here is a preview of how DeFi addresses these issues in each of the nine functions of the finance industry:

1. **Storing value:** Individuals and institutions can use noncustodial wallets like MakerDAO to act as their own banks, and third-party custodians can hold crypto at scale for institutions. For managing and protecting shared resources, Gnosis Safe has *multisignature* (multisig) capability, meaning that groups can program transactions to require more than one signature to execute them.[11] DAO treasuries are upending how organizations think of storing and allocating capital.

2. **Moving value:** BTC, MakerDAO's DAI, Terra Luna's UST, the Centre Consortium's USD Coin (USDC), Tether (USDT), and other stablecoins route around banks, PayPal's Venmo,

Early Warning Services' Zelle, the Society for Worldwide Interbank Financial Telecommunications (SWIFT) network, and other interbank settlement systems.

3. **Lending value:** Pooled lending protocols such as Compound (COMP) and Aave (AAVE) augment savings accounts at banks and other financial intermediaries and have better yields to boot.

4. **Funding and investing:** Investment aggregators such as Yearn Finance (YFI) and Rarible (RARI) could ultimately disintermediate investment advisers, mutual funds, *exchange-traded funds* (ETFs), and roboadvisers.

5. **Exchanging value:** Decentralized exchanges (DEXes) such as Uniswap (UNI), SushiSwap (SUSHI), and QuickSwap (QUICK) are competing with centralized cryptocurrency exchanges for liquidity and dollar volumes and will be the model for all exchanges, including today's centralized stock exchanges such as the New York Stock Exchange (NYSE) and the Nasdaq marketplace.[12]

6. **Insuring value and managing risk:** On-chain insurance such as Nexus Mutual and derivatives platforms such as the SX Network (SX), Perpetual Protocol (PERP), and dYdX (DYDX) could supplement or replace insurance policies and over-the-counter (OTC) derivatives.[13]

7. **Analyzing value:** On-chain data analysis such as DeFi Llama, DeFi Pulse, Open-orgs.info, and others produces a rich array of information on the movement, storage, and status of all digital assets. Messari and CoinGecko are the Bloomberg and Thomson Reuters of the new DeFi world.

8. **Accounting for and auditing value:** Block explorers such as Etherscan and PolygonScan track asset movements in

real time. Contract auditors such as Zeppelin and DeFi
Score could augment or even replace the key work of
the Big Four accounting firms Deloitte Touche Tohmatsu
(Deloitte), Ernst & Young (EY), Klynveld Peat Marwick
Goerdeler (KPMG), and PricewaterhouseCoopers (PwC).[14]

9. **Authenticating identity:** Accessing open-source DeFi
    protocols requires no formal verification. Pseudonymous
    or anonymous identities are common. Persistent, portable,
    blockchain-based identities are becoming more common
    online.[15] As DeFi scales with institutions and as regulators
    tighten rules, there is a growing need for a reliable,
    immutable on-chain identity system.[16]

As DeFi scales with institutions and as regulators tighten rules,
we need a reliable, immutable digital identity system. Protocols such
as Shyft and SelfKey are addressing this need. The lines between
traditional finance and DeFi will blur as DeFi adoption rates grow
in usage and TVL. As Robert Leshner, founder of Compound Labs,
a leading lending DeFi protocol, tweeted, "DeFi is not going to be
called DeFi in the next five years. It's just going to be called finance.
And all finance is going to run on blockchains; most assets will make
their way onto a blockchain."[17] In this chapter, we describe how DeFi
is disrupting every aspect of the industry.

A TAXONOMY FOR DIGITAL ASSETS

With DeFi, a new ecosystem of digital assets is emerging.[18] Our token
taxonomy has grown to nine assets:

1. **Cryptocurrencies (aka digital money):** Bitcoin is the
    mother of all cryptocurrencies with a market capitalization
    of over $1 trillion and tens of millions of users. It functions
    like cash for the Internet and a final settlement layer
    for the crypto economy. It's digital gold for investors

and a lifeline for many of the world's unbanked. Bitcoin is unrivaled in this role. Other cryptocurrencies such as Monera and Zcash tried to improve on bitcoin by enhancing privacy but remain minor players.

2. **Protocol tokens:** These are the native tokens of Layer 1 blockchains and are used to power transactions and secure these networks. Examples include ether, the native token of Ethereum; AVAX, the native token of Avalanche; and ATOM, the native token of Cosmos.

3. **Governance tokens:** Governance tokens such as Uniswap's UNI, Compound's COMP, and Aave's AAVE token give holders say in the governance of DAOs and dapps. As dapps gain users and increase TVL, their governance tokens often appreciate. For example, the value of UNI has grown from $2 billion to a decentralized exchange of over $15 billion in one year.[19] Protocol tokens also give holders governance rights but for convenience's sake we will not call them governance tokens.

4. **Non-fungible tokens:** NFTs are unique digital assets; they provide a means to verify the scarcity, provenance, and ownership of these assets. They can also represent physical assets such as sports memorabilia and luxury goods. Fine art NFTs alone are worth more than $65 billion a year.[20]

5. **Exchange tokens:** Crypto-exchange tokens such as Binance Coin (BNB) and the FTX Token (FTT), valued at $110 billion and $7.6 billion respectively, are native to centralized exchanges like Binance and the FTX ecosystem.[21] Typically, these tokens are essential to the exchange's functionality and incentivize adoption, but they are more centrally managed and confer no governance rights. BNB serves a dual purpose as an exchange token

and the native token of the Layer1 Binance Smart Chain, which is why it's so valuable.

6. **Securities tokens:** There are three kinds of securities tokens: *digitally native securities* such as DeFi investment funds, *synthetic securities* such as Mirrored Google (mGOOGL) and Mirrored Tesla (mTSLA), and *securities tokens* originated by traditional financial entities such as investment banks or asset managers.[22] They are transforming markets for stocks, bonds, and derivatives.

7. **Stablecoins:** Stablecoins are cryptoassets with stable value such as USDT and UST, with a total market value of $125 billion in early October.[23] They use different methods to stabilize their value. *Centralized* stablecoins are backed by deposits of cash and equivalents. *Decentralized* stablecoins are collateralized by cryptoassets held in smart contracts.

8. **Natural asset tokens:** These are digital assets backed by real-world commodities such as oil or gas, land, or carbon. For example, the blockchain-based ecology network Regen is connecting land stewards who protect and conserve ecosystems with buyers of offsets through the Regen registry, bringing transparency, liquidity, and verifiability to the carbon credit market.

9. **Central bank digital currencies:** CBDCs are crypto versions of fiat currency such as China's digital renminbi and South Korea's digital won.[24] Advocates tout their potential to reduce friction, improve stability, and broaden financial access; opponents point to their potential use for mass surveillance and political oppression.

FIGURE 1-1

DEFI ASSETS BY SECTOR

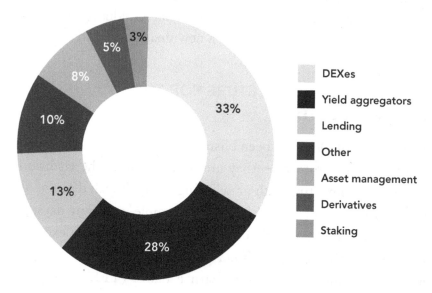

Sources of data: DeFi Pulse, *DeFiPulse.com*; and DeFi Llama, *DeFiLlama.com*, 30 Sept. 2021.

This taxonomy is not exhaustive or predictive of every use case for blockchain and digital assets. Unlike taxonomies in nature, it is also not completely mutually exclusive: one asset may fall into more than one category. However, any asset falls primarily into one of these categories. Overall, we have attempted to organize this ecosystem of disparate assets into a coherent structure so that we can better understand and discuss what's happening.

DECENTRALIZED FINANCE IS EATING WALL STREET

DeFi is not fintech. Fintech applications, although important, still require banks and other intermediaries to establish trust between parties, verify account balances, and perform the business logic—clearing, settling, contracting, and so forth—that makes the system work. In the end, most fintech innovation is digital wallpaper, a sleek user interface that conceals the Rube Goldberg contraption underneath. In this sense, DeFi is a new financial architecture.

DEFI: A NEW ARCHITECTURE FOR THE FINANCIAL SYSTEM

The growth of DeFi has been blistering. In under two years, many of these DeFi protocols—they aren't start-ups in the traditional sense—are competing with or eclipsing many fintech darlings and fast encroaching on Wall Street. For example, on many days, the volumes on the decentralized exchange Uniswap have exceeded those on Coinbase, a $60 billion NYSE-listed company.[25] The automated investment aggregator Yearn Finance (YFI, pronounced "Wi-Fi"), through which investors pool capital in a smart contract that invests on their behalf, hit $5 billion TVL within its first year.[26] By contrast, fintech company Wealthsimple took more than six years to reach the same value.[27] MakerDAO's stablecoin DAI (pegged to USD) does far more volume daily than Venmo.[28] In the second quarter of 2021, the Ethereum network settled $2.5 trillion in transactions, up 1,500 percent year over year, driven primarily by DeFi and stablecoins.[29]

In today's financial markets, value accrues to large banks and hedge funds, in part, because they can offer economies of scale and greater liquidity.[30] In the DeFi ecosystem, value accrues to protocols, not to corporations. Protocols can deliver the economies of scale and efficiencies of the big banks, but in a way that anyone can access. As Ethan Buchman, co-founder of DeFi leader Cosmos, a $10 billion blockchain, said, "Decentralization of finance is really the democratization of finance. It's about eradicating barriers."[31] Peng Zhong, chief executive officer (CEO) of Tendermint, put it this way:

DeFi democratizes access to financial products that most people around the world are barred from accessing, providing a level playing field to everyday services as well as exciting investment opportunities that were previously only in the domain of the ultra-wealthy. ... We want to empower people to control their own finances and understand that they no longer need the permission of banks or other gatekeepers to secure a better financial future.[32]

THE GOLDEN NINE: HOW DEFI IS REIMAGINING WALL STREET

Moving value

Digital assets are transforming how we move value in three important ways. First, usage of bitcoin and cryptocurrency is skyrocketing in many parts of the world, making it easier for millions of users to store, send, and receive money. In a way, Bitcoin is the original DeFi protocol—a censorship-resistant, decentralized version of cash. Second, stablecoins designed to hold a stable value have exploded in value. Earlier in the year, Visa's head of crypto, Cuy Sheffield said, "Stablecoins continue to grow rapidly, with over $50 billion of stablecoins in circulation that power $200 billion in payment volume each month."[33] Today the figures are much higher. They have obvious and widespread applications across a range of industries. Finally, applications like Chai, which uses the Terra Luna blockchain, are disintermediating traditional payment processors by undercutting fees and settling payments in real time.[34]

Bitcoin

Today, bitcoin secures $1 trillion in value and serves millions of people. According to Chainalysis, "Global adoption [of cryptocurrencies] has grown by over 2,300 percent since Q3 2019 and over 881 percent in the last year."[35] The report's authors argued, "In emerging markets, many turn to cryptocurrency to preserve their savings in the face of currency devaluation, send and receive remittances, and carry out business transactions."[36]

In June 2021, El Salvador announced that it would formally adopt bitcoin as legal tender.[37] Politicians in Argentina, Brazil, Mexico, Panama, and Paraguay also expressed their public support for bitcoin.[38] Could Latin America become the first economic region to embrace bitcoin at the state level? Perhaps. In many South American countries, the US dollar plays an outsized role. Until recently, it was El Salvador's only official currency. US dollar remittance payments, largely from the United States, constituted more than 20 percent of El Salvador's gross domestic product (~$24.6 billion in 2020).[39] Furthermore, 70.4 percent of Salvadorans are unbanked.[40] So the Bitcoin blockchain could serve more residents and potentially reduce fees for the poorest. Of course, a new government could reverse the decision. Still, it could prove to be a watershed for the world.

Bitcoin is known for its high energy consumption, low transaction throughput, and high fees, which limits its utility for different payment applications. For example, today's average transaction fee is $3.328, which would be prohibitive for the 22 percent of Salvadorans living on $5.50 a day.[41] The Lightning Network, a Layer 2 protocol developed on top of the Bitcoin blockchain, seeks to overcome these implementation challenges. With Lightning, parties can open payment channels between them and conduct off-chain transactions, which are batched and settled on the main chain.[42] The Lightning Network has grown rapidly. In mid-March 2020, the total capacity of the network was only $4.79 million; a year later, it was $64.93 million.[43] Then in September 2021, Strike, the leading bitcoin wallet developed on Lightning, launched its *application programming interface* (API) for Twitter users in the United States and El Salvador.[44] By mid-October, Lightning's capacity stood at $177.6 million.[45]

Stablecoins

Stablecoins hold the potential to transform legacy payments infrastructures such as SWIFT, the interbank network that handles global payments and more. They have also undeniably fueled the rise of DeFi. Stablecoins will almost certainly transform the payments industry by ushering in a new era of frictionless global real-time value settlement. They will lower barriers for individuals to access goods and services online and increase the metabolism of commerce. They will also help end the remittance rip-off, where annually people pay more than $60 billion in fees just to send money to family overseas. As Do Kwon of Terra Luna said, "For the financially disenfranchised, stablecoins represent a novel onboarding tool to a new, open, and more inclusive financial system."[46]

Blockchain-based payment applications

Finally, blockchains are enabling new applications that can compete outright with dedicated payment processing applications by reducing cost, friction, and time of settlement. For example, Terra's Chai App is a payment processor that is like PayPal or Alipay but can offer payment processing for a fraction of the cost by clearing transactions on its blockchain. Moreover, it can offer instant settlement compared to traditional payment processors that take days to settle. As of June 2021, Chai had more than 2.4 million users and processed more than 130,000 transactions per day.[47]

Storing value

In broad terms, there are several ways to store cryptoassets. Users can hold their own assets by keeping their own private keys in a software wallet like MetaMask, a hardware wallet like Trezor, or multisig wallet like Gnosis Safe.

In multisig wallets, accessing assets requires more than one person, sort of like safety deposit boxes that require two keys. Because multisig wallets are programmable, users can secure a multisig wallet any number of ways—for example, having five key holders and requiring at least three to move anything out of the wallet. Alternatively, users can rely on third parties to hold their private keys for them, such as the custodial services of cryptocurrency exchanges like Coinbase Custody or Gemini Custody, both regulated under New York State banking law.[48]

Users who hold their own private keys may do so in a hot or cold wallet. A *hot wallet* is a software wallet online, always connected to the Internet. For example, MetaMask is an Ethereum hot wallet created by ConsenSys. Users can access their MetaMask wallets via a browser extension or mobile app. It is an immensely popular gateway to the Ethereum ecosystem for its 10 million-plus monthly active users, especially the Philippines and Vietnam.[49]

Hot wallets are *noncustodial*: MetaMask holds no private keys yet is connected to the Internet. Similar wallets include Phantom (basically MetaMask for Solana), ImTOKEN, Trust Wallet, TokenPocket, Rainbow, and Coin98.[50] They have fewer users than MetaMask but are growing quickly. Phantom recently announced its weekly active users surpassed 500,000.[51]

In contrast, a *cold wallet* is not connected to the Internet. For example, hardware wallets such as Trezor or Ledger store keys offline, offering the kind of security that hot wallets can't. Similarly, third-party custodians may also keep keys in hot or cold storage. For example, Gemini Trust Company stores almost all the coins in custody in cold storage.[52] However, the coins of anyone who trades on Gemini are, by necessity, online in a hot wallet.

Gnosis Safe is a platform for securely storing, exchanging, and managing digital assets. Today it secures $100 billion in value across 23,500 safes, with the top twenty-five holding $4 billion. Many asset-rich entities trust Gnosis as an institutional and high-net-worth product. Users also have the option to buy insurance from Nexus Mutual. Gnosis employs an innovative "bug bounty" system, where it rewards $1 million per bug found. As of this writing, no one had uncovered any major bugs nor earned the million. Gnosis uses a variety of security protocols to secure assets, but the most well-understood is "multi-signature" verification. Rather than one single key residing with one individual, multi-signature requires that a certain minimum number of people approve before a transaction occurs.

FIGURE 1-2

WORLDWIDE BLOCKCHAIN WALLET USERS

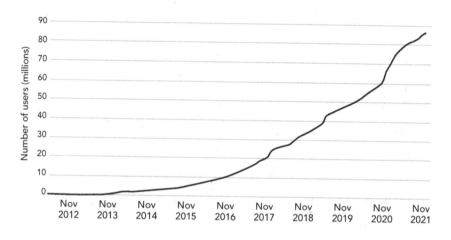

Source of data: "Number of Blockchain Wallet Users Worldwide," Statista.com, Statista GmbH, as of 3 Nov. 2021. www.statista.com/statistics/647374/worldwide-blockchain-wallet-users.

Many institutions and individuals still rely on centralized custodians who hold coins on their behalf (meaning they control the private keys). Gemini and Coinbase, two large fully regulated US-based institutions, have become leaders in this market. In May 2021, Gemini disclosed that it held more than $30 billion in custody.[53] Coinbase is even larger: according to its initial public offering (IPO) filing, it held 11 percent of all cryptoassets in the world.[54] As of September 2021, that would be around $200 billion.[55] Now many incumbent financial institutions want in on this market. Since 2020, banks have been scrambling to launch cryptoasset custody, including US Bank,

BNY Mellon, State Street, Cowen, Deutsche Bank, Bank of America, Union Bank of Philippines, BBVA (formerly a subsidiary of Banco Bilbao Vizcaya Argentaria), not to mention four of the five largest banks in South Korea.[56] These efforts were given a serious boost when the US Office of the Comptroller of the Currency (OCC) clarified regulations allowing federally regulated banks to engage in cryptoasset custody.[57] Here is a select list of financial firms planning cryptoasset custody services:

- Bitcoin Suisse – A "Swiss regulated financial intermediary" with over 5 billion Swiss francs in cryptoassets[58]
- BitGo – More than $40 billion[59]
- BNY Mellon – Formed digital assets unit to build industry's first multiple asset digital platform[60]
- Coinbase – $255 billion in assets[61]
- FireBlocks – More than $400 billion in assets as of March 2021[62]
- Gemini – $30 billion of cryptoassets[63]
- Kingdom Trust – $18 billion in its Choice offering[64]
- US Bank – Identified NYDIG, a subsidiary of Stone Ridge, as its first crypto sub-custodian[65]

These figures are large but pale in comparison to the total assets custodied by the world's largest financial institutions. US Bank's investment services division has more than $7.7 trillion in assets under custody and administration globally.[66] When all securities are digital assets, the figures across the board will only increase. Perhaps the biggest changes to how we store value are not happening at the individual wallet level but rather at the organizational level, thanks to the rise of DAOs.

A traditional company balance sheet is comprised of a mix of assets and liabilities. The cash balance, or current assets, refers to cash and equivalents sitting inside bank accounts, money market funds, and short-term government notes. However, DAOs turn that notion on its head. Andrew Young, CEO of Layer2 and co-founder of the SX Network, said:

> DAOs are on-chain entities that facilitate the governance and economic coordination of decentralized protocols. The typical DeFi protocol often collects a fee, which is then diverted to an on-chain treasury. Rather than having the core founders control this treasury, DAOs enable DeFi protocols to put tokens in control of them. Tokenholders vote on how to disburse funds, allocate budgets, and how to hire/fire contributors. DAOs are increasingly governing larger and larger DeFi protocols and their respective treasuries.[67]

Consider Uniswap, the largest decentralized cryptoasset exchange in the world. As Uniswap has exploded in size, so too has the "on-chain treasury" that holders of Uniswap's governance token (more on that later) have power over. Just how big is Uniswap's on-chain treasury? As of September 2021, it has more than $9 billion, a greater stockpile than all but the largest and most well-capitalized companies on the planet.[68] By comparison, according to its latest financial statement, Coinbase has less than half that.[69] To be clear, the assets Uniswap holds are not exactly like cash. Most of the value exists in UNI governance tokens, which are not the same as cash even though they're liquid. They are like treasury stock that holders can convert to cash quickly with other governance tokenholders' assent. Still, they are a powerful financial resource that users can deploy in multiple use cases. The section on governance tokens below expands upon the significance of DAOs in our economy.

Lending value

Measured by TVL, lending is one of the largest DeFi use cases. Decentralized lending platforms support users' desire to lend and borrow cryptoassets. These platforms flip the traditional model on its head: lenders and borrowers transact with each other through smart contracts, not intermediaries. These lending platforms have grown tremendously over the last year; Aave, the largest DeFi platform in the world, holds over $11 billion in assets.[70]

DeFi loans are typically overcollateralized, meaning for every $1 locked in a lending protocol, a user may get 50 cents of extra leverage. As lenders, users do not rely on borrowers' creditworthiness. Instead, credit works more like a margin loan: if the value of the assets locked in the protocol declines beyond a certain level, the smart contract automatically liquidates those assets and repays the lender. This kind of borrowing works well for traders seeking leverage to amplify their returns—and that's a big market. Wealthy individuals often borrow against their stock holdings to fund their lifestyles, avoid paying capital gains taxes, and get added leverage to improve their returns. In crypto, the situation is no different. To avoid paying capital gains taxes, and in the absence of traditional lenders willing to recognize digital assets, many successful crypto natives borrow against their assets.

An increasingly popular exception to overcollateralized loan is the *flash loan*, where a borrower puts up no collateral to borrow funds for a few seconds. However, the borrowing and repayment of the loan must occur within one transaction, meaning in effect that if the borrower fails to repay, then the transactions can be reversed. Why would someone want to borrow money for a few seconds? Likely to execute a short-term trade such as an arbitrage opportunity. Again, traders could potentially deploy this important innovation at scale in capital markets environments but it's not particularly useful for regular folks looking for a loan.[71]

Thus, as currently designed and implemented, DeFi lending does not yet work for most personal and commercial lending. For example, if we wanted to buy a house for $500,000 and we had $100,000, or 20 percent, ready to put down, the most we could get from this kind of DeFi loan is $50,000. That doesn't make much of a difference, but it still has some benefit: most DeFi lending today is overcollateralized, and so we don't need a credit check. Parties can transact pseudonymously or even fully anonymously. However, for broad mainstream adoption, DeFi lending needs to marry lending protocols with decentralized and reliable digital identities that parties can use for automated "credit checks." That's a multitrillion-dollar opportunity for whoever solves the problem.

Lending, like all other DeFi applications, must also overcome the interoperability challenge by enabling cross-blockchain lending. Various companies have set out to address this, such as Umee, which offers cross-ecosystem lending and borrowing.[72]

Funding and investing

DeFi is full of financial opportunities to earn attractive yields, and tokens have become an immensely powerful means of bolstering project balance sheets. However, finding the best returns can be time consuming and complicated. Enter yield aggregators such as Yearn Finance and Rarible, which hook into different DeFi protocols so that users can optimize yield. Users stake tokens in yield aggregators' platforms and permit the platforms to manage their assets. We can think of them as roboadvisers for DeFi. These yield platforms have grown tremendously, with over $20 billion TVL.

Complementing yield aggregators are DeFi index funds such as Index Cooperative, another emerging category of smart contract–enabled financial services. In the traditional world, an ETF is a publicly listed fund that tracks the performance of a given benchmark, such as the Standard & Poor's 500. ETFs generally allow for daily creation and redemption or destruction of units, based on the market demand. Other structures like closed-end funds or mutual funds can have more stringent redemptions, but the overarching goals are the same: to pool investor capital into a fund and then invest based on a set of criteria.

The DeFi system is no different. Smart contract–based index funds have been one of the fastest growing areas within the DeFi ecosystem. Like traditional ETFs, they create value for investors by packaging different assets (in this case, cryptoassets) into a basket or index, so that investors get passive exposure to an entire sector with a click of a button. DeFi index funds are entirely blockchain based: an open-source software protocol and a decentralized governance system oversee them, not a centralized asset manager.

Exchanging value

When cryptocurrency exchange Coinbase went public, its $60 billion market cap surpassed that of the NYSE—the exchange it had listed on—and Nasdaq combined. It was also the first large-cap crypto company that institutions felt comfortable owning. While Coinbase is an innovative and immensely valuable company, it is still fundamentally a centralized, regulated exchange and crypto broker, not unlike legacy firms like Morgan Stanley and Nasdaq.

DEXes also known as *automated market makers* (AMMs) such as Uniswap, SushiSwap, and PancakeSwap, could replace or enhance stock exchanges and centralized cryptoasset exchanges. AMMs like Bancor are open protocols that enable individuals to exchange any kind of cryptoasset peer to peer (or more precisely, peer to smart contract). These new platforms have grown so much that they are now competing for volumes with more established traditional rivals. None of the emergent DEXes are bigger or more important than Uniswap.

Bancor's Galia Benartzi explained the origins of AMM: "We understood that liquidity could be designed directly into tokens, and thus the Bancor Protocol was born, a formula and mechanism for making any currency, old or new, automatically liquid to any other—which would become known as the AMM, or automated market maker."[73] Today, Bancor is one of the leading DeFi protocols with $1.4 billion TVL.[74]

DeFi protocols are also all open source, inviting imitators and outright copycats. Uniswap had early success as one of the first AMMs to launch, and it was quickly copied in the summer of 2020 by SushiSwap, which duplicated Uniswap code line for line. SushiSwap volumes briefly competed with Uniswap, but Uniswap retained its lead. More interestingly, today Uniswap is much larger than it was in the summer of 2020. SushiSwap is also successful. The duplication probably helped Uniswap by increasing awareness for DeFi and drawing in more users. This is the power of open source. Famed entrepreneur and investor Naval Ravikant captured the essence of open source, tweeting the key to success is "solve your own problems and freely share the solutions."[75] This ethos has allowed DeFi to scale rapidly.

The typical DeFi protocol often collects a fee, which is then diverted to an on-chain treasury. Rather than having the core founders control this treasury, DAOs enable DeFi protocols to put tokens in control of them. Tokenholders vote on how to disburse funds, allocate budgets, and how to hire/fire contributors. We will cover DAOs and their corresponding governance tokens in detail in the token taxonomy. Not unlike their centralized counterparts in traditional financial markets, decentralized exchanges are often the most profitable DeFi protocols in the world.

Decentralized exchanges also make it easy for small and illiquid tokens to find a market. Traditionally, centralized exchange platforms would need to accept these tokens, but there would be no market maker to boost liquidity. Here's Benartzi's explanation:

AMMs eliminate the need for centralized exchanges and traditional order books by equipping digital assets with an inherent convertibility mechanism governed by a balancing formula, which can also be dynamically adjusted. This allows even new and small currencies to be easily bought and sold, a prerequisite for their use, growth, and sustainability. ... AMMs level the playing field for digital assets by removing barriers to entry for liquidity which governed traditional markets and exchanges for hundreds of years.[76]

DeFi protocols such as DEXes have several structural advantages over traditional financial intermediaries that allow them to scale quickly. For example, Osmosis, a decentralized exchange launched on the Cosmos Network in August 2021, had $500 million TVL within eight weeks.[77] In addition, DeFi protocols (i.e., Ethereum, Solana, Cosmos, etc.) have low infrastructure costs because their users pay the gas fees to support Layer 1 and extremely high margins because they have no head offices, very low headcount, and none of the regulatory fetters of traditional financial institutions.[78] Decentralized exchanges have all these advantages plus a high churn of transactions, where tiny transaction fees pile up quickly.

Insuring value and managing risk

On-chain insurance such as Nexus Mutual and derivatives platforms such as the SX Network, Perpetual Protocol, and dYdX could supplement or replace insurance policies and OTC derivatives.

Insurance and risk management is a $6-trillion market worldwide but underrepresented in the DeFi space. Decentralized insurance platforms and prediction markets enable the trading of *event risk* between participants.[79] These platforms upend the traditional model by allowing anyone to transact with someone else through smart contracts, not intermediaries like insurance companies for insurance or investment banks for derivatives. DeFi protocols like Uniswap and Aave have disrupted markets like trading and lending. Will decentralized insurance see the same kind of growth? What impact will these decentralized models have on legacy insurance institutions and business models?

Derivatives are the single largest asset class in the world, with an estimated notional value estimated to be over quadrillion dollars and used by traders and speculators.[80] By contrast, plenty of people and corporations use derivatives to hedge against risks to their portfolios and profitability.

In early September 2021, dYdX exploded onto the DeFi scene by offering an easy-to-use interface for trading perpetual futures contracts (known as *perps* in crypto trading circles). Historically, futures contracts have had an expiry date: a farmer agrees to sell a livestock business a commodity like corn at a future date. When that date arrives, the livestock owner expects the farmer to deliver the corn; otherwise, how will the livestock owner feed her cattle during winter? With cryptoassets (and, to be accurate, many traditional financial assets), there is no need for delivery, and so these contracts don't always need a fixed expiry date. Instead, they can be perpetual, where one side funds the premiums on an ongoing basis until it wants to exit the position, not unlike a swap in traditional finance. In its first quarter, dYdX has become one of the most profitable DeFi derivatives protocols in the world, outpacing more established players.[81]

Users turn to dYdX predominantly for trading and speculation. Why not for traditional insurance products such as life insurance? After all, life insurance is perpetual until the insured dies. Insurance premiums are similar to the premiums traders pay for short positions in perpetual futures contracts. Given that dYdX is barely a year old with a market cap of $1.2 billion, insurers ought to take notice.[82]

Prediction markets are financial marketplaces where people bet on the outcomes of different future events, from sports, elections, and the weather to the values of stocks or other assets. Unlike traditional betting platforms, they are fully peer to peer, transparent, and more flexible. SX Network is a leading prediction market platform, with $120 million in annualized prediction volume (in other words, wagers placed by others on the platform) as of October 2021.[83]

SX co-founder Andrew Young set his sights on predictions beyond betting. He said, "Prediction markets are already used in some forms of insurance and risk management systems today. For example, credit event binary options are a type of credit default swap that provide participants with an alternative way of hedging credit risk." The big target? "Using prediction markets, rather than voting, to determine policy" in DAO governance. "The idea is that prediction markets are superior to voting systems [because of] the introduction of gain and loss to governance systems."[84] Tokenholder apathy, it turns out, is as big a problem for DAOs as voter apathy is for democracies. We discuss these challenges in the section on governance tokens.

Analyzing value

Blockchains are transparent, searchable, verifiable, and trustworthy records of all economic activity in each network. They are constantly producing massive amounts of data that users can scrutinize, organize, analyze, and visualize. In other words, they offer users a view of the inner workings of DeFi and the digital asset ecosystem. The growth of DeFi has spawned a new industry of companies and open-source tools to properly analyze this information. Here are a few:

- Messari (Messari.io): This site has become the de facto second screen for most DeFi market participants. With an interactive interface with up-to-the minute data, analysis, and news, Messari's analysts break down on-chain data into clear and actionable research—like Bloomberg for DeFi with a bulge-bracket research department.

- DeFi Llama (DeFiLlama.com): With DeFiLlama, users can see how the TVL of their favorite DeFi project has changed day over day or month over month relative to its market capitalization. They can also search by project or by category such as lending, yield, options, indexes, and staking insurance. Uses can track changes in TVL over time for Layer 1 protocols such as Ethereum and Solana.

- DeFi Pulse (DeFiPulse.com): On DeFi Pulse, users can compare interest rates on various DeFi projects, see the DeFi leaderboard, or invest in a DeFi index fund.

- Etherscan (Etherscan.io): On Etherscan, users can see the entire Ethereum blockchain and check mined blocks, transactions, and addresses, gas (i.e., network fees), nodes (i.e., different participants on the network), and DEXes. Etherscan also covers all ERC-20 tokens (aka protocol tokens of DeFi apps).

- DEXTools (www.DEXTools.io): This site offers real-time data on DEXes so that users can develop strategies and anticipate market movements on platforms such Ethereum, Binance Smart Chain, and Polygon.

- Blockchain.com (www.Blockchain.com): The original site for analyzing on-chain data and still one of the best resources for bitcoin, Blockchain.com tracks every transaction on the Bitcoin blockchain as well as its transaction volume and hash rate (aka difficulty level for miners).

- Ethplorer (Ethplorer.io): This site tracks the price of a user's address balance and shows transfer volumes as well as prior balances, with totals received and sent.

- Blockscout (Blockscout.com/xDAI/mainnet): This open-source block explorer covers everything on Ethereum from transactions and block information to token values, sidechains, and private chains.

- ETHStats (ETHStats.net), Yield Farming Tools (YieldFarmingTools.com), and DeBank (DeBank.com) also offer their own levels of in-depth analysis and data gathering for the industry.

Accounting and auditing value

"Accounting is the language of business," said Warren Buffett. "You have to be as comfortable with that as you are with your own native language to really evaluate businesses."[85] It's so important that some consider double-entry bookkeeping one of the great innovations of all time.[86] According to economist Tim Hartford and others, it enabled Venetian and Tuscan merchants in the 1300s "to keep track of ... extraordinarily intricate web[s] of transactions" around the Mediterranean over time, laying the foundation for managing the modern global enterprise.[87]

Who invented it is unknown. But Florentine Friar Luca Pacioli wrote the book on it—that is, he devoted a couple dozen pages to it in his much "translated, copied, and plagiarized" tome on mathematics.[88] Since their publication in the late 1490s, those very lucid and illustrative pages have shaped how business owners have kept inventory and recorded transactions.[89] When they added up their transactions, both entries in the ledger had to "balance" out, which is where we get the term *balance sheet*, and why we "balance the books."

In the industrial age, we came to rely not just on accountants but comptrollers, auditors, and a vast army of analysts to capture complex financial information, verify its accuracy, and publish it in intelligible ways. Today accounting and auditing are massive industries. The Big Five accounting firms employ hundreds of thousands of people and serve every major corporation, government, and institution on the planet.

In *Blockchain Revolution*, we wrote about blockchains enabling triple-entry bookkeeping, with the third entry (or entries) appearing *on-chain*, that is, every transaction created an entry in a blockchain that anyone can see. At the time, this applied only to bitcoin. We based our hypothesis on the transparency of the Bitcoin blockchain, where anyone could see in real time all transactions on the network. We extrapolated that, if a distributed public ledger could work for bitcoin transactions, it could work for all transactions on-chain. We firmly believed that, if we could record most economic activity, not only the movement of money but also financial assets, IP, and even physical goods, in this way, then we could reinvent accounting.[90]

Fast-forward five years, and that prediction is playing out in real time in DeFi. As we saw in the section on analyzing information, even a novice can gather trustworthy on-chain data, and an expert analyst can create a financial statement at the protocol level with ease.

Some projects are taking it one step further. In addition to all the on-chain data readily available, Yearn Finance has made its GitHub repository a destination for data about the platform, all of which can be independently verified on-chain.[91] On it, we can track every single Yearn transaction in real time, get transaction records, and search protocol income, protocol expenses, income statements, end-of-month balances, and more. We can see revenue projections, charts, tables, and other useful data. In the future some mix of verifiable on-chain raw data, data analysis tools, and verifiable information curated by individual projects like Yearn will replace the quarterly statements and other financial paperwork of today.

In a world where on-chain data gives us a perfect snapshot into the financial health of an organization, what role is there for an auditor? Plenty, it turns out. However, instead of auditing data in a spreadsheet, auditors will have to vet and approve the code of smart contracts. After all, if DeFi is going to go institutional, then users and counterparties need confidence in underlying smart contracts' security.

Enter firms like Zeppelin, the leading cryptoasset cybersecurity company that safeguards billions of dollars on behalf of many of the world's leading crypto companies and DeFi protocols, such as Coinbase, Ethereum Foundation, Compound, Aave, and others. Zeppelin's goal is to solve for three security and usability concerns in the DeFi space:

- Security, namely exposure to hacking or attack
- Developer experience, namely lack of proper development and testing tools, which can create errors
- Operations, specifically managing and fixing problems in dapps once deployed, which can be very hard.

If this sounds a bit different from the average Big Four accounting firm's audit department, that's because it is. If most financial information is trustworthy and immutable, then auditors can focus on higher-order issues such as system resilience and security. To that end, Zeppelin security audits are becoming increasingly popular, giving users confidence in the platform. In the audit process, Zeppelin's engineers examine a system's codebase and architecture. They check whether the distributed system is working as intended and then generate a report including actionable tasks. Compound, Maker, Augur, Solidity, Brave, and others have all requested Zeppelin audits.

FIGURE 1-3

OPENZEPPELIN AUDIT PROCESS

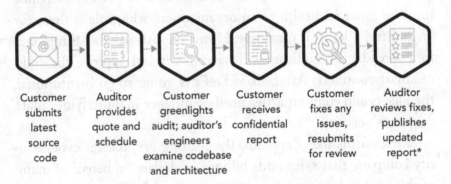

| Customer submits latest source code | Auditor provides quote and schedule | Customer greenlights audit; auditor's engineers examine codebase and architecture | Customer receives confidential report | Customer fixes any issues, resubmits for review | Auditor reviews fixes, publishes updated report* |

Customer has option to publish report on auditor's website

Source of information: "Security Audits for Distributed Systems," OpenZeppelin.com, Zeppelin Audits Ltd., as of 1 Nov. 2021. openzeppelin.com/security-audits.

Authenticating identity

Establishing a reliable and self-sovereign identity online proved difficult through the first era of the Internet. In the Web 2 paradigm, third parties like banks, social media companies, and digital conglomerates give us our identities and allow us to access their services. Web 2's Faustian bargain was signing our own data over to these intermediaries (via their terms of use and service). We gave them rights to use our data for their own gain, and they undermined our privacy in the process. We never get to own our identity. Rather, we simply rent it in these walled gardens. As data mining becomes more sophisticated, our rents keep going up. Like any rental, we always bear the risk of eviction—deplatforming, in Internet parlance. These are permissioned systems, and their owners decide whether we stay or go.

Blockchain remedies this situation in two ways. First, DeFi and most other blockchain dapps are open, permissionless, and anonymous: we need no third party to prove who we are. Anyone with a MetaMask wallet can access the DeFi world on Ethereum, for example, and needn't show any ID to do that. Second, blockchain enables us to bootstrap a self-sovereign digital identity. The data accruing in our cryptoasset wallets create a vivid chart of our financial past and present. We can use an NFT—an entirely unique digital asset—as an avatar to represent our digital self. These avatars can be fun, such as the Bored Ape or CryptoPunk NFTs. On the Internet, nobody knows you're a dog, but on Web 3, everybody knows you're a Bored Ape, CryptoPunk, or CryptoKitty.

We can now design our own identities and gather our own data rather than accept whatever a platform assigns to us so that it can track our behavior. We can use sovereign digital identities not only for protecting our data but for accessing more goods and services online. Chris Dixon of a16z tweeted, "NFTs give users the ability to own … credentials, governance rights, access passes, and whatever else people dream up next."[92] So our digital wallets could contain, among other things, our frequent flyer identities (IDs), our credentials to access banking, our proof of vaccination, or even our eligibility to vote in an election—in other words, all the components of our identity. However, many people may not want to be custodians of their own information, which could be irretrievable if hacked or stolen. This is a business opportunity for companies and protocols to build user interfaces and apps that are convenient, secure, and easy to use.

Could self-sovereign identities work in regulated environments, which require state-based identities? Joseph Weinberg thinks so. He's the co-founder of the Shyft Network, which he called a "decentralized version of SWIFT," referring to the SWIFT's financial messaging system launched in 1973 and widely used today for interbank settlement.[93] Through Shyft, Weinberg seeks to empower users with a decentralized identity framework robust enough to win over regulators and regulated financial institutions. Shyft works like other cryptoasset wallets, but for identity credentials—the critical information to access financial services from permissioned and centralized companies. Just as Fred Smith of FedEx said in 1978, "The information about the package is just as important as the package itself," the information about a payment is as important as the actual payment.[94]

Consider the Financial Action Task Force's so-called "travel rule," which requires financial intermediaries—including cryptocurrency exchanges Binance and Coinbase—to collect and transmit know-your-customer (KYC) data when executing a transaction.[95] Ignoring this rule could put a business in the crosshairs of regulators and law enforcers around the world. Compliance is increasingly important in certain DeFi environments, too, where the goal is to woo traditional financial firms (TradFi), other intermediaries, and their clients.

Various other projects and companies are targeting on-chain, self-custodied identities, among them BrightID, Identity.com, SelfKey, and Sovrin.[96] All are user provisioned, meaning that users decide whether to share their data and with whom. For example, Bloom is an identity solution for private data verification, distribution, and aggregation.[97] Global and tamper-proof by design, Bloom incorporates many attestations so that users can interact with DeFi platforms that require user ID. The Bloom team focuses on credit and hopes to offer credit scoring, KYC, account onboarding, and financial access using these data. Blockpass, with its PASS utility token, is another pioneer of on-chain KYC targeting regulated industries.[98]

A TAXONOMY OF DIGITAL ASSETS

As Harvard Business School professors Marco Iansiti and Karim R. Lakhani noted, "Contracts, transactions, and the records of them are among the defining structures in our economic, legal, and political systems. ... Yet these critical tools and the bureaucracies formed to manage them have not kept up with the economy's digital transformation."[99] Blockchain technologies bring asset creation and management into the twenty-first century. A cryptoasset is a digital asset defined by both public and private data and secured by cryptography within its ecosystem.[100] Thus far, we've identified nine asset categories, overviewed here and detailed throughout this book.

CRYPTOCURRENCIES AKA *DIGITAL MONEY*

Money has evolved from cowrie shells and clay tablets to pieces of eight, banknotes, and bank balances. With the Bitcoin blockchain, money became digital. Bitcoin is the most dominant digital cash, but there are other cryptocurrencies like Zcash and Monero. In general, they follow certain design principles:

- Resilient and open source: Parties should be able to use digital cash without relying on private banks, payment networks, or proprietary IP.

- Permissionless and low tech: Individuals or entities should need no IDs, bank accounts, large bandwidth, or complex or energy-intensive equipment to use it.

- Private and secure: Individuals must be able to hold and use it anonymously or pseudonymously.

- Accessible and easy to use: Digital cash must be easily attainable and require no special knowledge or expertise to use responsibly.

Yes, governments are eager to defend the status quo where states and state-based institutions have a monopoly on minting coins and printing bills, and corporations have their sights set on the reinvention of money. But numerous factors are working in cryptocurrency's favor. Consider bitcoin, by far the most valuable. Its community is zealous.[101] It is censorship resistant—holders can use it as they see fit—and it is emerging as a successor to gold as a store of value. It is also benefiting from the efforts of legacy fintech like PayPal, Square, and Visa, all of which are making bitcoin available to their hundreds of millions of users and millions of merchants.[102] Large public companies are also embracing it as a viable alternative to cash and other assets on their balance sheets or in their portfolios.[103]

Bitcoin usage is increasing rapidly. The banked and unbanked alike can use bitcoin without proof of identity or state censorship.[104] In Nigeria, for example, daily US dollar P2P trade consistently clocks in at over $1.5 million from a base of zero only a few years ago.[105] P2P bitcoin transactions can be zero-fee, a big break from the much higher fees many in Africa are forced to pay for basic financial services, such as those for remittances, which are on average close to nine percent.[106] Repressive regimes cannot easily throttle, control, or monitor usage of bitcoin for, say, a girl's education, birth control, or support of an opposition candidate as they can in the legacy financial world. In 2020, civil protests erupted in Lagos and across Nigeria because of the brutal and illegal actions of the Special Anti-Robbery Squad, a police unit. Within days, the government had frozen the bank accounts of groups supporting the protesters. So, they turned to the Bitcoin network, raising funds to sustain the movement.[107]

TABLE 1-1

CRYPTO OWNERSHIP BY COUNTRY

Crypto ownership is highest in middle- and lower-income countries.

COUNTRY	# CRYPTO OWNERS	% POPULATION
1. Ukraine	5,565,881	12.73
2. Russia	17,379,175	11.91
3. Venezuela	2,941,502	10.34
4. Singapore	549,903	9.04
5. Kenya	4,580,760	8.52
6. USA	27,491,810	8.31
7. India	100,740,320	7.30
8. South Africa	4,215,944	7.11
9. Nigeria	13,016,341	6.31
10. Colombia	3,122,449	6.14
11. Vietnam	5,961,684	6.12
12. Thailand	3,629,713	5.20
13. United Kingdom	3,360,591	4.95
14. Brazil	10,373,187	4.88
15. Pakistan	9,051,827	4.10

Source of data: Triple A, "Global Crypto Adoption," Triple-A.io, Triple A Technologies Pte. Ltd., 2021. triple-a.io/crypto-ownership.

PROTOCOL TOKENS

Protocol tokens are the native cryptoassets of the smart contracting protocols that support DeFi, NFTs, DAOs, and virtually every other major use case for blockchain except bitcoin, which is the original Layer 1. Whereas bitcoin serves as censorship-resistant cash for the Internet, protocols like Ethereum, Solana, Cosmos, Avalanche, and Polygon were designed to support dapps and smart contracts. Remember, smart contracts are self-executing pieces of software running in a decentralized trust-minimizing way on a blockchain.

FIGURE 1-4

TOP 10 ERC-20 VERSUS ETH

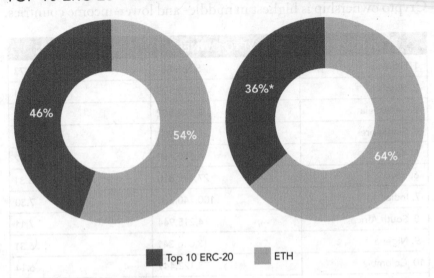

46%

54%

36%*

64%

■ Top 10 ERC-20   ■ ETH

*Not counting ERC-20 stablecoins

Source of data: "ERC-20 Token Tracker," Etherscan.io, Block Solutions SDN BHD LLC, as of 30 Sept. 2021. etherscan.io/tokens.

Nearly every single dapp, from Aave and Compound to Osmosis and Yearn Finance, runs on some protocol with its own native or protocol token, such as Ethereum and ETH. To run a dapp on these networks, dapp users and developers must pay for transactions, often using the network's protocol token. As a dapp, the protocol token constitutes the *transaction* layer of the platform. For example, to transact on Ethereum, users must pay transaction fees (aka gas fees) denominated in ETH, Ethereum's protocol token.[108] DeFi's viral growth has skyrocketed gas fees, driving the size of Ethereum's network to $454 billion accruing to ETH holders.[109] It has also opened a mile-wide lane for other DeFi protocols to capture market share by offering cheaper, faster, better options. Ethereum's share of DeFi TVL has dropped precipitously from 99 percent to 70 percent in less than a year, ceding ground to Solana, Binance Smart Chain, Terra, Avalanche, Cosmos, and others.[110]

In 2016, venture capitalist Joel Monegro posited that Web 3 protocols would capture far more value than those early iterations of the Internet.[111] The markets have put this "fat protocol thesis" to the test since. Over time, smart contracting platforms have exploded in value; however, their total share of the digital asset market is declining.

Still, Ethereum is larger than any project built on top of it. In fact, Ethereum's market capitalization is larger than that of the top ten projects on top of Ethereum *combined*. Ethereum's declining share of DeFi TVL compared to other smart contracting platforms is not a sign of waning Ethereum influence but a marker of DeFi's enormous growth. The Ethereum network processes more than one million transactions a day, which is not enough to support the future of financial services. Other protocols will emerge to fill the need. Peng Zhong, CEO of Tendermint, said this move away from "maximalism," this clinging dogmatically to one blockchain, is necessary for the long-term success of the technology:

> In five years' time, I see thousands of application-specific blockchains interconnected and flourishing from the ability to transact with each other. This has huge implications in many areas beyond DeFi, to decentralized organizations, gaming, identity, environment, supply chain, and so many use cases we can't even think of right now.[112]

Whereas many Layer 1 developers build the technology first and then hope applications will come, certain protocols have launched with a killer dapp. Terra Luna is one example. Terra's co-founder and CEO Do Kwon told us,

> Crypto has exploded over the last several years, with diverse types of assets, networks, and stablecoins booming in growth. However, many of the major [Layer 1s] and crypto networks like

smart contract platforms are focusing more on generalized computation. Terra is different in that it takes the reverse approach—creating and issuing a decentralized value-stable currency that can preponderate on multiple chains and is not beholden to the demand of a network's specific advantages.[113]

The trilemma

Launching a functioning smart contracting protocol is no easy feat, especially if the goal is to out-compete Ethereum on cost or throughput. In fact, Layer 1 developers face a choice called the "trilemma." It's a heuristic for judging the viability of different projects, and it will change as the facts change.

Given the choice among network security, scalability, and decentralization, developers must pick two. In other words, they can have a super-secure and super-decentralized protocol, but it may struggle to scale in transaction throughput, if not total volume. Bitcoin is a good example of such a protocol. On the other hand, we can have a very fast and decentralized protocol, but it may not be as secure. Some would put Solana in this category. It has millions of users and dozens of dapps, and its gas fees are a tiny fraction of Ethereum's. When it shut down for an entire day in September 2021, some questioned its durability.[114] But traditional financial markets shut down daily, and their systems undergo repairs and upgrades regularly. Blockchain and DeFi are 24/7/365, meaning that developers and code contributors—many of them volunteers—have no way to maintain, patch, or upgrade systems except on the fly.[115] In that context, Solana is an amazing accomplishment.

Layer 2 as scaling solution

One way to solve the scalability problem is to introduce Layer 2, which runs on top of or adjacent to Layer 1. Polygon is probably the most well-known. As Ethereum gas fees shot through the roof, many dapp developers, enterprises, and other users migrated to Polygon where the fees are cheaper. Polygon co-founder Sandeep Nailwal argued,

> With fees reaching as high as $200 earlier this year, staying on the Ethereum main chain has become unsustainable. By integrating Polygon, the average gas fee per transaction is just $0.00004. The average transaction time is also significantly lower with Polygon, clocking in at two seconds, versus five to ten minutes per transaction without Polygon.[116]

Similar to Ethereum, Polygon has a native token (MATIC) that acts as a transaction layer. So, the more transactions, the more value accrues to the token.

Because Polygon helped address this short-term bottleneck in Ethereum, there are now hundreds of projects using it. For example, high-end fashion brand Dolce & Gabbana released its debut NFT collection drop, Collezione Genesi, on a Polygon-based marketplace in September. According to Nailwal, other major projects using Polygon include Axie Infinity, DraftKings, Autograph, Lazy.com by Mark Cuban, CryptoPunks, Bored Aped Yacht Club, Beeple, and more.[117]

Interoperability through Multichain

Smart contracting platforms must interoperate seamlessly for DeFi and other new blockchain use cases to reach their full potential. Certain smart contracting platforms like Cosmos and Polkadot were developed at least in part to address this issue. Cosmos has been enormously effective in drawing app developers and services into its network. According to Peng Zhong, CEO of Tendermint, which builds the critical infrastructure underpinning many of Cosmos' applications, "There are already more than 250 blockchain apps and services in the network securing more than $125 billion of digital assets."[118] Here is Tendermint's vision:

> We're empowering people to build the decentralized web and create a transparent and accountable world through open, distributed, interoperable networks. We envision a sustainable multichain future in which all blockchain ecosystems can connect and thrive from their interactions with each other. This vision is collaborative, not competitive, and our industry-leading technology is already making it happen.[119]

CENTRAL BANK DIGITAL CURRENCIES

The rise of bitcoin and other nonstate-based monies compels central banks to confront the possible end to government monopolies on money. Christine Lagarde, president of the European Central Bank, captured the threat and opportunity of blockchain and cryptocurrencies in an interview with CNBC: "I think the role of the disruptors and anything that is using distributed ledger technology, whether you call it crypto, assets, currencies, or whatever ... [T]hat is clearly shaking the system." She added, "We don't want to shake the system so much that we would lose the stability that is needed."[120]

There is risk and opportunity for central bankers in this new future. Central bankers have often "failed to stem macroeconomic crises and may have, in fact, exacerbated negative outcomes by incentivizing excessive risk-taking and moral hazard via unconventional monetary tools such as quantitative easing and negative interest rates."[121]

Central bank digital money could improve the efficiency, reach, and responsiveness of financial markets. Its advocates in the United States and the rest of the Western world argue it could more easily accommodate unbanked people, reduce costs, add clarity and muscle to monetary policy, and reveal risk.

In China, a different picture emerges. People's ability to move and store value and fully participate in the economy already depends on their government-issued social credit score. Smoking in nonsmoking zones, driving recklessly, or playing too many video games could lower citizens' scores and decrease their access to flights, luxury goods and services, or the best colleges. Now China wants to kill cash and introduce a CBDC to keep a closer eye on how people spend money.[122] Without cash, the government could simply switch off a person's access to credit, payments, and savings if the person disagrees with the government, a form of financial deplatforming. Unsurprisingly, China has cracked down on bitcoin.[123] This battle between China, the most powerful surveillance state ever created, and bitcoin, the most powerful stateless money ever created, will be worth watching.[124]

FIGURE 1-5

STATUS OF CBDC EXPERIMENTS

Of the 90 countries exploring CBDCs, seven countries (8%) have launched their digital currencies.

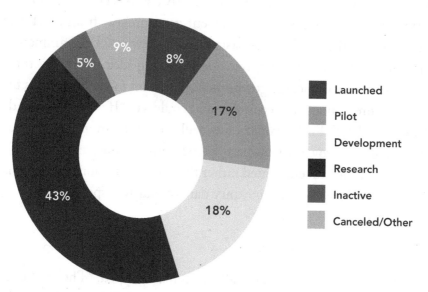

Source of data: "CBDC Tracker," AtlanticCouncil.org, Atlantic Council, as of 15 Nov. 2021. www.atlanticcouncil.org/cbdctracker.

Whichever path the United States and others choose—and they may not launch their own CBDCs—central banks must ensure that any CBDCs have similarities to cash. Cash is essential to financial freedom because it allows for anonymous transactions and private exchanges of money outside state surveillance.

But cash is in terminal decline. For decades, credit card payments have chipped away at cash's role in our economy. The pandemic accelerated that decline, as reports (later proved false) that cash was a carrier of COVID-19 caused many merchants to switch to card-only. The demise of cash highlights the need for a digital alternative to ensure private, safe payments between individuals. If cash disappears, as we argue it may, do we really want an administrative state imposing draconian rules that limit how we spend and save our money and suppress free trade? That is one future of CBDCs. If governments go down that path, more people will drop out of the formal economy.

Issuers of CBDCs in free societies like the United States or Canada must overcome several implementation challenges. For example, with CBDCs, how do users preserve their privacy for certain economic transactions? How do citizens prevent governments from blocking users, so that they can't access basic financial services? Programmable money has lots of benefits, but one troubling idea is "money that expires." For example, the government may want to get its citizens to spend more to boost the economy and could say, "If you don't spend $1,000 on Black Friday, your money will expire!" So money would be a privilege that governments bestowed. In other words, money would be an asset that citizens rented rather than owned. If money is speech, then this effectively puts an expiry date on our free speech rights.

NON-FUNGIBLE TOKENS

In 1964, media theorist Marshall McLuhan quipped, "The medium is the message."[125] At the time, print, radio, and TV were the dominant media. McLuhan's observation feels more prescient than ever.[126]

Consider NFTs, or non-fungible tokens, the provably scarce digital artwork and other digital goods that are enabled by blockchain.

NFTs have taken the art world by storm and are spreading through the culture. In Damien Hirst's foray into NFTs called *The Currency*, he sold 10,000 unique hand-painted variations on his "dot" works. Buyers also got an NFT of their piece. There was a catch: by 27 July 2022 (15:00 BST), buyers must choose between the physical painting or its NFT.[127] Hirst will destroy whichever the buyer doesn't choose.[128] So which medium will buyers choose? McLuhan would recognize the significance of that choice instantly.

Art and other so-called *crypto collectibles* are the main use case for NFTs today but that is quickly changing. In the not-so-distant future a wide array of unique digital goods and items will be NFT-based and allow individuals to move seamlessly their identity and digital possessions between different online ecosystems, platforms, games, and universes. Already, NFT-based video games are exploding in popularity as millions come online with the promise of having fun and making money. Brands are exploring NFTs to organize communities of fans. Culture at large is being transformed as musicians and other creators explore how NFTs can allow them to not only monetize their creations but also engage on a deeper level with supporters.

Let's focus on art. There are three main categories of art/collectible NFTs. The first are collectibles tied to familiar cultural assets. For example, NBA Top Shots NFTs capture highlights of favorite National Basketball Association players. The second are unique pieces of art, such as Beeple's *Everydays: The First 5000 Days*. The final and most viral category is generative art, often created algorithmically and usually issued in a series with a cap on the total supply, such as CryptoPunks. These have become the calling cards of online communities of early adopters and crypto-insiders and because of that cache, certain series have become increasingly valuable. So why would someone buy an art NFT?

- *First, NFTs are financial assets that we can buy and sell.*
  August 2021 smashed all records for NFT transaction values:
  OpenSea, a leading NFT platform, surpassed $3 billion in sales
  volume that month. Speculators are spending thousands and
  sometimes millions of dollars on the rights to own rare images.
  Tom Brady launched the NFT platform Autograph, and Steph
  Curry changed his Twitter avatar to an NFT he bought for
  $180,000 to align his brand with this emerging asset class.

- *Second, NFTs are status symbols.* As we spend a fourth of our
  time online, we care more about the presentation of ourselves
  in everyday *digital* life—the performative aspect of social
  interactions, as sociologist Erving Goffman described in his
  seminal work. Costumes matter. When someone's avatar is
  a provably scarce visual that the owner verifiably bought for
  $100,000, that image says a lot about its owner—namely, that
  the person is in on NFTs and immersed in cryptoassets (and
  probably wealthy).

- *Third, NFTs enable fans and artists to connect.* Of course, we
  could be cynical about NFTs as playthings for the super-rich.
  But most NFTs cost very little, and anyone can buy them.
  Many NFT collectors are fans; they don't expect to sell their
  NFTs at a higher price. And many NFT creators are bypassing
  galleries and auction houses—centralized intermediaries and
  gatekeepers to the collector world—to reach their fans directly,
  engage with them around art, and retain more of the value
  they create.

Today, innovators are using NFTs primarily for art and collectibles,
but we can harness them for greater ends. For example, NFTs will be
essential to the growth of the *metaverse,* a super-immersive shared
online state (perhaps one day paired with hyper-realistic virtual reality) where we can move digital objects between platforms in real time.
For example, in the metaverse pioneer Decentraland, we can buy and
sell virtual property, among other assets, using the native cryptocurrency MANA. It helped seed the development and adoption of some
of the more creative metaverse-crypto collaborations we've seen so far.

Consider Loot, created by prolific crypto entrepreneur Dom Hofmann, creator of Vine. Hofmann created 8,000 loot bags where fans could spend ETH (ether, the native cryptocurrency of Ethereum) to create lists of words such as *gold ring* and *divine hood*, for some future undeveloped videogame. Within moments, people snapped up all the loot bags. That's when the fun really started: communities of fans, artists, and creators emerged to imagine how these assets might look and to mint NFTs of these derivative works. The value of loot bags with rare words skyrocketed in value. A whole game of games arose around Hofmann's *idea* of a videogame—not an actual game.

Whereas Loot is still highly speculative, Axie Infinity is already an immensely popular NFT-based videogame that consistently draws over 1.5 million daily active users. Jeff Zirlin, co-founder and growth lead of Sky Mavis, said the goal with Sky Mavis' Axie Infinity was to "introduce the world to a scary and fun new technology through something relatable and nostalgic."[129] Players must first fund their entry into the game. Once they're in, they play and compete to earn Axies, the in-game assets. Axie are players in the game but also tradable assets that players can sell for hundreds or thousands of dollars. According to Zirlin, Axie NFTs have fetched $2 billion in the aggregate. By gamifying NFTs, Axie can retain players. Nine-tenths of people who play are still playing after 30 days.[130]

Axie's popularity is surging in the global south, particularly the Philippines where playing this game has become a lucrative job. Young Filipinos are earnings thousands of dollars staying home and playing Axie. Journalist Vittoria Elliott described how this surge has also created a new industry where "players are often sponsored by managers or guilds, who fund their entry into the game—a high barrier, with current costs that can go upwards of $1,500—in return for a cut." According to Elliott, "Guilds can sprawl hundreds of members managing various accounts, honing Axie characters and churning the value of the Axie Infinity Shard token ever higher."[131] Axie players have made so much money that the Philippine government now wants a cut of the action, claiming Axie rewards are income subject to tax.[132] Earning money for playing video games is not new. Twitch streamers and other e-gaming celebrities can make millions. But the NFT-enabled play-to-earn phenomenon is democratizing that.

The popularity of Axie has sent the value of its native token soaring. In early October 2021, the fully diluted market capitalization hit $40 billion.[133] That was as much as Electronic Arts, maker of popular titles like the Madden NFL game ($40.9 billion), and nearly as much as Roblox ($43.5 billion) and Nintendo ($53.8 billion), perhaps the best-known videogame company in the world.[134]

In McLuhan's day, an analog broadcast medium was transforming how we consumed information. NFTs and the underlying blockchain are a digital medium for value, changing the nature of digital goods and how we consume culture and interact online. Why is this important? Because it reveals the immense power of digital assets that we can own, trade, and transport across different environments and jurisdictions. Chris Dixon, a partner at Andreessen Horowitz said, "Tokens give users property rights: the ability to own a piece of the Internet."[135] The ability to own unique and scarce digital assets—such as our digital identities—and move freely around the Internet without the risk of duplication or seizure by a centralized platform is a profound shift from how finance works today. The medium is the message. Time to tune in.

STABLECOINS

Stablecoins are digital assets that track the value of some well-known and understood asset, typically the US dollar. They are, in effect, programmable fiat currency, but most governments don't recognize them as legal tender. Still, stablecoins are the dominant media of exchange in the digital asset ecosystem and have grown at a prodigious rate—surpassing $125 billion in circulating supply, compared with less than $2 billion two years ago.[136]

There are two kinds of stablecoins: centralized and decentralized. The larger category today is centralized stablecoins issued by companies, backed by reserves, and created largely to meet the insatiable demand for cryptoassets. To wit, Centre Consortium's USDC recently surpassed $30 billion in circulating supply and handles about $3.5 billion a *day* in volume—more than 10 times that of Venmo, the most popular payment app in the United States.[137]

Perhaps the most famous centralized stablecoin is Facebook's project, originally named Libra. Facebook had hoped to back Libra with a basket of other fiat currencies, including the US dollar and the euro. In Facebook's view, Libra would bank the unbanked, connect the unconnected, and position Facebook as a leader in the Internet of value, not just the Internet of information. The US government had other ideas. After much lobbying, Facebook cut the scope and ambition of the project, reimagining it as a US dollar–backed stablecoin called Diem. That didn't fly either. Regulators seem loath to green light any such coin while the name Facebook remains toxic. Instead, Facebook launched its digital wallet Novi and chose the Paxos Trust Company's US dollar–backed stablecoin (USDP) and Coinbase's custody services for its pilot in the United States and Guatemala.[138]

Representing only one percent of all stablecoins in circulation, the Pax dollar is a bit player compared to such centralized stablecoins as USDC or USDT. For Paxos, the deal is a potential game changer. "This news represents a tide shift in digital assets, as it's the first time that stablecoins are readily available in a consumer wallet outside of the crypto ecosystem," said Walter Hessert, head of strategy and business development at Paxos.[139] Paxos understands the significance of this deal, if not the risks associated with a tech giant so often in regulatory crosshairs, as they team up to integrate stablecoins into the payment landscape. (Facebook has since announced the change of its corporate name to Meta.[140])

Decentralized stablecoins have similarly exploded in value, though are still smaller than their centralized cousins. DAI, a decentralized stablecoin maintained by MakerDAO, has over $6 billion in circulation and does around $500 million a day in volume, which is more than Venmo.[141] Algorithmic stablecoins are a subset of decentralized stablecoins. UST, created on the Terra Luna blockchain, is one of the fastest growing and most widely used stablecoins in the DeFi ecosystem today. With over $2.5 billion in circulating supply, UST supports Terra Luna's burgeoning DeFi ecosystem, which has over $8.7 billion in TVL today. Do Kwon, the creator of Terra Luna, told us:

> From the start, building decentralized products that have the potential to augment the demand for UST, Terra's primary product, was our singular focus. Similar to the US dollar, ossifying demand for UST via a growing economy enveloping the currency is the best way to ensure the long-term success and sustainability of the ecosystem.[142]

Kwon's goal is to make UST the de facto stablecoin for the DeFi ecosystem, "with the mandate to issue the most robust, censorship-resistant stablecoin that DeFi requires to blossom."

There is some debate about how truly "decentralized" many of these algorithmic stablecoins are, leading the accusation by some that they're *decentralized in name only* (DINO), a clever acronym that riffs off the *Republican in name only* (RINO) tag of the Trump era. Any point of centralization gives regulators a way to crack down. This might soon be put to the test. Decentralized stablecoins help keep DeFi decentralized as well. After all, if the main payment rails for DeFi are centrally controlled stablecoins, how decentralized are they really? Or as Do Kwon said, "Without adequately decentralized stablecoins, DeFi will be subject to many of the same confined gateways and limitations of the legacy financial system for which it seeks to offer an alternative. Governments can force uptake of CBDCs."[143]

Centralized stablecoins are likely to face greater oversight of such regulators as the US Securities and Exchange Commission (SEC) and the CFTC. In early November 2021, the President's Working Group on Financial Markets, along with the OCC and the Federal Deposit Insurance Corporation, released a report on stablecoins.[144] They recommended that Congress swiftly pass laws that would subject custodial wallet providers to federal oversight and require stablecoin issuers to register as insured depository institutions and be supervised as such.[145]

Many industry watchers expect more stringent regulations to follow suit. SEC Chair Gary Gensler, who many hoped would be more open to the industry, has proven a tough critic. In a statement on the report, Gensler said, "We at the SEC and our sibling agency, the [CFTC], will deploy the full protections of the federal securities laws and the Commodity Exchange Act to these products and arrangements, where applicable."[146]

On various occasions Gensler has compared the crypto industry to the Wild West, repeating the comparison again in a recent interview with the *Washington Post*, "We've got a lot of casinos here in the Wild West .... And the poker chip is these stablecoins."[147] This comparison is unfair to the many regulated stablecoins such as USDC and trivializes the size, importance, and reach of the $125 billion stablecoin market. It's also just plain wrong—poker chips can be spent only in casinos, and sometimes only in the casino that issues them, kind of like Chuck E. Cheese money. Stablecoins are a highly liquid, widely accepted medium of exchange not confined to any one application or company.

A more nuanced critique of stablecoins was offered by Federal Reserve Board Governor Lael Brainard who said, "If widely adopted, stablecoins could serve as the basis of an alternative payments system oriented around new private forms of money," adding later that "a predominance of private monies may introduce consumer protection and financial stability risks because of their potential volatility and the risk of run-like behavior."[148] To be sure, centralized stablecoins should be fully backed by reserves, subject to regulation and periodic audits and fully transparent about their holdings to avoid these issues.

Some have suggested that stablecoins pose a threat to the government's monopoly on printing money. The opposite is probably true. Former Federal Reserve Board Governor Randal K. Quarles offered a starkly different view from his colleague Brainard, revealing, among other things, a clear lack of consensus in the world's most powerful central bank. In a recent speech, he argued that stablecoins could improve the speed and efficiency of the payments infrastructure and that innovation like this should be supported. He also quipped:

> We do not need to fear stablecoins. ...The Federal Reserve has traditionally supported responsible private sector innovation. Consistent with this tradition, I believe that we must take strong account of the potential benefits of stablecoins, including the possibility that a US dollar stablecoin might support the role of the dollar in the global economy.[149]

This makes sense. Banks have often worked hand in glove with the Federal government to extend United States influence into different parts of the world. Quarles added that "a global US dollar stablecoin network could encourage use of the dollar by making cross-border payments faster and cheaper, and it potentially could be deployed much faster and with fewer downsides than a CBDC." Quarles said, "The concern that stablecoins represent the unprecedented creation of private money and thus challenge our monetary sovereignty is puzzling, given that our existing system involves—indeed depends on—private firms creating money every day."[150] Indeed.

SECURITIES TOKENS

The securities market, which includes stocks, bonds, derivatives, and investment funds, is the mother of all markets. At its core, a security is nothing more than a contract. Take the humble stock—the bearer of a common share has a contractual right to a piece of a common enterprise, a right to a stream of cash flows, should that enterprise pay a dividend, and the right to vote on certain enterprise matters. We can program and automate each one of those concepts in a token so that securities markets run more efficiently, fairly, and inclusively because:

- Trades settle instantly rather than in days.
- Voting takes place instantaneously and transparently on-chain so that everyone can see results.
- Anyone with Internet access can trade them and participate in wealth creation.

However, which tokens are securities is open to interpretation. Three categories of tokens function like securities:

- *DeFi securities tokens and funds.* DeFi securities often take the form of pooled investment funds, such as DeFi index funds.
- *Synthetic securities.* These trade on centralized exchanges (e.g., FTX) and decentralized platforms (e.g., Mirror). They give investors a way to participate in securities markets that investors would not be able to access, such as the market for private stock (e.g., Coinbase pre-IPO) or shares listed in other countries.
- *TradFi-issued tokens.* Banks and other intermediaries issue these stocks and bonds, often on a crypto-native rail and a traditional rail, and then record ownership on a blockchain as well as on an off-chain registry.

DeFi index funds: Securitizing crypto

Many of the largest asset managers in the traditional financial world are passive ETFs and index funds. DeFi index funds are small relative to DeFi as a whole and subatomic compared to ETFs, which have over $7.5 *trillion* in assets.[151] The biggest one is Index Co-op, a DAO launched by Set Protocol. It teamed up with DeFi Pulse and other well-known entities to develop the DeFi Pulse Index. Today, Index Co-Op has around $400 million, which is small relative to the entire DeFi space. Despite its modest size today, Index Co-op has its sights set on a much bigger opportunity—to become the DeFi Blackrock, a decentralized autonomous asset manager that allows anyone to develop a passive investment fund.

Synthetic securities

Various exchanges and platforms offer investors synthetic versions of traditional securities in public companies like Apple or Google, or pre-IPO shares in upcoming listings such as Coinbase (Table 1-2).

TABLE 1-2

SYNTHETIC EQUITIES TRADING VOLUME

Select March 2022 futures, 24-hour trading period

TICKER	NAME	VOLUME
MSTR-0325	MicroStrategy	$1,897,795.96
BNTX-0325	BioNTech	$1,053,563.51
MRNA-0325	Moderna	$901,673.03
NVDA-0325	NVIDIA	$470,047.13
TSLA-0325	Tesla	$361,542.46
AMD-0325	Advanced Micro Devices	$214,131.59
AMZN-0325	Amazon	$198,468.22
GOOGL-0325	Alphabet	$186,506.02
UBER-0325	Uber	$176,847.51
SPY-0325	SPDR S&P 500 ETF	$176,597.35
FB-0325	Facebook	$167,803.92
ZM-0325	Zoom	$133,953.71
BABA-0325	Alibaba	$116,112.16
TWTR-0325	Twitter	$85,800.01
AAPL-0325	Apple	$31,417.05
ABNB-0325	Airbnb	$26,387.64

Source of data: Tokenized Stock Futures, FTX.com, FTX Trading GmbH, as of 19 Jan. 2022. ftx.com/intl/markets/future.

However, not all these assets are tokens, and none confer owner-ship of the underlying shares. In effect, holders have price exposure (i.e., they can make or lose money) but no rights or obligations of shareholders, such as voting rights.

Not unlike traditional equities market, the derivatives market asso-ciated with these synthetics is highly active. For example, the popular global exchange FTX offers nearly 50 USD synthetic pairs: inves-tors can trade around 50 different assets against the US dollar. In a recent 24-hour period, the total trading volume for synthetic equities hit $1.5 million. By contrast, the trading volume for synthetic equi-ties futures in the same period was nearly $5 million. Two lessons: first, derivatives are a more liquid market; and second, these figures are paltry compared to traditional cash equities markets. Still, the growth of such a new asset has been impressive.

For FTX, this is a sideshow to its main business as a cryptoas-set and crypto-derivatives platform. Not so for synthetic trading app Mirror built on the Terra Luna platform and designed exclusively for synthetic trading. Users of Mirror tokenize stocks by deposit-ing collateral such as the Terra stablecoins into Mirror contracts. Do Kwon of Terra Luna said:

Mirror is a decentralized, community-governed, synthetic assets protocol on Terra that provides an open-source framework for issuing and trading tokenized assets pegged to their real-world counterparts. Mirror provides asset exposure to many people in financially disenfranchised regions of the world who are blocked from major wealth-generating markets.

However, mAsset exposure is explicitly price exposure and does not confer ownership of the underlying asset, which simply uses oracles and arbitrage incentives to mediate its peg to the underlying real-world asset. Due to its open-source nature, myriad applications can be built on top of Mirror beyond its current iteration, such as options, futures, and more that wield the underlying mAssets of "synths."

Demand for synths is significant because it offers uncorrelated (top crypto markets) asset exposure on-chain—helping investors to diversify their portfolio risk and participate in both TradFi and DeFi simultaneously. Naturally, the potential TAM for synthetics is enormous, and we're only in the early stages of exploring their potential.[152]

mAssets are truly tokens, native to the Terra Luna blockchain and not derivatives on a centralized exchange. So, although they are basically an experimental market, they contain the blueprint for blockchain-enabled securities.

TradFi initiatives

Blockchain enables instant clearing, settlement, and record keeping for assets, including securities. Thus, TradFi institutions are looking to leverage it for their own businesses. However, there are various barriers to securities tokens scaling in this environment. First, legacy attitudes make some industry participants skeptical and reluctant to change. Second, installed market infrastructure and technologies make switching to a "crypto-native" format challenging. Third, customers are used to the old ways and may not want to switch over. Fourth, it is difficult to "tokenize" something that already exists in analog format. It's much easier to start from scratch with a new issue in a purely crypto-native format. Most financial assets already exist.

In spite of these challenges, there have been dozens of successful securities tokens offerings from entities in

- Australia—Commonwealth Bank of Australia, International Bank for Reconstruction and Development, Queensland Treasury Corp., RBC Capital Markets, TD Securities, and the World Bank

- Austria—Oesterreichische Kontrollbank AG
- Belgium, Luxembourg, and Spain—European Investment Bank, Euroclear, Banco Santander, and EY
- Canada—National Bank of Canada, J.P.Morgan, Bank of Montreal, and Ontario Teachers' Pension Plan
- France—Banque de France, EIB, Goldman Sachs, Santander, Société Générale Assurances, and Société Générale SFH
- Germany—Commerzbank, Daimler, DZ BANK AG, KfW Banking Group, Landesbank Baden-Württemberg, MEAG, Telefónica Deutschland Holding AG, and Vonovia
- Germany and Luxembourg—Continental, Commerzbank, and Siemens
- India—YES BANK and Vedanta Ltd.
- the Philippines—UnionBank and Standard Chartered
- Thailand—Bank of Thailand
- United Kingdom—Allen & Overy, LuxDeco, and Nivaura.[153]

Moreover, as regulated securities tokens become more popular, there is a growing demand for market infrastructure such as exchanges to transact in them. Tzero, INX, ISTOX, and others are trying to fill this gap, but they are still tiny compared to the broader cryptoasset ecosystem and financial markets in general. Perhaps securities like equities will become less relevant over time as we organize more economic activity in DAOs where governance tokens, not "common shares," give users and holders influence over the direction of these entities.

GOVERNANCE TOKENS

Recall that DAOs are on-chain entities that facilitate the governance and economic coordination of decentralized protocols, often with a large token treasury—effectively a war chest belonging to a piece of software (Table 1-3).

TABLE 1-3

LARGEST DAO TREASURIES

NAME	TOTAL TREASURY	LIQUID TREASURY
Uniswap	$7,059,549,080	$2,858,238,061
BitDAO	$2,518,235,477	$2,518,235,477
ENS	$1,820,387,081	$173,923,487
Gitcoin	$647,115,279	$103,524,706
GnosisDAO	$607,078,177	$607,078,177
Compound	$516,281,901	$36,417,249
Lido	$495,123,865	$495,123,865
Aave	$455,860,994	$455,860,994
Abracadabra	$412,240,397	$412,240,397
MakerDAO	$244,415,581	$244,415,581

Source of data: David Mihal, OpenOrgs.info, openorgs.info, as of 19 Jan. 2022.

MakerDAO, which maintains and regulates the DAI stablecoin, charges a small fee for minting DAI that accrues to the protocol's treasury as so-called "protocol revenue." As of August 2021, MakerDAO had earned over $63 million in fees for the year.[154] While modest compared to any large company, the MakerDAO model for a DAO, which can earn money and distribute funds, will become the model for the digital asset world and beyond.

Indeed, DAO treasuries are a by-product of this new model for organizing human activity. This is a radical departure from the traditional system, which relies on corporations as the main human artifact for creating value in the economy. Indeed, for a century, the main theories of management have enabled managers to build corporations, which have largely been hierarchical, insular, and vertically integrated.

However, DAOs allow us to rethink many functions of the firm beyond just storing value: how they are funded and managed, how they create value, who they employ, where they are domiciled, how they are regulated, and how they perform basic functions such as marketing, accounting, and incentivizing people (Table 1-4).

Marc Andreessen once explained why software is eating the world.[155] A prime example: DAOs are eating the corporation.

TABLE 1-4

DECENTRALIZED AUTONOMOUS ORGANIZATIONS

NAME	SYMBOL	PRICE	MARKET CAP	PURPOSE
Uniswap	UNI	$15.53	$9,768,361,591	Governs changes to protocol logic and allocation of governance funds
Aave	AAVE	$216.08	$2,919,567,330	Governs changes and upgrades to the Aave protocol
Maker	MKR	$2,031.54	$2,003,535,960	Governs policy for DAI stablecoin, collateral types, and governance itself
Curve DAO	CRV	$4.35	$1,970,070,448	Governs incentive structure, fee payment method, and long-term earnings method for liquidity providers
Dash	DASH	$128.99	$1,359,934,927	Governs budgets and projects funded
Compound	COMP	$171.63	$1,089,673,841	Governs adding assets, changing collateral factors, interest rate model, or other parameter/variable of protocol
Decred	DCR	$67.25	$924,201,193	Governs spending and changes to software and policy
SushiSwap	SUSHI	$6.09	$777,217,701	Governs changes to ecosystem
0x	ZRX	$0.6947	$590,200,255	Governs community treasury, not protocol upgrades
Synthetix	SNX	$4.96	$570,349,371	Governs ecosystem improvements and configuration changes

Sources of data: "DAOs," CoinMarketCap.com, CoinMarketCap OpCo LLC, as of 19 Jan. 2022, and each DAO's website. coinmarketcap.com/view/dao.

Whether DAOs are better suited for creating products and services and for delivering value to stakeholders remains unproven in a wider range of settings beyond DeFi protocols. But DAOs can perform many functions at least as well as traditional companies, including making money.

FIGURE 1-6

DEFI PROTOCOL ANNUALIZED REVENUE

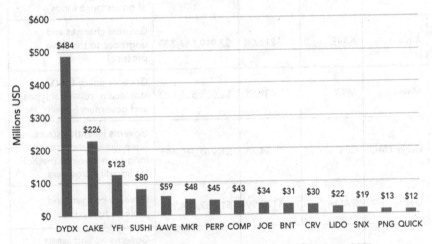

Source of data: "Protocol Revenue," TokenTerminal.com, as of 30 Sept. 2021. www.tokenterminal.com/terminal/metrics/protocol_revenue.

EXCHANGE TOKENS

Crypto exchange tokens are native to centralized exchanges, such as Binance and FTX (Table 1-5). Typically, these tokens provide rewards and discounts, improve liquidity, and provide other incentives to use a given exchange. They are similar to governance tokens of decentralized exchanges in that they are essential to the exchange's functionality and incentivize user growth. Unlike those tokens, however, they are more centrally managed and don't often confer governance rights.

The market capitalizations of the biggest exchange tokens have nevertheless exploded in value, especially as those exchanges launch

TABLE 1-5

TOP CENTRALIZED EXCHANGE TOKENS

EXCHANGE TOKEN	SYMBOL	PRICE	MARKET CAP
Binance Coin	BNB	$471.17	$77,672,705,991
Crypto.com Coin	CRO	$0.4337	$10,951,485,234
FTX Token	FTT	$46.19	$6,393,392,216
UNES SED LEO	LEO	$3.64	$3,480,673,417
KuCoin Token	KCS	$20.22	$1,619,388,681
Huobi Token	HT	$9.94	$1,557,373,117
OKB	OKB	$25.49	$1,530,295,133
LINK	LN	$138.04	$824,847,313
WOO Network	WOO	$0.7874	$696,207,914
GateToken	GT	$7.08	$552,661,906

Source of data: "Centralized Exchange," CoinMarketCap.com, CoinMarketCap OpCo LLC, as of 19 Jan. 2022. coinmarketcap.com/view/centralized-exchange.

adjacent DeFi projects where the tokens will have added utility, such as BNB, the native token for Binance. At the beginning of October 2021, BNB had a market capitalization of $70 billion.[156] That was more than twice as much as the market cap of Nasdaq ($31 billion) at the time, and BNB wasn't even equity in the company, at least not in the traditional sense.[157]

However, Binance is the largest and most profitable cryptoasset exchange in the world, and its native token has enormous utility inside the app and on its DeFi project, Binance Smart Chain. BNB is a utility token for discounted trading fees and referral levels: the more BNB tokens a user holds, the higher the percentage return for making referrals. As Binance grows and diversifies, holders of BNB will be able to use it for travel bookings, entertainment, online services, and other financial services. Every quarter, Binance uses one-fifth of its profits to destroy or "burn" its tokens permanently. In other words, the token has increasing utility (i.e., usefulness) and declining supply, which is generally a recipe for rising value.[158] In addition, BNB is the protocol token for the Binance Smart Chain, which supports its own ecosystem of dapps. This added functionality contributes to the immense value of BNB.

Though Binance is the largest exchange, FTX is rapidly gaining ground. FTX also has an exchange token whose value is geared to trading. FTX tokens serve as collateral for futures positions, discounts on trading fees, and staking and earning interest. Like Binance, FTX burns a portion of FTX periodically, banking on the same model of supply and demand to increase the aggregate value of the FTX token.

While FTX and Binance are the highest-profile exchange tokens, there are many others such as OKB, which offers discounts for trading fees, access to *initial coin offerings* (ICOs), and OKEx ecosystem access.[159] The Huobi Token lowers transaction fees, offers VIP discounts, and gives users access to exclusive events.[160] KuCoin acts like equity in that it pays a dividend to tokenholders based on trading fees.[161] In addition, holders get trading fee discounts, additional trading pairs, customer support fast passes, and other perquisites. Exchange tokens are a hybrid of loyalty points and equity: like loyalty points, they improve the quality of a customer's experience tremendously; and like equity, they offer users direct economic exposure to the success of the platform.

NATURAL ASSET TOKENS

At first glance, using a digital medium to manage a physical commodity seems a strange fit. How does one deliver physical oil, pork bellies, timber, or iron ore on a blockchain? However, we have various examples of using digital assets to express physical assets in the real world. Most commodities trade in the futures market, not the spot market, meaning when we buy oil, for example, we're buying a contract obligating us to buy oil at a future date. Futures are *contracts* and so we can make them smart. Earlier we discussed how decentralized futures markets such as dYdX are exploding in popularity as a way for speculators and investors to get exposure to cryptoassets. However, we can easily apply the underlying mechanics of a perpetual futures smart contract to virtually any futures market in the world, including commodities futures. Of course, this does not solve the physical delivery, but it could automate the front end of the market, improving speed and efficiency and perhaps even cutting down on risk.

Other nascent markets like carbon offsets could be scaled radically with the self-executing nature of smart contracts and immutable nature of blockchains. Global warming is a global crisis that requires a global solution. Carbon offsets could play an important role. Companies must offset their carbon footprint to meet standards set by governments, international accords, and increasingly many investors who are agitating for change. The best way to do that is by de-carbonizing our business model and our supply chain. That can take time. Carbon offsets can fill the gap in the meantime. There will be more demand for credits than what current projects, such as forestry conservation initiatives, can support.

What's required is a transparent, liquid market for carbon offsets with a common set of technical standards and a decentralized ledger for registering and retiring them. There are a few interesting projects addressing this issue. MCO2, a large global carbon market, is tokenizing carbon credits. XELS, which uses blockchain to trade carbon credits, listed recently on Bittrex, a large exchange. Single.Earth is trying to link carbon credits to token markets, and recently raised $7.9 million from EQT ventures. CarbonX wants to take this a step further, creating a way for individuals (and not just companies and governments) to earn credits as a reward for reducing their footprint.[162]

IMPLEMENTATION CHALLENGES OF DEFI

In *Blockchain Revolution*, we dedicated an entire chapter to reasons blockchain might fail or stall out. Let's revisit these with a focus on DeFi.[163]

THE TECHNOLOGY IS NOT READY FOR PRIME TIME

When we first raised this concern in 2016, the Bitcoin network was worth a few billion dollars and Ethereum had yet to launch. Dapps such smart contracts and DAOs had not yet been realized. Internet enthusiasts who used bitcoin were battling over its future—remember the block-size wars?[164] Corporations held few digital assets, and governments barely noticed the industry. We saw great potential but questioned whether the technology could cross the chasm to mainstream adoption.

After a decade, this industry is scaling rapidly. The value of the market today is over $2 trillion. Cryptoassets have created more value than every single unicorn launched after the financial crisis of 2007–2008. Today, 10 million people use MetaMask monthly. Nearly 30 percent of Nigerians use bitcoin as an alternative to banks. Gemini and Coinbase custody cryptoassets on behalf of Fortune 500 companies. El Salvador became the first country to make bitcoin legal tender. DeFi user growth is parabolic. NFTs have smashed into the mainstream, capturing the zeitgeist. DAOs have multi-billion-dollar treasuries. New protocols like Solana, Cosmos, and others are rapidly scaling Layer 1 throughput. Stablecoin values are over $125 billion. Coinbase went public. Every single corporation in the world is (or at least should be) developing a cryptoasset and blockchain strategy.

THE ENERGY USE IS UNSUSTAINABLE

The future of DeFi and dapps is *proof of stake* (PoS) and not *proof of work* (PoW). Just look at the stunning rise of Terra Luna, Cosmos, Solana, and other PoS networks supporting much of the DeFi innovation today. Even Ethereum is preparing to migrate to a PoS consensus mechanism. Still, bitcoin will persist as a significant asset and network in this ecosystem. Bitcoin miners harness vast computing power to secure the Bitcoin network.[165] Those computers use a lot of energy—by some estimates as much as the country of Chile.[166] This has led to charges of energy waste.[167] Something "wastes" energy only to those who think it serves no useful function. The Bitcoin network secures $1 trillion in value and serves millions of people, including many without access to traditional payment networks. Miners often co-locate to where power is abundant and free, which often means renewable hydroelectric or geothermal sources. Today, renewable energy powers at least 39 percent of Bitcoin mining, and that share is growing rapidly.[168]

Another solution is to offset the carbon footprint of the Bitcoin network with carbon credits. For example, Ninepoint Partners (where I work) has partnered with environmental fintech CarbonX to offset fully the carbon footprint of the Ninepoint Bitcoin ETF.[169] CarbonX, along with the Crypto Carbon Ratings Institute, will provide carbon emission analysis, carbon offsetting services, and carbon footprint analysis of the Bitcoin network.[170] Ninepoint is paying the costs of doing this. Making bitcoin greener may attract new investors to the asset class. In my view, Ninepoint's efforts are a form of environmental self-monitoring. We hope others will follow.

GOVERNMENTS WILL STIFLE OR TWIST IT

Governments will not kill blockchain and DeFi, but they may regulate it so that people, capital, and other resources move to other jurisdictions. This is a pivotal moment in this trajectory of digital assets, DeFi, and blockchain. Governments are used to traditional custodial financial intermediaries, but DeFi is noncustodial. Regulators are used to overseeing companies and individuals, whereas DeFi is built on clever code and math. By failing to understand how the technology works, governments could inadvertently derail one of the fastest growing and most promising sectors in the economy today. For example, policymakers want to designate many cryptoasset businesses as registered securities platforms. However, securities platforms need transfer agents and clearinghouses. As venture capitalist Adam Cochran explained:

> Both are centralized, custodial agents who sit between an exchange and customer. Transfer agents' jobs are essentially to record ownership, maintain records, distribute dividends, and cancel/issue various stock certificates. All things that DeFi replaces with the ERC-20 standard and a dashboard that queries the chain. A clearinghouse validates and finalizes the transaction ... something that is entirely unnecessary in blockchain land because of T-instant settlement.[171]

In other words, DeFi is irreconcilable with this requirement. Labeling every digital asset a security is problematic. Rep. Tom Emmer (R-Minn.), a member of the rapidly growing blockchain caucus in Congress, raised concerns with SEC Chair Gensler's approach: "If Gensler deems a coin with a $1 billion market cap and tens of thousands of investors a security, what happens to those investors? The value of the token will plummet, and retail investors won't be able to trade it."[172] At this point, government cannot stop any of this. Cryptoassets are systemically important and will be regulated. The devil is in the details.

POWERFUL INCUMBENTS OF THE OLD PARADIGM WILL USURP IT

Powerful incumbents of the old paradigm have adopted cryptoassets and are looking seriously at DeFi and other applications. They have not "usurped" anything. If they tried, they'd likely fail. Consider stablecoins, a tiny sliver of this whole pie: Stablecoins are integrating more into the financial system. AngelList, a leading platform for venture capital investment, now accepts stablecoins for eligible investments.[173]

MasterCard announced plans to integrate stablecoins into its network. It also plans to integrate with CBDCs if and when they come into existence.[174] VISA now supports transaction settlement with the USDC stablecoin, which crossed $30 billion in circulating supply.[175] PayPal, a longtime cryptoasset innovator, has explored its own stablecoin.[176] Payment giants want a firm foothold in the world of programmable fiat. Whether they're able to adapt in time is up for debate. At the time this book went to print, VISA announced it was taking another leap forward into stablecoins, by announcing it would launch its own Layer 2 "universal payments channel" where customers could use different stablecoins and CBDCs for payments globally.[177]

We've already covered how dozens of traditional financial firms have launched custody solutions for cryptoassets.[178] The integration of cryptoassets and DeFi into traditional industries is accelerating innovation, growth, and user adoption, not stifling it.

THE INCENTIVES ARE INADEQUATE FOR ADOPTION: THE BOOTSTRAPPING PROBLEM

Our concerns here proved unwarranted. The opposite is true: tokens serve as an immensely powerful incentive for mass collaboration and adoption by turning early adopters and users into economic participants in the network.

Chris Dixon tweeted, "In the Web 2 era, overcoming the bootstrapping problem meant heroic entrepreneurial efforts, plus in many cases spending lots of money on sales and marketing."[179] This difficult and costly process led to only a few networks reaching global scale. Once they were firmly entrenched, it became difficult for new networks targeting similar users to compete (think Facebook). Dixon continued: "Web 3 introduces a powerful new tool for bootstrapping networks: token incentives. ... The basic idea is: early on during the bootstrapping phase when network effects haven't kicked in, provide users with financial utility via token rewards to make up for the lack of native utility."[180]

Users have no barriers to launching a token and trying their hand at network building. More projects might fail than in previous technology cycles, since the denominator (y=projects launched) will be so much higher, underscoring tokens' role in incentivizing mass collaboration, coordination, and value creation.[181]

BLOCKCHAIN IS A JOB KILLER

In *Blockchain Revolution,* we questioned whether blockchain would disintermediate many white-collar jobs such as accounting, legal work, and even management. Yes, Web 3 is changing the nature of the labor market, but it appears to be creating more work than it is destroying. We're seeing new kinds of jobs such as digital artists, professional videogame players, liquidity miners, and NFT dealers. Software developers are working for DAOs.[182]

In the Web 2 era, a bright young person might set her sights on a career in Silicon Valley or Wall Street. But the large intermediaries considered graduates only from top schools, placing formal accreditations at the top of the list. They'd require a person to show up to an office, undergo intensive training, and report to a boss in a chain of command to the top.

Web 3, with such innovations as DAOs, has minimal formal hierarchy, management teams, home offices, and so forth. But traditional job postings in finance on sites like Indeed are soaring, up 118 percent from a year ago.[183] Given heightened concern of a regulatory crackdown, more companies are hiring compliance officers.[184] Yes, Facebook and Goldman Sachs still attract top talent, but their monopoly is weakening, evidenced by the flight of quality engineers to DeFi and other blockchain projects.

GOVERNANCE IS LIKE HERDING CATS

Blockchain and DAO governance are evolving in real time. Today, users and tokenholders manage a dozen DAOs with treasuries in excess of $1 billion. However, DAOs have limitations such as voter apathy.[185] Tokenholders often ignore governance approvals that require their assent, leaving decision-making to a few large, tuned-in stakeholders.[186] That's similar to most proxy votes for corporations in traditional finance. Moreover, radical decentralization may work for certain industries, but vertical integration may suit situations such as pharmaceutical manufacturing.

These governance challenges are familiar to any shareholder of a public company or citizen of a democracy. When we wrote *Blockchain Revolution*, we questioned the ability of PoS networks to push updates (i.e., the block-size debates) and the actual viability of PoS as a system for organizing and securing a blockchain. So, in comparison, today's problems stem from prior governance successes, such as the launch of dozens of working Layer 1 smart contracting platforms. Thus, DAOs still must overcome this challenge. SX Network's solution to tokenholder apathy is to use prediction markets to encourage DAO governance participation, effectively gamifying governance.[187] We'll see if that works or if some people by their nature simply do not care enough to participate.

CRIMINALS WILL USE IT

Let's put this fallacy to bed for good: *criminals use cash far more than crypto*. In fact, they use crypto a lot less. Why? Because blockchains leave a tamper-resistant digital trail that any half-decent Federal Bureau of Investigation agent can use to bust a would-be criminal. Chainalysis estimated that one percent of bitcoin transactions are linked to illicit activity.[188] Chainalysis has built an estimated $3 billion business using blockchains to bust criminals and keep institutions safe.

CONCLUSION: THE COMING CONFLAGRATION

The first era of the Internet upended information industries like news, advertising, and music. The second era of the Internet, enabled by blockchain and other digital assets will make those disruptions look quaint. Financial services, foundational to all industry, enterprise, and human economic activity, is undergoing a metamorphosis from a lumbering caterpillar, devouring everything in its path, to a soaring butterfly.

Yes, DeFi has its fair share of issues. Many of these applications are built on Ethereum, a network overloaded by the popularity of DeFi. Other platforms like Solana have had growing pains. Many dapps have clunky user interfaces, though that is changing rapidly. Let's not overstate their popularity today: Uniswap has only two million users. Regulators have questioned how decentralized some of these platforms truly are and have their sights set on tighter rules that could cause uncertainty and volatility. These are important implementation challenges to overcome. The winners will be those who overcome them.

British historian Eric Hobsbawm said the "short 20th century," which began in 1914 with the outbreak of the First World War, ended in 1989 with the collapse of the Soviet Union.[189] Francis Fukuyama called it "the end of history."[190] While the scales of geopolitics tilted dramatically that year, these forecasts for radical change were overstated. Perhaps the COVID crisis of 2020 marks the end of the long twentieth century and the true beginning of the twenty-first century.

While DeFi is inclusive, a new assertive cohort of (often young) crypto-native users is defining a financial counterculture analogous to the counterculture of the 1960s. Just as baby boomers rebelled against the institutions and cultural mores of their parents' generation, today's crypto-native generation is rebelling against a strict and permissioned financial system, the rigid hierarchy of institutions in art and culture, and the closed and stifling systems of Web 2. In 1960s, counterculture icon Timothy Leary encouraged his followers to "turn on, tune in, and drop out."[191] Today's youth are applying that mantra to technology—turning their brains on to digital assets, tuning into DeFi and its myriad applications, and dropping out of the legacy financial system. In the process, they are transforming every aspect of the industry.

The beginning of this new twenty-first century belongs to them.

If bitcoin was the spark for the financial services revolution, then DeFi and digital assets are the accelerant. The fire will engulf firms that fail to innovate, adapt, and embrace this hot new industry. The conflagration will suck oxygen from centralized systems and spread them into a new decentralized web. The financial and economic phoenix that rises will be virtually unrecognizable to the system we have today.

CHAPTER 2

COSMOS AND POLKADOT FOR THE ENTERPRISE

A Study of the Leading Blockchain Interoperability Solutions

Anthony D. Williams

 ## INTEROPERABILITY IN BRIEF

- Bitcoin, Ethereum, and Hyperledger are seeing enterprise adoption, but none offers a mechanism for communicating with or transferring value across other blockchains. Imagine if that were still true with email, where we couldn't send an email message to a Gmail address unless we had a Google account or Google's permission.[192]

- Cosmos and Polkadot represent their creators' efforts to enable cross-blockchain communication and tackle the scalability and throughput limitations that inhibited mainstream enterprise adoption. Their strategies for achieving these goals, however, differ significantly.

  - Dubbed the "Internet of blockchains," Cosmos is a network of independent, yet interoperable blockchains that can communicate in a decentralized way.

  - Polkadot offers tools that enable independent blockchains to communicate, exchange value, and share functionality via its central relay chain.

- Both Cosmos and Polkadot offer enterprise clients powerful and user-friendly platforms for building blockchains that can interoperate with a rapidly growing ecosystem of dapps.

- While Cosmos and Polkadot have much in common, each has trade-offs that relate to blockchain sovereignty, governance, security, and the fees required to run on the network. Neither addresses integration with existing enterprise systems.

THE CHALLENGE OF INTEROPERABILITY

Imagine email without simple mail transfer protocol, post office protocol, or interactive mail access protocol, or picture the Internet without transmission control protocol/Internet protocol, hypertext transfer protocol, or uniform resource locators.[193] These are the widely used standards for connectivity among email clients, websites, and applications that billions of us enjoy today. Without such ubiquitous communication protocols—or the nonprofit and open-source communities behind them such as the Internet Engineering Task Force (IETF)—each email client, website, app, or database would be an island unto itself and much less useful.[194]

Imagine nothing but a sea of such islands, some of them more populated than others, that cannot communicate among themselves. That's precisely the state of affairs with blockchain today. Bitcoin has proven to be a resilient store of value for both individuals and enterprises looking to protect their wealth from monetary inflation and macro-economic uncertainty. The Ethereum network is also seeing accelerating adoption of DeFi products. A handful of other blockchains and smart contract platforms such as R3 Corda, Ripple, and ConsenSys Quorum are also growing at a rapid pace. The trouble for enterprise adopters is that these blockchains are mutually incompatible systems: there is no seamless way to transfer data or value between them.

The Ethereum and Bitcoin networks don't communicate with each other, and neither do the dozens of other prominent blockchain networks still functioning today. Value recorded on one network is not visible on—or transferable to—other blockchains, making transactions difficult without centralized exchanges such as Binance, Coinbase, and Kraken acting as intermediaries to transfer funds.

In these early days of enterprise usage, no company wants to bet on a blockchain solution that won't interoperate with its supply chain partners, its customers, or any regulatory bodies that are using blockchain for official transactions. This lack of interoperability is what led to the creation of networks like Cosmos and Polkadot, both of which are designed to function as connectors, allowing blockchain networks to transfer value in a trustless and efficient manner.

Cosmos and Polkadot are similar in the sense that they enable cross-blockchain communication, but there are significant differences in their governance and network architecture that enterprise users should understand. Cosmos' founders are building the Cosmos network with the ethos of sovereign interoperability at its core. That means that anyone can leverage the complete stack of Cosmos' interoperability technology without vendor lock-in or network fees. Polkadot is building its network around the concept of Web 3.0. The idea is that anyone should be able to develop a dapp on the Internet— that is, it should be simple—and so Polkadot's software stack allows developers to create products without needing to build entire blockchain governance or security systems from scratch.

Both Cosmos and Polkadot have promising ecosystems, with hundreds of partners building products using their respective technologies across a wide array of industries. These projects are collectively valued at tens of billions of dollars, proving the market demand for interoperability is real.

INTRODUCING COSMOS

Cosmos is a decentralized network of independent blockchains called "zones" that can interoperate with each other thanks to the shared communication and consensus protocols of the Cosmos Hub. Dubbed the Internet of blockchains, the Cosmos network enables cross-blockchain communication while scaling network throughput beyond what most independent blockchains can handle on their own.

At the core of the Cosmos vision is the ethos of sovereign interoperability: the ability of independent blockchains to interoperate while maintaining control over the design and governance of their blockchain applications. The fundamental bet on Cosmos is that blockchains will work similarly to how the Internet works today. Just as the Internet provides permissionless access to billions of connected devices and people, Cosmos sees the future of blockchain as a loose network of interconnected and interoperable blockchains that will replace the few dominant and highly siloed blockchain platforms we have today.

COSMOS' ORIGINS AND ETHOS

In 2013, a blockchain software architect named Jae Kwon was researching alternatives to PoW, the core consensus algorithm for blockchains such as Bitcoin and Ethereum. For Kwon, PoW presented several limitations, but environmental concerns were top of mind. Because PoW requires cryptocurrency miners to solve computationally complex problems, it requires a lot of computing power that, in turn, consumes a great deal of electricity. In short, the enormous energy consumption needed to sustain a PoW approach to consensus at scale is wasteful and environmentally damaging, and Kwon thought more efficient mechanisms were possible. Proof of work has other well-documented limitations in security, efficiency, and performance that were also of concern as Kwon worked on alternatives using a PoS algorithm.[195]

The result of Kwon's work was Tendermint, a production-grade Byzantine-fault tolerant (BFT) consensus engine that uses PoS to achieve consensus and works not only in private, permissioned settings but also on public cryptocurrency networks.[196]

Launched in 2014, Tendermint is an incredibly resilient multinode database with applications that reach far beyond cryptocurrencies. As a consensus algorithm, Tendermint's PoS approach to consensus is less computationally intensive than PoW and thus significantly reduces energy consumption at scale. With the annual electricity consumption of Bitcoin miners rivaling that of small countries like Argentina and Sweden, this nontrivial win is less costly and considerably more environmentally friendly.[197]

Tendermint's PoS approach is also secure, fast, and scalable. Whereas the Bitcoin network handles seven transactions per second with about 60 minutes of confirmation time, and dapps built on top of Ethereum share a rate of 15 to 25 transactions per second and six minutes of transaction time, Tendermint has a block time of one to two seconds and can process thousands of transactions per second.[198]

In 2014, Kwon joined forces with Ethan Buchman to launch All in Bits Inc. (d/b/a Tendermint), a company that manages the ongoing development of the core infrastructure for Cosmos, including the Tendermint consensus algorithm. In 2016, Kwon and Buchman fleshed out a vision for an interconnected network of blockchains in a white paper, "Cosmos: A Network of Distributed Ledgers."[199] The white paper presented a road map for enabling independent blockchains to communicate and transact easily without relinquishing sovereignty. That same year, Kwon and Buchman launched the Interchain Foundation (ICF), a nonprofit organization with a mission to help fund ongoing development work needed to bring the Cosmos ecosystem to fruition.

THE CORE TECHNOLOGY COMPONENTS OF COSMOS

Tendermint packages the networking and consensus layer of a blockchain into a generic engine for the Cosmos ecosystem called the Tendermint Core. With the engine's handling of the complex underlying protocols, developers can focus on building applications on top of the Tendermint core. Cosmos claims its platform reduces the time to develop new blockchains from years to weeks.[200] In addition to the Tendermint Core are Cosmos' native token ATOM, Cosmos' *software development kit* (SDK), and IBC protocol.

ATOM, the native Cosmos token

In April 2017, ICF held an ICO for ATOM, the native currency of the soon-to-be launched Cosmos network. Through the ICO, ICF raised $17 million, an amount that quickly accrued as the value of ATOM and other cryptocurrencies increased.[201] In the last public report, ICF's $17 million had grown to $104 million by November 2019, with ICF treasurer Arianne Flemming telling *CoinDesk*, "To date, we still have over 1,400 BTC, over 50,000 ETH, and just over 20 million ATOMs in the treasury."[202] With cash on hand, and after almost two years of development work, Tendermint launched the Cosmos Network in March 2019.

The ATOM has three uses.[203] First is to prevent spam. Users pay fees in ATOMs in proportion to the amount of computation their transactions require, and so spamming the network would be costly. Second is staking tokens. Users who stake or bond quantities of ATOMs to validators of transactions not only ensure the economic security of the hub but also make them eligible for block rewards. Third is governance. ATOM holders who've staked ATOMs can vote on proposals.

Cosmos software development kit

The Cosmos SDK is a framework that simplifies the process of building blockchain applications on the Tendermint Core.[204] It puts the Cosmos principle of sovereign interoperability into practice by enabling enterprise users to build on top of Tendermint in any programming language they choose.[205] On Ethereum, developers must write apps using programming languages that can be compiled down to byte code that the Ethereum virtual machine can understand.[206]

The Cosmos SDK is also designed to be modular, meaning that it comes equipped with many of the core modules that an enterprise might need to launch its blockchain application, such as a coin distribution algorithm, the Starport command-line interface, and a PoS governance mechanism, which—as we've noted—uses far less energy than PoW.[207] That appeals to enterprise stakeholders who have committed to sustainable development goals and have been reluctant to experiment with or adopt blockchain solutions.[208] Tendermint CEO Peng Zhong said that the SDK makes enterprise adoption as attractive as possible:

> As an enterprise, investing into blockchain technology shouldn't require massive amounts of time or capital. With the current version of Starport, you're able to build a new blockchain in minutes. My goal is to make the Cosmos platform easy enough to use so that any enterprise team can spin up a new chain to solve their business problem, as they do with Google Sheets or Airtable today.[209]

As testaments to its usability, two of the world's largest cryptocurrency exchanges, Binance and OKEx, built their blockchain-based exchanges with the Cosmos SDK.[210] As Binance explained in its acknowledgments, "Projects like Binance Chain and Binance DEX are often built as forks of Bitcoin or as smart contracts on platforms like Ethereum. With a foundation of clean, well-structured code from Cosmos SDK, we were able to build on a codebase that we saw as a better alternative."[211]

Interblockchain communication

The IBC is a protocol for relaying messages or transferring data and value (i.e., tokens) between independent blockchains. In essence, IBC is the foundation of blockchain interoperability in the Cosmos network, the equivalent of transmission control protocol/Internet protocol (TCP/IP) for the Internet.[212] Buchman explained in an interview:

> IBC is designed a lot like TCP/IP was designed, as a base-layer transport network for the Internet that many applications can be built on top of, like HTTP, SMTP, and many others. IBC has core transport logic built in and allows anyone to build applications for different purposes on top. IBC is even designed to be able to accommodate different consensus engines outside of Tendermint.[213]

In the Cosmos network, IBC acts as a connective web between "zones" and "hubs." Zones are independently maintained blockchains, and hubs are connectors of heterogeneous zones. When a zone creates an IBC connection with a hub, it can automatically access (i.e., send to and receive from) every other zone connected to that hub. A constant stream of recent block commits from zones posted on the hub allows the hub to keep in sync with the state of each zone. Likewise, each zone keeps directly in sync with the state of the hub (and indirectly with other zones through the shared hub).

In this sense, Cosmos is a stark departure from the ambitions of some blockchain platforms to become the "single dominant blockchain" with total global transaction ordering.[214] With IBC, Cosmos permits many blockchains to run concurrently while retaining interoperability. This decentralized, interoperable architecture is key to Tendermint's claim that Cosmos is more scalable than monolithic blockchains like Ethereum and Bitcoin. Kwon and Buchman wrote in their white paper:

This architecture solves many problems that the blockchain space faces today, such as application interoperability, scalability, and seamless upgradability …. Cosmos is not just a single distributed ledger, and the Cosmos Hub isn't a walled garden or the center of its universe. We are designing a protocol for an open network of distributed ledgers that can serve as a new foundation for future financial systems, based on principles of cryptography, sound economics, consensus theory, transparency, and accountability.[215]

Although IBC was part of Kwon and Buchman's vision from beginning, they took several years to develop it and 18 months to test it before IBC was ready for production. Tendermint officially launched IBC on 18 February 2021. By 29 March 2021, ATOM holders had voted overwhelmingly (112 million votes to 75) to activate IBC functionality on the network.[216]

For the Cosmos community, IBC's launch marked the beginning of a truly interblockchain age and, as such, it is possible that new applications will be built on IBC in the future that aren't even being considered today. Dean Tribble, CEO of Agoric, an application built on Cosmos, told *CoinDesk,*

It's like dropping a crystal into a supersaturated solution: the pent-up need for interconnection between chains will be unleashed. Some of the most interesting connections will be between chains that we have never heard of, accomplishing things not currently feasible.[217]

With the infrastructure and essential development tools in place, Tendermint, ICF, and the other key Cosmos players are focusing on growing the ecosystem and increasing their impact. ICF offers funding and support to developer teams and enterprises that are realizing ideas and creating the software and applications that ICF deems critical to the success of the Cosmos ecosystem. "We encourage people to build their own decentralized organizations, governance platforms, social networks with the open-source Cosmos tools that we provide," said CEO Zhong. "For the best projects, we provide mentoring, marketing support, and capital investment to help them get their new projects off the ground."[218]

METRICS OF COSMOS SUCCESS

For measuring impact of the ecosystem to date, two metrics are key: the market capitalization of ATOM and the collective market cap of the broader community of Cosmos applications. ATOMs, the native currency of the Cosmos blockchain, are valued at just over $9 billion today (up from $2.93 billion when this paper was originally published).[219] However, the broader Cosmos ecosystem has become far more valuable than the ATOM token prices captured by Cosmos investors.

Just as companies like Microsoft, Apple, Shopify, and other tech giants have helped their partners create multiples of the revenue the platforms collect themselves, Cosmos' enterprise users have launched products with tokens valued at $165.65 billion to date, such as Binance's native token BNB, ThorChain's RUNE, Terra's LUNA token, and OKEx's blockchain token.[220] The strategic decision of major crypto players to anchor their platforms to Cosmos is evidence of the growing utility and influence of the ecosystem. As Buchman put it, "It goes to show how useful this Cosmos technology is, when the biggest exchange in the world can just decide to host [its] own native blockchain and currency on it, and it's one of the biggest [cryptocurrency projects] in the world."[221]

Beyond the market capitalization of tokens are less quantifiable metrics such as the utility of Cosmos-enabled services and applications and the social and economic value they generate for their users.

As of mid-January 2022, 262 apps were leveraging Cosmos technology, spanning use cases from decentralized exchanges and privacy applications to Internet infrastructure and more.[222] See Table 2-1 for a select list of Cosmos applications.[223]

TABLE 2-1

SELECT COSMOS APPLICATIONS

APPLICATION	LAUNCH DATE	DESCRIPTION	FOUNDER(S)	KEY METRICS
Althea Network (Hawk Networks Inc.)	2018	Mesh network; distributes fast, affordable, locally run Internet services to communities in need.	Jehan Tremback, Justin Kilpatrick, and Deborah Simpier, Oregon	As of June 2021, Althea had operationalized 14 community mesh networks in Nigeria and the United States.
Bluzelle	2018	Decentralized cloud storage; stores data across several nodes around the world, eliminating single points of failure.	Pavel Bains and Neeraj Murarka, Singapore	As of Jan. 2022, the native BLZ token had a market cap of $94 million.
FOAM	2016	Crowdsourced map and location-based services; alternative fault-tolerant system delivered over open network of terrestrial radios.	Ryan King, Kristoffer Josefsson, and Katya Zavyalova, New York City	In June 2020, FOAM installed a proof of concept in the Brooklyn Navy Yard for field testing.
Regen Network	2017	Incentivizes land stewards to sell ecosystem service credits to buyers around the world.	Gregory Landua, Brecht Deriemaeker, and Will Szal, Massachusetts	In April 2021, Regen Network raised $10.5 million from 216 investors in a private token sale.

APPLICATION	LAUNCH DATE	DESCRIPTION	FOUNDER(S)	KEY METRICS
Secret Foundation	2020	Blockchain network of privacy-preserving smart contracts; users exert full control over how their data are used.	Tor Bair, Chicago	In May 2021, a syndicate of venture capitalists led by Arrington Capital and Blocktower Capital invested the equivalent of $11.5 million into native coin SCRT.

Sources: _Blog.Althea.net/NetEquity-and-Althea_; _CoinMarketCap.com/Currencies /Bluzelle_; _Foam.Space Blog_; _BanklessTimes.com_; and _TechCrunch.com_, accessed 15 Jan. 2022.

In the social good arena, there are projects like the Regen Network, an open network for climate solutions that enables "land stewards" (i.e., farmers and ranchers) to sell their ecosystem services directly to buyers around the world. A business looking to offset its carbon footprint, for example, could buy "ecosystem service credits" to support biodiversity or carbon sequestration projects.[224] There is also She256, funded by ICF to encourage greater diversity and gender representation in the blockchain ecosystem. Among its initiatives, She256 runs mentorship programs and educational events such as hackathons and coding camps for a community of some 3,500 members.[225]

INTRODUCING POLKADOT

Polkadot is a project built by the Web3 Foundation to enable a functional, user-friendly, and decentralized Internet for everyone—in other words, a layer-zero technology, a fabric, or a set of protocols that facilitates the transfer of data and tokens between independent blockchains. Like Cosmos, Polkadot's protocols support transmissions across public, open, permissionless blockchains as well as private, closed, permissioned blockchains. In doing so, Polkadot seeks to unite a diverse network of purpose-built blockchains on a shared infrastructure, so that they operate seamlessly together at scale as the Internet does today.

Beyond protocols, Polkadot is also a blockchain development platform that supplies the core modules, such as shared security and an easy-to-use launchpad, for blockchain developers to build on. Plug-and-play modules like a consensus engine, networking, and added security are available so that developers can focus on their specific area of expertise and save substantial time and effort in the development process.

In a tangible way, we could just as easily describe Polkadot as an embodiment of a libertarian-inspired philosophy. In essence, the team and community behind Polkadot want to break what they describe as a "corporate stranglehold on the Web" and replace it with an open, decentralized alternative that hands individuals control over their digital identities and data.[226] The founders articulated this philosophy in the opening pages of Polkadot's white paper:

> Every day we interact with technologies controlled by a handful of large companies whose interests and incentives often conflict with our own. If we want the benefits of using their proprietary apps, we're forced to agree to terms that most of us will never read, granting these companies complete control over the data we generate through each interaction with their tools ... . [With] open source and decentralized technologies like blockchain, we can build systems that prioritize individual sovereignty over centralized control. With these new systems, there's no need to trust any third parties not to be evil.[227]

POLKADOT'S ORIGINS AND ETHOS

Polkadot is the creation of three blockchain pioneers: Gavin Wood (a co-founder and chief technology officer for Ethereum and creator of the Solidity smart contract language), Robert Habermeier, and Peter Czaban. Like Kwon and Buchman at Cosmos, the Polkadot team set out to tackle some critical issues that were stymieing mainstream blockchain adoption, namely interoperability, scalability, and shared security.

As key players in Ethereum, the co-founders realized early on that the lack of interoperability between independent blockchains was hampering the development of a decentralized Internet infrastructure. Not only are value and data stuck within individual blockchain silos but also performance and functionality limitations are inherent in the status quo of autonomous, yet mutually incompatible blockchains. Independent blockchains can process only a small number of transactions, they are hard to customize for particular use cases, and any builders trying to launch new blockchain networks from scratch face difficult security and incentive problems.

Polkadot offers a set of protocols and a central hub designed to connect disparate blockchains and address these limitations:

- *Interoperability:* With Polkadot's protocols, blockchain applications can transfer value and data across chains—no data siloes.

- *Customization:* With Polkadot's development framework, developers can optimize blockchains for specific use cases but exploit a shared infrastructure for consensus and security.

- *Scalability:* Polkadot spreads transactions across multiple chains, so that far more transactions can be processed in parallel.

Implicit in the Polkadot model (and in the Cosmos model as well) is that no single blockchain fits all user needs. None can adequately address the manifold uses of decentralized ledger technologies. On the contrary, chains will specialize over time as blockchain developers make trade-offs to support specific features and use cases. This specialization, in turn, will increase the need for interactivity and interoperability between a growing and diverse population of blockchains. For example, with true interoperability, a university's private, permissioned academic records chain could send proof to a credential-verification smart contract on a public chain as part of an employment application process.

Like the Cosmos ecosystem, Polkadot is stewarded by a mix of nonprofit and for-profit entities. The core development team is housed in Parity Technologies, a software development company founded by Wood and Jutta Steiner, former chief of security of the Ethereum Foundation.[228] Research centers such as the French National Institute for Research in Computer Science and Automation (Inria) are contributing research on emerging blockchain standards and technologies.[229] The Web3 Foundation, set up by Wood to nurture an array of decentralized Internet protocols, provides funding for the Polkadot ecosystem, including its network of app developers.[230]

In describing the long-term vision for Polkadot, Wood told *TechCrunch* the project is ultimately contributing to the development of an open and more decentralized Internet. As Wood put it, Polkadot is no less than "a substrate of trust-freedom underpinning the economic activity between people, business, and organizations; changing the landscape of bureaucracy, trade, and industry as much as Google, Facebook, and Wikipedia changed the landscape on which the telephones, libraries, and the post office operated."[231]

THE CORE TECHNOLOGY COMPONENTS OF POLKADOT

Polkadot relay chains and bridges

The center of the Polkadot system is the Polkadot relay chain, which handles the network's security, consensus, and cross-chain interoperability. In so doing, the relay chain unites many independent blockchain "shards" (called *parathreads* or *parachains*, short for parallel block-chains), which can have their own native tokens. Parathreads and parachains connect to Polkadot's main relay chain by paying fees for usage per block or by leasing the rights to a relay chain slot.

Bridges are specialized protocols that connect Polkadot block-chains to blockchains outside the Polkadot ecosystem, including Bitcoin, Ethereum, and Tezos. In short, bridges enable Polkadot blockchains to communicate with and transfer value or data to and from external block-chains, including the growing number of DeFi apps on Ethereum.[232]

Toronto-based blockchain developer ChainSafe has been leading some of the most advanced work on Polkadot bridges to date. For example, one of the first implementations of ChainSafe's bridging functionality was Moonbeam, an Ethereum-compatible smart contract platform on Polkadot. A multidirectional bridge between Ethereum and Moonbeam will allow asset transfers between the two indepen-dent chains. ChainSafe founder and CEO Aidan Hyman called the bridging capability an imperative for open-source collaboration in the blockchain ecosystem: "Collaboration is good for the whole garden, and it gets competitors to see value beyond zero-sum thinking."[233]

In addition to enhancing interoperability between economi-cally sovereign and technologically diverse chains, Wood and other Polkadot enthusiasts believe that a combination of network sharding and bridging with external chains will address the scalability chal-lenges that have plagued Bitcoin and Ethereum.[234] (*Sharding* here means partitioning the Polkadot network and its data into special-ized parachains to distribute storage and computational workloads across the nodes of the network so that no single node must process all transactions.[235]) More specifically, Wood argues that the ability of interoperable chains to process transactions in parallel will eliminate the throughput limitations and bottlenecks that occur on blockchain networks that process transactions one by one.[236]

Substrate

Substrate is Polkadot's development framework that anyone can use to build a blockchain. It allows a developer to pick and choose quickly from numerous features for specific use cases and then deploy the resulting blockchain under Polkadot's shared security model. The Polkadot runtime environment is coded in Rust, C++, and Golang, making it accessible to a wide range of developers.

More than 130 projects are already using Polkadot's Substrate technology to build their own blockchains today, with such notable projects as Chainlink, Edgeware, Polymath, and SushiSwap.[237] We look at some of these applications in the ecosystem overview below.

DOT, the native Polkadot token

DOT is the Polkadot network's native token. In October 2017, Polkadot put 10 million such tokens in supply. The Web3 Foundation reserved about 30 percent of these tokens for founders and the foundation's own use. It held an ICO of DOT in which it sold roughly a quarter of this supply for $140 million.[238] It sold the remainder in two private sales in 2019 and 2020.[239] In August 2020, the community voted to redenominate DOT, which increased the supply of tokens from 10 million to one billion.[240]

DOT serves three distinct purposes in the Polkadot ecosystem. DOT holders are entitled to take part in the governance of the Polkadot platform. DOT also plays a key role in the consensus mechanism that underpins Polkadot, as participants must put their DOT at risk (referred to as *staking*) to validate new blocks. Finally, participants seeking to add parachains to the relay chain are required to bond DOT tokens for as long as their chain is connected.

Consensus and governance

Consensus on the Polkadot network is achieved by the cooperation of four distinct ecosystem participants. They are called collators, nominators, validators, and fishermen.

- *Collators* are responsible for maintaining network shards, which Polkadot calls parachains. They do this by collecting transactions from users on a specific shard, producing blocks, and packaging them up into proofs for validators on the relay chain.

- *Nominators* help secure the relay chain by choosing trustworthy validators and staking DOTs.

- *Validators* secure the Polkadot relay chain by staking DOTs and updating the global state. They do this by validating the proofs produced by collators on individual parachains.

- *Fishermen* monitor the network and report bad behavior to validators. Any parachain full node or collator can perform the fisherman role.

Polkadot uses a variety of governance mechanisms so that community participants can play active roles in decision-making as the network evolves over time. Updates to the protocol, for example, happen fork-free via transparent on-chain voting, so protocol development never stalls due to the lack of a clear process. The on-chain voting mechanisms include stake-weighted referenda, which depending on circumstances, can be implemented with different approval thresholds, including simple majorities and super majorities. In all cases, DOT tokens are required to participate in governance decisions, including tabling proposals, voting, and bonding.

While parachains must use the Polkadot shared security, they are free to implement their own designs, tokens, and governance processes. With this flexibility, for-profit enterprises or nonprofit communities can run parachains as permissioned or permissionless networks, as platforms for others to build applications on, or as common good utilities that benefit the entire Polkadot ecosystem. We list select Polkadot applications in Table 2-2.[241]

TABLE 2-2

SELECT POLKADOT APPLICATIONS

APPLICATION	DATE	FUNCTION	FOUNDERS/ LEADERS	METRICS
Edgeware	2018	Smart contract chain enables developers, creators, and members of its community to build, fund, and manage their projects effectively.	Commonwealth Labs, San Francisco	In 2019, it dispersed EDG tokens to more than 15 million unique addresses via a lockdrop, a method of distribution without raising money.
ExeedMe	January 2021	Gaming platform uses non-fungible tokens (NFTs) and DeFi; gamers can monetize their skills and earn crypto while playing their favorite games.	Nuno Fernandes and Francisco Varela, Portugal	Still in the start-up phase, ExeedMe held its first live tournament in February and March 2021.
Ocean Protocol	2017	Decentralized data marketplace allows data owners to monetize their data while creating new data sources for data scientists and AI practitioners.	Bruce Pon and Trent McConaghy, Singapore	As of May 2021, Ocean Protocol had more than 3,000 users in 100 countries and partnerships with such enterprise users as Daimler, IBM, and Roche.
Polkastarter	2020	Protocol built for cross-chain token pools and auctions; blockchain projects can raise capital in a decentralized and interoperable environment.	Daniel Stockhaus and Tiago Martins, British Virgin Islands	In September 2020, Polkastarter raised $875,000 in a seed/ private sale backed by NGC Ventures, Moonrock Capital, Signum Capital, and Astronaut Capital.

APPLICATION	DATE	FUNCTION	FOUNDERS/ LEADERS	METRICS
Polymath	2017	This app makes it easy to create, issue, and manage tokens on the blockchain by solving the inherent challenges with public infrastructure around identity, compliance, confidentiality, and governance.	Chris Housser, Adam Dossa, and others, Toronto	Polymath raised $59 million through an ICO in 2018; innovators deployed more than 200 token projects; launched Polymesh, an institutional grade blockchain built specifically for regulated assets.

Sources: *Edgewa.re*; *Hackernoon.com*; *OceanProtocol.com*, *GlobeNewswire.com*; *Polymesh White Paper*, *PRNewswire.com*; and *CoinDesk*, accessed 23 June 2021.

HOW ENTERPRISE CAN USE POLKADOT

Enterprise users and other entrepreneurs and organizations looking to build on Polkadot can do so in one of three ways. They can

- Build an independent substrate blockchain (with independent security) connected to Polkadot using a bridge.
- Use Substrate to build a parathread for applications that don't require immediate state updates.
- Use Substrate to build a parachain for applications that do require immediate state updates.

Independent blockchains

Teams can leverage the Substrate development framework to build an independent blockchain, connect it to Polkadot with a bridge, and still retain control over their validator set. Enterprises choosing this option get the benefits of interoperability; they can access the functionalities of other parachains using the Polkadot Network via a bridge. This solution does not leverage Polkadot's shared security model, nor does it require an enterprise to pay for parachain or parathread usage.

Parathreads

The next level of integration with the Polkadot ecosystem is the use of a parathread to leverage Polkadot's shared security model. Parathreads are appropriate for enterprises that want to be secured by the Polkadot relay chain but can't or don't want to commit to the DOT tokens required to run a full-time parachain or don't need to sync to the relay chain every six seconds.

For example, weather trackers or payroll systems implemented using smart contracts wouldn't need to update the network state every six seconds. Parathreads are a great solution for applications that require less immediacy, as they can leverage Polkadot's security, consensus, and interoperability protocols for a lower fee than parachains.

Parachains

Enterprises that require regular state updates for their dapps can build on Polkadot using a parachain. Parachain slots are leased by bonding DOTs on the Polkadot network. While the goal is to have 100 parachain slots available on Polkadot, the Web3 Foundation has opted to make slots a scarce resource in the early stages of the ecosystem's development. Because of this limited number, organizations and other users must bid to secure a slot via a parachain slots auction.[242] (For a detailed explanation of this auction, please see the Polkadot wiki.[243]) To make sure enterprise users have continuous access to the Polkadot relay chain, Polkadot will auction parachain slots in leases of six months to two years. In exchange for leases, enterprises must lock up their winning bid of DOTs for the same period. At the end of their lease, they get their DOTs back.

Enterprises can decide to increase their Polkadot usage in phases. They can build an independent substrate chain, and if needed in the future, they can transition to a Polkadot parachain or parathread, should they decide that they no longer want to host their own validator set.

THE POLKADOT ECOSYSTEM AND ITS IMPACT

Compared to Cosmos, Polkadot is in an earlier phase of its ecosystem: it launched the genesis block of its relay chain in May 2020. Nevertheless, the community has made impressive progress since then, both accruing considerable value and growing its roster of compatible applications (Table 2-3).

Measured by market capitalization, Polkadot's native DOT token rose to $27.4 billion (from $20 billion in June 2021), making it the world's ninth most-valuable cryptocurrency. No doubt some of the rapid price gains are due to the central role of the DOT token in Polkadot network fees and governance, whereby only DOT holders can add new parachains and parathreads to the network or vote on changes or updates to Polkadot protocols.

Just as important, numerous institutional investors are taking sizable DOT positions to diversify their cryptocurrency holdings. In May 2021, Osprey Funds, a New York–based hedge fund specializing in digital securities, launched a Polkadot Trust, which gives accredited investors exposure to DOT prices.[244] Earlier in 2021, Swiss issuer 21Shares AG launched its own DOT ETF on the Swiss SIX exchange, attracting investment from global investment banking heavyweights such as Goldman Sachs, J.P.Morgan, and UBS.[245]

The market will judge the ultimate value of Polkadot by the scope, quality, and performance of applications that the Polkadot ecosystem hosts. Several teams are already building impactful solutions for Polkadot. Projects include cloud storage, digital identities, finance, gaming, social networking, and supply-chain management. Like the ICF for Cosmos, the Web3 Foundation offers grants to teams building Polkadot functionality. To date, the foundation has directed much of the funding to core infrastructure projects and ecosystem components such as wallets, bridges, and tooling.[246]

TABLE 2-3

TOP POLKADOT ECOSYSTEM TOKENS BY MARKET CAPITALIZATION

RANK	PROJECT	TOKEN	PRICE	MARKET CAP	CIRCULATING SUPPLY OF TOKENS	AUDITED?
10	Polkadot	DOT	$27.89	$27,540,216,657	987,579,315	
18	Chainlink	LINK	$25.24	$11,763,855,582	467,009,550	
56	Kusama	KSM	$287.52	$2,432,295,789	8,470,098	
85	Compound	COMP	$190.88	$1,206,975,261	6,332,744	
109	Ankr	ANKR	$0.09317	$760,848,171	8,162,899,378	
122	0x	ZRX	$0.771	$657,784,183	847,496,055	
127	Celer Network	CELR	$0.09963	$610,427,519	6,135,981,458	CertiK
129	Ontology	ONT	$0.653	$572,132,233	875,249,524	CertiK
136	Ocean Protocol	OCEAN	$0.8343	$511,492,027	613,099,141	CertiK
140	Ren	REN	$0.4761	$477,461,739	997,764,051	

Source of data: CoinMarketCap.com, as of 15 Jan. 2022.

WHAT DO DECISION-MAKERS NEED TO KNOW?

Cosmos and Polkadot have much in common, but there are also some notable differences in how each solves the problem of connecting independent blockchains. In this concluding section, we briefly review some of the key similarities and differences between Cosmos and Polkadot with respect to blockchain sovereignty, governance, network fees, and security.

KEY SIMILARITIES

Mission

Both Cosmos and Polkadot were established to improve the interoperability and scalability of the blockchain ecosystem. Both sets of founders see the proliferation of specialized, but interoperable, chains as the best solution for users who want not only to transfer data and assets across chains but also to tailor functionality and governance to specific use cases. Both platforms address the throughput and scalability limitations of monolithic blockchains by enabling specialized chains to process multiple transactions in parallel. Finally, both pitch themselves as user-friendly platforms for building the decentralized Internet of the future—one where users have more control over digital assets, identities, and data.

Origins and operational structure

Both Cosmos and Polkadot were founded by blockchain pioneers with deep experience and well-recognized credentials in the blockchain community. Both founding teams established for-profit software development companies to do the heavy lifting of developing the core technology platforms and tools for their respective ecosystems. Both founding teams also created foundations to provide neutral forums for ecosystem governance and to disperse funding to developer teams intending to build useful tools and applications for the respective platforms.

Hub-and-spoke architecture

At a high level, both Cosmos and Polkadot deploy a hub-and-spoke architecture as the foundation for an interoperable blockchain ecosystem. In Polkadot, the relay chain is like the command center. It controls security, consensus, and cross-chain communication between the parachains.

The Cosmos Hub is similar to the relay chain but much less prescriptive with respect to security and governance. Indeed, many of the key differences between Cosmos and Polkadot concern nuances in the relationships between the hubs and spokes in the respective ecosystems.

Development platforms

For blockchain application developers, both Cosmos and Polkadot offer powerful tools that make it comparatively easy for users to build fully featured blockchain applications. Separating the infrastructure (i.e., the communication protocols and the consensus algorithms) from the applications means enterprise users can devote their energies to the business logic and the features that support their use case. Both the Cosmos SDK and the substrate provide plug-and-play modules or ready-made components (e.g., consensus algorithms, authentication models, and voting systems) that help developers reduce app development time from years to months. Both Cosmos and Polkadot also offer protocols to enable interoperability with external blockchains such as Bitcoin and Ethereum, and so developers can integrate their apps with these established entities.

KEY DIFFERENCES

Membership and sovereignty

Cosmos is deeply committed to the principle of sovereignty and grants as much autonomy to its ecosystem participants as possible. There are no fixed rules or fixed fees for membership in the Cosmos community. Any entity can launch a hub or zone in Cosmos for free. Although Tendermint launched the first Cosmos Hub, the system can accommodate multiple hubs, and others have launched hubs since. The IRISnet, for example, launched in 2019 and plans to connect blockchains operating in China and other parts of Asia.[247]

Peng Zhong, CEO of Tendermint, said the notion of unfettered access to interblockchain communication and full control over one's applications resonates deeply with the decentralized ethos of the blockchain community. As Zhong put it, "Unlike Ethereum, Polkadot, or Avalanche, you don't have to buy our token to be a part of the Cosmos ecosystem. You and your community of tokenholders have sovereignty—absolute ownership—over your foundations."

In Polkadot, there is only one relay chain, and parachains have less sovereignty than Cosmos counterparts because they must adhere to Polkadot's shared security model. Membership is also restrictive— that is, there are limited parachains slots that Polkadot will auction to the highest bidders—and scarcity could make them expensive, depending on demand. It's difficult to determine because the project hasn't held its first parachain slot auction yet.

Governance

Both Cosmos and Polkadot invite active participation in ecosystem governance. Both platforms provide transparent on-chain governance mechanisms, including referenda, to enable users to propose and approve/deny changes to the underlying protocols. However, there are some key differences in how governance is fulfilled in each ecosystem.

Polkadot uses stake-weighted voting, which means that ecosystem participants with the most DOTS call the shots: larger, wealthier members have the opportunity to control changes to the protocols, the rules of membership, and other ecosystem parameters. However, Polkadot established a council elected by tokenholders to represent passive stakeholders and minority interests in the community.[248]

By contrast, Cosmos leaves governance up to the individual hubs and zones. There is no single set of rules or a uniform process for making decisions across the ecosystem. However, the Cosmos Hub does have a stake-weighted voting process for making changes to its core protocols. As with Polkadot, participants must put their ATOM tokens at risk to table proposals and vote in referenda.

Fees

Polkadot's system requires that all parachains and parathreads connected to the relay chain pay a fee in DOTs. As noted, parathreads pay a fee for usage, while parachains must bid for a leased slot on the relay chain for a period of up to two years. The fees allow enterprises to leverage Polkadot's security without the cost of running their own validator sets.

By contrast, Cosmos is building an open ecosystem that acts almost like a public good. Developers can fork its software, and any enterprise can build its own blockchain using Cosmos zones without paying fees or holding ATOMs. "That's true by design because an enterprise could not do sovereign interoperability honestly if that weren't the case," said Buchman. "The alternative would be a domineering political economic environment like Avalanche, Polkadot, or Ethereum, where an enterprise is forced to use the platform's token and governance."[249]

Participants must hold ATOMs *only if* they want to connect their zone to the Cosmos Hub and leverage its security or participate in Cosmos Hub governance. Otherwise, users can transact with other blockchains through the IBC protocol. As Buchman explained, "If you want to interoperate with other blockchains, you can do that with IBC and have nothing to do with ATOMs."[250]

Security

Another major difference between Cosmos and Polkadot is the model used to secure the chain. Parachains in Polkadot operate under a "shared security" model, in which the relay chain deploys thousands of validators to provide a highly secure environment. Any parachain can benefit from this strong security simply by connecting to the relay chain, but each parachain retains sovereignty over its functionality, transaction cost structures, and other application design features. In exchange for strong security, parachains use DOT tokens to pay for network access.

For some applications and enterprise users, shared security is a highly convenient service. It lessens the burden and cost of retaining an independent set of validators. It also provides a uniform level of security across the network, which may increase enterprise users' trust in the platform to protect their exchanges of assets and data. Other entities—and particularly large enterprises—may find this approach less than ideal, as it means they relinquish some control to the main relay chain's validators who have final say over state changes in any parachain.

What could go wrong? In theory, validators could opt to reject blocks that come from collators of a specific parachain and thereby block the parachain from including its activities in the global state. However, Polkadot attempts to limit the scope for malicious behavior by deploying fishermen to police the ecosystem.

On Cosmos, each zone has complete flexibility to run its own consensus and recruit its own validators to secure the application. With the latest version of Cosmos, smaller applications and enterprises can opt to purchase security from the Cosmos Hub in much the same fashion as parachains on Polkadot.[251] However, for a larger entity like Binance, which might prefer to have full control of its Binance Chain and has no problem building its own validator set, the flexibility to manage its own security is a great feature.

TABLE 2-4

COMPARISON OF COSMOS AND POLKADOT

	COSMOS	POLKADOT
Origins	2014 (Tendermint); 2016 (Cosmos white paper v1); 2017 (token sale); 2019 (network launch)	2016 (white paper v1); 2017 (Web3 Foundation, 1st token sale); 2019 (2nd token sale); 2020 (mainnet launch)

	COSMOS	POLKADOT
Founders	Jae Kwon, Ethan Buchman	Gavin Wood, Robert Habermeier, Peter Czaban
Headquarters	Switzerland	Switzerland
Website	https://cosmos.network/	https://polkadot.network/
Key funder	Interchain Foundation	Web3 Foundation
Token/role	ATOM (for the Cosmos Hub) • Governance • Staking	DOT • Governance • Staking • Bonding
Circulating supply of tokens	226,226,028	987,579,315
Market cap	$9,049,025,593	$27,445,713,166
Consensus	Tendermint BFT	GRANDPA consensus algorithm
Transaction time	7 seconds	6 seconds
Transactions per second	1000s	1000s
Intellectual property?	Open source	Open source
Who stewards the technology?	Interchain Foundation, Tendermint	Web3 Foundation, Parity Technologies
Who reaches consensus?	Validators on independent Cosmos zones and hubs	Validators on the Polkadot relay chain
Staking mechanism	Bonded proof of stake	Nominated proof of stake
Security	Decentralized security or shared security via the Cosmos Hub	Shared security via the relay chain
Public or private	Public/Permissionless	Public/Permissionless
Fees	• Transaction fees	• Transaction fees • Parachain slot auctions
Method of interoperability	• Interblockchain communication protocol	• Polkadot relay chain for parathreads and parachains • Bridges for external blockchains
For developers	Cosmos SDK	Substrate
GitHub site	https://github.com/cosmos	https://github.com/paritytech/polkadot

Sources of data: "About Cosmos," Cosmos Network, Tendermint Inc., n.d. v1.cosmos. network/about; "Cosmos ATOM," CoinMarketCap.com/Currencies/Cosmos; "Polkadot DOT," CoinMarketCap.com/Currencies/Polkadot-new; and "Polkadot Profile: History," Messari.io/Asset/Polkadot/Profile, as of 15 Jan. 2022.

CONCLUSIONS ON INTEROPERABILITY

Both Cosmos and Polkadot offer viable solutions to the interoperability challenge. These are exciting because, as Rafael Belchior and his colleagues at the University of Lisbon put it, they allow us "to explore synergies between different solutions, scale the existing ones, and create new use cases."[252] In other words, they take us to a new level of discovery. Belchior's team also argued that interoperability could also "promote privacy by allowing the end user to use different blockchain for data objects with different privacy requirements."[253]

"But interoperability is just the ante," said Cory Doctorow, an activist and special adviser to the Electronic Frontier Foundation. "For a really competitive, innovative, dynamic marketplace, you need *adversarial* interoperability: that's when you create a new product or service that plugs into the existing ones *without the permission* of the companies that make them."[254] He has written extensively on the value created through this type of interoperability in markets for operating systems, personal computers, and cable television, to name a few.

"Adversarial interoperability was once the driver of tech's dynamic marketplace," Doctorow wrote. "But the current crop of Big Tech companies has secured laws, regulations, and court decisions that have dramatically restricted adversarial interoperability." No innovator can create an app that interoperates with Facebook and then expect Facebook to sit back and watch it become hugely popular. "From the flurry of absurd software patents ... to the growing use of 'digital rights management' to create legal obligations to use the products you purchase in ways that benefit shareholders at your expense, Big Tech climbed the adversarial ladder and then pulled it up behind them." By acquiring the best of its rivals such as Instagram, WhatsApp, and Oculus VR, Facebook has grown into a behemoth.[255] But it's still an island.

It is a cautionary tale for creators and users of blockchain innovation in the second era of the Internet. Our hope is that these interoperability solutions will encourage more participation, experimentation, and competitiveness, where the market decides the winners but doesn't strand those who supported platforms that never gained traction; users should be able to port their assets.

Also, platform governance is important, and both Cosmos and Polkadot teams have been quite thoughtful, deliberative, and transparent in their design. Might these become standards or models for governance of blockchain interoperability in general? In a recent study, the World Bank Group (WBG) underscored the need for interoperability not just between blockchains but also across different legacy interfaces, organizational infrastructures, and sources of data. "The idea of a heterogeneous future state with more than one tech platform is inevitable. Ensuring they can work together is key," the WBG concluded. "A governance group is needed to oversee data sharing, monitor interoperability standards from standard-setting bodies, refer to the technical framework to find an appropriate approach, and examine security and legal framework to check the design and implementation."[256]

A working group in the spirit of, if not within, such bodies as the Internet Engineering Task Force, the International Telecommunication Union Telecommunications, or the Worldwide Web Consortium—and with participation from industry groups such as the Enterprise Ethereum Alliance, Hyperledger, and the InterWork Alliance—could build on these solutions in ways that benefit the whole ecosystem.

CHAPTER 3

THE PROMISE OF COMMUNITY-OWNED PREDICTION MARKETS

Why Decentralized Crypto Networks Are
Inevitable and Important to Society

Andrew Fennell Young

 ## PREDICTION MARKETS IN BRIEF

- Big tech platforms have rapidly evolved and created rich markets in the virtual space. They've also monetized corporate access to prospects through advertising revenue and fees. This business model has generated large profit margins for these platforms but raised barriers to entry for newcomers wanting to compete in the same space.

- A crypto network encompasses everything surrounding cryptocurrency. It consists of technology, a community, and developers. Each crypto network is its own "bubble" in this way. But as an ecosystem, it represents a fundamental change in societal interactions, organization, and workflows.

- Each crypto network has its own incentive system, governance mechanism, and monetary policy. Many are decentralized: users are the primary owners, and no central group controls or earns profits. User ownership intensifies loyalty to the network and among its community members.

- Global prediction market protocols allow anyone to create a community-owned-and-operated market. Sports and political betting are the most popular forms of prediction markets today. The next multibillion-dollar sports betting market will be a smart contract protocol deployed as a sports betting public utility on the Ethereum blockchain.

- Community-owned, open-source betting platforms give their members the best odds, whereas centrally owned and controlled betting platforms favor the house. These traditional for-profit entities will likely not adapt—or be able to adapt—to offer their users the benefits of the community-owned model.

- Decentralization is not without its flaws. Crypto networks still face such implementation challenges as stakeholder alignment, funding, and upgradability because of their decentralized and open-source nature.

THE PROMISE OF PREDICTION MARKETS

Prediction markets are those where people bet on the outcomes of different future events, from sports, elections, and the weather to the values of stocks or other assets. Among the most famous are the Iowa Electronic Markets, a set of futures markets where traders "buy and sell real-money contracts based on their belief about the outcome of an election or other event," and the Hollywood Stock Exchange where participants "trade on movies and their box office returns" using the virtual currency H$.[257] Prediction markets on real-world events contain uncertainty; market actors with differing information, views, intuitions, and levels of expertise and any number of other factors may affect the outcome.[258]

Cisco, Google, and Microsoft are among the companies that have experimented with prediction markets to gather information in real time from a wide range of participants about, for example, project management, product quality, and the impact of external events on the enterprise—and they typically preserve anonymity so that participants can bet on the truth, not on what management wants to hear.[259]

With the Internet, people can communicate across borders, but the number of global markets with significant liquidity across borders is quite limited. Thus far, social (trust) and political (regulation) factors have limited the success of such global markets. Moreover, centralized entities (e.g., the University of Iowa) have owned and operated traditional prediction markets. The social and political limitations of their centralized products have in turn limited the types of markets, liquidity, and geographic reach.

CLASSIC USE CASE: SPORTS AND POLITICAL BETTING

Human beings love to bet on contests. As a species, we have been betting on outcomes since the creation of contests for entertainment. The ancient Romans used to bet on horses, chariot races, and gladiator fights.[260] For the most part, people bet on sports because they enjoy it.[261] Having money on an event directly aligns the bettor's monetary interests with the outcome of the event. It makes the event far more interesting and stimulating.

Some market participants also bet on sports as part of a risk-management process. For example, ticket scalpers with an excess inventory of tickets for Game Seven of the NBA finals would be in deep trouble if the series ended prematurely.[262] Ticket scalpers could, however, lock in their revenue by betting on the series to end in fewer games. If it didn't happen, the winning bet would offset the loss in ticket revenue.

Another example is Jim "Mattress Mack" McIngvale, owner of one of the largest Houston-based furnishing companies. As part of a marketing campaign, he offered full refunds to customers who spent at least $3,000 on mattresses in his Gallery Furniture stores if his hometown Houston Astros won the Major League Baseball World

Series. To hedge his economic loss in case the Astros won, he also bet on the Astros to win.[263]

Sports and political betting are among the most popular forms of prediction markets today. Their creators typically structure them as *dealer markets*, in which single market-makers (commonly called *book-makers*) offer liquidity on both sides of the market.[264] There are a few *open-auction style markets* (commonly called *betting exchanges*), but they make up less than 10 percent of total sports betting volume today.[265]

THE PROBLEMS OF SPORTSBOOKS

Most sports and political betting today happens on sportsbooks. Sportsbooks operate almost like an e-commerce store: they host products on their site (i.e., sports events to bet on), set the price (i.e., the odds), and have a definite amount of inventory (i.e., the amount you're allowed to bet).[266] Like any e-commerce store, sportsbooks compete against each other by offering more selection (i.e., markets), lower prices (i.e., better odds), and better inventory (i.e., higher betting limits).

Sportsbooks operate like casinos: when a user bets on an event, the sportsbook takes the opposite side of the bet. So, when users win their bets, the sportsbook loses and vice versa. Its profit is directly inversely proportional to its users' losses. It's a parasitic relationship in which the only way for a sportsbook to make money is for its users to lose. That's the sportsbook model's unavoidable conflict of interest. For users to lose enough money to pay for the massive salaries, overhead, and satisfactory shareholder returns, sportsbooks systematically tilt the playing field in their favor, pushing users to the limit of what most bettors would consider acceptable behavior. As for-profit businesses with an inherently zero-sum relationship with its users, bookmakers go above and beyond to make sure their users lose.

Sportsbooks charge high transactions costs to their users in a sneaky way. Rather than charging a set fee, sportsbooks simply bake the fee into the odds they offer users; and these implied fees are much higher than what bettors would normally accept. Bettors often unwittingly pay transaction costs of five percent per transaction, with some high-cost sportsbooks charging upward of 10 percent.

Sportsbooks do whatever they can to keep their users in the dark. Users cannot find valuable information that traditional financial markets would ordinarily disclose such as customer order flow, betting volume, or dealer exposures because sportsbooks do not and need not by law disclose such. This information asymmetry makes it harder for users to transact intelligently.

Finally, sportsbooks tend to have highly discriminatory practices toward users. However, rather than discriminating based on race, age, or sex, they discriminate based on users' profitability. Users who consistently win their bets routinely face reduced market selection, lower betting limits, and sometimes outright bans. Bookmakers also make it difficult, slow, and expensive for users to withdraw their money.

Given the high fees, information asymmetry, discriminatory practices, and high switching costs, we need not wonder why many sports bettors lose money over the long term. So why do users continue to bear these costs? Why not just leave?

THE PERILS OF CENTRALIZED BETTING EXCHANGES

Given the rampant problems of sportsbooks, innovators launched a new kind of sports betting platform at the turn of the century: the sports betting exchange. Sports betting exchanges are set up in a similar style to the stock market: they are marketplaces where users bet against each other rather than against the platform operator. In theory, this model resolves the conflict of interest between the platform operator and user in a traditional sportsbook. Rather than acting as the direct counterparty to every bet, the exchange operator serves as an impartial regulator of the system and, in exchange for this service, charges a small fee on every trade.

Exchanges are set up as two-sided marketplaces, so that users can compete to provide better offers to each other.[267] This competition decreases transaction costs for users and leads to better liquidity for everyone. Transactions are public as bettors are betting against each other, giving users better information on volumes and order flow. Finally, exchange operators have little incentive to discriminate against winning bettors as operators don't lose when bettors win.

The two-sided nature of betting exchanges creates a tremendously powerful network effect: as more users enter the system, liquidity improves, the public dataset reflects real trends, and winning bettors have more opportunities to make money. This leads to a virtuous cycle: as an exchange gains users, liquidity, data, and better opportunities, it attracts more users, grows more liquid, and generates more data and better opportunities.

This tremendously powerful network effect protects the exchange from competitors, thereby centralizing power in the hands of the exchange operator. Like any for-profit entity with monopolistic power over its platform, betting exchange operators have historically abused their position (Figure 3-1).

"Centralized platforms follow a predictable life cycle. When they start out, they do everything they can to recruit users and third-party complements like developers, businesses, and media organizations," noted Chris Dixon, partner at Andreessen Horowitz. "When they hit the top of the S-curve, their relationships with network participants change from positive-sum to zero-sum."[268] Extracting data from users and competing with complements become the easiest path to continued growth.

Betfair is a classic example. After securing a position as the most liquid betting exchange in the industry, it has slowly been squeezing its users with higher fees, new taxes on winning bettors, and more. Eventually, Betfair decided that these revenues were insufficient and created a proprietary (*prop*) trading desk to begin trading against its own users, completing the life cycle from exchange to sportsbook.[269]

FIGURE 3-1

A CENTRALIZED EXCHANGE'S RELATIONSHIP TO USERS
AND COMPLEMENTS

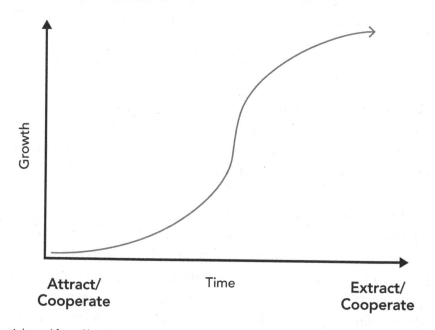

Adapted from Chris Dixon, "Why Decentralization Matters," One Zero Blog, Medium Corp., 18 Feb. 2018. onezero.medium.com/why-decentralization-matters-5e3f79f7638e.

While sports betting exchanges hold promise, we have little reason to expect their for-profit owners to improve upon sportsbooks in the long term; they have no incentive to do so. Their interests diverge from the interests of their users. If anything, they are likely to exploit their market position further as the network effects inherent in running an exchange protect them from competition. In short, centralized betting exchanges have mostly failed in their mission to level the playing field for users.

THE CENTRALIZED GOVERNANCE PROBLEM

As we discussed, single entities control and govern most online markets today. To summarize, these entities carry out several functions: they

(1) create the markets, (2) open these markets to users, and (3) ensure the resolution of transactions according to user expectations. In return for these services, users often pay these entities some form of value because they are for-profit legal entities set up explicitly to maximize shareholder value by extracting more value from customers than they spend in delivering products and services. While a company's interests often align with the interests of its customers, its shareholder interests can and often do diverge.

Online markets have large network effects. Each additional user who joins an online market adds liquidity to it. With greater liquidity, users can transact in the market quickly and cheaply. The market becomes increasingly attractive for other users to join, generating a positive feedback loop of liquidity and usage. As a market develops liquidity, its dominance grows, and less liquid markets have trouble competing against it. To a certain extent, it also locks in users, as the number of alternative markets with similar liquidity dwindles. This cycle typically results in one company with monopoly power over the whole online market, which it can govern in ways that extract more value from its user base with little negative consequence.

THE FUTURE IS CLEAR: COMMUNITY-OWNED BETTING MARKETS

Even though they are different market structures, the problems that plague sportsbooks and betting exchanges are similar in nature. The reasons are deeper than the individual market structure and more fundamental to the business model: sports betting markets are inherently zero-sum. Unlike other asset classes (e.g., equities or bonds) where aggregate financial returns of all market participants can be positive, sports betting (e.g., derivatives) inherently nets out to zero.

This underlying fact underscores the importance of marketplaces where participants can transact with trust, fairness, and low costs. Yet, the inverse seems true: sports betting market operators have far bigger conflicts of interest, more aggressive rent seeking, and more central governance than traditional financial markets. At this point, sports betting markets are fairly mature with greater consolidation in the online betting space. To gain market share in this industry, any upstarts in the industry must offer better value propositions for sports bettors.

INTRODUCING THE CRYPTO NETWORK

Crypto networks have taken the world by storm.[270] Here *crypto network* refers to everything surrounding an individual cryptocurrency—its underlying technology, community, developers, and so forth. Many people don't understand what is happening and have rushed to describe the phenomenon as a bubble. They are partly right: there are some clear signs of speculative excess in the crypto space.[271] But this view misses a far deeper point. Crypto networks represent a fundamental change in how members of society transact, organize, and collaborate with each other.

Over the last ten years, many of the world's largest technology companies have been technology platforms.[272] The typical platform business model involves setting up an online exchange or two-sided market for buyers to interact with sellers. The company's platform acts as an intermediary and charges a transaction fee. Here are a few well-known examples:

- *Facebook/Instagram/Twitter:* Platforms for users to exchange relevant content with each other. Transaction fees come in the form of advertisements.

- *Uber/Lyft:* Platforms that match riders with amateur drivers through smartphone global positioning system and mapping. Transaction fees come in the form of commissions.

- *Airbnb:* Platform for users to find and buy hospitality services from other users with rooms or homes to rent. Transaction fees come in the form of commissions.

This type of business model, sometimes referred to as *network orchestration*, creates huge network effects that protect those who use it from competition.[273] These barriers allow such firms to generate large profit margins, and public markets have responded by valuing them at far higher multiples than other business model types (Table 3-1).[274]

TABLE 3-1

AVERAGE REVENUE-TO-MARKET CAP RATIO (X:X)

Technology providers (1:4)	Exponential platforms (1:8)
"Monetize technology" model	"Monetize network effects" model
Microsoft, Salesforce, IBM	*Alphabet, Amazon, Meta*
• Productivity and business processes	• Social media
• Personal computing	• Digital search
• Cloud services	• Cloud services
Asset pipelines (1:1)	**Service providers (1:2)**
"Make (or move) one, sell one" model	"Sign one, serve one" model
Barrick Gold, Exxon Mobil, Caterpillar	*McKinsey, J.P.Morgan*
• Mining	• Product/consulting services
• Energy	• Asset management
• Manufacturing	• Law firms

Crypto networks are similar to platform companies. But rather than having a central owner that coordinates activity between users, they are decentralized systems with efforts coordinated by an underlying blockchain-based cryptoasset (i.e., the cryptocurrency). This currency acts as the incentive mechanism to ensure that all stakeholders work toward the success of the network.[275] In contrast, platform owners are for-profit companies that can generate revenue only by reducing the utility of the platform to its users in the form of transaction fees.[276] This business model severely misaligns owner incentives with those of platform users.

Crypto networks have several advantages. First, they solve the misalignment problem by decentralizing ownership among its users. Second, because users have tied up their net worth (and, therefore, to a certain extent, their self-worth) in the network, they often have extreme levels of loyalty to its success. This loyalty can lead to rapid viral growth as users evangelize others to join. Third, because of their unique structure, they support new types of decentralized business models that we haven't yet imagined.

The crypto network is a radically new system for human beings—and possibly artificial intelligence (AI) and smart things—to coordinate and create economic value. Investors looking to evaluate crypto networks on their investment potential should focus on the technological utility of the protocol, the size and veracity of the surrounding community, and the short-term pricing dynamics of the cryptoasset.

Centralized products have the benefits of a high degree of coordination, fast decision-making, and mature infrastructure and tools. Decentralized protocols have few of those, and their progress tends to be slower as a result. A global open-source prediction market protocol would allow anyone to create a prediction market for anything. There would be no single entity that controlled the protocol; it would be community owned and operated (Table 3-2).[277]

TABLE 3-2

COMPARISON OF CENTRALIZED AND DECENTRALIZED PREDICTION MARKETS

	ADVANTAGES	DISADVANTAGES
Centralized Betfair Iowa Electronic Markets PredictIt	High degree of coordination Fast decision-making Mature infrastructure and tools	Proprietary protocols Single entity owns and controls the markets Not censor resistant
Decentralized Augur Polymarket SportX	Open-source protocols Anyone can create a prediction market for anything Community owned and operated	Slow decision-making Nascent infrastructure and tools Not always lower fees

That was what SX Networks set out to accomplish in the design and development of SportX betting platform owned and governed by holders of the SX token. SportX is a smart contract protocol deployed on the Ethereum and Polygon blockchains. This protocol serves as the world's first sports betting public utility, with potential to grow into a multibillion-dollar sports betting market. On this protocol, Ethereum's network of miners validate transactions, thereby guaranteeing fairness and timely settlement. Transaction data are pseudonymous but public by default to give everyone fair and ungated access to data.

Fees are low—currently a four percent fee on winnings compared to Betfair's commissions of five to seven percent—and applied directly to finance upgrades to the underlying market structure.[278] Developers building on this protocol need never worry about a centralized party's blocking APIs or market data access. No central party can prevent someone from accessing the SportX platform or otherwise discriminate unilaterally against market participants.

Governing this protocol is the network of stakeholders using the platform. They agree to lock their economic stake into the protocol; therefore, they have incentive to act with the long-term interests of the protocol in mind. What's more, the platform gives its members the best odds and runs on open-source technology. The interests of the community influence governance decisions; the decision-making process is open to any SX tokenholder and auditable by anyone. In short, it is a sports betting market owned, operated, and governed by its community of users.

Numerous studies have shown that the armies of democratic governments fight better than the armies of autocratic ones: soldiers fight harder, take more initiative, and organize themselves better.[279] Enfranchisement is a competitive advantage on the battlefield. The SportX community members are making the bet that enfranchising bettors will motivate the same behavior on the sports betting platform as on the battlefield.

The biggest advantages of this community-owned model are disincentives for traditional for-profit entities to adapt. To embrace this model, traditional incumbents would need to let go of the ownership, profit margin, and IP of the businesses they created. Any for-profit entity with millions of dollars in revenue will find that challenging. For this reason, we believe community-owned betting platforms will be an extinction-level event rocketing toward traditional bookmakers who cannot or will not adapt.

Just as the extinction of dinosaurs created the conditions in which large mammals could take over the earth, the demise of traditional bookmakers will open up opportunities for fairer, more trustworthy, community-owned betting platforms such as SportX.

PROBLEMS WITH DECENTRALIZED GOVERNANCE

Crypto networks have a similar exponential growth dynamic to platform companies, but without a central owner that coordinates activity among users. Instead, they are decentralized systems coordinated by an underlying public blockchain-based token (such as the SX token on SportX).

We can think of crypto networks as their own enclosed economies, each with its own incentive system, governance mechanism, and monetary policy.[280] In a real-world economy, we measure economic activity using gross domestic product (GDP), the sum total of all goods and services produced in an economy. Using the expenditure approach, we measure it by summing the amount spent by all ultimate or final consumers of products and services. The higher the expenditure (i.e., transaction) volume, the larger the economy.

We use a similar process for measuring the economic activity in a crypto network. The only difference is that a crypto network records all transactions within it on a transparent, shared public database (i.e., blockchain) such as Ethereum. Transactions are simple to understand—buyers provision money to sellers in return for a good or service. In traditional economies, the scope is vast of products or service on offer. In contrast, the scope of products or services provisioned by crypto networks can be much narrower and highly dependent on the focus of the network.

Just as the competence of governments plays a crucial role in the formation of a national economy, the effectiveness of governance mechanisms plays a critical role in development of blockchain economies. By shifting ownership of the network to users as the network scales, governance mechanisms attempt to resolve the conflict of interest that naturally arises among the people governing an online market, its usage, and its users.

Governance, however, can be a tool for good or bad. Most crypto network governance models are either (1) *informal* with core developers and/or off-chain legal entities making and implementing decisions or (2) *formal* with whale tokenholders controlling the network on-chain through forks.[281] Crypto networks face huge challenges such as stakeholder alignment, ongoing funding, and upgradability because of their decentralized and open-source nature. The informal off-chain governance systems of open-source software aren't well suited to manage these implementation challenges because of the large economic stakes involved and the coordination problems inherent in decentralized networks. We identify three core challenges:

1. Voter apathy

While tokenholders benefit from good governance, these benefits are dispersed across all tokenholders while the cost of governance research falls entirely on the individuals conducting it. For holders of few tokens, the impact of their participation is very small relative to the cost of participating, and so they have very little incentive to participate in voting-based governance systems. The result is widespread voter apathy and a governance system highly susceptible to special interests and the whims of a minority of the largest tokenholders.

2. Ambiguous objectives

For the most part, governance systems rarely have clearly defined, desired outcomes or goals. For example, governance proposals often request millions of dollars in liquidity mining funding, with a broad goal of "increasing liquidity" without bothering to quantify exactly what that means in practice. Smallholders have little incentive to monitor proposal success, and whales have no metrics to do so systematically against defined goals. This intuitively makes sense: if we don't define the characteristics of a "successful proposal," then we can't easily review any proposal's performance. This lack of review and clear performance feedback on activities also means that DAOs lose out on valuable stakeholder insights that could improve the governance process over time.

3. Lack of penalties

Few (well-run) companies would ever spend millions of dollars on a specific growth campaign without clear goals, constant performance review, and clear accountability in place. Yet, that's the norm in DAO governance today. Crypto-network participants often make proposals that clearly fail to achieve any success commensurate with their cost, but tokenholders face no direct penalty for voting in favor of objectively "bad" proposals. While a bad proposal may damage the reputation of whoever submitted it within the community, those who voted in its favor suffer the same loss of value as those who voted against it.

INTRODUCING PREDICTION MARKET-BASED GOVERNANCE

Markets by themselves offer no protection against fraud, theft, and violence; and a failure to regulate free markets properly leads to a loss of trust in these markets. We need governance systems to ensure trust in markets through the creation and enforcement of rules. Market participants typically pay for this service in the form of fees, taxes, and/or data.

Prediction markets may hold the key to the age-old problem of governance: the free market. Utilizing a native prediction market allows us to create one of the world's first market-based governance systems, also known as *futarchy*.[282] This involves using a voting system to determine objectives, and then using a prediction market to determine the optimal policy for achieving that objective. By doing so, it prevents governance systems from political capture and replaces it with an objective, market-based system in which bettors with real skin in the game, rather than politicians, make decisions.

The fundamental design philosophy guiding prediction market governance is that any stakeholder who can significantly influence the direction of a collective must have skin in the game. According to this principle, such stakeholders are the first ones to bear the consequences—similar to how a general leading an army into battle faces the greatest danger out in front the troops. In other words, they must have measurable risk when making major decisions, ensuring that decisions lead to fair, transparent, and efficient outcomes.

GOVERNANCE DESIGN FOR A SIMPLE PREDICTION MARKET

The key to a prediction market-based governance system getting any real level of adoption is dependent on the actual design of the system. Figure 3-2 is a simplified four-stage betting-based governance design outlining how this would work.

1. Proposal

The proposal is similar in structure to a traditional governance proposal but must contain two key metrics: *objective key performance indicator* (KPI) and *proposed policy*.

The objective KPI is the desirable goal of the proposal. They must be unambiguous, measurable, transparent, and economically costly to manipulate. On-chain metrics are thus the ideal candidates here, as they fit all four criteria. Common examples would be TVL, pooled

FIGURE 3-2

SAMPLE GOVERNANCE DESIGN

1. Proposal	2. Settlement rules	3. Market action	4. Settlement
Fund SX/ETH Uniswap pool with 100,000 SX	TVL over/under $50 million, expires inone month	If market likes proposal, then proposal passes	If TVL increases to $50 million, then over bettors win bet
		If market dislikes propsal, then proposal fails	If TVL falls short of $50 million, then under bettors win bet

liquidity, and on-chain token trading volume. Each of these metrics is quantitative, transparent, and very costly to manipulate (i.e., doing so involves decentralized exchange trading fees, gas costs, and capital opportunity cost).

The proposed policy is the actual action taken to help achieve the objective KPI and the funding (if any) required from the community to reach it. The policy could involve a liquidity mining budget, a treasury investment, a parameter change (e.g., protocol fee, staking yield, etc.), or the underlying product (e.g., deploy on XYZ chain, add XYZ token to application, etc.).

2. Settlement rules

The settlement rules dictate the parameters of the betting market, including

- Market duration—the period in which the market will be live for trading
- Settlement date—the date on which the market settles
- Settlement terms—the rules by which the market pays out.

For market duration and settlement dates, the rules should prioritize shorter over longer durations because of the opportunity cost of capital and prediction market traders' natural preference for shorter-duration markets. These rules are customizable and will require much experimentation to figure out which combination works best. For now, somewhere between 1–7 days for market duration and 14–28 days for market settlement are in line with the structure of other prediction markets.

The market terms can range across a variety of exotic flavors. However, a binary option on the objective KPI is usually the simplest. That is, if the objective KPI is hit, then YES bettors win; otherwise NO bettors win.

3. Market action

Once a party has created a viable proposal with an objective KPI and proposed policy and has set the settlement rules, the governance market is ready for the party to list its proposal on the prediction market and begin trading.

During this process, market-makers provide liquidity to the market while directional traders take opinionated positions in the market. Trades occur when, given the adoption of a proposed policy, traders' individual opinions on the likelihood of the proposal's hitting its objective KPI diverge from the market consensus.

Since prediction markets are inherently zero-sum (negative sum, once we factor in transaction and other costs), the market must receive some sort of liquidity mining subsidy to motivate both sides of the market to take part. This is natural. If betting-based governance systems are indeed more accurate than traditional voting-based systems, then projects will provide liquidity incentives to these markets because project proposers are receiving valuable insight from them. Within that context, liquidity mining rewards are the DAO equivalent of executive management salary expenses.

At the end of the market duration, the protocols determine a time-weighted price based on all the trades that took place in the market to derive the final governance market closing value. This closing value represents the market consensus' probability that the objective KPI will be met because of the level of adoption of the proposed policy.

The protocols then compare this closing value to the bar by which the governance system adopts proposals to determine whether the proposal has passed. Most governance systems today use a simple majority rule; therefore, if the closing value exceeds 50 percent, then the proposal has passed, and the community will implement it. If the closing value proposal falls short of this bar, then the system refunds traders their positions and doesn't implement the policy.

4. Settlement

This is the simplest stage. If the proposal meets its settlement terms (e.g., it exceeded its objective KPI), then the YES bettors receive the stake of the NO bettors as a reward, and vice versa. See Figure 3-3 for the process end to end.

FIGURE 3-3

SIMPLE GOVERNANCE PROCESS

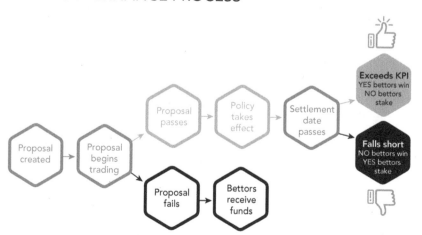

CONCLUSION: THE INEVITABILITY OF CRYPTO NETWORKS

We can think of crypto networks as their own enclosed economy with their own unique incentive systems, governance mechanisms, and monetary policies.

In a real-world economy, we measure economic activity by GDP, the total of all goods and services produced in an economy. Using the expenditure approach, we sum up the total amount spent by all ultimate or final consumers of products and services. The higher the expenditure (i.e., transaction) volume, the larger the economy.

The process of measuring economic activity is similar for a crypto network. The only difference is that all transactions happening in a crypto network are recorded on a transparent, shared public database (i.e., a blockchain).

Transactions are simple to understand—buyers provision money to sellers in return for a good or service. In traditional economies, the scope of products or service offered is vast. In contrast, the product or service provisioned by a crypto network can be much narrower in focus and highly dependent on the focus of the network.

CHAPTER 4

GOING CASHLESS WITH CBDCS

The Digital Dollar in the Face of Global Disruption

J. Christopher Giancarlo, Alex Tapscott,
and Don Tapscott

On 28 April 2020, the Blockchain Research Institute hosted a webinar, "Going Cashless: The Digital Dollar in the Face of COVID-19." The guest was J. Christopher Giancarlo, former chair of the US Commodity Futures Trading Commission and co-founder of the Digital Dollar Project. Alex Tapscott moderated the conversation, which was introduced and summarized by Don Tapscott of the Blockchain Research Institute. This chapter is an edited transcript of the proceedings.[283]

INTRODUCTION: A NEW PARADIGM FOR MONEY

Don Tapscott: We face major challenges, related to the pandemic and global recovery. COVID-19 has had and will have a profound and irrevocable change in the world.

Economic costs are devastating. The human costs are unfathomable. The crisis is challenging many institutions. They're coming under scrutiny and, we hope, will change for the better. The world will be a different place when the dust settles, as it surely will.

Blockchain and related technologies—AI, the Internet of Things (IoT), augmented and virtual reality, autonomous vehicles, and so on—are becoming more relevant than ever, not just to business and the economy but also to the future of public health and the safety of global populations.[284] From a lack of data to the breakdown of supply chains, traditional systems are failing us.

It is time for us to think about a new paradigm. To build on Victor Hugo, "Nothing's more powerful than an idea that has become a necessity."[285] When the pandemic loomed, we evolved the BRI business model to offer full digital delivery of our research and services.

So, today's topic is the digital dollar, digital money. If supply chains are the machinery of global commerce, then money is its lubricant. But money itself has been a source of confusion and strain during this crisis. Some have criticized cash as a carrier of disease, and the drumbeat to abolish it altogether has loudened. Many countries are exploring the notion of digital cash or cryptocurrencies. We think in terms of three types:

- *Community-based cryptocurrencies*, of which Bitcoin was the first, is the largest, has a number of use cases, and actually works.[286]

- *Emergent corporate cryptocurrencies*, such as Diem that Facebook had planned.[287] If some version of it ever succeeds, and that's a big if, Facebook would become the largest financial institution in the world.

- *State-based or fiat cryptocurrencies* like the dollar, the euro, the pound, the yen, the renminbi, the peso, and so on.

These fiat currencies could become digital currencies different from what we have today.

Our guest today is the Honorable Christopher Giancarlo, former chair of the United States Commodity Futures Trading Commission. During his tenure at the CFTC, the agency published primers on virtual currencies and smart contracts and launched LabCFTC, as the agency's stakeholder in the digital evolution of derivatives trading market.[288] On Twitter, he's known as *Crypto Dad*. Chris established the Digital Dollar Foundation, which recently unveiled suggested principles for a central bank digital currency in the United States.[289]

Driving our fireside chat is Alex Tapscott, who is co-founder of the BRI and co-author of *Blockchain Revolution*.[290] Alex has a new book out, *Financial Services Revolution*.[291] Alex, over to you.

DISRUPTIVE TECHNOLOGY MAKES FOR NEW POLICY OPTIONS

Alex Tapscott: Thank you, Don. This is an area that we've been researching extensively and one of the areas where the rubber is really hitting the road in this space.

Chris, you've emerged as one of the most vocal advocates for blockchain and cryptocurrencies to emerge from the traditional world of financial services. How exactly does the head of one of the largest and most mission-critical financial regulators in the world, the CFTC, which oversees what some people call "the biggest financial market you've never heard of," which is the commodities futures market, become such a big fan of crypto and blockchain?[292]

Chris Giancarlo: Sure, thanks. First, let me say what a pleasure it is to be here with the BRI. Thanks to you and Don for making this happen. I'm so glad to see what a great audience we have today—folks from all over the world, from the Congo, India, Europe, and the United States. Thank you to so many people for joining us today and giving us an opportunity to talk about this.

I had an interesting journey to government. I never set out as my career journey to go into government. I spent 16 years practicing law in New York and London, mostly at the intersection of technology and markets. Then, in 2000, I teamed up with a group of entrepreneurs, and we built a company that launched the first electronic trading platforms for OTC derivatives—not derivatives changed on an exchange like futures, but derivatives known as *swaps*, which are traded directly between financial institutions.[293]

Over the early 2000s, we raised several rounds of private equity. In 2005, we took the company public. It was a very successful IPO. Over that time, we built trading platforms in over 18 cities around the world, most of the major financial centers of the world. We conducted a secondary offering in 2006. By 2008, we had emerged as the world's leading platform for trading a type of swap called a *credit default swap*.[294] We probably saw 80 percent of the marketplace trade on our platforms.

I remember a call—a few days before Lehman collapsed in September of 2008—from a senior official at the New York Federal Reserve, asking us, "What do you guys do again?" As I had explained to him at a Fed reception a few months before, we were the world's largest trading platform for credit default swaps.

Just so your [readers] understand, credit default swaps are a proxy for the health and safety of financial institutions. The price at which these instruments trade indicates how the market perceives the creditworthiness of large institutional debtors. Credit default swaps trade at a spread to the lowest risk instrument, which is considered US treasuries.[295] So, the greater the spread, the more the belief is that that issuer of debt could be in serious financial trouble.

He said, "Right, that's what I thought you did. So, what are you seeing in the market?" I said, "Seeing now? Or seeing earlier today? Or what I expect to see at the end of the day? Because they may be dramatically different." We had a good conversation and he understood. A few days before Lehman Brothers fell, we saw Lehman Brothers' credit default swaps on its debt trading at hundreds of basis points over treasuries.

But we also saw the same thing happening in name-your-favorite household money center, investment bank. And so our trading floor became the bellwether of what was happening in the global financial center, in the risk of bank failure.

At that moment, it struck me that regulators had no better way of knowing about the likelihood of failure of some of the world's largest banks than to call around shops like mine and ask, "What do you guys do again, and what are you seeing in the market?" At that time, based upon notional outstanding amounts, the world thought that there was around $400 billion in credit default swap protection written against the failure of Lehman Brothers.

If there was that much on Lehman Brothers, then the amount written against Morgan Stanley might have been $800 billion and the amount written against J.P.Morgan might have been $1.2 trillion. That's why we had the [Troubled Asset Relief Program].[296] That's why the central bank had to flood banks with capital, because of the fear of failure.

Alex: To put that into context, the size of the insurance written against those banks was many times their market cap at that point.

Chris: That's exactly right. Here's the salient point: through the work that we did at the CFTC, netting down all the shorts and longs for the failure of Lehman Brothers, we now know that the net amount, not the gross amount, of protection was only about $9 billion. Not $400 billion. Had we known that Lehman Brothers would have led to about $9 billion in outstanding loss, the Federal Reserve could have dealt with that net exposure in an instant.

I'm not saying that was the policy choice that should have been made; however, without the visibility, it was a policy choice that *could not have been made*. There's a big difference. What we know is that the crisis was really a crisis of the opacity of credit risk among major financial institutions. That's how I get to the blockchain. If we'd had a blockchain, if all those obligations had been recorded to a blockchain, then we wouldn't have guessed at the outstanding total amount. We would have known in an instant what the net exposure was. And we would have had policy choices that were not available to us then.

Over the next several years, I became a huge believer in the potential of the blockchain to bring precision, transparency, and visibility to financial markets. Out of my experience in 2008, I followed the passage of the Dodd-Frank legislation very closely.

I served as head of a trade association for platforms like ours and testified multiple times before Congress on how the swaps market worked. In 2010, when the Dodd-Frank law passed, I put out a statement commending President Obama for its passage.[297] In 2013, perhaps as a reward for that statement, the president asked if I would serve on the commission. He was looking for someone who was a supporter of the law to serve on the commission, and I was delighted to serve.

Over the next few years, I came out with several statements calling for a do-no-harm approach to blockchain innovation.[298] In 2016, President-elect Donald Trump asked me to stay on the commission, and I assumed the role as chairman of the agency. In 2017, as we witnessed the rise of bitcoin, several of our largest exchanges approached us about self-certifying bitcoin futures, and we did.[299] Those products have demonstrated their value proposition in the marketplace. My term ended in July 2019, and I elected not to serve a further term and to step down and return to the private sector. That's my journey.

Alex: That's terrific. The company you built was one of the largest marketplaces for OTC derivatives, which are derivatives not traded through an exchange or a centralized clearinghouse.

They're two different counterparties, financial institutions, right? And so, in the financial crisis of 2008, the Federal Reserve, probably the US Treasury, and other groups were trying to figure out who had what exposure to certain asset classes and where the counterparty risk existed.[300] And the only way they could do that was by contacting them. A lot of those agreements were done over email, with spreadsheets, that made understanding the totality of the risk really hard to capture at that moment in time. Having a trusted, distributed record of who owns what and who owes what to whom would have been extremely helpful.

OVERVIEW OF THE DIGITAL DOLLAR

HOW DIGITAL CURRENCIES DIFFER FROM OTHER FINANCIAL ASSETS

Alex Tapscott: Let's move on to the dollar. Money markets are quite different from derivative markets, and we're seeing this huge amount of growth in digital currencies. Some people think of money as being digital in some ways—we use credit cards, debit cards, our online bank account, contactless payments, and so forth. And so what exactly is a digital dollar? How is that different from what we have today?

Chris Giancarlo: I'm so glad you asked me that. I get comments all the time saying, the dollar is already digital. Let me use an example that somebody gave me. Faxes are digital, but they're representations of documents. They're not the original documents. What we're talking about is something that is actually the instrument itself. That's what tokenization is. It's not a representation of it. It *in itself* is the thing of value. That's the big difference.

When we're talking about the digital dollar, we're not talking about something like a stablecoin that's tied to something of value. We're not talking about a representation of something of value. We're talking about the thing itself of value. Now, the monetary system that exists today has some things of value in it like dollars and coins, and lots of things that are representations of value.

If I write a check to you, the check is a demand on an institution to pay you money. If it's endorsed, it may become a thing of value, but initially it's a demand on an institution to pay you something of value. Institutions record things of value on their books, but that value is an obligation of the institution. It's not an obligation of the sovereign as fiat currency is.

So, when we talk about the digital dollar—we use *digital dollar* because it's an alliterative phrase that can capture the imagination—we are actually talking about something much bigger than that, which is known by the cognoscenti as CBDC, or central bank digital currency. I spend a lot of time talking to folks on Capitol Hill in Washington. If you use terms like "tokenized central bank digital currency." you can see their eyes glaze over.

So, we use the phrase "digital dollar." By that phrase, we are referring to something that is of itself the fiat currency in a digital format. It's very different from representations of value.

Alex: Someone on Twitter asked, "Which would you trust more, a stablecoin or your deposits at your bank of choice?" A lot of people prefer the stablecoin. They don't realize that the deposits backing that stablecoin are sitting in a bank somewhere. And so there's that same level of counterparty risk or default risk to owning a stablecoin.[301]

Chris: In those places you're relying on an intermediary to validate that the money is there, that you're entitled to it, and that it has value. You're always reliant. When we talk about a digital dollar, we're still talking about reliance, but you're reliant on the sovereign, and that is the United States of America. Since the Second World War, that has been recognized around the world as the most valuable backstop that any instrument of value can have.

Alex: Yes. T-bills [Treasury bills] are used as the risk-free rate, because they're considered to be undefaultable.[302]

ATTRIBUTES OF THE DIGITAL DOLLAR

Alex Tapscott: There are two angles from which I want to approach the subject of the digital dollar. First, some people are saying that cash is potentially a bearer of disease, that it could help to spread the coronavirus, and that we should replace or eliminate it altogether. I find that troubling, because several attributes of cash are very important, such as privacy, the ability for individuals to do private transactions. And so we abolish cash at the risk of our own economic freedom.

You've said that the digital dollar is not a replacement for cash, banknotes, coins, and so forth. But do you think of the digital dollar as having those same privacy and freedom-enabling attributes that cash today has? Or can that never really be the case because there's always some level of traceability?

Chris Giancarlo: No, privacy is vitally important to a successful digital dollar. If we get it right, we could make the digital dollar potentially the most attractive sovereign currency in the world, compared to other sovereign currencies. Notwithstanding the dollar's economic power, simply because of the privacy issues. Let me explain what I mean.

Let's start with the premise that cash provides absolute privacy. It doesn't. Cash is already a balance between privacy and state law enforcement and other restrictions. Right now, any cash transactions over $10,000 are recorded by banks and reported to federal authorities. So, cash does not provide absolute privacy, but there is a zone of privacy under a certain amount for cash. We also know that cash is used in many cases in large amounts outside the purview of law enforcement. And so there is a zone of privacy, but it's not absolute.

Alex: I like that expression, the "zone of privacy." We know that privacy is important for individuals doing normal day-to-day transactions, but we also know the criminals use cash to evade taxes, law enforcement, and so forth. So we have to figure out a way to strike that balance.[303]

Chris: Let me tell you how I think we can strike that balance, and why I think a US digital dollar could be superior in privacy rights to all other sovereign currencies. It starts on the following basis, and reasonable people can disagree, that there must be a balance. They may put the balance in different places, but there must be a balance between the individual's civil rights to a degree of privacy in transactions and the sovereign's right to conduct law enforcement, national defense, and so forth—to make sure that the fiat currency is not used for money laundering, human trafficking, or [illicit] drugs.

So, we've got to balance it. We've got to find that right balance point. For over 200 years in the United States, there's been a search for that balance. Here's where I think the United States could have superior privacy rights. The United States has written into its Constitution, in the Fourth Amendment, protections against the government's infringement of reasonable expectation of privacy.[304]

That traditionally has given people the right to their commercial activity using the sovereign currency. We think that, if Fourth Amendment rights and the jurisprudence around them are properly developed, then there could be a zone of privacy in the use of a digital dollar that could be superior to others.

Why do I say that? Europe has a strong privacy protection law, GDPR [General Data Protection Regulation], but I understand that it protects against only *commercial* invasion of privacy, not *government* invasion. China, in its development of a digital yuan, is claiming that there will be a zone of privacy. Yet we know in an authoritarian system, all civil rights are compromised when it comes to state security issues. And so, at the Digital Dollar Project, we believe that developing the jurisprudence around the US government's approach to commercial activity using the sovereign currency, if it's done right, could be a feature of a digital dollar that could be superior to other global reserve currencies.

Alex: That's music to my ears, because that's one of the big hurdles to implementing the digital dollar effectively.

THE NEED FOR INFRASTRUCTURE INNOVATION

ROAD MAP TO A NEW BANKING SYSTEM

Alex Tapscott: The second angle I want to explore, in the context of COVID-19, is financial infrastructure. Right now, the Federal Reserve and the government in concert are pumping a record amount of stimulus money into the economy.[305] Congress has authorized issuing money to individuals, providing emergency relief.

But you have different states with different financial infrastructure. You have people with bank accounts, some without accounts. People who paid the IRS [Internal Revenue Service] last year, some who didn't. The system is very balkanized and inefficient. And so people are not getting the money on time.

Is one of the potential benefits of the digital dollar, that every individual could have a digital account with the Federal Reserve?

If you needed to put liquidity into the economy or provide emergency relief, then could you—to borrow an expression from the blockchain industry—*airdrop* that money into their accounts?[306] In the past, you've said that Federal Reserve accounts are not one of the main benefits of the digital dollar. But can you see such accounts as part of a road map at some point?

Chris Giancarlo: At the Digital Dollar Project, we do not propose Fed accounts. We propose that digital dollars be distributed through the two-tiered banking system in the same way that fiat cash is distributed now. It works like this. Physical US dollar bills are minted for the Federal Reserve. The Federal Reserve distributes those bills through regional Fed banks and then through the commercial banking system, in return for reserves. The banks distribute those bills as a public good to their automated teller machine users and otherwise. That's how cash gets into the marketplace.[307]

We propose something very similar. Policymakers may find that digital currency provides them with more tools than the traditional system. As you mentioned, the government may find this to be a superior way of delivering helicopter money. But we're talking about architecture. How policymakers use that architecture is for the political process to determine.

Let's get the most modern architecture we can, so that policymakers have those tools. In terms of monetary policy, we're not making recommendations as to what the size of the money supply would be, or what the balance between digital fiat and cash fiat would be—those are for policymakers to determine. But we absolutely need the most modern digital architecture possible for a modern digital economy. And that means a digital dollar.

If you look around, systems that were once state of the art in the twentieth century like transportation infrastructure—roads, bridges, tunnels, airports—have been allowed to age, decay, and, in some cases, become obsolete.[308] The same is true about much too much of our financial market infrastructure. As we go into a digital age, into the Internet of value, these analog-based systems are not up to the challenge. Nowhere is anything more central to a digital marketplace, a world of digital assets, than a digital unit of account—a digital dollar.

Today, the world's commodities—whether they're soybeans, cotton, wheat, oil, or natural gas—are priced in US dollars. Most of the world's important large contracts are accounted for in US dollars. As all those things become digitized, how long can the dollar remain the world's major unit of account, and therefore the reserve currency, if it remains analog? It needs to become a digital instrument, to be the unit of account for digital instruments.

Alex: That's incredibly well said.

ATTRIBUTES OF A DIGITAL GLOBAL RESERVE CURRENCY

Alex Tapscott: Let's go down that path for a second. Mark Carney, the former governor of the Bank of England—I'm sure you know him personally—

Chris Giancarlo: I know him well.

Alex: Last year at the Jackson Hole event that the Fed hosts for global central bankers, he gave this speech—you probably remember this—

Chris: I remember.

Alex: Carney said that the US dollar was the reserve currency because, at Bretton Woods [in July 1944], the United States was the biggest creditor nation with all that gold, it had the biggest military, and after the Second World War, it had the largest economy by far. And so it was able to exert its will. But these days, the situation is quite different. We have a multipolar world. In terms of global trade, half of global trade or more is denominated in US dollars, even though the US economy represents only about 10 percent of the global economy.

During his speech, Carney argued that we should move on from the US dollar standard, but not to some other sovereign currency—not the renminbi or the euro or other fiat currency. Instead, it should be what he called a *synthetic hegemonic currency*, a unit of account based on a basket of sovereign digital currencies.[309] So, I want to get your perspective on that. If the United States retains its status as the global reserve currency, then is that good for the world or just good for the States? What do you think of the idea of a synthetic hegemonic currency?

Chris: I'm so glad you asked that. So, a disclaimer to your audience is, at the end of the day, I've just finished five years' service as a US regulator. I'm a US citizen. I have to view the world from my perspective. Our audience members all have their own perspective. I believe that the prevalence of the US dollar as a global reserve currency from the mid-twentieth century is unique in human history.

Throughout most of human history, we've had multiple sovereign currencies competing for market share in the world. The predominance of the dollar is relatively unique. Yet, during that period, a global world economy has emerged. As part of that emergence of a global economy—what we used to call *globalization*—more people have moved out of poverty, into the middle class, than ever before in human history. With that has come fewer child deaths and greater life expectancy.[310]

At the same time has come greater enjoyment of civil liberties and freedom. US values have accompanied the dollar's role around the world. That's not to say it has been perfect. There are many complaints, reasonable complaints about the dollar's use of sanction activity and so forth. I don't deny that. I'm talking about something that, on balance, is a net good.

I believe that, over the last several generations, the dollar's role in the global economy has been a net good for the world. If it's not the dollar, if it's another sovereign's instrument, then what values would come with that? Mark Carney is not proposing some other sovereign. He's proposing something that is a global world order, perhaps rules out of Basel by the FSB [Financial Stability Board] or other body, that would set the terms of such a [synthetic hegemonic] currency.

But one of the core values that's driven the dollar has been democracy, some degree of representative interest. And so my question for Mark is—who elected those people at FSB?[311] What's their representation? Do they determine this basket of values? How?

If we could solve that, then maybe that's what the future looks like. But I'd be cautious about that because I believe that, at the end of the day, all government must be accountable to people. That's democracy. And so my question about his proposal is the representativeness of it, or its lack of. Is it to be central bankers who themselves are not terribly accountable to a voting population? So, if we could get that right, then maybe there's something in that.

I'm of the mind that the US dollar has a generation or more left to go, because its value proposition is still superior to alternatives coming from authoritarianism countries. I think of the democratic values of private enterprise, free capital markets, rule of law, free speech, and economic liberty, of a broad durable good for all participants, of public and private partnerships, of a balance of privacy and national security. Looking at some of its competitors, I ask how are privacy rights abrogated and when? Do they take a rule-of-law approach, or is it down to state supremacy?

So, if we could address all those issues, then I think something could replace the dollar. But right now, there's a reason—and not just an economic reason—that the dollar has enjoyed the world's patronage. It also has to do with some of the values that went into it.

THE GOAL OF MODERNIZING GLOBAL ECONOMIC ARCHITECTURE

Don Tapscott: China is moving quickly toward its DCEP [digital currency electronic payment], a fiat cryptocurrency system. President Xi Jinping has said blockchain and AI are the two dominant technologies for China to build an innovation economy. Has that announcement really stimulated things in the United States? The threat to the US dollar as the currency of record is clear. China has rolled out its One Belt One Road initiative into Southeast Asia, Africa, the Middle East, and South America. All of a sudden, the Chinese currency, in theory at least, could become a dominant currency globally. Is that helping you in your efforts with the digital dollar?

Chris Giancarlo: Don, I think there's been a series of events: bitcoin first, perhaps China next, then Libra Coin, and now COVID-19. Those four events have woken up people who might not otherwise want to do early adoption of this new technology. But it's more than those developments—it's about modernization of architecture.

Bridges and airports need to be modernized. Every 50 years they need to be torn down and reengineered. At the heart of it, currency is about infrastructure. It's a public good on which an economy is built, on which people start businesses, realize their dreams, and aspire to a greater financial security. It relies on the security that it's fit for purpose.

I'll talk for a moment about history. At the time of the European exploration of the east coast of the Western Hemisphere, in the sixteenth and seventeenth centuries, there were multiple currencies in use. Some were sovereign—French francs, Dutch guilders—and some were commercial. The [Dutch] West India Company issued its own script.[312] So, there was a balance of commercial and sovereign instruments. (We can analogize to our own time, when we've got perhaps Libra Coin as opposed to sovereign CBDC, all competing for commerce.)

During that 150-year period, the one instrument, the one coin that was the most desirable, was the dollar—not the US dollar but the Spanish dollar—for three reasons.[313] One, it was minted from New World silver, which was purer than Old World silver. That meant it used less alloy, which made it lighter to travel, whether in your pocket or in a trunk. Two, it was more consistently pure and, therefore, more fungible. One coin was the same as another, and you had to do less weighing. Three, it was more technologically advanced than the others—it was minted in such a way that you could break off eight equal pieces, known as pieces of eight—so that you could fractionalize it to do smaller transactions.

That's what digitization of our currency is all about, right? It's a technological advance. Think about the dollar today. It's an analog instrument. We're going into a digital world, and so we need to futureproof the dollar. We need to modernize it with the times. So, despite the challenges posed by commercial instruments like Libra Coin or something as deep as bitcoin, or something as sovereign as China, this is about modernizing something that has served so well in an analog economy, modernizing it for a digital economy. It's worth doing in its own right, notwithstanding what may be happening elsewhere in the world.

Alex: That's a terrific analogy. The piece of eight was the first form of fractionalization of a single unit of currency. That's always been one of the criticisms of precious metal, that it's hard to fractionalize. Fiat currencies are fractionalizable. But digital currencies can be fractionalized to any specific amount, which enables other kinds of use cases like micropayments. So, as the piece of eight was better than what came before, the US dollar was better than the pound sterling, with these attributes.

THE NEED TO MODERNIZE GLOBAL FINANCIAL REGULATION

Alex Tapscott: There are a couple of ideas there. In the twentieth century, we talked about American institutions. Many institutions that emerged from the Second World War were American by design, such as the financial system based around the US dollar. But securities regulation was also American by design. After the crash of 1929, the Securities Act of 1933 became state of the art, in terms of how we think about public disclosure, insider information, market transparency, and so forth.

Yet, that's almost 100 years old. Would you argue that the regulatory infrastructure—similar to the bridges, roads, and tunnels—and even the underlying financial system, are antiquated and in need of modernization?

Chris Giancarlo: One hundred percent, what you said. Having run the world's preeminent derivatives regulator, the CFTC, I'm acutely aware that, over the decades, regulatory agencies have developed bodies of regulation that can become increasingly antiquated, especially when facing a new technological paradigm, as we are seeing with the IoT, the Internet of value.

That's very much the case at the Securities Exchange Commission, chaired by my good friend, Jay Clayton. As an independent agency, the SEC is older than the CFTC. The CFTC, which I chaired, is a *principles-based* regulator, which means that we look at our rule set on a principle basis and adapt it for changing times and changing paradigms. The SEC is *rules based.* It builds rules on top of rules, often written to correspond to the prevailing architecture, the prevailing technological paradigm, and it's very hard to adapt that paradigm for new technology.

Despite some very good work at the Securities Exchange Commission by Chairman Jay Clayton and commissioners like Hester Peirce [aka *Crypto Mom*], the SEC is struggling with almost 100 years of rule sets.[314] Decades of rules built on top of rules written for an analog securities trading world. Going into a digital world is a challenge. There needs to be a reset, a reengineering of those rule sets to match this new paradigm.

I'm somewhat envious of emerging economies that are writing their securities rules for the first time now and can write these rules based upon that new paradigm. Look at what Singapore is doing. It's not exactly a new economy, but it's very forward-looking, and it's writing rules for this new paradigm very well. We must wake up to that in the United States. Just as we need to modernize our airports, our bridges, and our currency, we need to modernize our securities regulation.

Alex: There's an old joke that God may have invented the world in six days, but he didn't have an installed base.[315] We see this after the Soviet Union fell in the late 1980s, early 1990s, certain countries like Estonia emerged without rule sets or institutions at all. And so they started on a digital forward path. Many aspects of how Estonia's government interacts with its people are more advanced than in Canada or the United States.[316] I wonder whether that creates a drag on the US' maintaining its advantage in money and financial services globally.

CONCLUSIONS: THIS IS JUST THE BEGINNING

DIVERSITY MAKES FOR A HEALTHY MARKETPLACE

Alex Tapscott: I want to get to the [audience's] comments and questions about Libra, a proposed type of corporate currency. One of the criticisms of Libra was that, by having a basket of currencies, Libra was in effect creating money, which is a role normally confined to governments and central banks, at least for the past 150 years or so. Yet there was no democratic accountability for where those deposits sat, what monetary policy it would have, whether Libra could start or cut off service in certain countries, and do whatever usually and hopefully requires the consent of the governed using that currency. And so Congress and certain US regulators have been very vocal in their opposition. More recently, Libra has scaled back and is going more the route of creating stablecoins for different kinds of currencies like the US dollar and hoping that it will be more palatable.[317] What was your view on the original design?[318]

Chris Giancarlo: At the Digital Dollar Project, we have taken a foundational position, that we don't seek either to criticize or to call for the restriction or suppression of any other instrument, whether it be a commercial instrument, another sovereign, or a DeFi instrument like bitcoin. The market's always healthier and healthiest when there's a multiplicity of trading instruments for market participants to choose from. Choice is a good thing.

So I don't want to sound as a critic of any element of Libra, either its initial one, or where it's migrating to. But I would say this: even in a world of CBDCs, of sovereign central bank digital currencies, there will be a need for other instruments. If one constructs a good basket of currencies to backstop a stablecoin, then investors might say, "This is a good hedge against the failure of any one currency or, if I'm engaged in global commerce, this is a better way of hedging my currency risk in the world." In some ways, it becomes like an ETF or a mutual fund. It's not *if* but *when* the United States develops and rolls out a digital dollar, you will still see stablecoins available.

There won't be myriads of them, but there may be a few key ones that folks engaged in international commerce may see as a way of hedging a particular currency risk. But construction will be very important, just as investing in a fund is. You have to read the fine print. Where are the reserves held? Who holds them? Who are the trustees? What risks of loss are involved when you're not having actual fiat, but something tied to fiat?

BLOCKCHAIN WILL TRANSFORM OTHER FINANCIAL ASSETS

Alex Tapscott: We've been talking about money, and money makes the world go 'round, as they say. There are so many other kinds of financial asset classes. The notional value of derivatives outstanding is in the hundreds of trillions of dollars. The net amount is smaller, which people fail to realize, but it's still a lot. Global equity markets are $60 trillion, $70 trillion. One of the big promises of blockchain is that we could apply these underlying properties, which seemed to work so well for money, to other financial assets like stocks and bonds specifically, since they settle to cash and there's no physical delivery—the perfect kinds of assets that ought to be tokenized.[319]

I spent almost a decade in the stock market. A stock is really a contract. It's an instrument that entitles the bearer of the contract a share of a common enterprise to cash flow if the company pays dividends and to vote on certain decisions. Why should we have share certificates, clearinghouses, and myriad institutions inside the securities industry? Why has the pace of innovation not been faster? Is it a technical question or a regulatory question?

Chris Giancarlo: I think it was Bill Gates who said, when you view things forward-looking, it always seems as if it takes longer to get there. Then, when you look back, wow, it happened fast. The front offices of our financial markets are probably 90 percent automated now. Yet, when I began my career on Wall Street 35 years ago, the ferries, the subways, and the trains were letting off tens of thousands of people to go to the front office and the floors of the exchange in lower Manhattan. They're all gone now, all that floor trading. The floor of the New York Stock Exchange is a TV studio. It's not really where trading takes place. The front office has been automated. Now we're talking about the middle and the back offices.

It took a generation for the front office to transition. I don't think it will take a full generation for the middle and the back offices to transition, because of Moore's Law. Just as the SEC and regulation didn't stop the transformation of the front office, I don't think it will stop the transformation of the middle office. Because markets are always searching for greater efficiency, and the pressure for efficiency will push aside barriers, whether they be regulatory or institutional. It is happening, it will happen, and the Internet of value is going to accelerate that happening.

Alex: It's a great point. People hear about high-frequency traders who put their trading desks next to server farms in New Jersey rather than in midtown Manhattan, because the signal for trade travels along fiber optic cable. If you're eight miles closer along the speed of light, you can beat the market by picoseconds. Yet, those trades take T plus three days to settle.

Chris: Do you know why it's three days? Because the standard delivery for US first-class mail used to be three days. Today we send everything in an instant, electronically, yet we have a settlement cycle based upon a modality of delivery that nobody uses anymore.

Alex: Unbelievable. I remember reading that it was only after 9/11, when all the airlines were grounded, that the Fed finally allowed for same-day settlement of transactions because, otherwise, you had to budget for the time it would take to fly a check across the country.

Chris: That's fascinating—it took a crisis to realize that a methodology was inadequate and needed to be replaced. I think COVID-19 is going to show the inadequacy of the account-based system as a delivery mechanism for federal benefits, and the need to move to a digital-based system. That's why you now see in Congress these initiatives called "digital dollar wallets." They are not CBDCs; they are a recognition that the accounts-based, paper-based, check-based delivery mechanism for money, for federal benefits, is out of place, especially in a crisis. If you're going to fix it for a crisis, let's just fix it for everything.

Alex: Absolutely. Crises tend to change the course of history. Bills and laws that would take months or years to pass, pass in days or hours. Changes to our behavior, like work from home or using Zoom, happen overnight. Those same emergency conditions could lead to a real shift in our thinking about money and value, which is quite exciting. Never let a good crisis go to waste.

CURRENCY INNOVATION WILL UNLEASH
ECONOMIC INNOVATION

Alex Tapscott: I want to talk about those three kinds of currencies: community currencies, corporate currencies, and CBDCs. It seems as if this unstoppable force of technology is on a collision course with all this legacy infrastructure in the financial services industry. Most of the time, collisions are violent, but sometimes they're not. When two galaxies collide, they actually interact in this beautiful way—they coalesce around a new center of gravity—and very few stars are destroyed because there's so much space between them.[320] We get something that's bigger and stranger but different. So, what's the collision going to look like? Is it going to be violent? Are vested interests going to push against change? Are we going to see them fighting to defend their territory, or could this collision create something beautiful?

Chris Giancarlo: I think it can create something beautiful. For the effort that's needed to create a digital dollar, the two analogies that I draw on are the 1960s space programs and the 1990s and 2000s development of the Internet as a public good. In both cases, what I think the United States did very well was to build partnerships between the public and the private sector. When China does something big, whether it's building a blue-water navy or creating a digital renminbi, it's a top-down approach driven by the Communist Party. When Europe does something big, it's often the public sector that lays out a framework and tells innovators, "Okay, here's the framework. You need to innovate to this framework."

When we do big things in the United States and Canada, we tend to blend public and private. That's what the space program was. Think of all the good that came from that for the private sector—all the new businesses, all the entrepreneurial activity that flowed from that. Certainly, the same was true of the Internet as well.

I think that should be the model for developing a US CBDC. What may flow from it is a lot of innovation for commercial currencies and DeFi experiments.[321] Just as I think a US CBDC can learn from bitcoin, bitcoin could learn from the work that would go into creating a US central bank digital currency. So it doesn't have to be worlds colliding. It could be a beautiful flowering of innovation, with one side informing the other and vice versa, and with all the good that could come out of that.

Alex: Well said. We've often advocated for a multistakeholder approach to problem-solving. You mentioned a couple of great examples of collaboration between public sector, private sector, and nongovernmental organizations even. Many governance organizations in the Internet ecosystem played an important role in developing standards, shaping policy, and so forth. I think you're right: we need that all-hands-on-deck approach for this as well.

Chris: One of the silver linings of the COVID crisis is how the public sector and the private sector are working together. There are all kinds of innovation in building respirators, PPE [personal protective equipment], vaccines. The large pharmaceuticals and biotech companies are doing work that normally takes years, if not decades, to get done. It's remarkable. There's an amazing amount of cooperation going on. We should look to those models as our edge.

Alex: Where can people learn more about the Digital Dollar Project? Where can they follow what you're doing?

Chris: Thank you, we have a website DigitalDollarProject.org. I use Twitter actively to report on what we're doing, and my handle is @GiancarloMKTS. Follow me on Twitter and follow the Digital Dollar Project. Check out our white paper on the Digital Dollar Project.[322] It's a fairly thoughtful review of not just how a digital dollar should look but also what use cases can be done. It also proposes a series of pilot programs that the US public sector could do with the private sector in rolling this out.

We don't think a digital dollar should be done in a big bang, overnight. It should be done thoughtfully, carefully, in an iterative process. Just as the decision to go to the moon was taken in the late 1950s, the landing on the moon didn't take place until ten years later. Along the way, there were multiple programs—the Mercury mission, the Gemini mission, the Apollo mission.[323] All different rollouts of the technology before the technology was perfected.

We're proposing that the development of a digital dollar be a similar developmental effort across the private and the public sectors, in a series of pilot programs and iterative structures. We'll be laying that out in our white paper and publishing it on our website. We welcome thoughtful input. Again, we want to learn and to educate at the same time. So, thank you.

Don: What we have today is not a digital dollar but a bearer instrument. Privacy can be a competitive differentiator for the US dollar, privacy built into the architecture. A system like this could defend the privacy of individuals and still deliver extraordinary transparency. Central bankers could have a lighter touch on regulation, fewer rules upon rules. Sunlight is a great disinfectant. If you make institutions naked, then they've got to get buff.

Regulation is the number one implementation challenge. It's a new paradigm bumping up against an old, causing dislocation and conflict, confusion and uncertainty. New economies have new opportunities to leapfrog established ones. We saw that with mobile technology in emerging markets. When we have a new paradigm, we have a leadership crisis. A new paradigm calls forth new leaders, and Chris Giancarlo is at the top of our list.

CHAPTER 5

INTRODUCTION TO STABLECOINS

Providing Price Stability in Decentralized
Financial Systems

Alyze Sam

 ## STABLECOINS IN BRIEF

- Invented to support more everyday use cases and attract more users, stablecoins are digital money with many of the benefits of cryptocurrencies like bitcoin and without their drawbacks such as price volatility. But great are the technical challenges of developing a stablecoin system strong enough to weather market turbulence.

- There are several types of stablecoins: those backed by well-known assets such as fiat currency, precious metals, or other cryptoassets (asset-collaterized); those backed by no asset (non-collaterized, aka seigniorage supply or algorithmic stablecoins); and hybrids that combine collateral and algorithms to manage supply and price. For stability, their value is often pegged to a well-known asset with a steady price, like US dollars or gold.

- The top ten stablecoins by market capitalization have some features in common. For example, all are dapps running on top of a blockchain rather than native tokens to that blockchain, and many are ERC-20 tokens running on the Ethereum network. Several have distinct features, such as reserves held by third parties (e.g., financial institutions) and audited by independent accountants, to increase user trust.

- The use cases for stablecoins are as numerous as the use cases for fiat currency with stable value, but mass adoption will take time. Implementation challenges are well known in terms of user understanding and experience, scalability, and interoperability of systems. In the meanwhile, the authors suggest additional uses in shoring up losses when the cryptocurrency market is volatile, making a profit when the market declines, and protecting cryptoasset value in general.

THE CONTEXT FOR STABLECOINS

While Satoshi Nakamoto proposed bitcoin (BTC) as "a purely peer-to-peer version of electronic cash [that] would allow online payments to be sent directly from one party to another without going through a financial institution," BTC is rarely used as a medium of exchange.[324] Price volatility and high transaction fees make many BTC and other cryptocurrencies impractical for daily transactions. Instead, people buy and hold them as electronic stores of value rather than use them as digital money.

In 2014, Vitalik Buterin wrote, "Given the high level of interest in 'blockchain technology' coupled with disinterest in 'bitcoin the currency' that we see among so many in the mainstream world, perhaps the time is ripe for stable-currency or multi-currency systems to take over."[325] He suggested three categories; "Stable assets for trading, speculative assets for investment, and bitcoin itself may well serve as a unique Schelling point for a universal fallback asset, similar to the current and historical functioning of gold."[326]

The stablecoin concept first appeared in J.R. Willett's 2012 white paper, "The Second Bitcoin White Paper," where he described a Mastercoin protocol that would "improve the stability of Bitcoin."[327] In 2013, Dan Larimer, Charles Hoskinson, and Stan Larimer published a white paper on BitShares, a digital asset exchange designed "to embrace the innovations divined from bitcoin while ... addressing both volatility and illiquidity without introducing the need for trust ... ."[328] On the BitShares exchange, digital assets could "track the value of gold, silver, dollars or other currencies while paying dividends to holders and avoiding all counterparty risk."[329]

TABLE 5-1

TYPES OF STABLECOINS

CATEGORY	TYPE	CHARACTERISTICS
Asset Collateralized	Fiat-collateralized	• Centralized; backed by government currency, ensuring its store of value • Convenient, fast, and secure conversions • Easily understood by the average consumer
	Crypto-collateralized	• Decentralized; backed by another cryptocurrency, not a central government • Convenient, fast, and secure conversions • Easily used in leveraged or margin trading related to over-collateralization • Transparent; with transactions recorded on a public ledger
	Metal- or commodity-collateralized	• Backed by real-world asset or tangible commodity • Convenient, fast, and secure conversions • Greater liquidity to commodity markets • Easier price discovery • Easily understood by the average consumer
Non-collateralized	Seigniorage supply (algorithmic)	• No tangible asset required • Autonomous; not influenced by outside markets • Decentralized; no government control • Automatic value adjustments based on the market • Transparent; transactions recorded on public blockchain
Hybrid	Collateralized and non-collateralized	• Characteristics of both categories above • Meets the needs of a variety of users

The associated coin, bitUSD, was defined as a collateralized asset that would be "highly correlated by self-enforcing market feedback to the value of USD and backed by BitShares."[330] So the idea was to create a digital currency backed by another cryptocurrency and pegged to precious metals or *fiat money*, that is, "government-issued currency that is not backed by a physical commodity, such as gold or silver, but rather by the government that issued it."[331]

That's essentially what a *stablecoin* is: a cryptocurrency with some of the benefits of BTC—such as cryptographic security, distributed rather than centralized governance, transparent and publicly auditable, P2P digital asset exchange, and speedy settlement of transactions—but without the price volatility of BTC because the value is pegged to an asset with an established and fairly steady value like gold, corn, oil, sugar, diamonds, wheat, fiat currency, or other *fungible* asset, meaning an asset that is interchangeable, substitutable, or uniform with other assets. When two commodities are considered fungible, they are identical in specification; we can substitute one unit for another in a contract.

A cryptocurrency that's backed by a stable asset and pegged to a well-understood unit of value such as the US dollar makes it more understandable and acceptable for everyday transactions and recurring payments, from credit cards and mortgages to rent and subscriptions. The most cited use cases for stablecoins—as for BTC itself—include

- Dealing with hyperinflation in countries such as Argentina, where governments restrict residents' use of cash and citizens want to hold assets of more stable value

- Banking the unbanked or under-banked people who lack the official paperwork or minimum required balances to open bank accounts

- Transferring remittances cheaply, securely, and easily between countries

- Converting from crypto to locally acceptable currencies as easily as possible.[332]

But start-ups are getting creative in stablecoin usage. For example, Blockimmo, a real estate company focused on tokenizing real estate, initiated an online property sale where investors could buy a piece of the building.[333] Blockimmo used XCHF, a stablecoin tied to the Swiss Franc (CHF) as a payment option, keeping the price steady during the entire transaction process. The XCHF is pegged 1:1 to CHF. Use cases for stablecoins will likely multiply as the public becomes more aware of them.

Tyler and Cameron Winklevoss, co-founders of the cryptocurrency trading platform Gemini, told *Fortune* that "stablecoins amount to 'dollars on the blockchain'" and are a "bright spot" in the crypto space.[334] To summarize, a stablecoin attempts to:

- Facilitate the adoption and use of digital currencies.
- Support effortless transactions like traditional currencies.
- Contribute to a new DeFi ecosystem.
- Create stability among cryptocurrency trading pairs in foreign exchange–style trades.
- Reduce risk and diversify portfolios during critical junctures.
- Assist in investment predictions by increasing transparency and minimizing market volatility.
- Provide global access to a stable currency, protecting nations plagued by hyperinflation.

THE ECONOMICS BEHIND THE PROTOCOLS

Satoshi constructed a digital system for making impervious money and payment transactions feasible to all, despite location. In Satoshi's vision, the cryptocurrency community saw the potential for DeFi, also described as "open finance." The Ethereum blockchain breathed life into this future of finance with its easily integrable smart contract system. The community imagined a world of programmable money, where independent people could effortlessly log into an open alternative to every financial service available today: not just payments but savings, insurance, loans, and more.

According to *BlockGeeks.com*, "a *smart contract* is a computer protocol intended to digitally facilitate, verify, or enforce the negotiation or performance of a contract. Smart contracts allow the performance of credible transactions without third parties."[335] A smart contract program is a dapp operating on a blockchain that can execute transactions automatically when coded conditions are met. This system lets developers construct functions that go well beyond digital assets, on a decentralized technology rather than built and controlled by a centralized entity.

Technologists and economists imagined the future operating effortlessly with protocols like these, but it is no longer relegated to the realms of science fiction. The authors of many a stablecoin white paper claim that they were inspired by the quantity theory of money—that is, the monetarist's hypothesis that "changes in the general level of commodity prices are determined primarily by changes in the quantity of money in circulation."[336] Early in the twentieth century, economist Irving Fisher developed an equation of exchange to represent this mid-sixteenth-century idea:

$$M*V = P*T$$

where *M* is the supply of money,
V is the velocity of circulation,
P is the level of price, and
T is the volume of market transactions[337]

In theory, if M doubles while V and T remain constant, then P should double, cutting the value of each individual unit of currency in half. In practice, central bankers try to stabilize prices (i.e., minimize inflation) by controlling the amount of fiat currency in circulation.[338] Charles Kim, co-founder and chief operating officer of Decon, a blockchain technology advisory firm in South Korea, gave this Korean Republic won (KRW) example: "In the long run, currency value, like commodities, can change in accordance with supply. If the exchange rate today is $1 = ₩2000 (weaker KRW), the exchange rate could become $1 = ₩1000 (KRW appreciates) by decreasing circulating KRW by half."[339]

Many economists accept the Fisher equation as valid.[340] This model suggests stablecoins could be programmed to keep drastic price swings at bay by adjusting units in circulation. If a stablecoin's value dropped below a certain price point, the smart contract would curb the total number of tokens circulating and stabilize its value. If the token's value rose beyond a certain price point, the smart contract could incorporate more supply to keep cryptocurrency at desired market value.

Most economic models are imperfect. This model assumes that the velocity of circulation and the volume of transactions are proportional. Blockchain technology is still in its infancy, and cryptocurrency projects are rapidly changing; therefore, we cannot easily calculate token velocity and transaction volume, let alone make any assumptions about constancy. Considering V and T, we may want to add more variables to the equation.

For example, with BitShares, Dan Larimer was trying to solve for the hidden costs of securing the Bitcoin blockchain through hash power. He suggested that BTC advocates were ignoring *marginal utility*, the economic theory that "the value of a good or service decreases as the quantity consumed or available increases. ... Unfortunately, each additional unit of security provides less value and costs more money."[341] He estimated that BTC holders were paying about 10 percent of their BTC savings each year to protect BTC's market capitalization.

Larimer asked prospective users to "think of a cryptocurrency as shares in a *decentralized autonomous corporation* (DAC) where the source code defines the bylaws."[342] The BitShares DAC's code would pay for security but only the necessary amount to maximize shareholder value. Larimer believed that, instead of distributing coins solely to miners, "paying shareholders dividends will result in a better long-term viral marketing campaign and increase the demand for shares of the DAC. This increase in demand will bid up prices beyond competing DACs that do not offer dividends. As a result, miners make more money despite having a smaller share of the pie."[343]

In its survey of stablecoins, BitMEX Research concluded that stablecoin innovators often miscalculate the technical challenges of creating a stablecoin system "robust enough to withstand cycles or the turbulence and volatility linked to financial markets."[344] They pointed out that "most forms of fiat money, even the US dollar itself, have not even achieved that, with credit cycles putting US dollar bank deposits at risk." BitMEX's takeaway: a stablecoin system built on USD may never be more reliable than the current banking system.

GOVERNANCE OF STABLECOINS

Controversy has stirred in the crypto communities over stablecoin design. Some have questioned the logic of pegging and using an algorithm to adjust pricing. "Fiat-world examples of pegged assets form an object lesson in why you don't try to peg currencies: because you are unable to hold the peg any longer than you can afford to subsidize your differences of opinion with the market," wrote Preston Byrne, co-founder of enterprise blockchain start-up Monax.[345] He later blogged that stablecoins were "the techno-magical idea that a cryptocurrency can tell the market what its price should be, rather than the market determining what a cryptocurrency's price should be."[346] He put it another way in an email to *Technology Review*: "Price is determined by a meeting of the minds of a buyer and seller, not by an algorithm. ... All that is required for these systems to fail is for people not to buy the product."[347]

Not all stablecoin projects are transparent and decentrally governed. Adam Back, known for the Hashcash "proof of work" system, said that stablecoins intrinsically fall short of BTC because of their custody risk. He believed existing stablecoins lacked the self-sovereignty properties of BTC and expected central government–operated ones in the future similarly to lack in self-sovereignty.[348] Finally, he added, publicly auditable blockchains provide more value.[349] According to PricewaterhouseCoopers, most stablecoin developers have built their projects on Ethereum using Solidity, a programming language that makes the resulting smart contracts more difficult to verify.[350]

BitMEX Research distinguished distributed stablecoin systems "from tokens such as Tether, where one entity controls a pool of USD collateral, ultimately making the system centralized and thus susceptible to being shut down by the authorities."[351] In 2017, rumors surfaced about Tether's not being fully backed 1:1 by the USD as Tether had claimed. Tether representatives eventually admitted that Tether was backing only 74 percent of its coin by USD, making it a fractional reserve stablecoin. Bitfinex, which shares a parent company with Tether, reported an $850 million loss in Tether funds that it planned to supplement with its new asset exchange token, LEO.[352]

In the fourth quarter of 2019, two members of the US House of Representatives Financial Services Committee, Rep. Sylvia Garcia (D-Texas) and Rep. Lance Gooden (R-Texas), proposed the Managed Stablecoins are Securities Act of 2019 on the day of a committee hearing on the role of big data in financial services.[353]

Rep. Garcia said managed stablecoins "are clearly securities under existing law. ... Bringing clarity to the regulatory structure of these digital assets protects consumers and ensures proper government oversight going forward."[354] Rep. Gooden brought to light the necessity of the bill in helping consumers understand the financial assets they were buying:

In what are called "managed stablecoins," we have trusted brands marketing digital assets to consumers as secure and stable ... . Everyday investors need to know they can trust the issuers behind their financial assets. This bill would bring them the security they deserve by applying the laws we use to regulate financial securities to this new breed of digital currencies.[355]

TABLE 5-2

A LOOK AT STABLECOINS IN GENERAL

ADVANTAGES	DISADVANTAGES
• Easier to understand for fiat and digital currency users • An acceptable bridge from fiat to cryptocurrency • Potentially low-fee, secure, and partially or completely anonymous digital transactions peer to peer • Censorship resistant • Potentially strong governance with transparency and accountability • Use of in-dapp purchases over utility tokens when token volume is low, volatile in price, or a combination of both • Offers a hedge against fiat currency in countries with challenging economic conditions • Use of smart contracts to protect all parties with interest in investments • Asset-backed, potentially reducing market fluctuations • Likely regulated to protect users • Potential to transform remittance transactions	• In some countries, users must buy stablecoins through their bank accounts • Custody risk in projects controlled by a single entity or backed by centrally managed assets; requires trust in a third party • External audits needed to ensure that entity is holding stated amount of assets • Pegging to a fiat currency that faces inflation or other shock to its value • Over time new markets tend to decrease in price volatility; if BTC value stays relatively stable, then demand for stablecoins may decrease • New technology takes time to mass adoption • Reduced return on investment; traders look to other means for financial gain • Likely regulation could increase costs and reduce user anonymity; in some countries, users must buy stablecoins through their bank accounts

GOLD OR BITCOIN, A STABLE COMMODITY?

The goal of monetary policy is to prevent not only inflation but also deflation, while promoting a stable monetary environment. In the nineteenth and twentieth centuries, governments adopted the "gold standard" for their monetary systems, in which their standard economic units of account derived from a fixed quantity of gold.[356] The gold standard appealed because it moved control from human beings to market forces. The physical quantity of gold acted as a limit to currency issuance, thus curtailing inflation. Most nations abandoned the gold standard in the 1930s, although many still hold substantial gold reserves.[357] By the 1930s, gold coins were no longer a circulating currency, and the world abandoned the gold standard.

Practical uses aside, gold has kept its value largely related to tradition—that is, its perceived scarcity and the difficulty of mining it.[358] Many believe that, during times of economic downfalls, gold is still a safer investment, provided that no majority owner or block of owners can control the market. For example, King Mansa Musa of the Mali Empire (1312–1337 CE) spent so much gold in the markets of Cairo that the value of the precious metal plummeted by 20 percent.[359] Ranked as the twelfth richest man ever to walk the earth, Mansa Musa had hauled over 16 tons of gold with him on his annual pilgrimage from Timbuktu to Mecca. It was on his return trip to Mali through Egypt that he stopped to shop, and his Cairene shopping spree triggered an economic downturn in the Middle East.

Notwithstanding this example to the contrary, humankind has recognized gold as a precious asset with a stable value for five millennia. But can we formulate stronger digital currencies and protocols to prevent such devastating events in the crypto space? Some have argued that BTC is a better investment asset than gold because private companies, governments, and banks cannot control its quantity.[360]

According to *Cointelegraph*, Nick Szabo predicted that, in countries on economic sanctions lists or "where economic mismanagement has precipitated ruinous national currency devaluation or inflation," people would adopt cryptocurrencies such as BTC over gold in particular because central powers have proven themselves untrustworthy stewards of value. As an example, Szabo cited, "the Nazis' looting of Europe's gold reserves, beginning with Austria's in 1938."[361]

Bitcoin is governed by computer science, cryptography, and mathematics, not by politicians. It's run by a social consensus implemented through the Hashcash PoW system as part of the BTC mining algorithm. That's the consensus mechanism through which members of the distributed Bitcoin network decide upon unitary rational action. In general, consensus technology enables truly democratic governance and the coordination of free market activity. The Bitcoin network was the first to integrate a fully distributed consensus method for facilitating the transfer of value more efficiently P2P through electronic communications. The PoW structure that secures and maintains the Bitcoin network is one way of organizing individuals who do not necessarily trust each other to act in the best interest of all participants of the network.

Bitcoin advocates have compared the market performance of gold over the last 43 years with that of BTC over the last six years and proclaimed an "uncanny resemblance" in the resulting charts of their respective prices.[362] Perhaps it is because Bitcoin's creator capped BTC quantity at 21 million, released steadily over time, and so it is finite like gold.

Once all 21 million bitcoins are minted, there will be no more to mine and its value will increase as demand grows. Crypto fanatics relish their proposed new gold standard. They can melt gold down to power the *application-specific integrated circuit* (aka ASICs) devices used to mine and transfer BTC, thereby unleashing a new digital gold rush.

So which is more beneficial to invest in—BTC or gold?[363] Remember, BTC and gold are completely different assets with different use cases. BTC will never be a tangible commodity, while volatility limits BTC's ability to be a haven for investors. Today we can invest in either one, or we can obtain both by investing in a legitimate gold-backed and gold-pegged stablecoin.

TYPES OF STABLECOINS

In this section, we develop a basic taxonomy of stablecoins for comparing and contrasting those in use and in development.

ASSET-COLLATERALIZED STABLECOINS

The socially agreed-upon currency in most countries is termed *fiat*, meaning something created without effort, by dictate or decree.[364] Until 1971, most nations applied a gold exchange standard or else pegged foreign currency exchanges to the price of gold or silver.[365]

Shifting from an asset-backed currency to the current fiat system left centralized banks, governments, financial technologists, private entities, and economic experts with the concept of asset-collateralized stablecoins. Their purpose is to tokenize stable assets on a blockchain, and so serve as a means of speedy, secure, and stable daily transactions. Stablecoins in this category may guarantee to exchange one stablecoin for one unit of its underlying asset.

Fiat-collateralized stablecoins

The most basic type of stablecoin is a fiat-collateralized stablecoin. This token is a 1:1 ratio cryptocurrency backed by fiat like the US dollar or the Japanese yen. Stablecoins are created when a fiat asset is deposited to a distributed platform or centralized issuer and destroyed when the fiat asset is withdrawn: the stablecoin protocol or issuer accepts a deposit in fiat and issues the depositor one unit of stablecoin for every dollar deposited. The 1:1 ratio holds. The digital currency is effectively an IOU for its underlying asset. If depositors decide to liquidate their stablecoin tokens, the stablecoin protocol or issuer transfers the fiat currency and then "burns" the stablecoins representing the fiat currency transferred.

This digital currency system makes transactions safe, fast, and secure, making it useful as a medium of exchange as well as a short-term store of value. In addition to price stability, stablecoins are convenient and easier to convert back into fiat, and consumers are acquainted with government-backed assets. The disadvantages are several:

- Centralized systems are prone to certain vulnerabilities (i.e., single point of failure, bankruptcy of the central entity, and moral hazards); using a centralized structure negates the decentralization principle of cryptocurrency.

- Users must trust some third party to hold sufficient fiat collateral for the system to function optimally; again, this idea goes against the principle of cryptocurrencies, which are traditionally *trustless media* of exchange.

- Governance must include external audits to verify transparency in fund accounts. Auditors can determine whether the issuer is holding the appropriate amount of collateral. Auditing can be a tedious and expensive process.

- Processes involving fiat currency require greater oversight and more regulations, which could complicate and possibly compromise the efficiency and the anonymity of the cryptocurrency adoption process.

- Fiat-backed coins rely on traditional fiat currency payment systems, which tend to rely on older, slower, and more expensive technologies.

Let's look at a well-known corporate example. JPMorgan Chase is the largest bank in America with $2.5 trillion worth of assets.[366] In 2017, Australia's ANZ bank and the Royal Bank of Canada co-launched the Interbank Information Network on JPMorgan Chase's Quorum blockchain and integrated with Microsoft Azure to streamline an array of financial processes such as compliance, settlement, origination, and interest rate payments.[367] Now rebranded Liink by J.P.Morgan, the platform connects over 400 banks worldwide.[368] (ConsenSys acquired Quorum in August 2020 and is now managing the underlying technology for the bank.[369])

JPMorgan Chase has integrated real-time settlements, indicating it has successfully launched a digital currency, which surprised many in the fintech sector.[370] The results were exciting for those awaiting

JPM Coins. J.P.Morgan's official website states, "We have always believed in the potential of blockchain technology and we are supportive of cryptocurrencies … ."[371]

Some would disagree. Jamie Dimon, the bank's chair and CEO, called BTC a "terrible store of value" as early as 2014.[372] A year later, he said, "Bitcoin will not survive."[373] In September 2017, he very publicly dismissed BTC as a "fraud" and threatened to fire any staff members who used it. Dimon later said he regretted making this statement.[374] During the "Delivering Alpha" conference in 2018, Dimon announced, "My daughter bought some bitcoin and it went up and she thinks she's a genius now."[375]

However, for the underlying Bitcoin blockchain, Dimon never had anything but praise, evidenced not only by his words but also his actions. JPMorgan Chase had been experimenting with distributed ledger technology for several years. Anticipating cryptocurrency regulation, J.P.Morgan plans to evolve with financial trends. In February 2019, its site proclaimed, "J.P.Morgan this month became the first US bank to create and successfully test a digital coin representing a fiat currency. The JPM Coin is based on blockchain-based technology enabling the instantaneous transfer of payments between institutional clients."[376]

Despite Dimon's disdain for BTC, JPM Coin tries to imitate the technology for trust. It will be a fiat-collateralized stablecoin pegged to the US dollar.[377] On 28 May 2019, JPMorgan Chase announced that its "blockchain team [had] developed a privacy feature for Ethereum-based blockchains," an open-source extension to the Zether protocol that masks user identities and amounts of transactions.[378] Oli Harris, then head of digital-assets strategy and Quorum at J.P.Morgan, explained the extension's function to *CoinDesk*:

> In the basic Zether, the account balances and the transfer accounts are concealed but the participants' identities are not. So, we have solved that. In our implementation, we provide a

proof protocol for the anonymous extension in which the sender may hide herself and the transaction's recipients in a larger group of parties.[379]

JPM Coin went live in October 2020.[380] Although JPM Coin made headlines, it was not the first stablecoin launched by an American bank. The first was actually Signet, launched by Signature Bank in January 2019 with the regulatory approval of the Department of Financial Services of the State of New York.[381]

Financial service providers in the digital asset industry like OKCoin (USDK), Huobi Group (HUSD), and Binance USD (BUSD, launched in collaboration with Paxos Trust Company) have all launched stablecoins. The coins are tradable at their parent company's asset exchanges as well as other platforms that offer other stablecoins. USDK, HUSD, and BUSD are all ERC-20 tokens issued on the Ethereum blockchain. They are all pegged 1:1 to the US dollar.

TABLE 5-3

FIAT-COLLATERALIZED STABLECOINS

STABLECOIN	SYMBOL	ISSUER	RELEASED	NOTES
AUD Ramp	AUDR	OnRamp Technologies	2018	ERC-20 compliant; backed by and pegged to AUD
Gemini Dollar	GUSD	Gemini Trust Co. LLC	2018	ERC-20 token; backed by and pegged to USD; publicly available monthly audit by accounting firm
Globcoin	GLX	Reserve Currency Solutions SA	2018	Backed by 15 fiat currencies
HUSD Token	HUSD	Stable Universal Ltd.	2018	ERC-20 token; backed 1:1 by USD
JPM Coin	JPM	JPMorgan Chase	2020	Backed by and pegged to USD

STABLECOIN	SYMBOL	ISSUER	RELEASED	NOTES
Nollar	NOS	NOS Stablecoin	2018	Backed by EUR; pegged to USD and other fiat currencies
Paxos Dollar	USDP	Paxos Trust Co.	2018	ERC-20 token; backed by and pegged to USD; audited by WithumSmith+Brown PC
Reserve	RSV	N/A	2020	ERC-20 token; backed by fiat currency
Stably USD	USDS	Stably Corp.	2018	ERC-20 token, BEP-2 token (Binance); backed by and pegged to USD; supply adjusted via open market operations
Stasis Euro	EURS	STSS Ltd.	2018	ERC-20 token; backed by and pegged to EUR; verification streams supported by Stasis
Tether	USDT	Tether Holdings Ltd.	2014	ERC-20 token; backed by and pegged to USD; built on Omni chain; formerly Realcoin
TrustToken	TrueUSD	TrueCoin LLC	2018	Backed by and pegged to USD; built on Ethereum; focused on transparency; also TrueAUD, TrueCAD, TrueGBP, TrueHKD
USD Coin	USDC	Centre Consortium	2018	Co-founded by Circle and Coinbase; ERC-20 token; backed by and pegged 1:1 to USD; audited by Grant Thornton
USDK	USDK	OK Group, Prime Trust	2019	ERC-20 token; backed 1:1 by USD; exchange rate with USD; third-party auditors of accounts and smart contract

Sources: CoinMarketCap.com, Etherscan.io, and individual token websites, as of Nov. 2020.

Crypto-collateralized stablecoins

Crypto-collateralized stablecoins are tokens backed by other cryptocurrencies. Typically, they are backed by a mix of cryptocurrencies. This tethering of value allows for better risk distribution: the volatility risks for a single cryptocurrency is much higher than a basket of such currencies. They resemble mutual funds or exchange-traded funds (ETFs) depending on risk management, respectively.[382]

Crypto-collateralized coins are often over-collateralized to withstand price fluctuations of underlying cryptocurrencies. The most common form of crypto-supported stablecoins require users to stake (vault) a certain amount of digital currencies according to the specifications of a smart contract, which will result in a fixed ratio of stablecoins.

TABLE 5-4

CRYPTO-COLLATERALIZED STABLECOINS AT A GLANCE

ADVANTAGES	DISADVANTAGES
• Potentially decentralized underlying asset with transparent and secure structure and no central party to trust • Convenient and fast conversions occurring on a blockchain • Easily used in leverage trading related to the over-collateralization • All transactions recorded on a public blockchain for accountability	• Complex elements that can obfuscate the minting process • Excess collateral required to secure • Possible instantaneous liquidation if value falls below a certain threshold • Backed by multiple cryptos; selecting the right coins for maximal price stability can be challenging

This approach is on-chain, trustless insurance. The system uses the stablecoin when assets are pledged as collateral on the network. The token maintains stability through over-collaterization, market efficiencies, profit motives, complementary incentives, as well as fallback procedures such as global settlement.

Venture capitalist Haseeb Qureshi pointed out two disadvantages of crypto-collateralized coins: they are more vulnerable to price instability than fiat-collateralized coins and can automatically revert to the underlying cryptocurrency if the crypto's price drops far enough. "This could be a dealbreaker for exchanges," Qureshi wrote. "In the case of a market crash, they would have to deal with stablecoin balances and trading pairs suddenly mutating into the underlying crypto assets."[383]

TABLE 5-5

CRYPTO-COLLATERALIZED STABLECOINS

STABLECOIN	SYMBOL	ISSUER	RELEASED	FEATURES
Alchemint	SDUSD	Alchemint Foundation	2018	Backed by a pool of assets; fiat and cryptos; built on top of NEO
Augmint	A-EUR	Augmint DAO	N/A	Pegged to EUR and backed by ether (ETH); planned to replicate fiat using stability reserves and smart contracts
bitUSD	BITUSD	BitShares	2014	Collateralized 1:1 by USD; backed by BTS, fiat, silver, gold, and other assets; uses derivative instruments; also bitCNY (BITCNY)
Dai	DAI	MakerDAO	2017	ERC-20 token; backed by ETH, eventually backed by multiple assets; 1:1 soft peg to USD; maintained by MakerDAO community, governed by MKR holders; assimilable to derivatives
EOSDT	EOSDT	Equilibrium Lab	2019	EOS-based; pegged to USD; collateralized by other digital assets
Neutral Dollar	NUSD	Neutral	N/A	Backed by basket of other stablecoins; Ethereum smart contract; maintained by "profit-seeking arbitrageurs"‡; auditable on-chain custody

‡*NeutralProject.com*, as of 1 Nov. 2020.

Commodity-collateralized stablecoins

Commodity-collateralized stablecoins are cryptocurrency backed by commodities; that is, assets that are undifferentiated from each other in an asset class and are therefore fungible for convenient trading and transactions.[384] Investors will still invest in gold and other precious metals when every other market is bearish or struggling because they generally view precious metals as reliable stores of value and largely recession-proof.

Anthem Blanchard, CEO and founder of the commodity-collateralized stablecoin Anthem Gold, told us, "Gold is a recognized store of value ingrained in our DNA. Bitcoin has freed gold to become a currency again by creating a better way of accounting. We utilize public protocols, including Bitcoin's, to ensure the most transparency in the history of gold currency."[385]

Backing these cryptocurrencies by commodities with long-term stable market prices helps to ensure that their prices won't fluctuate wildly and that their carrying costs are lower, since users need not hold the commodities themselves in inventory. Consider the logistics of delivering and storing goods: transporting physical assets like precious metals can be costly, time consuming, and ecologically irresponsible.

TABLE 5-6

COMMODITY-COLLATERALIZED STABLECOINS AT A GLANCE

ADVANTAGES	DISADVANTAGES
• Backed largely by established tangible commodities rather than intangibles like computing power or communications bandwidth • Converting into and out of these tends to be convenient, fast, and secure • Average consumers can understand commodity structure • The tokenization of commodities increases market liquidity and improves price discovery	• Centralized systems are prone to various vulnerabilities and risks (e.g., single point of failure, incompetence, or corruption of the central entity, etc.) • Using these requires trust in a third party to hold enough fiat collateral • For greater transparency, governance includes external audits to verify account balances

A commodities-backed stablecoin represents a specific amount of a commodity. For example, we could peg one stablecoin to one gram of gold. Its owner would store the physical asset in a trusted third party's vault. Whenever someone invested in a commodity-collateralized stablecoin, the network would mint a new token. Conversely, when the stablecoin was liquidated, the network would burn the token and release the collateral.

Commodity-collateralized stablecoins have value because they are digital representations of a different asset, therefore, some would say, it is an inherently centralized design. A mix of enthusiasts believe cryptocurrency should always be trustless, in other words, beholden to no external authority. Requiring a third party and audits is time intensive, costly, and leaves room for error. Intense regulation is needed to maintain transparency, which is why so many fail.

TABLE 5-7

COMMODITY-COLLATERALIZED STABLECOINS

STABLECOIN	SYMBOL	ISSUER	RELEASED	FEATURES
Anthem Gold	AGLD	Anthem Vault Inc.	2019	Backed by 1.0 g tangible gold; fully insured; vaulted securely in nonbank
AurusGOLD	AWG	Aurus Technologies	2020	Software offering established gold traders tokenization service; ERC-20 token; 1 token to 1.0 g 99.99% LBMA approved gold; currency transaction fees pay for insurance and storage; user can withdraw gold at any time
Digix Gold Digix DAO	DGX DGD	Digix Global	2016	Backed by gold; crowd sale raised 465K ETH; two ERC-20 tokens: DGX pegged to 1.0 g 99.99% LBMA gold vaulted in Singapore; and DGD to reward users quarterly based on total DGX transaction fees

STABLECOIN	SYMBOL	ISSUER	RELEASED	FEATURES
DinarCoin	DNC	Harimau Mint Gold	2019	ERC-20 token equal to a gold spot contract offered by company's forex liquidity provider; gold smart contract: gold in 1.0 g, 100 g, or 1.0 kg; silver in 100 oz., and 1.0 kg
G-Coin Responsible Gold	XGC XRG	Emergent Technology Holdings LP	2020	Backed by 1.0 g conflict-free gold; stored in an approved vault; blockchain used to track gold from mine to vault before tokenized
Goldmint	MNTP	Goldmint PTE Ltd.	2018	ERC-20 token; reliant on Graphene technology; pegged to gold and/or ETFs
OneGram	OGC	OneGram Project	2018	Backed by 1.0 g physical gold; vaulted near Dubai airport; compliant with Islamic Sharia; max number of OGC coins is 12,400,786; smart contract burns unsold coins after ICO
Puregold Token	PGTS PGPAY	Puregold Group	2018	Two ERC-20 tokens: PGTS for transactions, PGPAY backed by physical gold, equal to cost of 1.0 g gold plus 5% commission for fiat
Royal Mint Gold	RMG	The Royal Mint Ltd.	On hold	Backed by gold reserves in UK Royal Mint vault; CME Group stepped back
Sudan Gold Coin	SGC	Sudan Gold Coin	2020	ERC-20 token pegged to 0.05 g gold; backed by Sudanese gold mining business 100% controlled by Dubai SG Mining Co.
The Midas Touch Gold	TMTG	Digital Global Enterprise Ltd.	2020	ERC-20 token pegged to 1.0 g gold; Digital Gold Exchange is platform for exchanging cryptocurrencies for gold

STABLECOIN	SYMBOL	ISSUER	RELEASED	FEATURES
Xaurum	XAUR	Auresco Institute	2016	ERC-20 token backed by gold owned by Xaurum CommonWealth; 1 coin worth 1.0 g 99.99% gold; users can exchange XAUR for physical gold, deliverable to any destination

Sources: All trade data from Etherscan.io, as of 1 Nov. 2020. Another resource worth checking is "ICO Scams – Fake Initial Coin Offering Tokens List," BitcoinExchangeGuide.com/Cryptocurrency/ICO-scams.

NON-COLLATERALIZED STABLECOINS

Critics sometimes disparage the inherently centralized nature of asset-backed stablecoins. If one company owns a large amount of a desired asset, the company can control the stablecoin's price fluctuations and policies. This ownership model becomes a risk if users cannot exchange the coin for fiat or have low confidence that the central entity actually holds the amount it claims to hold. It also may operate on a fractional-reserve system, in which the platform backs only a fraction of its holdings by actual fiat currency on hand and available for withdrawal.[386] Fiat-collateralized stablecoins are also prone to destabilization by external factors like geopolitics and new regulations.

Tether (USDT), the first fractional reserved stablecoin, has long been subject to accusations. One study found that a single entity used Tether to increase the price of BTC.[387] Parties to a class action complaint accused Tether Limited and Bitfinex of holding insufficient USD reserves, and both came under investigation regarding the reserve funds.[388]

Tether had a $2 billion-plus market capitalization, which meant that Tether Limited, in theory, should have had an equal amount of fiat in one or more of its accounts. Legal documents showed that the stablecoin was only backed 74 percent by the US dollar.[389] Hence, there was not enough currency in the reserve fund to ensure all token holders can convert their USDT to USD. Tether Limited adjusted Tether's terms so that it was not guaranteeing tokenholders a 1:1 conversion rate.[390]

The seigniorage supply stablecoins, also called algorithmic stablecoins, are the only noted type of non-collateralized cryptocurrency. *Seigniorage* is generally considered the difference between the price of the coin and the cost of creating it; if the creation cost is lower than the price, then the system makes a profit. Modeled after central banks' approach to managing money supply and discouraging price fluctuations, seigniorage supply stablecoins rely on algorithms to auto-adjust the number of stablecoins in circulation.

The algorithms apply what Robert Sams called an "elastic supply rule that adjusts the quantity of coin supply proportionately to changes in coin market value." In such a system, there are two types of coin: a cryptocurrency that acts like money and a stablecoin that acts like shares in the system's seigniorage—a seigniorage share.[391] Vitalik Buterin thanked Sams for his insights into the role of these seigniorage shares in valuing coins with volatile prices in multicurrency systems.[392]

In seigniorage supply stablecoins, the algorithms are written into and implemented through smart contracts. Let's say a stablecoin is one dollar per unit. The price drops to 80 cents, indicating that supply is outstripping demand. The algorithm uses seigniorage to buy the stablecoin, thereby decreasing supply and pushing the price back to one dollar. If the price remains below one dollar, there are no profits to purchase excess supply, and so the algorithm issues seigniorage shares. These serve essentially as bonds used to raise funds for network users.

Bonds promise seigniorage profits to buyers. Users are essentially investing in the growth of an algorithmic stablecoin supply. When the stablecoin trades above a dollar, the algorithm issues additional tokens to increase supply until price returns to a dollar.

TABLE 5-8

SEIGNIORAGE SUPPLY STABLECOINS AT A GLANCE

ADVANTAGES	DISADVANTAGES
• Absence of collateral; no tangible asset required • Created or destroyed by an algorithm, reducing or eliminating the potential of human error • Autonomous, not easily influenced by outside markets • Decentralized to the extent that the protocols are transparent, on-chain, and governed by users • Theoretically protected against volatility, with automatic value adjustments to supply and demand • Supported by fintech experts	• Rule-based system integrated with complex logic, making it difficult for some to understand • Somewhat untested methodology based on a novel concept; one or more failures could hamper further attempts • Regulated in that real-world bonds are considered securities, and algorithmic stablecoin bonds will likely classify as such

This method of stabilizing coin value is not without its critics. In a research paper on stablecoins, the Swiss Finance Institute's Didier Sornette and Richard Senner discussed the use of *quantitative easing* (QE), a monetary policy in which a central bank creates new money for itself to buy assets from a particular sector, thereby stimulating consumer prices.[393] Let's say the asset is a government bond. If demand for bonds increase, their price should increase, and interest rates should fall, thus stimulating purchasing.[394]

However, as Sornette and Senner concluded, "QE was not overly effective because it did not channel new liquidity to ordinary people, who would have a high propensity to consume."[395] In other words, if the scheme didn't stimulate buying in the real world, then why should it do so in a digital one? Preston Byrne alluded to Ponzi schemes in his description of a failed algorithmic stablecoin: "An investment scheme backed by introducing new investors ... and not backed by income-generating assets can be called a number of things. I leave it to you, dear reader, to decide what name you will choose to give to this one."[396]

Patrick Devereaux, CEO of Aperum and a contributor to this research, agreed with these assessments: "If there isn't a financial incentive to the risk, people are not likely to buy the bonds. The only way for there to be a manageable level of income to cover risk costs, is if the stabletoken seeks profits. If it is seeking profits, it is not a stablecoin."[397]

"A reserve is not an end-all solution, but it's a safety net that enables flexibility in managing any given currency," investor Nat Wittayatanaseth wrote. "If executed well, this type of stablecoin will unlock rich possibilities for crypto holders since it will be decentralized, efficient, and free of counterparty risk. The approach is promising, albeit in need of testing."[398] It could potentially collapse during a black swan event, such as war or pandemic, but this is no different from other assets.

TABLE 5-9
SEIGNIORAGE SUPPLY STABLECOINS

STABLECOIN	SYMBOL	ISSUER	RELEASED	FEATURES
Ampleforth	AMPL	Ampleforth Foundation	2019	Formerly µFragments; pegged to USD; security audit by Certik; monetary policy where supply adjusts to demand
BitBay	BAY	BitBay Official	2015	Uses dynamic pegging to manage liquidity; decentralized governance mechanisms
NuBits	USNBT	NuBits	2014	Stabilized by issuance mechanisms and custodial grants; no vendor fees; no customer chargebacks
Steem Dollars	SBD	Steemit Inc.	2016	Stabilized on Steem blockchain with 1:1 USD; based on a convertible notes system

Sources: Ampleforth, TechCrunch.[399]

HYBRID STABLECOIN MODELS

Hybrid stablecoins combine two or more of the aforementioned crypto models (fiat, crypto, or commodity-collateralized and algorithmic) in one token. While the resulting combination of advantages may meet the needs of a greater diversity of users, these are more difficult to understand because of the basket of assets backing them or the mechanisms governing them. Also, financial regulations may limit hybrid stablecoin projects.

Sam Trautwein, founder and CEO of Carbon-12 Labs, observed, "While algorithmically backed stablecoins are superior in terms of the lack of centralized fail points, on the consumer side, they are initially inferior to fiat-backed stablecoins."[400] The downside of fiat-backed tokens is their inherent unscalability. He recognized that users wanted both price stability and redeemability—in other words, liquidity—in stablecoins, whereas investors in stablecoin projects tended to prefer rising prices. That tension was difficult to resolve. In Trautwein's view, "The fiat-backed algorithmic hybrid approach is by far the most elegant solution to this tension, maintaining a perfect reserve ratio and not misleading investors." That is what he has strived to achieve in CarbonUSD.

Sam Kazemian, co-founder and president of Everipedia, said, "Stablecoins, as an asset class, are the next big thing in crypto and will lead to a new bull market in the next six to 18 months."[401] Kazemian concluded that a hybrid stablecoin was the most promising and joined Mahbod Moghadam and Stephen Moore in announcing the launch of the stablecoin Frax.[402]

In an interview with *Fortune*, Moore said his libertarian views led him to support cryptocurrency, which he believes is an important alternative to state-backed money. "I've followed monetary policy for 30 years and always been troubled by the government monopoly on currency, which is unhealthy for markets," said Moore. "It's very healthy for private competitors to challenge central banks over the money supply."[403] In the next section, we'll take a closer look at Frax.[404]

TABLE 5-10

HYBRID STABLECOIN MODELS

STABLECOIN	SYMBOL	ISSUED BY	RELEASED	FEATURES
Aurora DAO IDEX Token	AURA IDEX	Aurora Labs SA	2018	ERC-20 token rebranded IDEX; backed by a basket of ETH reserves, debt from loans, and dapp endorsement
Celo	CUSD	Celo.org	2020	Pegged to fiat; backed by a diversified, over-collateralized, and auditable cryptoasset reserve
Frax	FRAX	Frax Cryptocurrency	N/A	Fractional-algorithmic stablecoin system; the protocol adjusts the collateral ratio of Frax based on the market price
Jibrel	JUSD	Jibrel Network	N/A	Also JGBP, JEUR, and JKRW; ERC-20 tokens pegged to fiat currency; and backed by Jibrel Network Token (JNT)
LBXPeg	LBX	London Block Exchange	2018	Backed by GBP; stored in auditable UK bank account; ERC-621 token
Saga	SGA	Saga Foundation	2019	Pegged to the International Monetary Fund's *special drawing rights* (SDR), which is in turn tied to an underlying basket of currencies
Tiberius Coin	TCX	Tiberius Group AG	2018	Backed by a combination of seven precious metals; tradable on the Estonia based LATOKEN exchange

TOP STABLECOINS

Here is a brief look at the stablecoins with the highest market capitalization as of this writing.

TABLE 5-11

TOP STABLECOINS BY MARKET CAP

	SYMBOL	TYPE	MARKET CAP	ALL-TIME HIGH PRICE	ALL-TIME LOW PRICE
Tether	USDT	Centralized	$78,328,993,477	$1.21	$0.5683
USD Coin	USDC	Centralized	$45,519,400,088	$2.35	$0.9292
Binance USD	BUSD	Centralized	$14,303,480,913	$1.11	$0.8861
TerraUSD	UST	Decentralized	$10,762,094,902	$1.05	$0.7929
Dai	DAI	Decentralized	$9,677,990,134	$3.67	$0.9455
Frax	FRAX	Decentralized	$2,221,814,048	$2.19	$0.7805
TrueUSD	TUSD	Unclear	$1,437,214,279	$1.36	$0.9179
Paxos Dollar	USDP	Unclear	$945,252,148	$2.02	$0.8728
Neutrino USD	USDN	Decentralized	$528,325,372	$1.20	$0.7343
Fei USD	FEI	Decentralized	$422,537,243	$2.46	$0.6914
Reserve Rights	RSR	Centralized	$327,735,179	$0.1189	$0.001247
Gemini Dollar	GUSD	Centralized	$208,833,988	$1.27	$0.8521

Source of data: Stablecoin View, CoinMarketCap.com, CoinMarketCap OpCo LLC, as of 17 Jan. 2022. coinmarketcap.com/view/stablecoin.

TETHER (USDT)

In 2014, then-Bitcoin Foundation Director Brock Pierce, software engineer Craig Sellars, and entrepreneur Reeve Collins launched Realcoin, which they claimed to represent "the first dollar-backed cryptocurrency." Collins told *Cointelegraph*, "We are digitizing the dollar and giving that digital dollar access to the Bitcoin blockchain."[405] He also said that they planned to keep a "real-time record" of the firm's "dollar-based reserves, all held in conservative investments," and would "subject that record to the blockchain's authenticating system."

A few months later, they rebranded their token to Tether to dissociate it from altcoins. "We're not our own blockchain. We're a service, a token that represents dollars," Collins explained to *CoinDesk*. "*Tether* means a digital tie to a real-world asset, and the digital assets we're focused on are currencies."[406]

They wanted to create a fast and efficient way to transfer value from one crypto exchange to another without using a more volatile digital asset. Tether's convenience as well as its link to the US dollar appealed to stock magnates and everyday traders. The first stablecoin to be listed on exchanges, USDT started trading in February 2015.

Tether falls under the stablecoin category because it was originally designed to keep $1 in reserves for each Tether issued. Initially it issued only a couple of tens of millions. It stated that it would not increase the money supply of stablecoin. In early 2017, USDT authors began to "print money" as traditional banks in the United States and other countries do. In November 2017, it was allegedly hacked, and $31 million worth of Tether coins were stolen, prompting a hard fork.[407] Tether became a stablecoin market monopolist and started releasing USDT coins without retaining an equivalent US dollar backing.

In January 2018, it hit another hurdle as a necessary audit never took place. Instead, it announced that it was parting ways with the audit firm, after which it was issued a subpoena by regulators.[408] Yet, over the summer, Tether facilitated about 80 percent of all BTC trading, ensuring liquidity on the crypto market.[409] According to *The Wall Street Journal*, David Gerard said that Tether was "sort of the central bank of crypto trading ... [yet] they don't conduct themselves like you'd expect a responsible, sensible financial institution to do."[410]

In November 2018, *Bloomberg* reported that US federal prosecutors were investigating whether anyone had used USDT to manipulate the price of BTC. After several fraud allegations, Tether's price fell from $1 per token to 85 cents.[411] Tether had initially claimed that it backed each token with one US dollar. But on 14 March 2019, it changed the backing to include loans to affiliate companies. On 30 April 2019, Tether International Limited's lawyer claimed that each Tether was backed by 74 cents in cash and cash equivalents.[412] But owners of Tether tokens had no contractual obligation to guarantee that users could redeem or exchange Tether coins for fiat.[413]

In 2019, USDT surpassed BTC in trading volume with the highest daily and monthly trading volume of any cryptocurrency on the market. It has since become one of the most traded assets on the market. In April 2019, New York Attorney General Letitia James accused iFinex Inc., the parent company of Tether Ltd. and operator of cryptocurrency exchange Bitfinex, of hiding a loss of $850 million of commingled client and corporate funds from investors. Court filings claimed that the company had given these funds to a Panamanian entity called Crypto Capital Corp. without a contract or agreement to handle withdrawal requests.[414]

Bitfinex allegedly took at least $700 million from Tether's cash reserves to hide the gap after the money went missing. In a statement, Bitfinex said the NYAG's filings "were written in bad faith and are riddled with false assertions."[415] It explained that "these crypto capital amounts [were] not lost but have been, in fact, seized and safeguarded. We are and have been actively working to exercise our rights and remedies and get those funds released."

As of this writing, Tether's terms state, "Tether Tokens are 100 percent backed by Tether's Reserves [and] denominated in a range of Fiat, but Tether Tokens are not Fiat themselves. ... The composition of the Reserves used to back Tether Tokens is within the sole control and at the sole and absolute discretion of Tether."[416] Tether's site describes the token as "money built for the Internet. ... Whatever you can do with digital currencies, you can now do with digital cash."[417]

USD COIN (USDC)

In 2013, Internet entrepreneur Jeremy Allaire founded Circle Internet Financial to focus on digital currency innovation.[418] A Bitcoin blockchain advocate, he distinguished himself by underscoring the importance of compliance with national and local financial rules and regulations.[419]

By 2015, Circle had raised over $50 million from such respected investors as Accel Partners, Breyer Capital, General Catalyst Partners, Goldman Sachs Group, China's IDG Capital Partners, and Oak Investment Partners.[420] With this funding, Circle planned "to expand beyond bitcoins to provide services in US dollars." The goal was to enable customers "to keep accounts in dollars, eliminating the risks associated with bitcoin price volatility, while still being able to send and receive currency both in dollars and bitcoins."[421]

In 2018, Circle launched its USD Coin (USDC), an ERC-20 compliant stablecoin pegged to the US dollar. Through Circle's platform, users could begin converting US dollars from their bank accounts into USDC tokens, and Circle's banking partners would hold the equivalent USD in reserve so that USDC could easily redeem them for US dollars. Tokenizing dollars was free, but users paid a 0.1% fee to redeem USDC for dollars.[422]

It also formed the Centre Consortium as a multi-stakeholder operations, governance, and standards-setting body. Among the consortium's ongoing goals is to establish best practices for commercial issuers of fiat-based digital currencies, including "requirements for licensing, compliance, and proof of reserves."[423] Others are providing research and development to Centre's open-source software project, business development for the Centre Network, optional certification testing for node owners, and engineering expertise to the infrastructure on which it operates.[424]

USDC reserves are subject to regular audits and public reporting. Its site states that licensed and regulated financial institutions issue USDC and hold full reserves for any new coin issued. Each month, the accounting firm Grant Thornton LLP audits the dollar reserves, attests to the amounts, and writes a report that Circle publishes so that users can see whether they can redeem their coins for dollars.[425]

USDC has continued growing despite the occasional token burn, as the asset works like a fiat off-ramp in crypto trading. According to the Centre Consortium, "USDC has established itself as the second most popular stablecoin in the world; it has unparalleled support from more than 100 companies across the global crypto ecosystem, and it's the first stablecoin to reach $1 billion in issuance in less than a year."[426]

Critics have pointed out that USDC is a centrally controlled token with anti-money-laundering/counter-terrorist financing verification: users must provide personal information to use this stablecoin. Users do not have full pseudonymity or control of their funds as they do on the Bitcoin blockchain; and Circle can block or freeze accounts on Circle's balance sheet.[427]

Circle and Coinbase have continued to engage with financial oversight bodies. In 2020, they recommended that "relevant authorities across jurisdictions mutually agree on the principles, criteria and, where possible, measurable thresholds at which point a stablecoin is deemed to be a [global stablecoin or GSC] and, as a result, the GSC arrangement subject to additional regulatory requirements."[428] They advocated for a rapid shift to digital payment systems amid the COVID-19 crisis:

> By expanding access to digital dollars and other reserve currency-backed stablecoins, through a system that has the reach and accessibility of the Internet, companies can partner with regulators and supervisors to create a fundamentally more open, inclusive, efficient and integrated world economy.[429]

In December 2020, Circle announced that it had joined "Visa's Fintech Fast Track program" with "plans to issue a Visa corporate card enabling businesses to spend USDC anywhere Visa is accepted" and supporting "USDC payouts to Visa's growing network of digital currency wallets."[430]

BINANCE USD (BUSD)

Binance is a blockchain ecosystem composed of several arms to serve the greater mission of blockchain advancement and the freedom of money. The Binance ecosystem includes Binance Labs, the venture capital arm and incubator; Binance DEX, its decentralized exchange feature developed on top of its native, community-driven blockchain software system, Binance Chain; Binance Launchpad, the token sale platform; Binance Academy, its educational portal; Binance Research, the market analysis; Binance Charity Foundation, the blockchain-powered donation platform and nonprofit for aiding in sustainability; and Trust Wallet, its official multi-coin wallet and dapps browser.

The BUSD stablecoin was Binance's first step toward its cryptocurrency exchange ambition. Its leaders wanted to create a portfolio of stablecoins pegged to different fiat currencies on the Binance blockchain.

The Binance Jersey Exchange, a fiat-to-cryptocurrency exchange that accepts euros (EUR) and British pounds (GBP), first announced that it was testing a GBP-backed stablecoin in June 2019. Binance CEO Changpeng Zhao confirmed that the company had issued only £200 worth of the stable asset.

In July 2019, the Binance Jersey Exchange announced the listing of its GBP-backed token, the Binance GBP stablecoin (BGBP). An ERC-20 token based on the Ethereum platform, BGBP is pegged 1:1 to GBP and backed by fiat in reserve in Binance's bank.[431] At the time of the BGPB launch, only two other venues provided GBP-pegged stablecoins: the TrueGBP project and the eToro GBP stablecoin project.[432]

Binance reported that it wanted to continue offering more options in the cryptocurrency space and provide its European users with better trading experiences. Wei Zhou, chief financial officer of Binance, said:

> There has been an overwhelming demand in the market and Binance community for more stablecoin diversification, including a GBP-pegged stablecoin, and listing BGBP is in response to it. Use cases and the utility of stablecoins have increased as well as BNB, which has tripled since the beginning of the year and continues to grow rapidly with the advancement of Binance Chain.[433]

This development was significant because, at the time, Binance was one of the leading global cryptocurrency exchanges by trading volume with users from over 180 countries. Capable of processing more than 1.4 million orders per second, Binance remains among the fastest cryptocurrency trading platforms in the world.

In September 2019, Binance received clearance from the New York State Department of Financial Services (NYDFS) to issue its stablecoin (BUSD) in partnership with the Paxos Trust Company.[434] In October 2020, Binance decided to close Binance Jersey to deposits, shut down the specialized exchange in November 2020, and take over the secure and reliable trading of EUR and GBP with BTC and ETH in addition to digital asset management services for users around the world.[435]

DAI (DAI)

Founded in 2014 by Rune Christensen and launched in 2015, MakerDAO is both an open-source project and a DAO dedicated to DeFi on the Ethereum blockchain. Its protocol is among the largest dapps running on Ethereum and gaining traction in the DeFi space. MakerDAO issued its governance token, MKR, in 2017.[436] Among early buyers of MKR in a $12 million sale were Andreessen Horowitz and Polychain Capital.[437]

Members who hold quantities of MKR make decisions about the Maker protocol, including key parameters (e.g., fees, collateral types, rates, etc.) and responses to problems that crop up such as malicious attacks, black swan events, user migration to a better stablecoin, or dissolution of the Maker Foundation. The governance system is scientific: it involves voting and polling of MKR holders. The more MKRs a person holds, the greater the weight of the person's vote in decision-making.[438] It is also distributed, to the extent that MKRs are distributed among independent and diverse parties, where none has majority control over decisions.

One of the project goals was to design a stablecoin—the Dai (DAI), pinyin for the Chinese character meaning "loan" and issued at the end of 2019—that people could use to take full advantage of cryptocurrency payment and investment infrastructure without worrying about asset price volatility.[439] To access liquidity, users can either buy Dai through exchanges or generate them by depositing collateral assets into "Maker Vaults" within the Maker Protocol; and they burn Dai tokens by withdrawing their deposit.[440] In that sense, DAI is more decentralized because only users have power to create and destroy DAI. For the generation of DAI tokens (ERC-20), users must purchase and stake an equal value (in USD) of ETH tokens. When the cost of DAI rises, users will have incentive to create more. If the price falls, users will want to sell their DAI back to the pool.

Regarding the "collateral assets," the Maker Foundation selected the first types of collateral—all cryptocurrencies—to test in its Multi-Collateral Dai (MCD) system. The selection criteria included the "average daily volume of several million US dollars, and the relative stability of each token."[441]

The protocol has set the DAI's target price at $1 (i.e., a 1:1 soft peg to USD) to calculate the value of collateral assets that DAI holders would receive, in case of an attack on the Maker Protocol infrastructure or to facilitate a system upgrade.

There are two foundations to the MakerDAO protocol. The first is the Maker Foundation, which works with the "MakerDAO community to bootstrap decentralized governance of the project and drive it toward complete decentralization."[442] To protect the IP that MakerDAO founders couldn't technologically decentralize in the Maker Protocol, they set up a second governance body, the Dai Foundation. Independent of the Maker Foundation, "it operates solely on the basis of objective and rigid statutes that define its mandate," as set forth in the Dai Foundation Trust Deed.[443] Those include keeping the protocol "free of charge, as open source and without restrictions, on equal terms and for anyone," with a "a high degree of access and distribution to the unbanked and financially underserved."[444]

With DAI, the team at Maker hopes to overcome the sometimes-violent price swings associated with cryptocurrency. In its white paper, the team cites examples like BTC falling 25 percent in one day or rising more than 300 percent in one month.

External market factors such as collateralized debt positions, autonomous response mechanisms, and external economic incentives also help to stabilize the DAI's price. Issued on the MakerDAO platform, the DAI is transparent: the smart contracts that run operations are publicly available to read. DAI is a good fit for betting, financial markets, international trading, and transparent auditing. Going forward, Maker plans to give users a chance to choose the ecosystem's expanding set of collateral types.[445]

FRAX (FRAX)

Frax co-founder Sam Kazemian is known for launching the blockchain Wikipedia competitor, Everipedia, and Mahbod Moghadam, for co-founding Wikipedia and Genius.com, the world's largest collection of song lyrics and music knowledge.[446] Together they launched Frax with Stephen Moore. Kazemian and Moore said that Frax didn't have any outside investors. They launched the algorithmic stablecoin in February 2021. The overview on Frax's website described it as "a new paradigm in stablecoin design … the first and only stablecoin with parts of its supply backed by collateral and parts of the supply algorithmic."[447]

Many existing stablecoins are pegged to a 1:1 pool of reserve dollars, whereas Frax relies on a fractional reserve. Algorithms loan out its reserves and collect interest so that the value of Frax can maintain its peg to fiat. Kazemian claimed this system would eliminate the need for central banking entities, as users would record all transactions safely on a blockchain. Critics argued that a guarantee of 1:1 backing could be a challenge: tokenholders might decide to sell all at once, leading to collapse. Kazemian contended that Frax's loan mechanism would ensure its stability.[448]

Moore has made it known he feels cryptos can be valuable when governments follow misguided monetary policies. Moore, well-versed in economic history, warns governments have and may continue to deflate their currencies to pay back their debts. In his opinion, if users receive an alternative means of barter, governments could be less likely to pursue deflationary policies.

For now, senior US officials, many of whom have expressed deep skepticism about cryptocurrencies, do not appear to share his view. Central banks in other countries, however, have been more open to the potential of cryptocurrency. The Bank of Canada and the Bank of Japan, for instance, have been experimenting with crypto versions of their national currencies while Switzerland has created a special legal regime to foster the development of the crypto ecosystem.

Moore told *Fortune* that he hoped the Federal Reserve would eventually follow suit: "If I had been on the Fed, I would like to have seen encouragement for the development of cryptocurrencies like Frax. It can be a check and balance against runaway currencies."[449] Protocol Frax will be a fractional-reserve, algorithmic stablecoin.

According to the Frax team, "The basic premise is that we layer this over a collateralized stablecoin such as Dai and use interest from Compound.Finance loans to stabilize the price to one dollar to 1 Frax algorithmically changing the supply of Frax."[450] There is a two-token system in place: the stablecoin (FRX) and the investment token (FXS). The system starts 1:1 backed (reserve ratio of 100). For every 100 Dai put in, there are 100 FRX minted. The Dai is then lent out (either through the compound finance smart contract itself or the exact implementation within the Frax contract). The cash flow from the interest rate earned through the loan is accrued into the smart contract. Once there is a sufficient amount of interest earned, the reserve ratio goes down by X. If X = 1, then for every 99 Dai put in, 100 Frax are minted. The difference in the reserve ratio (aka X) must be paid in FXS as a fee (which is burned from circulation) so that value isn't leaving the system but instead is being captured by the investment token.

The governance token, FXS, is essentially valued as the net future fiat value creation of the network in perpetuity. If the market price of FRX holds at $1, 1 FRX then the reserve ratio becomes more fractional by increasing X as more interest cash flow comes in. If the FRX price drops because the market only values FRX based on backing collateral, the accrued cash flow is used to buy back FRX and "walk back" the reserve ratio to the market's value of 1 FRX.

At all times, there is a small amount of Dai that is always kept in the contract to exchange out for FRX for easy redemption. Essentially, this is a system to algorithmically measure the market's value of the "monetary premium" of a currency. This can be used to scale Dai and allow DeFi loans to provide monetary policy and stability.

TRUEUSD (TUSD)

TrueUSD (TUSD) was the first stablecoin fully backed by the US dollar held in escrow accounts by third parties. Created by TrustToken Inc. and launched in 2018, TrueUSD is an ERC-20 token project unrelated to TrustUSD (TRUSD), which launched in 2019 by the United Trust Company.

Transparency was paramount from the start of this project. The founders wanted investors and users to be able to trust that TUSD was fully backed 1:1 by USD. That required third-part attestation. Every month from March 2018 to March 2020, the independent US certified public accounting firm Cohen & Company audited and attested to the funds held in escrow as collateral to all the TrueCurrencies (TUSD, TGBP, TCAD, TAUD, and THKD) in circulation.[451] Cohen conducted its first audit on 1 March 2018 and determined that $4,777,750 were deposited in Prime Trust LLC in anticipation of the TrueUSD token launch four days later.[452] A week later, Cohen confirmed that the number of TrueUSD tokens issued did not exceed the $6.6 million balance held in escrow. Two years later, there were over 137 million TUSD tokens issued and in circulation and over $138 million held in escrow, meaning that $1.01 was backing each TUSD. In other words, TUSD was 101 percent secured by US dollars in legally protected escrow accounts.

In April 2020, TrustToken started pointing to TrustExplorer, a blockchain-based assurance dashboard launched by accounting firm Armanino LLP in December 2019.[453] Armanino recognized the need for third-party assurance of private and hybrid blockchains that weren't transparent or decentralized enough for prospective users in the space. To the Armanino team, "stablecoins minted on public blockchains [presented] a unique use case for assurance."[454]

The first version of TrustExplorer was a simple dashboard that confirmed the issuance of stablecoins. The second version provides near-real-time attestations according to American Institute of Certified Public Accountants Auditing Standards.[455] To implement this new service, Armanino decided to host and control a full Ethereum node. There are two parts to the balance sheet, so to speak.

On the left side are current wallet balances and the total circulating supply of tokens. To get those numbers, "a microservice within the application ... extracts new and existing blockchain data, translates it to a readable format, and writes that data to a database. The application layer of the dashboard can then query the database to populate the left side of the dashboard with the total circulating supply of ERC-20 tokens."[456] Since the Ethereum protocols add 12 blocks to Ethereum every 10 or 20 seconds, the service "parses and indexes blockchain data every 15 seconds."[457]

On the right side is the total balance of dollars held as collateral. To get this number, a representational state transfer API (REST API 13) pulls account balance data every 30 seconds from the trust company's database of accounts and writes the data to the TrustExplorer database.[458]

In November 2020, TrustToken collaborated with Armanino and Chainlink, a decentralized oracle network, to introduce "proof of reserve" and "proof of supply" contracts running on Ethereum. A deviation in the balance of TUSD supply and USD reserve triggers an on-chain transaction update and proof of reserve that dapps can query before processing transactions. If TUSD supply exceeds USD reserve, then a dapp can reject the transaction. If the reserve exceeds the supply, then a dapp can approve the transaction. According to TrustToken, "With the support of Armanino and Chainlink, TUSD becomes the world's first stablecoin with live, on-chain attestations."[459]

PAXOS DOLLAR (USDP)

In 10 September 2018, the Paxos Trust Company LLC announced the launch of its ERC-20 stable token, the Paxos Dollar (USDP), which sought to combine the efficiency of blockchain technology with the stability of USD.[460] Its press release stated that USDP would be "the world's first regulated crypto asset. The Paxos Dollar token is fully collateralized 1:1 by the US dollar, ... and approved and regulated by the [NYDFS]," which oversees the asset's issuance and trading.[461] Nomic Labs conducted two security audits of the Paxos system and found no vulnerabilities but recommended changes to improve its interoperability and sustainability, which Paxos addressed.[462]

The Paxos Trust Company positioned itself as "a fiduciary and qualified custodian of customer funds [that could] therefore offer greater protections for customer assets than any other existing stablecoin."[463] Paxos co-founder and CEO Charles Cascarilla said, "In the current marketplace, the biggest hindrances to digital asset adoption are trust and volatility. As a regulated trust with a 1:1 dollar-collateralized stablecoin, we believe we are offering an asset that improves on the utility of money."[464] Cascarilla is also CEO of Kabompo Holdings Inc., Paxos' holding company registered in the Cayman Islands.[465]

Since Paxos is an ERC-20 token, users of Ethereum wallets can send and receive it, conduct all their transactions according to the rules of the Ethereum network, and share all its features including smart contracts. US government treasuries or Federal Deposit Insurance Corporation (FDIC)–insured US banks collateralize the dollar deposits held by the Paxos Trust and accounted for as property of the tokens' holders. Moreover, the number of USDP in circulation corresponds to the number of dollars held in reserve. Upon redemption for dollars, USDP tokens are immediately destroyed.

USDP retains simple integration with Paxos payments. Users trade USDP with other assets available on the site. In particular, USDP users can buy or sell BTC, ETH, Binance Coin (BNB), Ripple's XRP, as well as Stellar's XLM.

Compared to fiat currencies in cryptocurrency exchanges, USDP is faster and cheaper to use—a positive for those who want to buy and sell quickly and inexpensively as well as safely and reliably. Paxos has other favorable attributes including:

- No transaction fees
- 24/7 customer support for Ethereum-based transactions
- Monthly attestation of reserves by the accounting firm WithumSmith+Brown PC[466]

- Reliable in a number of use cases such as remittances and payments

- Suitable for cryptocurrency traders during volatile periods

- Useful as a cash component of a transaction outside of traditional banking hours, as an alternative to Tether (USDT).

Paxos Trust Company has issued two other ERC-20 tokens, both asset based. The first is Binance USD (BUSD), also pegged 1:1 to USD, with monthly attestations available.[467] The other is Paxos Gold (PAXG) pegged to gold. Specifically, its redemption value is "strictly pegged at 1:1 to the number of troy ounces of gold held in custody by third parties," and its supply did "not exceed the balance (in troy ounces) of gold on hand at third parties ... specifically segregated for Paxos Trust Company LLC" as of 30 October 2020.[468]

GEMINI (GUSD)

In 2014, Cameron and Tyler Winklevoss founded the Gemini Trust Company LLC "with a 'security-first' mentality and ethos of *asking for permission, not forgiveness*," from its customers and regulators.[469] Gemini began adding to its financial services thereafter, with a series of innovations, such as the Financial Information eXchange protocol and API support early on. The innovations kept coming.

In May 2016, then-New York State Governor Andrew Cuomo announced Gemini as the first licensed exchange of ether (ETH) based in the United States.[470] Under the New York Banking Law and under the Investment Advisers Act of 1940, Gemini was authorized to act as a custodian of digital assets, and it complies with anti-money laundering (AML) and KYC requirements. It began operating its exchange continuously, with full reserves, for buying and selling digital assets.

In December 2017, Gemini worked out the details of a licensing and information sharing agreement with the Chicago Board

Options Exchange (Cboe) for "a cash-settled bitcoin future to be traded on [Cboe Futures Exchange LLC]," and Cboe submitted the terms and conditions to the Commodity Futures Trading Commission for certification.[471] Cboe called this new financial product "Cboe Bitcoin futures" (XBT), that is, cash-settled futures contracts "based on the auction price of bitcoin in US dollars on the Gemini Exchange" and "designed to reflect economic exposure related to the price of bitcoin."[472] Gemini was the first exchange to launch BTC futures contracts.

In April 2018, Gemini began offering *block trading*, where users can program orders to buy or sell specific quantities of assets with a minimum acceptable quantity and a maximum acceptable price.[473] Block trading enables users to buy and sell large quantities of digital assets outside of Gemini's continuous order books, which creates additional liquidity mechanisms when trading in greater amounts. Also in April 2018, Nasdaq reported that Gemini would use Nasdaq's SMARTS technology to monitor trades and combat fraudulent activity and price manipulation on its exchange.[474]

In May 2018, the NYDFS announced that it had approved Gemini to offer Zcash (ZEC) on its platform. The NYDFS commented that its decision was a "continuation of New York's longstanding commitment to innovation and leadership in the marketplace."[475] Gemini's CEO Tyler Winklevoss said that Gemini was "proud to be the first licensed exchange in the world to offer Zcash trading and custody services."[476]

After laying all the groundwork, Gemini received NYDFS' approval in September 2018 to launch a stablecoin, the Gemini Dollar (GUSD), collateralized 1:1 by USD held in reserve by State Street Bank and Trust Company.[477] GUSD launched shortly after.[478] According to the Gemini dollar white paper, the stablecoin "combines the creditworthiness and price stability of the US dollar with the technological advantages of a cryptocurrency and the oversight of US regulators."[479] Gemini created it to address the existing "implementations of fiat-pegged stablecoins" that lacked "some combination of *supervision, transparency,* and *examination*."[480] Its white paper elaborates on its stablecoin solution:

> Building a viable stablecoin is as much of a trust problem as it is a computer science one. While Bitcoin created a system based on cryptographic proof instead of trust, a fiat-pegged stablecoin requires both due to its reliance on a centralized issuer. Desirable outcomes in a system that relies (at least in part) on trust requires oversight. In the context of a stablecoin, we submit that the issuer must be licensed and subject to regulatory supervision. From this, transparency and examination become requirements of the system, ensuring its integrity and engendering market confidence.[481]

Gemini did everything required to obtain the necessary licenses and maintain registrations to issue GUSD legally. From a technical standpoint, GUSD is an ERC-20 compliant token that Gemini customers can transfer across the Ethereum network. They can trade USD and GUSD at a 1:1 exchange rate, creating or destroying GUSD by depositing or withdrawing USD from their Gemini accounts, and the platform updates their Gemini account balances accordingly.[482]

To summarize, here are GUSD's advantages. First, GUSD is under supervision of the NYDFS and compliant with US laws and regulations. Second, the number of dollars in the account strictly corresponds to the number of tokens in circulation, and those dollars are held by State Street. Third, in October 2018, Gemini obtained insurance covering digital assets held on its exchange. Aon, a London-based public risk consulting company, brokered the insurance underwritten by a consortium of global underwriters.[483] Fourth, BPM LLP, an independently registered public accounting firm based in California, examines the deposit balance each month to verify the necessary 1:1 peg and attests to what Gemini calls *proof of solvency*.[484] Users can review the monthly audits online.[485]

USING STABLECOINS: A FEW IDEAS

As the Sufi scholar Muhammad Tahir-ul-Qadri once said, "If knowledge is not put into practice, it does not benefit one."[486] Users might consider experimenting with stablecoins as part of their crypto portfolios. Here is a review of stablecoin's uses.

1. TRADING FIAT TO CRYPTOCURRENCY QUICKLY

Nearly every exchange in existence allows crypto-to-crypto trading. Very few exchanges allow users to trade crypto directly for fiat currency. Now they can go from fiat to stablecoins quickly to the digital currency trading market. Many stablecoins are 1:1 equivalent to fiat; therefore, users can almost instantly sell crypto for stablecoins and convert to fiat without leaving their preferred exchange.

2. MAKING PAYMENTS

There's no question digital currency is the future. In 1999, Nobel Laureate Milton Friedman said, "I think the Internet is going to be one of the major forces for reducing the role of government. The one thing that's missing but that will soon be developed, is a reliable e-cash."[487] Daily use of stablecoins allows for riskless, secure, and interchangeable payments with fiat. Users will adopt stablecoins initially for convenience. This usage may serve to educate consumers on cryptocurrencies overall, as blockchain technology matures.

3. PROTECTING ASSET VALUE

Some users have found the following methods effective in managing their cryptoasset portfolios. Timing one market correctly is difficult, let alone two markets. No one wants to watch profits disappear. Less advanced crypto traders tend to use cryptocurrency exchanges but should be aware of fees for each transaction. Here is a typical process:

1. Obtain BTC or altcoin with centralized fiat-to-cryptocurrency exchange platform that allows deposits.

2. Transfer cryptocurrency to preferred digital currency exchange.

3. Trade, obtain, exchange, and so forth on the exchange.

4. Trade crypto back to BTC or altcoin on preferred trading exchange in a fluctuating market.

5. Transfer cryptocurrency to centralized cryptocurrency-to-fiat exchange that allows withdrawals.

6. Sell BTC or altcoin on exchange and withdraw to bank account.

7. Wait three to seven days for bank transfer.

4. STOPPING A LOSS IN A VOLATILE CRYPTOCURRENCY MARKET

In the stop-loss method, users exchange digital currency for stablecoins. Seasoned users know to refresh their browsers regularly for enough confirmations to approve a transaction. Then the asset becomes tradable. Historical charts show that the price of BTC can change in a short amount of time. A crypto buyout, another country ban, or major headline has prompted a 30 percent drop. Stablecoins, while not guaranteed to hold their value, provide a more likely way to retain value.

5. GAINING A PROFIT IN A DECLINING MARKET

Exchanging fluctuating cryptocurrency investments into stablecoins allows users to rebalance a portfolio during market dips to secure more investments. Users can then reinvest these profits gained during market highs.

One strategy is hedging with stablecoins, using them "to reduce the risk of adverse price movements in an asset."[488] Investors use different financial instruments when hedging that risk. A successful hedge minimizes portfolio losses. For example, let's say we hold a portfolio of $1,000: 50 percent BTC and 50 percent stablecoin. If the cryptocurrency market decreases by 20 percent in value, our portfolio is over-allocated in stablecoin (55.56%) and under-allocated in BTC (44.44%). To rebalance the portfolio, we can buy $50 worth of BTC with stablecoins. Our portfolio is once again 50/50.

Thanks to stablecoin security, we lose only 10 percent in overall portfolio value. Rebalancing the portfolio gives the investor more BTC during market dips. This is beneficial in a market increase and our harvesting scenario.

TABLE 5-12

HEDGING WITH STABLECOINS

HEDGING EVENT	BITCOIN	STABLECOIN	PORTFOLIO
Balanced portfolio	50%	50%	Total: $1,000
Crypto market decreases 20% in value	44.44%	55.56%	Total: $900
Rebalance portfolio	Buy $50	Sell $50	Use stablecoin to buy BTC at a lower price
Ending portfolio	50%	50%	Increase BTC investments Total: $900

Another strategy is harvesting BTC profits while hedging with stablecoins. According to *Investopedia*, the harvesting "method is commonly referred to as an exit strategy, as investors seek to exit the investment after its success. Investors will use a harvest strategy to collect the profit from their investment so that funds can be reinvested into new ventures."[489] Employing a harvest strategy could allow users to harvest maximum profits before the market starts to decline.

Since 2017, the US Internal Revenue Code Section 1031 does not apply to nested portfolio gains.[490] Crypto users are left with alternative means to balance profits, losses, and US tax implications. The IRS issued present guidance in IRS Publication 2014-21 and as clarification in 2019.[491]

Cryptocurrency is not inherently considered a security and therefore is not subject to wash-sale loss limitations.[492] Therefore, crypto users could harvest losses in a crypto market downturn and use those capital losses to offset current year capital gains. Furthermore, taxpayers can use up to $3,000 in annual losses to offset ordinary income or carry it forward to offset future capital gains. Hire a certified tax professional before executing any tax mitigation strategy.

TABLE 5-13

HARVESTING PROFITS WHILE HEDGING WITH STABLECOINS

HARVESTING EVENT	BITCOIN	STABLECOIN	PORTFOLIO
Balanced portfolio	50%	50%	Total: $1,000
Crypto market increases 20% in value	55.56%	44.44%	100%
Rebalance portfolio	Sell $50	Buy $50	Sell BTC at a higher price, yielding $50 in profit
Ending portfolio	50%	50%	Total: $1,100

Here's another example. If the cryptocurrency market increases by 20 percent, the portfolio will hold more value in BTC. Harvesting consists of taking the BTC profit and reinvesting. Rebalance the portfolio by taking 20 percent of the BTC profit to purchase stablecoins. Portfolio is once again 50/50, however, the return on investment (ROI) has risen.

CONCLUSION AND REVIEW

As stablecoins advance, many question where they are heading. In its survey of stablecoins, BitMEX Research concluded that "the transformative nature of such a technology on society would be immense, perhaps far more significant than Bitcoin or Ethereum tokens with their floating exchange rates."[493] *Cointelegraph* reported:

> Various models of stablecoins have surged in popularity last year ... research firm Diar published an analysis saying that the adoption of stablecoins is growing based on the increasing number of on-chain transactions. As per the study, the same four major stablecoins to date have broken the $5 billion mark in on-chain transactions within the three-month period.[494]

Stablecoins are already considered commodities and traded among crypto exchanges. Naturally, during cryptocurrency market fluctuations, stablecoins do a better job of holding their value. For example, during the largest cryptocurrency market crash of all time in 2018, many currencies lost 30 to 70 percent of their value whereas Tether's stablecoin held within eight percent. Still, critics raise three concerns about their design and governance.

1. *Many are centrally controlled.* Can binding to a traditional banking system foster a decentralized ecosystem and still retain users' anonymity? BitMEX Research concluded that distributed stablecoins more so than centrally controlled ones "could have the advantages of bitcoin ... without the difficulties of a volatile exchange rate and the challenge of encouraging users and merchants to adopt a new unknown token."[495]

2. *Many are not backed by true assets.* If fiat currency is backed by government promises rather than gold, then what type of backing is sufficient for nongovernmental stablecoins? According to one governor of the US Federal Reserve System, people use fiat currency because they "are confident that they can convert it on demand to the liability of another commercial bank or the central bank, such as physical cash. ... because bank deposits are insured, and commercial banks are subject to supervision, regulation, and deposit insurance requirements."[496]

3. *Many are not necessarily transparent.* Transactions on public blockchains are recorded on inviolable digital ledgers. If we back a stablecoin with a traditional asset, which often requires off-chain storage and related costs, then users may expect a third party to audit those reserves for full transparency of system.

A high-quality stablecoin could allow the use of fiat currency on crypto exchanges in today's rapidly changing financial landscape. With stablecoins, users could control their assets while taking advantage of many positive aspects of a crypto economy. People can use stablecoins with real-world value assets in everyday life, which opens the floodgates to mass adoption.

After a majority use digital cash, say, in the form of stablecoins, the cryptocurrency community can inform the public about the benefits of decentralization and need for trustless cash exchanges. With digital cash experience, there's less to learn in a new, highly complex, and ever-evolving fintech ecosystem. Crypto enthusiasts can't disagree; stablecoins could be the key to getting more people to use BTC and altcoins in the future.

In all likelihood, stablecoins will be a critical part of the future as bridges toward more decentralized digital currencies and in their own right as sensible investments. We may need a wave of stablecoins now to encourage adoption and later, perhaps in perpetuity, to hedge against risk. Let's remember, stablecoins are designed not to be speculative instruments for investment but to maintain a steady value for payments and exchange.

CHAPTER 6

FINANCIAL DERIVATIVES WITH BLOCKCHAIN AND SMART CONTRACTS

Massimo Morini

 ## BLOCKCHAIN-BASED DERIVATIVES IN BRIEF

- This research explores how blockchain technology is relevant to the world of financial derivatives, with derivatives written as assets on blockchain ledgers, and blockchain technology used to increase the efficiency of derivatives processing.

- It covers the initiatives that standard-setting bodies and banking institutions are taking to exploit smart contracts and blockchain networks in satisfying the regulatory requirements of standardization, transparency, and interoperability across firms and platforms.

- The author analyzes the current issues in managing derivatives and controlling risk via collateral and identifies solutions that exploit automation and efficiency of smart contracts and blockchain technology.

- The case also covers the initiatives in the public blockchain space that mimic the logic of financial derivatives, their strengths and weaknesses, and how regulators are dealing with some of these initiatives.

DERIVATIVE CONTRACTS ON BLOCKCHAINS

Derivatives are contracts to transfer risk from one person to another. To make it possible, they require the parties to agree on future payments whose amount depends on the value taken by some financial variables in the future. The financial variables that define the future payments are called the *underlyings* of the derivative. For credit derivatives, the underlying is the event of default of one or more borrowers. Credit derivatives (including more complex products such as synthetic collateralized debt obligations) were at the heart of the Great Financial Crisis that started in 2008. After that, all derivatives have been subject to new, pervasive regulations regarding both derivatives traded on regulated exchanges and, even more, derivatives traded bilaterally outside exchanges. The latter are called OTC derivatives.

What have derivatives to do with blockchain? There are at least two possible relevant connections.

1.   Cryptocurrencies based on public blockchains are a natural underlying for derivatives. Everyone can invest in cryptocurrencies, but cryptocurrency prices are volatile and the investment is risky. Investors can be happy to buy protection on this risk via derivatives, allowing simultaneously their counterparties to take additional risks with particular profiles. Bitcoin futures are offered by Chicago Mercantile Exchange and by the Chicago Board Options Exchange, with full US regulatory approval by the CFTC.

     LedgerX was the first US Swap Execution Facility and Derivatives Clearing Organization specialized in options whose underlying is the rate of exchange between the US dollar and bitcoin.[497] In June 2018, they claimed clearing a maximum of $50 million in option volumes per month. Other non-US companies enjoying less restrictive regulations and offering cryptocurrency derivatives are

BitMEX based in Seychelles, and Deribit based in the Netherlands.[498] All these companies offer derivatives on cryptocurrencies, but they make no use of blockchain technology. While they are an important step in making finance and crypto words more connected, the market is still small.

2. Blockchain technology that makes cryptocurrencies possible can be applied in regulated financial markets to change the rules for settlement, the nature of the contracts, and the role of intermediaries. Derivatives are a natural use case since they are purely monetary products, where the technology of digital currencies—sometimes called *distributed ledger technology* (DLT)—can be applied without linking blockchain events to material goods having an *independent life* outside the blockchain.

Derivatives are natively digital products where the only input required from outside the blockchain are prices of the underlyings. Then all transactions related to derivatives can happen on the blockchain as digital records of money transfers. McKinsey stated, "DLT may have the most potential among the technologies fintechs are deploying in capital markets solutions," and that "markets showing the most promise include OTC derivatives."[499]

The first connection pertains to derivatives that are negotiated and managed with traditional contracts and intermediaries, but where the underlying is a cryptocurrency. The second connection regards derivatives where the underlying is a traditional asset negotiated in a traditional market, such as a stock or a bond, but the derivative itself is managed using blockchain technology.

We focus on this second connection, since it has the possibility to transform the market of OTC derivatives, which was valued at $544 trillion at the end of 2018, according to the Bank of International Settlement.[500] But we will also cover the first connection in part, since the borders are blurred and companies are now offering derivatives on cryptocurrencies managed with blockchain technology.

In February 2018, Christopher Giancarlo, then-chair of the CFTC, spoke before the US Senate about blockchain and DLT. He said:

> These technologies are having an equally transformative impact on US capital and derivatives markets. ... DLT will likely develop hand-in-hand with new "smart" contracts that can value themselves in real-time, report themselves to data repositories, automatically calculate and perform margin payments and even terminate themselves in the event of counterparty default.[501]

He explicitly quoted one of my earlier papers written with Robert Sams, "'Smart' Derivatives Can Cure XVA Headaches."[502] Since then, I have been involved in several experiments to apply blockchain technology to improve one or more aspects in the life cycle of a derivative project. By my analysis, there are different levels of application of blockchain to the derivatives business that address different problems in this market.

LEVELS OF APPLICATIONS

STANDARDIZATION, TRANSPARENCY, AND INTEROPERABILITY

The first issue is lack of standardization and interoperability, which brings about a need for frequent reconciliations, and a transparency issue. Derivatives are complex products. It happens often that the consequences of a specific part of the agreement are not fully anticipated by the parties, and it is easy to have disagreements in interpreting contracts, and almost surely two implementations of the same product will differ greatly.

To avoid these conflicts, there has been an intense regulatory effort. For example, the requirement to trade through central counterparties imposes a strong incentive to use the standards defined by the central counterparty. Regulators also require parties to report all traded derivatives to official trade repositories for regulatory transparency, which is a cumbersome procedure with today's technology.[503]

One blockchain initiative in the direction of transparency and standardization is the introduction of the Common Domain Model (CDM) by the International Swaps and Derivatives Association (ISDA), an organization of the main players in derivatives markets.[504] ISDA had an important role in standardizing contracts from 1990 to 2002: it introduced the Master Agreement, the Credit Support Annex, and related derivatives collateralization practices. It also had an interest in standardizing the digital representations of derivatives contracts, which are fed to the IT systems that manage the life cycles of derivatives. Since 2000, ISDA has managed *financial products markup language* (FpML), a standardized digital representation for derivatives—a sort of XML scheme, a data model to represent a derivative transaction.[505]

The CDM is a new ISDA effort, and it is the next step in the same direction. It is explicitly described as "a blueprint for how derivatives are traded and managed across the trade life cycle."[506] The goal is to provide "a single, common digital representation of derivatives trade events and actions [to] enhance consistency and facilitate interoperability across firms and platforms, providing a bedrock upon which new technologies [e.g., cloud, distributed ledger, and smart contracts] can be applied."[507]

The CDM extends FpML toward the representation of not only derivative agreements but also events and actions related to the life cycle of a derivative, such as novations (substitutions of new contracts for old ones), amendments, terminations, reporting, valuation, and collateralization. It makes use of more modern data representations such as JSON files; and it aims to create a unique IT representation of derivatives processing so that each step in the process is represented in an efficient, standardized fashion—one single machine-readable representation of data, events, and actions on the life of a derivative. Two major features of the CDM are

1. *Consistency*, which means that same code on same data give exactly the same result on any node/machine, so that a computation can be perfectly replicated across network nodes. This is an obvious requirement if derivatives computations are distributed across the nodes of a blockchain that then have to reach consensus on the result of the computation themselves.

2. *Lineage*, which means that every piece of information can be traced to its ultimate inputs, through the chain of copies and transformations. Lineage is obtained through a chain of hashes similar to the ones used in blockchains, where every block contains a hash of the previous block. I am part of the working group, and I have seen the debate evolve from traditional solutions, such as giving version numbers to the different versions of a contract, toward blockchain solutions such as making sure that every version contains a hash to the previous version.

Even beyond blockchain application, an amazing feature of the CDM is to create interoperability among different applications by creating a market standard. Everyone working in banks knows that lack of interoperability is one of the big issues of legacy infrastructure, with almost 80 percent of IT resources spent on integration of scarcely interoperable solutions. The CDM can be a game changer in this respect.

In 2019, Barclays organized a hackathon to select the best application of the CDM to the management of derivatives transactions. Dr. Lee Braine—from the chief technology and innovation office of

Barclays and one of the judges at the London event—declared that the CDM was approaching maturity, thanks also to contributions from the open-source community. Now the most important objective is adoption by financial institutions, in particular by financial market infrastructures. When the adoption process is completed, interoperability and automation will greatly increase in financial markets, and savings will be in the billions. The current derivatives infrastructure is very complex, and that CDM would be a radical simplification of the workflow.[508]

These companies participated in the hackathon: IBM teams working with Fabric, R3 teams working with Corda, teams working with Ethereum and J.P.Morgan Quorum (now ConsenSys Quorum), and the Digital Asset Holdings team working with the *digital asset modeling language* (DAML), a smart contract language that won the main award with an implementation supporting provision of digital trade data, pre-trade negotiation automation, atomic exchanges, and regulatory reporting for mock derivatives to be cleared with a central counterparty.

Interestingly, when derivatives are implemented as a detailed smart contract, the regulatory reports can be automatic. When both parties use a single digital representation, there is no need for reconciliation.

Digital Asset Holdings had already developed the first live application of blockchain to the financial market, developing a new system for Australian Securities Exchange (ASX) to clear cash equities. The most interesting innovation was the creation of the Global Synchronization Log, a chain of public *hashes* of every transaction executed through ASX, increasing transparency, reducing the risk of errors, and helping reconciliation.

Judgments of these advances are mixed. Definitely, the blockchain is the right technology for such issues as standardization and transparency. However, the industry can do more with blockchain.

COLLATERAL, SETTLEMENT, AND AUTOMATION

The next level of issues regards the financial risks associated to derivatives, in particular counterparty risk. The market addresses this issue by requiring all parties to post to their counterparties an amount of liquid collateral that needs to be in line with the counterparty's exposure to default (i.e., the amount of money that would be lost in a failure to pay). Unfortunately, the provision of collateral is affected by several technical imperfections:

1. *Technical complications in collateral provision:* many parties do not have the technology to revalue exposures frequently, and they lack the capability to set up the accounts and the regular liquidity flows required by collateralization.

2. *Slow collateral settlement:* in the traditional payments system, collateral takes one to three days to move from one party to the other. This delay misaligns collateral with exposure.

3. *Lack of automation in collateral exchanges:* collateral should move in lockstep with derivatives cash flows, since cash flows change exposures and should be readily available if the counterparty fails to pay. In today's business model, cash flows and collateral are not moved atomically: when the counterparty fails, those involved must perform long default procedures.

To address these problems with blockchain technology, we require more than a common representation of derivatives as smart contracts, and the use of a distributed ledger as a golden source. We must manage the whole life cycle of derivatives on the blockchain, with payment automatically triggered by smart contracts in the form of digital currency transfer. Therefore, in my experiments, we implemented derivatives in Ethereum, using ether as a digital currency.

1. Since smart contracts manage the whole process and can calculate how much margin must be transferred, all parties can join this market since smart contracts handle the complexity. Smart contracts also manage the different forms of collateral and the different rights associated to them.

2. The settlement time in blockchain depends on the speed of the consensus algorithm. In Ethereum, the speed of settlement is measured in minutes; a party waits for a few confirmations to consider the transaction final. The typical settlement delays are eliminated in this way.

3. The smart contract automatically executes collateral updates atomically with derivative cash flows. It also monitors the payments of the parties, and if one party misses more than a fixed amount of payments, it terminates the contract and uses collateral to compensate for the lost payments.

This is a radical approach where blockchain operates all aspects of the business model. Today, however, regulations still constrain the possibility to use digital currencies, and to replace some legal procedures with automated smart contracts.

The Depository Trust & Clearing Corporation (DTCC) is taking an intermediate approach: it is transforming the Trade Information Warehouse, its previously centralized credit derivatives platforms, into a distributed ledger.[509] Worried by scalability and privacy limitations of public blockchain, DTCC built this distributed ledger as a private, permissioned blockchain, reaching the high level of scalability it requires, that is, up to thousands of transactions per second.

The project addresses regulatory reporting, sourced from a unique "golden source" of data: it includes the custodians that hold collateral and integrate external settlement operators. Since custodians and settlement are integrated as external parties, the project does not address the slow collateral settlement, but it certainly reduces the technical complications in collateral provisions and may introduce some automation. Release had been announced for mid-2019, but it has been delayed to the end of 2019.

When regulated digital currencies are introduced, and regulations are adapted accordingly, the Trade Information Warehouse ledger could be upgraded to introduce blockchain settlement and full automation.

DERIVATIVES ON PUBLIC BLOCKCHAINS

We are left with analyzing what is happening outside the world of financial institutions. There are a few start-ups offering cryptocurrency derivatives making use of public blockchain technology.

The first is VariabL.io, a ConsenSys start-up using the Ethereum blockchain.[510] The team has, overall, a few years of experience in finance. The main product it offers is a *contract for difference* (CFD) on the ether/dollar rate of exchange: one party pays/receives from the other the return/loss of an investment on the rate of exchange between dollars and ethers.[511] There is a return when the value of ethers in dollar goes up, and loss in the opposite case. Here the two parties put their funds in the blockchain, and it is a smart contract that moves the funds when payments have to be done. This way, VariabL.io is really making use of blockchain technology to avoid the need to trust an intermediary, or legal recourse, to have the confidence that the counterparty will pay its dues. It is the network, executing the smart contract on the funds held on the blockchain, that triggers payments.

However, this business model is heavily collateralized: everyone must lock in the blockchain an amount of money equal to the maximum loss they can bear, for the whole life of the contract. This is rather inefficient, since players do not like to lock so much margin for trading. In fact, to make this requirement less undesirable, the maturity of VariabL.io CFDs is limited to 24 hours.[512]

The second is dYdX, also an Ethereum-based start-up that provides a decentralized derivatives exchange: parties can post orders on the blockchain, and then a smart contract will automatically bid, match, and offer prices.[513] However interesting, it is so far offering simpler products, such as short selling and loans, rather than real derivatives. The volumes have been near $10 million over six months.[514]

Decentralized applications

Even if the dapps that explicitly propose derivatives are still far from mass usage, other applications show how derivatives, if supported by regulations and the investment of institutions, can become a killing app for blockchains with smart contracts. If we look at the reality of blockchains featuring smart contracts, what are the most popular dapps?

The blockchain analysis company Diar showed back in 2018 that $1 billion worth of Ethereum transactions were related to gambling, and that gambling dapps represent around 50 percent of all Ethereum dapps.[515] Pulling no punches, the technical features of gambling dapps are similar to those of derivatives dapps: both are applications that represent no material good outside the blockchain, but pure monetary flows triggered by external events. In both cases, the blockchain is used to make payments automatic, through a smart contract, once the relevant external events have been observed. Nowadays, gambling applications have migrated toward the EOS blockchain, and represent the lion share of EOS applications.

MakerDAO

The most popular new application in Ethereum, however, is MakerDAO, an application based on monetary flows triggered by external observations that allows players to speculate or to get protection against volatility, exactly like a derivative. MakerDAO now holds around two percent of all circulating ether. MakerDAO users can create a smart contract holding Ethereum collateral, called *collateralized debt position* (CDP), that allows issue of MakerDAO's token, Dai.

Dai is considered a stablecoin because it is supposed to have a value on par with the dollar: if the dollar value of the ether collateralizing one Dai falls dangerously near to one, then the collateral is sold to Dai holders.[516] Therefore, Dai holders know that they can always transform each Dai into an amount of ether worth at least one dollar, either by dismantling the original CDP or through liquidation of failing CDPs.

The Dai is structured as a derivative contract written on the ether/dollar rate of exchange, and gives users an amount of ether valued at least one dollar when the price of ether falls, while the user gains proportionally when ether price increases. As in a call option, the user has limited downside and unlimited upside. Here the smart contract that holds the funds (the ether collateral) guarantees the payout.

We spoke with the MakerDAO team, which confirmed that it sees its work as both an example of a derivative and a very useful tool to introduce further derivatives.[517] Derivatives investors may be interested in speculation or protection of the most diverse assets, and they want payment in a stable currency, where stability is often measured relative to large currencies such as the dollar. This is what Dai provides. The team confirmed that the massive decline in the dollar value of ether during the so-called crypto winter did not put the payoff of CDPs under stress: they kept their promise to guarantee an approximate dollar-Dai parity (Figure 6-1).

One more analogy emerged in the conversation with the MakerDAO team. The working of MakerDAO resembles in part a decentralized central bank in its mechanism for stabilizing Dai, and in part a decentralized central counterparty.[518]

For example, the design of MakerDAO includes a second token, MKR. In normal times, MKR represents administrative rights for the working of the application. If ether collateral loses value and

FIGURE 6-1

THE DAI VALUE AFTER CRYPTO WINTER

Dai value in US dollars between 18 March and 19 August 2019.

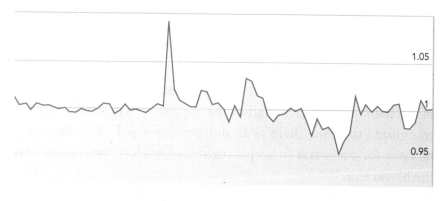

Source of data: CoinMarketCap.com/Currencies/Maker.

becomes insufficient to back the Dai, MKR will serve as a collateral of last resort. This design bears some analogy to the mechanics of default funds in derivative central counterparty clearings (CCP): funds made available by CCP members as a collateral of last resort, used jointly to cover any additional losses when the collateral provided by members against their own specific risk of default is completely depleted. One final note: overcollateralization remains a feature of blockchain applications that resemble derivatives. But MakerDAO has found a relatively efficient solution.

Nivaura

Last, let's consider what blockchain start-up Nivaura did to issue bonds in Ethereum to pave the way for managing any financial product on the blockchain, including derivatives. In derivatives, only investors properly profiled through KYC are authorized to trade. Working with UK Financial Conduct Authority (FCA) in a regulatory sandbox program, Nivaura showed first that it could easily perform KYC for assets in a blockchain. The smart contracts it used to issue the bonds had a list of the public keys properly identified and profiled as authorized investors: transactions were set to fail automatically if they involved any public key not listed among those who had passed KYC. Nivaura embedded this limitation into the code, thus guaranteeing that only authorized investors could trade—which was easier to do in a blockchain-based market than in a traditional one.

Equally important, the FCA acknowledged the blockchain as an official ledger in Nivaura's bond implementation: "The transfer of the securities from the issuer to the investors was recorded on the blockchain, which functioned as the register … . Because the FCA recognized the blockchain as an independent third party, there was no need for a registrar to keep a register of holders; the register was the blockchain."[519]

Such recognition could be crucial in simplifying the management of derivatives. We have already mentioned how cumbersome the reporting process for derivatives is. If a derivative is traded on a blockchain via a smart contract, all the details of the trade and the identities of the parties are notarized in the blockchain.

If the blockchain is officially recognized as an independent third party, then we can overcome the need for parties to provide notarization via a plethora of inefficient, corruptible, and difficult-to-reconcile reports. I confirmed this in conversation with Nivaura, which is now working with the London Stock Exchange on equity issuance but plans to address derivatives as the next step.[520]

LUXDECO AND THE WORLD'S FIRST CRYPTOBOND

Anthony D. Williams

Nivaura made history by issuing the world's first legally compliant cryptocurrency denominated bond. In 2017, LuxDeco, an online retailer of luxury furniture and home decor accessories, issued two blockchain-enabled bonds using Nivaura's platform: a control bond and an experimental bond. The control bond was a traditional sterling bond and structured in a conventional manner. The experimental bond was an ether-denominated bond that was structured, executed, and administered through the Nivaura platform and cleared and settled on the Ethereum public blockchain. While the transactions were true financings for the issuer, they were also experiments designed to see what the industry can achieve using blockchain.

THE CONTROL BOND

The typical issuance process involves several key market participants, and in many cases one party performs several roles:

- The issuer is the party issuing the debt security.
- For a local private placement, the registrar maintains a record of the legal owner of the instrument.
- For a public instrument, the central securities depository acts as the trusted intermediary for registration and settlement of trades in international debt securities.
- In cases of public issuances, the common depository holds the global certificate evidencing legal ownership of the instrument.
- The custodian (typically a bank or broker) is the account holder in the clearing system and maintains the register of beneficial ownership of the bonds and holds them for end investors.
- The paying agent distributes payments to the bond holders on behalf of the issuer.
- The trustee represents the interests of the bond holders.[521]

As Richard Cohen and his co-authors explained in their white paper on automation and blockchain in securities issuances, this constellation of actors executes securities issuances and administration in a complex web of transactions: "Payments must go from the issuer to the paying agent to the clearing systems and then possibly to one or more custodians before it eventually arrives at the person entitled to it. Some market participants also opt to have a trustee represent the bond holders and protect their interests."[522]

With the LuxDeco control bond, the parties documented and structured the GBP-denominated transaction in a conventional way, but Nivaura substituted its platform for the conventional clearing system and acted as paying agent. Nivaura also recorded all the transactions on a blockchain to demonstrate how a blockchain-based bond would work.[523] Cohen et al. detailed the control bond's issuance on the Nivaura platform. First, investors made a bank transfer to Nivaura's client account. Upon receipt, Nivaura credited the investors' cash accounts with the amount invested. On settlement, Nivaura issued the bonds into LuxDeco's securities account, then transferred them to the investors' securities accounts, simultaneously moving cash from the investors' cash accounts to LuxDeco's cash account. The Nivaura platform automatically recorded these transfers on a blockchain, which functioned as the register.[524]

The approach used to issue the control bond also provides a model for the tokenization of fiat currency. Investors paid sterling into Nivaura's client account for LuxDeco. The cash was locked in the client account and then tokenized on the blockchain; that is, on receiving cash in a real-world bank account, Nivaura credited LuxDeco's blockchain wallet with that cash in the form of a token. In a world with widespread blockchain-based commerce, LuxDeco would be able to spend that tokenized cash on its business and then make sales, which would generate more tokenized cash for payments of interest and, ultimately, principal.

When it comes time to repay the bond, LuxDeco would pay cash from its blockchain wallet to its investors' wallets. The real-world cash remains in the Nivaura client account, and at this point investors could keep their blockchain representation of it (in the form of tokens) or redeem that cash from Nivaura's client account into their real-world bank accounts.

AN EXPERIMENTAL BOND

LuxDeco also issued an experimental bond through Nivaura's platform but denominated it in ether, the native cryptocurrency of the public Ethereum blockchain. Not only was this the first time a bond has actually been denominated in cryptocurrency and fully settled on a blockchain, it was also the first instance of a financial services company issuing a cryptobond in full compliance with the UK regulatory framework. As Nivaura and its partners pointed out, this milestone is significant because the cryptobond made it possible to issue and pay for a legally enforceable financial instrument without using any of the traditional financial infrastructure.

The structure and issuance of the experimental bond was also considerably simpler than a conventional bond issuance.[525] As Cohen and his co-authors explained, "investors transferred ether from their existing blockchain wallets … to their Nivaura cryptocurrency wallets. On settlement, ether transferred from investors' cryptocurrency wallet addresses to LuxDeco's address, and the bonds transferred from LuxDeco's securities wallet address to the investors' addresses." Nivaura recorded these transfers on the Ethereum blockchain; investors could see them through the Nivaura blockchain interface on the Nivaura platform.[526]

◈ KEY TAKEAWAYS ON CRYPTO DERIVATIVES

The world of regulated institutions is actively researching blockchain technology to increase standardization, transparency, and interoperability in derivatives processing.

A predominant example is the CDM, the smart contract protocol that ISDA is developing. The CDM can be a game changer in financial markets: even before derivatives are moved to a blockchain infrastructure, this new standard can solve the fragmentation of derivatives processing across hundreds of tech platforms that do not communicate with each other. We are far from general adoption, yet everyone in fintech is advised to be compatible with this standard.

Even so, this effort appears to underuse blockchain technology in derivatives. As the experiments on Ethereum demonstrated, smart contracts can also reduce the specific financial risks of derivatives products by changing key pieces of the business model—such as the speed of settlement, the coordination between cash flow and collateral payments, and the automation of break-up clauses that allow participants to terminate an agreement and settle collateral before the counterparty enters into an irreversible default state.

We don't expect anyone to implement these advances soon. Regulators must first understand them and adjust the regulatory framework so that financial counterparties may benefit fully from this new technology. The first application that gains enough traction and full regulatory recognition can make derivatives less risky from a systemic viewpoint.

The ecosystem of public blockchains is looking with interest at developing financial products that match, or resemble, the derivatives products traded in traditional financial markets. In this use case, we covered the most interesting initiatives and showed how they embed the same financial logic as derivatives.

An important example is MakerDAO. The blockchain infrastructure allows us to increase efficiency and automation. Even regulators have recognized these benefits, as in the Nivaura case. If an investor is looking for derivatives available and managed through blockchain technology, then the public blockchain is probably the place to look.

CHAPTER 7

OIL, NATURAL GAS, AND BLOCKCHAIN

How PermianChain Creates Value
through Natural Asset Tokens

Mohamed El-Masri

 ENERGY USE CASE IN BRIEF

- Energy companies are exploring the possibilities of blockchain. One of the most-investigated blockchain applications is energy trading; a convoluted process dominated by a large number of intermediaries and burdened by back-office costs that blockchain technologies could mitigate.

- The adoption of blockchain and smart contract solutions could give rise to:

  - A trustworthy primary market for issuing *natural asset security tokens* (NASTs) to enhance natural resources investment environment and attract smart and sustainable private capital.

  - *Natural resource tokens* (NRTs) with utility coded in *smart offtake agreements* (SOTAs) for a more efficient natural gas trading environment, with near real-time blockchain-enabled tracking system and improved digital currency payment mechanism.

- A digital energy conservation solution for natural gas-powered data mining operations that could provide an auxiliary source of revenue to oil and gas operators.

- If oil and gas operators adopt NRT with SOTA frameworks, then stakeholders and traders (who ultimately become the NRT holders) can purchase the utility tokens that underpin holding rights to verified natural gas reserves, whether in production or not. NRTs are convertible into electricity for powering on-site data mining containers.

- Potential new business models range from sourcing commodities from producers to transferring and converting natural gas for a clean, reliable energy source. Parties could eliminate the need to transport and track assets by land and sea; store assets in terminals, tanks, and warehouses; blend assets to meet customer specifications; or deliver assets to the right places at the right times.

- PermianChain's blockchain-integrated solution could reduce holding period returns for accredited investors. It could also optimize stakeholder value while reducing the potential of smuggling, raising red flags on black market participants, and enforcing international sanctions.

INTRODUCTION TO THE OIL AND GAS MARKET

We have been studying the use of blockchain in the oil and gas market for two years. The existing platforms that are live, in test mode, or under development have functions that relate to inventory, logistics, and post-trade efficiency. Our research did not identify an oil and gas blockchain platform dedicated to investing in *and* trading oil and gas with an integrated natural gas marketplace for power generation and data mining operators. So, we created one.

TABLE 7-1

BLOCKCHAIN INITIATIVES IN OIL AND GAS

COMPANY	LOCATION	DESCRIPTION	STATUS
Ponton Enerchain	Hamburg, Germany	Blockchain-based platform for P2P wholesale trading of natural gas	Live
Energía Abierta	Chile	Regulator tracking national energy data for oil and natural gas	Live
Fujairah Oil Industrial Zone, S&P Global Platts	Fujairah, UAE	Oil terminal stock levels reporting	Live
Mercuria, ING, Société Générale	Africa	Use of digital documents for oil cargo traded three times en route to China	Test
BTL OneOffice (Canada)	Europe	Use of BTL's Interbit platform to cut post-trade reconciliation costs for natural gas	Shuttered
Sinochem Group, Xiamen Customs, and HSBC	China and Singapore	Simulated gasoline export from Quanzhou to Singapore	Test
VAKT consortium (BP, Chevron, Shell, and others)	London, England	Platform to cut post-trade costs for oil	Live

Source of data: S&P Global Platts, "Blockchain for Commodities: Trading Opportunities for a Digital Age," foreword by Martin Fraenkel, S&P Global Inc., Sept. 2018. s3-ap-southeast-1.amazonaws.com/sp-platts/Blockchain.pdf. Table updated 19 Jan. 2022.

The PermianChain is a permissioned *blockchain platform-as-a-service* (BPaaS).

- It solves the funding challenge by simplifying how *exploration and production* (E&P) companies and registered *exempt market dealers* (EMDs) work together.

- It solves the market challenge by allowing E&P companies to sell field-generated electricity digitally to data center operators for powering on-site remote data mining farms.

The BPaaS uses Hyperledger Fabric blockchain integration to allow E&P companies to catalog, manage, and create value from their proven oil and gas reserves (Figure 7-1).

FIGURE 7-1

PERMIANCHAIN BPAAS ECOSYSTEM

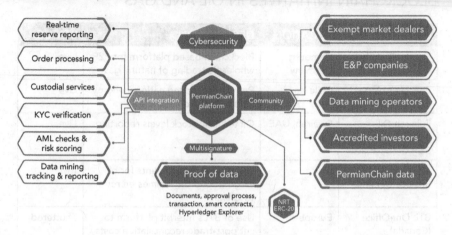

The BPaaS leverages the tokenization process. It features two ERC-20 tokens developed on the Ethereum protocol and compatible with the PermianChain platform:

- NASTs address the funding challenge. These digital securities enable issuers to offer debt and equity investment opportunities to accredited investors under available prospectus exemptions.

- NRTs address the market challenge. These utility tokens enable users buy and sell natural gas operators' field-generated power instantaneously.

All transactions, once executed, are immutable and recorded in the distributed ledger and reflected on the token register of the platform. The data registered on the BPaaS are updated by authorized verifiers and users on the platform. For example, once the dealing representative of a registered EMD verifies a NAST transfer, the data are updated on the Ethereum network as well as on the platform's real-time token register in compliance with securities regulations. When E&P companies must upload or update oil and gas reserve reports and company valuations, authorized petroleum consultants must verify them on the platform before these data are pushed to Hyperledger Explorer. Petroleum consultants contributing to the platform receive NRT tokens.

Oil and gas data reports are uploaded and accessible to accredited investors in a private virtual data room. Accredited investors must first be admitted to the PermianChain's primary digital securities issuance platform to subscribe for NASTs by their registered EMD. Key data from these reports (e.g., proven reserves, barrels of oil equivalent, valuations, etc.) appear on the investor dashboard so that investors have key indicators relevant to the value of their holdings.

In the PermianChain marketplace, the use of NRT utility tokens provides buyers of transformed natural gas the access to data related to these natural gas assets, reserves, and the amount of power generated in kilowatts. Users can access data relevant to pricing, supply, demand, and production to exercise SOTAs; they do not have access to proprietary information.

INVESTING IN OIL AND GAS

Investors have several options for getting involved with oil investing. These methods come with varying degrees of risk and range from direct investment in oil and gas as a commodity to indirect exposure through the ownership of energy-related equities.

One direct method of owning oil is through the purchase of oil futures or oil futures options. Futures are highly volatile and involve high risk. Additionally, investing in futures may require the investor to do much homework and invest a large amount of capital.

Another direct method of owning oil is through the purchase of commodity-based oil ETFs. ETFs trade on a stock exchange; investors can buy and sell them similarly to stocks. For example, buying one share of the US Oil Fund (USO) would give an investor exposure to roughly one barrel of oil.

In addition, investors can gain indirect exposure to oil through the purchase of energy sector ETFs, like the iShares Global Energy Sector Index Fund (IXC), and to energy sector mutual funds, like the T. Rowe Price New Era Fund (PRNEX). These energy-specific ETFs and mutual funds invest solely in the stocks of oil and oil services companies and come with lower risk.

THE DOWNSIDE OF CONVENTIONAL DIRECT INVESTMENTS

Many private oil and gas opportunities are structured with upfront fees. Advisers and brokers profit just by placing investors' money in the deal. That means fewer investor dollars go into the project, and it motivates the offering company to fill the deal quickly for fast profits rather than stay engaged with investors or offer deals more likely to yield better returns on production. Any innovation must address these issues in the oil and gas private capital market:

- Convoluted transaction processes
- High barriers to entry
- Long holding periods for private investors without expectations of dividend distributions
- Uneconomic infrastructure requirements to bring natural gas to market
- Wasted and stranded natural gas resulting in lost profits and opportunity costs

An array of operational problems from equipment repairs to dry holes can negatively affect shareholder returns. Companies should address these with investors in near real time, yet companies may go silent when problems arise, particularly if they downplayed the risks when soliciting investors. Too many companies fail to provide their investors access to important project updates. Consequently, investors have less confidence in the performance—even the legitimacy—of oil and gas investments.

The upstream Canadian oil and gas sector has become a less attractive investment in recent years, whereas major production areas in the United States have become more attractive. One of the largest foreign holders of Canadian energy stocks is Darren Peers, an analyst and investment manager in Los Angeles. In an open letter to Prime Minister Justin Trudeau, Peers warned that investors and companies will continue to avoid the Canadian energy sector unless more is done to improve market access.[527]

STREAMLINING DIRECT INVESTMENTS THROUGH BLOCKCHAIN

PermianChain developed its solution for conventional direct investments to solve the capital requirements of oil and gas exploration and production. To a certain extent, its development democratized direct investment for accredited investors. Using smart contracts, blockchain, and other digital innovation, PermianChain expects to streamline inflow of capital. The benefits are several:

- Buyers of blockchain-based digital securities have an immutable proof of ownership, whereas buyers of paper share certificates rely on third-party transfer agents to ensure that the issuer has not sold the same certificate to multiple people.

- Scaling up or down according to the number of parties involved improves the system's efficiency without more paperwork.

- Storing data in an encrypted, digital distribution ledger improves accessibility for every party in the blockchain. Key stakeholders will be able to access status updates and track performance of underlying assets in real time.

- Implementing *electronic* KYC requirements helps to determine viability and raises red flags for regulated activities. EMDs registered on the platform can provide access to relevant regulators, auditors, and compliance personnel.

- Cryptography and key-based encryption thwart efforts to tamper with documents and contracts within the blockchain.

DIGITAL SECURITIES AND TOKENIZATION

Tokenized securities are transforming oil and gas campaigns into digital assets. Digital securities (aka *security tokens*) are financial instruments created through smart contracts representing rights to financial securities. Transactions with the token recorded on the distributed ledger cannot be undone or erased. Access to the information is customizable based on the ledger setup (e.g., public, private, or hybrid). The tokenization process allows private companies to issue a digital token, which can represent equity in proven oil reserves and ongoing oil and gas production campaigns. The objective is for E&P companies to meet working capital requirements by efficiently implementing capitalization events and monetization strategies on their proven oil and gas resources.

Using smart contracts, we can now replace paper and complex agreements that are cumbersome, difficult to transfer, and hard to track for buyers of exempt securities. PermianChain's solution for investing in exploration and production of oil reserves allows upstream companies to digitize the private placement process under a compliant framework that leverages the blockchain (e.g., Ethereum, Hyperledger), resulting in a digital security that represents ownership (e.g., equity, shares) in reserve-based assets on a dedicated digital platform.

The natural gas tokenization process is a positive cycle: investors subscribe to NASTs to supply private capital, natural gas operator deploys power generation infrastructure to convert gas to electricity, and operator enters into *power purchase agreements* (PPAs) as SOTAs, deploys remote and portable data centers, and distributes portions of proceeds to NAST holders.

Now let's consider that, according to the Central Intelligence Agency, there are 1.665 trillion barrels of oil recoverable globally.[528]

The United States represented approximately $182 billion in capital expenditure while Canadian capital expenditure stood at approximately $38.5 billion at the end of 2018.[529] For the oil and gas industry as a whole, capital expenditures in Canada in 2018 were about 21 percent higher than in 2016; capital expenditures were also about 21 percent higher in the United States.[530]

IPOs for small to midsize oil and gas companies have declined, and other factors have affected the continuous flow of capital requirements for E&P companies to scale and meet production capacity (Figure 7-2). Tokenization of natural gas and oil assets as well as the electricity they help to generate could be a more suitable alternative. Adoption of digital securities in the natural resources sector could increase liquidity in the industry. It could meet working capital and capital expenditure requirements by reducing the barriers to entry and digitally streamlining financing and investment processes through tokenization.

FIGURE 7-2

HISTORICAL US EXPLORATION AND PRODUCTION IPO ACTIVITY

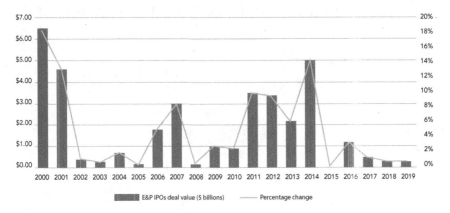

Source of data: James Chenoweth et al., "IPOs and Capital Markets Developments in the Oil and Gas Industry," GibsonDunn.com, Gibson, Dunn & Crutcher LLP, 26 Feb. 2019. www.gibsondunn.com/wp-content/uploads/2019/03/WebcastSlides-IPOs-and-Capital-Markets-Developments-in-the-Oil-and-Gas-Industry-26-FEB-2019.pdf.

E&P companies usually reinvest their cash flows into new projects where they must purchase property, equipment, infrastructure, and so forth. These large upfront capital expenditures eat into an E&P company's cash. E&P companies frequently require taking on the equity and debt positions placed by lenders and private investors. Before their investors realize a return, E&P companies aim to recoup their expenses first, plus servicing the debt. E&P companies will need to present a differentiated growth story and a clear strategy for the energy transition, and to show that they are taking measures to meet environmental, social, and governance criteria that command investors' attention.

To support such efforts, E&P companies can issue digital securities to capitalize on their oil and gas reserves to support related assets and operations. The digital security enables the shares of a privately-held upstream company to be digitally bought, sold, and transferred with the capability of automating dividend distributions in the form of digital currency (e.g., ETH, BTC) from oil and gas blockchain-integrated framework (OGBiF) and SOTA revenue models (Figure 7-3).

FIGURE 7-3

OIL AND GAS BLOCKCHAIN-INTEGRATED FRAMEWORK

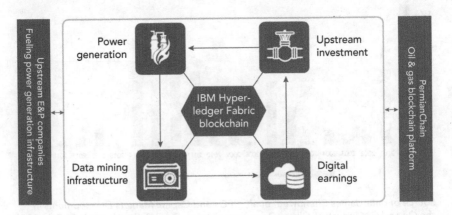

As the only reserve-focused tokenization platform, PermianChain expects that NASTs can become a critical instrument for attracting private capital and offer an ever-expanding range of investment exposure to the oil and gas sector using blockchain technology.

TRADING OIL AND GAS

The process leading up from extraction to trading of oil and gas includes a lengthy process that spans upstream integration, joint ventures, prepayments on offtake agreements, and technical support requirements. Oil and gas companies can benefit from a streamlined approach on a blockchain-enabled digital platform that enforces the functionalities of a smart contract.

Trading firms aim to maximize difference between the price they pay for (untransformed) commodities and the revenue they earn by selling (transformed) commodities. Their priority is minimizing the overall cost of acquiring commodities. They work with producers to secure a long-term, cost-effective supply.

Processing quality is equally important. Trading firms must be careful where they source these. Some oil fields, especially in conflict areas, do not conform to international health and safety standards. In a world that is moving toward increased transparency, suppliers that source from oil fields with poor social, environmental, and production performance run a significant reputational risk.

POOR INTEGRATION, LONG-TERM CONTRACTS, AND OPACITY

Keeping up with capital requirements over time is a real challenge. Upstream integration is a cash-intensive business and requires ongoing access to capital and various sources of financing to maintain production growth to meet offtake and demand. An offtake agreement is an agreement between an oil and gas producer (upstream) and an oil and gas buyer (midstream) to sell some or all of the production expected from the upstream company's production campaigns.

A long-term PPA is also known as a form of an offtake agreement, usually used for purchasing electricity between utility companies and power-generation facilities; or, in our case, natural gas operators with power generation as a line of business. Conflicts related to offtake agreements can arise from termination, price review negotiations, unforeseen events, compliance, regulations, accountability, dispute resolution, and more. All are major challenges to consider for energy trading.

The lack of transparency throughout the supply chain, from extraction and power generation to trading, can lead to the mismanagement and misappropriation of revenues. Ongoing reporting obligations (e.g., Canada's Extractive Sector Transparency Measures Act) can burden small and medium-sized enterprises (SMEs) in this sector.

SMART CONTRACTS

Imagine a group of companies that want to trade oil and gas with one another. Normally members of this group would exchange paperwork and keep their own lists of trades. If they could move to a blockchain-based system for trading their oil and gas, they could potentially reduce paperwork and have more robust record-keeping. Many conglomerates form to replace paper trading systems with blockchain trading systems. They rarely aim to tokenize real-world assets directly; instead, they use a blockchain system for trading real-world assets. This is a hybrid of the old paper-record approach and the new blockchain approach. The tokens have value only within the context of a contractual system involving all the past and future participants.

Now let's add fungible and tradeable smart contracts to such a system. The SOTA is intended to function as a smart contract that facilitates transactions between natural gas producers and data mining companies to enforce trading of field-generated electricity. SOTA's benefits allow multinational SMEs to cut costs on legal barriers allowing well-enforced, cross-border transactions and provide encrypted digital signature capabilities. SOTAs can be programmed using Solidity language on the Ethereum network. The deployment and compatibility of SOTAs on the PermianChain platform will allow buyers and holders of natural resource utility tokens to exercise their business-to-business (B2B) offtake agreements. Each SOTA transaction will be registered on the Ethereum network. Reports of other relevant resulting data are also published on the PermianChain platform using IBM's Hyperledger for enterprise and private blockchain solution. Here is how the PermianChain ecosystem works:

1. Supplier gathers documentation on reserves for PermianChain's due diligence prior to adding a production campaign to the PermianChain platform.

2. Supplier uploads documents through PermianChain's dashboard.

3. PermianChain compresses, encrypts, and saves documents in decentralized cloud storage.

4. PermianChain notifies experts and advisers (e.g., geologists, petroleum engineers, acquisitions and divestitures consultants) of a new submission. They conduct due diligence on each supplier in exchange for NRTs. Experts also monitor the decision-making process to ensure that it meets ethical standards and yields the proper number of tokens.

5. If at least two experts approve the submission, then proof of submission, proof of approval, and hashes of supplier's datasets are automatically published to PermianChain's blockchain explorer (IBM Hyperledger Fabric).

6. The PermianChain-appointed treasurer unlocks a quantity of NRTs and makes the tokens available for sale.

7. Data miner buys tokens to secure power from natural gas resources.

8. Data miner submits purchase order and sends order amount to custodial account to hold in escrow until miner receives natural gas power.

9. Supplier processes order to deliver power via on-site power generation. That is, the miner must ship equipment (i.e., mining servers) to the supplier for installation in supplier's containerized data centers.

10. Data miner confirms receipt of power on the platform once the mining equipment is up and running.

11. The confirmation of receipt releases funds in escrow to the supplier.

PermianChain's BPaaS also serves as a blockchain-enabled private B2B marketplace. It offers a trading system with redemption rights to data mining companies that seek to buy cleaner and more economic sources of electricity from natural gas operators. It allows independent oil and gas companies to sell proven reserves not yet produced, and natural gas that is in production but is wasted because of the lack of capital or sales pipeline infrastructure. BPaaS addresses working capital requirements without changing any business operations; suppliers can more efficiently monetize their resources. On the other hand, the adoption and integration of such technology allows suppliers to maximize on market volatility and generate higher and more stable revenues when they enter into early offtake agreements with oil traders. By using blockchain, suppliers can dramatically reduce their operational expenses by effectively eliminating the need for brokers.

THE UTILITY OF NATURAL RESOURCE TOKENS

Offtake agreements are an attractive alternative method of financing for oil and gas companies. By adopting smart contracts and blockchain solutions, upstream companies and offtakers can efficiently transact using NRTs as a bridge currency governed by a smart contract from within the suppliers' closed-loop B2B exchange. This allows for a stable and increasing token price on the platform.

If an oil and gas company owned land with proven reserves of 100 million *barrels of oil equivalent*, it could tokenize those barrels, though not yet produced; the resulting NRTs would give token purchasers exercisable rights for a fraction of the assessed value of the barrel of oil.

CONSUMING AND CONSERVING NATURAL GAS

WASTE AND INEFFICIENCY

There are two main forms of natural gas waste: (1) the controlled release of produced gas, commonly known as *flared gas*, burning into the atmosphere and (2) *stranded natural gas*, which is untapped gas that cannot be extracted because of logistical and economic barriers. These are traditional practices for dealing with the excess gas produced. Because of the high cost of infrastructure, stranding or burning the gas on-site often costs less than taking it to market for many oil and gas companies upstream. An investment in gas pipelines is a sunk cost, usually irrecoverable. Around the world, the industry flares approximately 150 billion cubic meters of natural gas at a cost of over $16 billion.[531] That's a high opportunity cost.

A separate but relevant data point is the energy consumption of commercial data centers and data transmission networks: combined, they need roughly two percent of the world's electricity.[532] About 40 percent of that goes to cooling.[533] But environmentalists worry about the lack of transparency in reporting exact amounts of energy that these data center and data network operators use and the impact of this usage on climate change.[534]

FIGURE 7-4

GLOBAL GAS FLARING VOLUMES

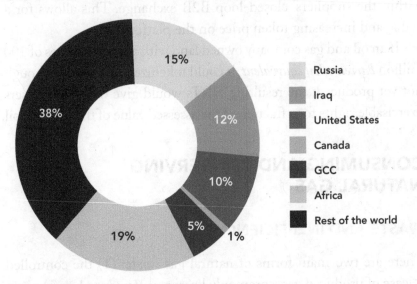

GCC = Gulf Cooperation Council (Saudi Arabia, United Arab Emirates, Kuwait, Bahrain, Oman, and Qatar)

Source of data: Zubin Bamji, "Global Gas Flaring Inches Higher for the First Time in Five Years," Open Data Blog, Global Gas Flaring Reduction Partnership, World Bank Group, 14 June 2019. blogs.worldbank.org/opendata/global-gas-flaring-inches-higher-first-time-five-years.

Some data center and network operators share this concern. Microsoft for one has pledged to cut its carbon emissions by 75 percent of its 2013 level over the next decade.[535] Toward that goal, it chose natural gas to power the fuel cells feeding a small server farm in Seattle.[536] It was a test of what Microsoft could do to make its data centers more cost-effective and energy efficient and to reduce its dependence on the electrical grid.[537]

Another relevant data point is the energy consumption of blockchain solutions. Unlike enterprise servers where we can't easily draw a one-to-one correlation between server energy use and financial return, we can easily obtain this correlation from cryptocurrency mining operations, partly because cryptomining servers do only one thing—mining—whereas enterprise servers may handle many different applications.

In one 30-month study, Bitcoin mining consumed an average of 17 megajoules (4.72 kWh) of electricity to generate one dollar, whereas conventional mining of gold used only five megajoules (1.39 kWh) to yield the same value.[538] The same study concluded that the Bitcoin network emits far more CO^2 than Ethereum, Litecoin, or Monero. Combined, the four cryptocurrencies produced as much as 15 million tons of CO^2 in the period studied.

According to the International Energy Agency, recent estimates of Bitcoin's electricity consumption range from 20 terawatt-hours (tWh) to 80 tWh per year.[539] That's about 0.1 percent to 0.3 percent of global electricity use, compared to the 10 percent consumed by air conditioners and electric fans deployed to cool various environments such as homes, commercial buildings, and industrial systems.[540] If we understand how different variables affect the costs of a new data center for bitcoin mining, then we can identify ways to maximize the owner's ROI.[541]

NATURAL GAS–POWERED DATA CENTERS

PermianChain sees data center operations as an opportunity for natural gas operators with power-generation capabilities. In 2019, the global data center construction market grew to an estimated $22.73 billion.[542] Data centers consumed roughly 200 tWh of energy, almost one percent of global demand for electricity.[543]

Data center operators require locations for scalable operations, ongoing flow of electricity, and efficiency that reduces downtime and reliance on the electrical grids. Electrical grids power virtually all these data centers: electricity flows from a power plant, through multiple substations and transmission lines, and then is converted into the right voltage for a data center. Operators can manage data centers remotely with scheduled maintenance requirements or on-site management during emergencies. By getting power directly from a natural gas line, we can streamline the power chain and minimize the energy leakage over long-distance transmission. Reducing the waste of natural gas is a new market for upstream companies, increasing netback and net benefits. It significantly reduces the amount of energy lost in power generation, transmission, and conversion.

Bitcoin mining is a reasonable gateway for natural gas E&P companies to enter the data center powering business. To be a viable source of revenue, it requires a clean source of low-cost electricity, which natural gas operators can supply. We can mitigate operational unknowns by using standard mining server design such as ASICs, standard data center structure and envelope (e.g., containerized units), and standard cooling equipment. Additionally, we can more easily account for energy consumption and cost through upfront analysis on location, system type, and server performance.

Finally, we can implement OGBiF and introduce a new oil and gas business model wherein we transform excess or wasted natural gas into electricity that powers on-site data centers with ASICs connected to the Bitcoin network. In exchange for bitcoin mining rewards and transactions fees, the ASICs would solve algorithmic equations that make bitcoin transactions possible. Oil and gas operators could:

- Register natural gas reserves and conserve energy on the PermianChain blockchain, which uses Hyperledger to store data transaction hashes.

- Receive an auxiliary source of revenue in the form of bitcoins that they could liquidate into cash flows for operational expenses and/or distribute to shareholders as dividends.

By deploying on-site power-generation infrastructure to convert natural gas to electricity, oil and gas operators can power on-site data centers for various data mining operations and conserve natural gas, thereby increasing netback and net benefit. By using NRTs and SOTAs, they can create a new market for natural gas trading in the form of electricity. Bitcoin miners can now purchase cost-effective sources of electricity, and producers can meet regulations on wasted natural gas.

PermianChain ran a pilot project with Brox Energy Holdings Ltd. (Brox), an Alberta-based energy company. Brox deployed a 100-kilowatt bitcoin mining data center using as little as 30,000 cubic feet of natural gas to power 26 ASICs. This proof of concept (POC) was registered on the PermianChain platform so that Brox could sell power in kilowatts to third-party bitcoin miners.

In many cases, Canadian natural gas operators usually sell their gas into the Alberta market based on the Alberta Energy Company (AECO) benchmark price. Our analysis showed electricity costs as low as $0.01 to as high as $0.05 per kilowatt-hour compared to the usual $0.07 to $0.12 per kilowatt-hour on the market today. For mining data centers, a significant reduction in operational expenses makes for higher profits and lower payback periods. Brox's pilot in rural Alberta proved the gas-to-power and power-to-bitcoin arbitrage. Brox used stranded and suspended natural gas reserves to generate electricity and earn bitcoin revenue of up to seven times AECO market spot prices.[544]

The result on shareholder returns derive from converting clean natural gas into electricity and delivering a cost-effective energy source that can power the world's data storage centers and data mining farms. By providing cheaper and more reliable computing power for data mining operations on-site, we can reward shareholders with an auxiliary source of income, through company-owned bitcoin mining operations or third-party electricity sales.

IMPLEMENTATION CHALLENGES

Attracting capital while remaining competitive in global markets is challenging. Despite its relatively large size compared to other industries within Canada, the oil and natural gas industry will continue to compete for investment and capital in an increasingly globalized world that still needs oil and gas to meet the growing energy needs.[545]

To compete in the global economy, we must first address the regional challenges of achieving a prosperous oil and gas industry. Blockchain companies planning to deliver a user-friendly experience and industry standard processes must consider platform development costs, appropriate systems, and efficient and reliable networks. Oil and gas companies must also develop patient strategies when applying blockchain and digitization methods to solve the industry's funding and market challenges.

Consider Envion AG, a start-up based in Berlin. In early 2018, the Envion team registered in Switzerland to raise $100 million in an ICO. The funds were to support Envion's development of mobile blockchain data centers that would operate on-site at power plants. Laurent Martin, Envion's former vice president of special projects and strategic growth, said that Envion's designers had to consider, for example, the proper air-flow dynamics and the control of heat moving through the data mining units. Laurent's team also focused on energy efficiency so that its fabricator could manufacture the design cost-effectively.[546]

According to Envion's ICO prospectus, the team came up with "a proprietary combination of technologies for the crypto mining industry," which Envion called *mobile mining units* (MMU) housed in standard twenty-foot freight containers and featuring "proprietary pattern of air flows and high performance fans."[547] Its choice of and modifications to hardware reduced the unit's power consumption further.[548] The MMUs would run autonomously with minimal overhead expenses. The start-up had rolled out plans to build and distribute these MMUs strategically worldwide to take advantage of cheap energy sources.

Of PermianChain's OGBiF and SOTA applications, Martin said, "It is a good time—and there is room for profit—if we apply the pricing mechanism from the gas-to-power businesses. Natural gas conversion is key to take advantage of the economics of mining bitcoin."[549] Unfortunately for Envion, the start-up went into liquidation after a dispute between its CEO and its founders.[550] Envion's founders have distanced themselves from the former CEO and are seeking opportunities to put their MMU designs to work.[551]

SCALABILITY OF THE PLATFORM

E&P companies can scale this new-generation oil and gas business by collaborating to consolidate assets on the PermianChain. They can implement an integrated solution for oil and gas that includes digitization of energy resources coupled with fintech that opens access to private capital for innovative on-the-ground operations and increases the bottom line and netback per cubic feet of gas. The sector can achieve scalability by satisfying growing demand from:

- Investors seeking upside value under a trusted, reliable, and environmentally conscious business model

- Data center operators looking for remote locations and PPAs as a package allowing for more efficient methods of purchasing electricity under a controlled pricing model

- Bitcoin mining operators seeking economic sources of power to sustain their long-term operations and high volatility of bitcoin

A bottom-up approach would more likely engender loyal and scalable adoption of such a platform. We see the pressing demand for this solution coming from SMEs in the upstream sector across Canada and the United States. Any platform must successfully address efficient, smart, and patient capital needs. Kris Jones, former ministerial assistant to the Honorable Lori Carr of the province of Saskatchewan, said, "Overall investment is a concern for CAPP [Canadian Association of Petroleum Producers] members. ... Operators are already using flare gas at well sites and might be interested in the mining on-site solutions in addition to a platform for tokenized reserves project."[552]

Adoption of such a platform needs the support of the private capital markets. EMDs who are authorized and regulated by their province's financial regulator to market exempt securities are key to sponsor such initiatives. For a digital securities issuance platform to comply with regulatory requirements, EMDs must sponsor the offering of those oil and gas companies' digital securities and support raising capital for those companies on a best-effort basis. Including EMDs brings about a more well-rounded consensus among industry participants as EMDs can instill credibility and ensure compliance with securities regulations.

GOVERNANCE OF AN INVESTMENT PLATFORM

The platform is governed by its users, which include expert petroleum consultants, oil and gas companies, investors, and shareholders who subscribe to the NAST issued by oil and gas companies; they are registered on the platform and by the EMDs that foster platform compliance and facilitate NASTs under strict securities regulations. Holders of NASTs own a digital representation of shares, which give them rights to equity in the oil and gas companies registered on the platform.

The platform operates under a set of predefined governance and reporting frameworks that are brought forward by registered EMDs to comply with securities regulations and that are coded into the platform's functions and the NAST smart contracts. The functions on the platform are executed with the participation of third-party verifiers (e.g., dealing representatives, compliance officers, custodians, trustees, etc.) to ensure regulatory approvals, compliance, and standard reporting. Each verified function or transaction on the platform is then pushed to the platform's blockchain and distributed ledger (i.e., Ethereum network for token register and Hyperledger blockchain for time-stamped data and transparent reporting).

INTEROPERABILITY WITH OTHER PLATFORMS

On-site data mining operations capture data on natural gas consumption. Through the platform, a company and its shareholders can access and use these data to track conservation and natural gas revenues in real time. Likewise, blockchain data mining on the Bitcoin network can provide holders of NRTs and NASTs with real-time data on revenue generation from natural gas, and the platform can distribute dividends in real time to shareholders. Furthermore, the integration of remote sensors and remote monitoring application on-site that are connected to existing enterprise resource planning software, such as Oracle NetSuite, can reflect key data to stakeholders and have such data pushed on a blockchain-enabled platform via an API.

We can digitize oil fields to supply real-time tracking of select data that would bolster investor sentiment. Upstream companies could attract more sources of capital as they optimize revenues through proper data analytics and simulation. Commercializing such interoperability is a work in progress requiring industry participation. We believe that to adopt, integrate, and test the potential of different systems for interoperability would require a minimum user base that could produce around 1,000 barrels of oil equivalent per day.

REGULATION AND REGULATORY UNCERTAINTY

Regulation of digital securities depends on the structure of each offering. The global standard is to regulate according to the rules of jurisdiction in which the company will issue and distribute the financial security. The current paper-based regulation sometimes does not work well for all-digital securities, though regulators have granted exemptions from certain requirements as long as they don't undermine investor protections. In Canada, provincial and territorial regulators generally collaborate with each other through the Canadian Securities Administrators (CSA) Regulatory Sandbox so that they treat novel applications uniformly across Canada.[553] The hope is that the CSA's sandbox can deal with issues faster to provide service to this fast-paced part of the financial industry.

As for regulations around the natural gas market, the solution of OGBiF with on-site data mining addresses concerns around gas flaring volumes. It is a positive response to the industry's wasted natural gas resources.

Forester Yang, head of blockchain application development for Sinochem Energy Technology in China, shared his views on how the political challenges of governance would create uncertainty for such a platform in countries where oil and gas are national commodities and where private investors do not own mineral rights.[554] He elaborated on how distributed ledger technology platforms should always include the human touch in their governance frameworks to comfort stakeholders.

A balance between human responsibility and digital automation is how the PermianChain platform implemented its functions. As an aggregator of oil and gas data sets owned by its users, PermianChain must ensure the quality and veracity of information recorded on its platform. That's why experts (e.g., petroleum consultants, geologists, engineers, and landsmen) must verify the data sets before they are recorded to the blockchain. Proof of ownership of each set is also recorded to PermianChain's distributed ledger.

 IMPLICATIONS AND KEY TAKEAWAYS

Managing execution risk for upstream companies as they consider shifting and transforming their business into an OGBiF is a growing concern because of the nascency of the technology. The rise of big oil consortia within this space is a validation of a gradual internal move between companies and their stakeholders to test and implement trading activities on the blockchain, where they have proven to cut post-trade costs by almost 40 percent.[555] Leaders within the industry should carefully plan and implement a gradual shift before going to market.

Rigorous planning and coordination. The OGBiF model requires careful planning relative to cybersecurity, physical security, crisis management, and regulations, from exploration and production of oil and gas to financial securities. With a close-knit industry participation, bringing a more commercially viable and compliant platform to the data mining market—one that is accessible by investors globally—is a very achievable task. PermianChain is a pioneer member of the Blockchain Research Institute and a start-up member of the Petroleum Technology Alliance Canada (PTAC), gaining key stakeholder feedback to commercialize its application.

Diversity of talent. The success of OGBiF depends on a variety of experts. The implementation phase relies on the skills and knowledge of electricians, petroleum engineers, technicians, and data center ecosystem professionals. Leveraging investments after implementation requires the expertise of investment advisers, information technology professionals, and natural gas field operators. PermianChain was founded by a corporate finance regulation professional, a legal specialist, and a petroleum geomechanics engineer. These practitioners help to ensure economies of scale, economic growth, and profitability of the OGBiF business model.

Compliant frameworks. Business models must comply with laws across industries and jurisdictions. To that end, PermianChain has been in close and ongoing discussions with regulatory bodies in Canada and the United Arab Emirates. Likewise, current oil and gas blockchain consortia such as Vakt and OOC Oil and Gas Blockchain Consortium are addressing use cases around post-trading efficiencies, data management, dispute resolutions, and project management. Sinochem Energy Technology is also developing its own post-trading platform focused on petrochemicals in the Chinese market.[556]

Research and development. Ongoing R&D is critical, and it includes prospective user feedback. For example, PTAC hosted an online webinar that showcased PermianChain's OGBiF business model and the advantages of blockchain adoption for resource financing and cash-flow optimization.[557] According to participants, natural gas–powered blockchain data mining would need an ultra-low emissions power source so that adopters could earn emissions credits. If we can profitably use gas to generate electricity, then why would we want to sell gas if we can sell power? However, we see little synergy between gas producers and power generators, perhaps because of the lack of openness in local markets for innovation.

Industry consensus. Consortia and showcases under PTAC can bring industry players together to drive technological innovations that attract new sources of capital and maintain growth of clean energy in domestic and international markets. The focus here is on consolidating small and medium-sized oil and gas companies that need to revive their businesses. To solve their funding and market challenges and to manage execution risk, the industry needs to support the use of one platform for B2B transactions. Philip Collins, CEO of Brox Energy Holdings Ltd., summarized the situation nicely:

The industry faces many challenges including capital constraints and fast evolving environmental policies. This has left many small and mid-cap E&P companies cash-strapped despite their significant growth potential, proven reserves, and quality assets. Digital transformation, blockchain adoption, and power generation facilities are becoming key growth drivers for the future of the oil and gas industry ... to create a new market for our region's [Canada] wasted and stranded natural gas while digitally transforming our business model to focus on efficiency and increase shareholder value. These are desperate times for North American oil and gas.[558]

Through its proof of concept, PermianChain demonstrated that it could support innovative ways of doing business for many undervalued companies that joined its platform. The goal is a circular economy in which consumers of electricity subscribe to NRTs to supply funding; natural gas operators deploy power-generation infrastructure, convert gas to electricity, and send it to the power grid; and NRT holders consume, resell, or use power for data centers, bitcoin mining, and so forth.

CHAPTER 8

NON-FUNGIBLE TOKENS

An Enterprise View of Programmable Digital Assets

Alan Majer

 ## NFTS IN BRIEF

- In information-poor environments, we try to eliminate differences. Standards remove the need for data and complex coordination. But it needn't be this way. NFTs embrace the reality of uniqueness and give us new means of value creation that mass manufacturing and commoditization have pushed aside.

- NFTs breathe life into digital notions of ownership. We can represent virtual game loot and IP—copyrighted work, patents, and designs, some in the form of 3D print files—as NFTs, pushing the boundaries of what ownership means in terms of usage, sharing, licensing, printing, and additive manufacturing.

- Enterprise leaders must start thinking creatively about tangible and intangible property rights. Which bundles of rights might the enterprise manage, monitor, and enforce via NFTs? While blockchain technology secures select ownership and usage rights, what or who might secure the rest? That's unclear. We must rely on the promises of the issuer, artificial forms of scarcity, and interpretations of the law.

- In many economic and social circumstances, beliefs alone (such as self-fulfilling prophecies) may alter the course of events. NFTs can catalyze communities and encourage economies of participation toward community goals such as systemic change and sustainable development.

- Enterprise can use NFTs to engage stakeholders—such as employees and consumers—in the enterprise ecosystem and give them a stake in cocreating success. Organizations can actively harness NFTs to create the dynamic feedback loops that their entire ecosystem needs for success.

INTRODUCTION TO NFTS

In a few years, the market has expanded and matured for NFTs, which are unique digital tokens secured cryptographically on block-chain ledgers. From marginal beginnings as blockchain-powered collectible cats, NFTs have diversified into a network of assets, some auctioned at speculative heights (Figure 8-1). Gartner expects half of all publicly listed companies to issue some sort of NFT as a marketing tool by 2024, not just to underpin their brands but to expand their presence in digital ecosystems or metaverses and to improve enterprise valuations, potentially putting them among the most valued companies by 2026.[559]

In 2018 and 2019, the market capitalization of NFTs grew 17 percent, from $180 million to $220 million, with the user base growing from 111,640 to 113,287, as the overall market value for cryptoassets plummeted 56 percent during crypto winter.[560] Then, in the first quarter of 2021 alone, $2 billion worth of NFTs changed hands. That's 131 times as many NFT sales as in Q1 2020, along with a 269 percent growth in active NFT wallets.[561]

Since 2020, the market distribution of NFTs has shifted dramatically as well. In the second quarter of 2021, $754 million worth of NFTs changed hands on Ethereum, with art (14%) and collectibles (66%) making up the bulk of sales. Yet, today's art and collectibles are only the tip of a valuable iceberg. Gauthier Zuppinger of NonFungible.com said, "We still need to explore the last 95 percent remaining."[562] While usability of NFTs is miles ahead of where it was, innovators have plenty of room to create superior user experiences (UX). With mainstream adoption, subpar UX won't cut it anymore.

FIGURE 8-1

NFT SALES IN USD BY CATEGORY

This chart includes ERC-721 tokens on the Ethereum blockchain only—no sidechain or off-chain activity, no ERC-1155 or ERC-998 tokens, nor NFTs on other blockchains.

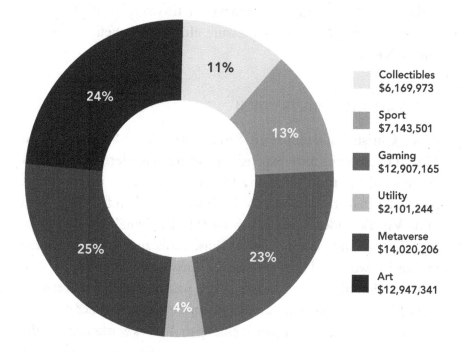

Popularity comes with a price. It can cost $300+ to mint an NFT, depending on the contract.[563] As NFTs go mainstream, the transaction fees—known as *gas* on Ethereum—have increased. In May 2021, gas cost 144 gwei, while a year ago it was 16 gwei. In many cases, trading a low-value NFT isn't worth the gwei. Even a simple ether transfer costs around $7.50.[564]

In other cases, mainstream adoption has watered down the purported benefits of NFTs. Developers have prioritized accessibility and ease of use over strong ownership rights (e.g., cutting costs by storing data off-chain in central databases rather than on-chain), and limitless NFT issuance has surfaced the speculative greed that often ends in disappointment. Some suggest that an NFT speculative bubble is nearing its end. A song called "NFTs Are Dead" appeared in June 2021, sold as an NFT, and fetched two ether (approx. $5,000 at the time).[565] As with the crypto winter, these cycles sift the wheat from the chaff. The selective pressure ultimately benefits the evolution of NFTs.

THE SALVATOR METAVERSI

When Christie's auctioned off *Salvator Mundi* for $450 million in 2017, it became the most expensive painting in modern history. This figure is all the more shocking for two reasons: (1) experts aren't convinced that it's a Leonardo da Vinci original and not the work of da Vinci's students and (2) two art dealers bought it for a mere $1,175 at an estate sale in New Orleans, Louisiana, in 2005.[566] Some restoration work and a few deals later, *Salvator Mundi* took its place in art auction history.[567] The tale of this painting and its provenance reads like a high-stake detective mystery. Its current owner declined the Louvre's request to display it among da Vinci's works because the museum wouldn't confirm it as a da Vinci original, thereby ensuring its value.[568] The deeper we dig, the more interesting the story becomes—and the truth, more elusive.[569]

NFTs meet the needs of art collectors who want indisputable evidence of a work's authenticity *before* they submit their bids.
Salvator Metaversi is an NFT that riffs on this concern. Its creator
Ben Lewis issued a blatantly copied and modified version of *Salvator
Mundi*, to which he held no copyrights. (If da Vinci or his students
had indeed painted it, then it would be deemed in the public domain.)
We might interpret Lewis' treatment of the image as transformative,
a critique of current art world practices, but a court might find in
favor of the photographer of the painting.[570] The provenance of the
original may be in dispute, but the origin of *Salvator Metaversi* is
indisputable. (To see work online, see https://opensea.io/collection/
crypto-leonardo-masterpieces.)

Lewis tweeted that he would give the proceeds of the sale to the
New Orleans family that sold *Salvator Mundi*.[571] At auction, Lewis'
work fetched 1.8 ether (around $3,700), more than the family received
for the original.[572] Equally illuminating was the perspective of the buyer,
Christian S., who wrote in a direct message, "I love ART because it
gives me joy having it around the house [and] looking at it."[573] When
asked why he bought *Salvator Metaversi* in particular, he said, "I loved
the combination of Ben Lewis giving back to the family who sold the
initial piece, but I also liked the look of *Salvator Metaversi* holding
dollar notes, which is a great representation of our time."[574]

Artisans in museum-grade framing have an opportunity to team
up with innovators in touch screen display technology and develop
customizable screens for exhibiting NFTs. Ditto for three-dimensional
projections of digital sculpture, in a real space or virtual reality (VR).
We can anticipate VR experiences of museums, with NFTs displayed
among well-known pieces of art, as with the Met 360° Project.[575]

Also taking an interest in NFTs are such cultural institutions as
Beijing's UCCA Center for Contemporary Art, which recently hosted
the first major NFT art exhibition.[576] Numerous NFT innovators are
now fielding interested queries in all kinds of industries and areas of
application, from social media and game development, to consumer
brands, sports, and entertainment as well as from the brokers, law

firms, and sports and talent agencies that represent rights of publicity, IP, and other intangibles.

In May 2021, when conventional intermediaries were getting into the game, online marketplaces for NFTs were doing a steady volume, from OpenSea ($136M), NBA Top Shot ($45M), and Rarible ($25M) to AtomicMarket ($12M) and SuperRare ($5M).[577] By October, volume had dropped considerably: OpenSea was still on top ($60.64M, down 44%), then Axie Infinity ($15.81M), CryptoPunks ($5.76M), NBA Top Shot ($839K, down 98%), and SuperRare.com ($412K).[578] See Table 8-1 for a comparison of standards.[579]

While NFTs started as ERC-721 tokens on the Ethereum blockchain, more use cases have catalyzed NFT options. New token standards created greater flexibility in token options and features as well as lower costs via smart contracts and entire blockchains optimized to NFT applications.

EASE OF USE: THE TRADE-OFFS

In 2018, buying an NFT was somewhat complex. Users needed to convert dollars into crypto via an exchange, transfer them into a suitable wallet, and make a purchase. Some advances like the MetaMask wallet, a browser extension in use at the time, were huge improvements over blockchain user interfaces. In a couple of years, users could buy NFTs directly, that is, without conversion to crypto. In many cases, buying an NFT today is as simple as pulling out a credit card. In other cases, crypto itself has become easier to purchase. Companies like Coinbase accept debit cards, and PayPal accountholders can buy bitcoin, ether, litecoin, and bitcoin cash directly via their PayPal accounts. These alternatives improve the user experience; minimize friction, complexity, and hassle; and encourage mainstream adoption.

Yet, some user interface improvements come at a cost, often weakening ownership rights. For example, to expedite the purchasing process, many NFTs are held in escrow. What if the escrow service provider goes bust or a founder absconds with the assets? Those building NFT tools, experiences, and communities are wise to uphold ownership rights. For example, Valuables.com holds NFTs of tweets in custody via Cent's digital wallet, but users can request transfers to a personal wallet without a fee.[580]

TABLE 8-1

COMPARISON OF FUNGIBLE AND NON-FUNGIBLE TOKEN STANDARDS

STANDARD	DISTINGUISHING FEATURE(S)
ERC-20	Original fungible token standard, adopted by Ethereum.
ERC-420	PepeDapp's token standard for its collectible trading cards, Rare Pepes, which are hybrid: each card is fungible with cards of the same type, but different types are non-fungible.
ERC-721	The first NFT standard, adopted by Ethereum and used in games such as CryptoKitties.
ERC-721x	Backward compatible with ERC-721, this token standard offers advanced features such as batched transfers and the creation of multiple classes of items.
ERC-994	Delegated NFT (DNFT) standard, a proposed extension of ERC-721 for registering land and physical property.
ERC-998	*Composable NFT* (CNFT) standard, a proposed extension enabling any NFT to own another fungible ERC-20 or non-fungible ERC-721 token.
ERC-1155	Like ERC-721x, this token standard offers batched transfers and group transfer features. Created by Enjin, it is not backward compatible with ERC-721. Gamers and companies such as AgriDigital have embraced it.
Flow NFT	Founded by Dapper Labs, the Flow blockchain supports NFTs with many of the features of ERC-721 and ERC-1155. Users can import CryptoKitties NFTs and run NBA Top Shot.[581]
Paratokens Efinity	This token standard for Polkadot supports fungible tokens and NFTs. Enjin's Efinity token standard is a utility Paratoken, for game developers and others to work more easily with NFTs such as an ERC-1155 bridge between Ethereum and Polkadot.
rwaNFT	Mattereum's *real-world asset* NFT backed by a physical asset with warranties, insurance, and legal enforceability to create trust in trade.
SimpleAssets dGoods	Other blockchains are supporting NFTs such as SimpleAssets and dGoods developed for use on the EOS blockchain.
Tezos FA2	NFTs on Tezos use FA2 (the TZIP-12 standard), which permits both fungible tokens and NFTs with a consistent interface and offers capabilities similar to ERC-20, ERC-721, and ERC-1155.

Another usability challenge is gas itself. Gas is the quasi-transaction fee users pay out when consummating a transaction on the Ethereum blockchain. Understanding what exactly gas is, applying enough of it for a transaction, and then paying the fees all create other barriers. Even then, blockchain transactions are far from instant on Ethereum. Consider the lengthy loading times of blockchain games like Nine Chronicles and imagine waiting for certainty on in-game transactions.[582]

While Ethereum developers are moving toward new models that expedite throughput at lower costs, these options are not yet available. Newer NFT standards already help with that issue. ERC-1155 offers a more flexible token standard and has optimized contracts for affordability; users can transfer multiple token types at once. To lower transaction fees, others are using sidechains as Valuables does with Matic (Polygon).[583] Still others are creating entirely separate blockchains better suited to the application, such as Dapper Labs' Flow or Enjin's Efinity on Polkadot.[584]

Witek Radomski, chief technology officer of Enjin, explained the importance of reducing these transaction costs: "It's the community coming together saying ... we don't want to spend $50 or $100 to interact with our NFTs. Make this happen. So that's why we're doing Efinity."[585] In addition, Radomski said that NFTs shouldn't be limited to a single blockchain. "You should be able to bring your NFTs into other chains," he said. "We'll have standards ... so that it's easy to port these things and make them cross-chain compatible."[586]

EARLY ADOPTION OF USE CASES

NFT adoption remained strong throughout crypto winter. Developers expanded the range of their use, users produced a steady volume of transactions, and NFTs reached entirely new markets. A surge in NFT news in the first half of 2021 attracted an entirely new segment of users.[587] NonFungible.com analyzed user wallets by different applications, and the overlap of projects is relatively small or clustered.[588]

Distinct types of NFTs and applications are appealing to different user segments, which typically indicates a higher level of market maturity. As the number of use cases and applications expands, we can reasonably expect more niches and communities to emerge. To figure out which categories have the highest level of user interest and activity, we look at the percentage of daily return visitors (Figure 8-2).

FIGURE 8-2
DAILY VISITOR RETURN RATES

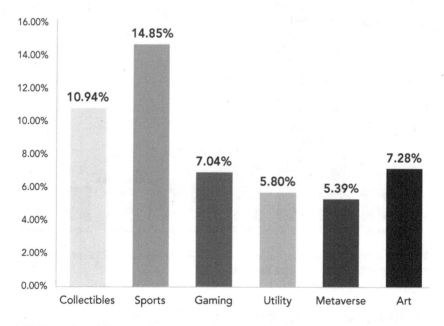

Those results are also consistent with the popularity of markets like NBA Top Shot, developed by DapperLabs in partnership with the NBA and its player union (Figure 8-3).[589] Coming soon for cricket fanatics are NFTs of cricketing feats on the Rario platform, with the Abu Dhabi T10 joining the Hero Caribbean Premier League and the Lanka Premier League in issuing these digital sports collectibles.[590]

Through NFTs, enterprises can generate new types of assets, launch creative endeavors, connect with existing customers, and reach new audiences. Fans want to connect with the teams, characters, brands, causes, alma maters, and people they admire or care most about, and NBA Top Shot clearly demonstrates that.

FIGURE 8-3

NBA TOP SHOT SALES VOLUME IN 2021

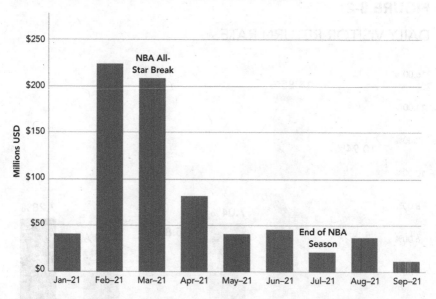

Source of data: "NBA Top Shot Sales Volume," CryptoSlam.io, as of 25 Sept. 2021. cryptoslam.io/nba-top-shot/sales/summary.

CHRISTIE'S: A CASE STUDY OF INCUMBENT INNOVATION

Most NFT intermediaries are start-ups. Some offer marketplaces for NFTs (e.g., OpenSea, Rarible, and SuperRare); several have set up new games, tools, or ecosystems for these assets (e.g., Axie Infinity,

Ethereum Name Service, and Decentraland); and others have created new blockchains or currencies (e.g., Enjin and Dapper Labs).

Christie's is an exception. An auction house incumbent, the company likes to think of itself as an innovator, pointing to its 2018 sale of artwork generated by AI named GAN (for Generative Adversarial Network) and sold for 45 times its initial estimate.[591] GAN's creator, the Paris-based collective Obvious (formed by Pierre Fautrel, Hugo Caselles-Dupré, and Gauthier Vernier) holds the copyright to GAN's art and, we presume, receives its proceeds, since courts in the United States and the United Kingdom have thus far recognized only "natural persons" in the form of human beings, not other primates or AI software, as creators of IP.[592] It is a relevant area of the law to watch, in anticipation of the types of digital assets that a DAO can originate and manage.[593]

Christie's NFT exploration began with its sale of a Barney A. Ebsworth collection: with each piece sold, Christie's included "a secure, encrypted certification of the sale … providing a permanent digital record of relevant information about the artwork" on the blockchain start-up Artory's registry.[594] In that same year, the company participated in an art and technology summit, "Exploring Blockchain."[595] In fall 2020, Christie's sold its first NFT, Robert Alice's *Block 21*, for seven times its initial estimate.[596]

All these experiences prepared Christie's for the record-setting sale of Beeple's *Everydays* NFT for $69 million. The company's leaders knew it was entering an unfamiliar domain—it was the first time Christie's estimated the value of a work as "unknown," said Noah Davis, Christie's specialist in post-war and contemporary art.[597] At the same time, Christie's saw a clear opportunity: Beeple had established a following through his NFT sale on the Winklevoss twins' Nifty platform in late 2020.[598] The *Everydays* auction attracted a new generation of collectors—of the 33 bidders, all were millennials or younger, 91 percent were first-time Christie's bidders, 55 percent lived in the United States, 27 percent lived in Europe, and 18 percent lived in Asia.[599]

Justin Sun, founder of the Tron cryptocurrency, lost in his bid to acquire digital artist Beeple's *Everydays* but went on to buy a pair of physical art—a Picasso and a Warhol—for $22 million, a bargain by comparison.[600] Christie's went on to auction *Larva Labs sold CryptoPunks* for $16.9 million and an Emily Ratajkowski NFT for $175,000 on 13 May 2021.[601]

Sotheby's quickly spun up its own business, selling a Larva Labs *CryptoPunk #7523* for $11.8 million, an NFT of the original source code for the World Wide Web for $5.4 million, and a set of NFTs from the *Bored Ape Yacht Club* collection for $24.4 million.[602]

Why should enterprise leaders care about these NFTs, if they work outside the creative industries? "It has always been impossible to monetize works of purely digital means because it's easy to duplicate works on [a] computer," said Christie's spokesperson Rebecca Riegelhaupt in an interview with *Barron's*. "With the introduction of NFTs and blockchain technology, [we]'re able to make a work that is incapable of being duplicated and holds all of the relevant information ... prominently encrypted onto the file."[603]

That's great news for incumbents with valuable brands. They have another opportunity to innovate, to introduce cutting-edge technology to established audiences, and to attract new, well-heeled clients, geographically dispersed and already engaged with blockchain or NFTs. While NFTs have features that relate to providence and strong ownership rights, enterprise leaders still have important roles to play in overcoming the implementation challenges of NFTs. For example, a trusted organization like Christie's could vet the series of events that lead to an NFT's minting and add specifics about the bundle of rights the NFT's code contains.

THE REALITIES OF NFT OWNERSHIP

When a company buys an NFT, what exactly does it own? It's a simple question, too often pushed under the rug. Jon Sharples, an IP lawyer, outlined the problem: "Licensing intellectual property rights can be a complicated business and is usually the subject of detailed negotiations with lawyers involved. The frothy world of NFTs does not lend itself to that dynamic, and there is a lot of potential for misunderstandings."[604] Unresolved, many of these issues present barriers to commerce and hinder wider adoption of NFTs. If we address them appropriately, then we can realize new use cases and categories of opportunity.

WHAT EXACTLY IS OWNERSHIP ANYWAY?

We take ownership notions for granted. Yet, ownership is not some kind of empirical truth; it's a human notion supported by legal and institutional structures. Technically, NFTs have strong ownership rights that most physical assets do not, but NFT creators may not codify the bundle of rights transferred via an NFT. So, ownership rights default to those enshrined in law, and those laws often impose limitations on those rights. For example, the limitations can be at odds with rights that we want to protect, such as indigenous knowledge that's viewed as holistic and inseparable from the communities in which it originates.[605] In other cases, existing laws are inadequate because they've never contemplated certain rights or use cases. Consider the ownership of property by smart contracts functioning as DAOs, which are not yet recognized as legal "persons" as corporations are.[606] NFTs fall closer to the latter.

On one hand, NFTs appear to offer a strong form of title and ownership; on the other, they are still subject to the rules and regulations governing tangible property rights, IP rights, and, in some cases, moral rights. See Table 8-2.[607]

TABLE 8-2

DIFFERENCES BETWEEN PHYSICAL OWNERSHIP AND NFT OWNERSHIP

ATTRIBUTE	PHYSICAL	NFT
Who owns it	Whoever holds the deed, title, or receipt	Whoever holds the private key
Who has rights to it	Whoever holds a license or agency agreement	Whoever has a key to a smart contract
Are those rights exclusive?	Exclusive ownership by legal "person" is required, such as a corporation.	While non-human forms (e.g., software) can hold or own assets, they don't have legal standing.
Transaction costs	Internet platforms have minimized costs of search, negotiation, performance, and post-performance; still need intermediary for authentication, payment, settlement (if not cash), and disputes.	Blockchain platforms have minimized costs of search, authentication, negotiation, performance, and post-performance; may need off-chain intermediary for disputes.
Accidental loss	Institutions can often restore ownership.	If a key is lost, no power on earth can restore ownership.
Durability/longevity	Wear and tear; restoration periodically required	Immutable and forever
Title system	Is paper-based or a central database; represents ownership rights	Is blockchain-based, where the NFT itself contains terms of property rights
Provenance	May require research as chain of custody and quality of evidence vary	Stored on the blockchain
Fraud	Provenance or authenticity may be in question	Provenance provable, but are parties who they say they are, and do they own the rights?
Enforcement	Theft is punishable by law; holders must return lost or stolen property.	Cryptographic keys offer strong ownership but make recovery of lost or stolen property difficult.
Loans	Possible, but requires possession (e.g., pawn shop) or legal complexity (e.g., lien)	Exhibition rights of NFT owner may be uncertain; logistics for digital works far clearer
Intellectual property/ Moral rights	Not included by default, arranged by buyer and seller	Not included by default, arranged by buyer and seller
Identity	May have a physical tag, machine readable code, or serial number	Must link NFT to digital or physical asset it represents

Delving into ownership differences between digital and physical items offers us some clarity when examining NFT possibilities. While NFTs offer key features such as strong ownership rights and immutability, prospective NFT buyers have as-yet unanswerable questions about enforcing real-world ownership rights and legal dependencies. Who owns the copyright? Can the owner of the art use it for commercial purposes? What degree of exclusivity does the owner have, and are there any guarantees of that exclusivity over time?

THE BUNDLE OF RIGHTS FOR NFTS

In September 2020, Emily Ratajkowski penned an interesting article called "Buying Myself Back, When Does a Model Own Her Own Image?"[608] She reflected upon her career as a model and her lack of ownership or control of her images. In May 2021, Ratajkowski decided to sell her own NFT via Christie's for $175,000.[609] But did Emily really own the NFT? She based it on a photograph of her standing in front of what appears to be a canvas blowup of a screenshot of one of her Instagram posts containing a *Sports Illustrated* photo of her. (The magazine paid her $150 for the shoot.) But it was a copy of a painting by Prince—an artist notorious for wandering into the grey areas of copyright law—that Emily bought for $81,000. Emily didn't own copyright to the *Sports Illustrated* photo in the post or Prince's painting of the post. Whether Emily held the rights necessary to issue an NFT is difficult to answer.

For would-be NFT purchasers, the case exemplifies how copyright law may align or not with the ownership rights offered in NFTs. At its core, an NFT is a sequence of cryptographic data in a smart contract. Since blockchain storage is costly, few NFTs store much data (let alone high-resolution images) on-chain, and so buyers usually purchase pointers to images rather than the images themselves. If the web server at that URL goes down, the image may simply disappear, too. So much for immutability. A more considerate NFT content creator may store the image via a service with some longevity like InterPlanetary File System.[610] Even then, there are no guarantees. To benefit from strong ownership, the NFT must be in the buyer's wallet, which is one more factor to double-check, since many systems host NFTs in an escrow account to save on transfer fees.

Then there are questions around ownership itself. The simple, yet difficult to decipher, question in Emily's case: does the person minting the NFT own the rights to the content? Is this NFT exclusive, or one of a series? What exactly is she selling, which set of rights, what type of ownership? In some cases, what a person is buying is clear. Cameron Hejazi, co-founder and CEO of Cent, mentioned that when we purchase the NFT of a tweet on Valuables, we're not getting the copyright, and we don't get the commercial rights either (e.g., we can't make money printing out a tweet on a T-shirt). Instead, we're buying a connection to the person who tweeted it, plus a promise of exclusivity. But even that's based on the honor system, said Hejazi: "Really it's their reputation, that they're saying, 'I'm signing this tweet to you as a one of one.' To break that contract would damage their reputation."[611]

Ownership questions grow more complex still when physical property is involved. What happens when a physical piece of property leaves possession, but the NFT doesn't? Or how do we determine (with some kind of physical fingerprint or other measure) whether an NFT pertains to a given object? Imperfections in manufacturing become an asset rather than a liability: the difference of a few grams, the natural grain of a piece of lumber, and surface imperfections are useful identifiers, not just sources of variation. Also, makers can manually introduce the variations such as micro dots, etching, or other hidden identifiers. Even the addition of a quick response code can aid identity.

Now we're applying these ideas to digital entities. "We've always had non-fungible physical objects," said Irving Wladawsky-Berger, research affiliate at MIT Sloan School of Management. "[Now] we are bringing more and more of the practices of the physical world into the digital world." [612] Since NFTs are digital, do we get anything real when we buy one? That's a question art lovers often ask NFT artists. How is a purchase of an NFT of a photo different from a download or screen snip of the same photo on social media? Here's Beeple's response:

> You'll always be able to view these things on Instagram, just like you can pull up a picture of the *Mona Lisa*. But that's very different [from] owning the *Mona Lisa*. You can pull up a picture of a bunch of different famous paintings ... but you don't own those paintings. And if you did own those paintings, then it would feel very different [from] looking at [them].[613]

But Beeple himself has reservations about selling digits alone. He has offered physical versions of several NFTs along with locks of his hair: "With the physical piece, ... I'm trying to bring it back a little bit more to the traditional world of art. Don't worry about any of the blockchain stuff, you own this physical piece. It's signed by me and it's got authentication markers."[614]

NFTS AS ASSETS

On 21 March 2021, Jack Dorsey sold a tweet for $2.9 million.[615] It was an impressive tweet to be sure, the first one ever recorded—but what exactly did Dorsey sell, how could anyone own a tweet (let alone a signed tweet), and what did the buyer of that tweet come to possess? "What you're getting is real estate in your mind and other people's minds around this interaction," said Cameron Hejazi, whose company Cent auctioned off Dorsey's tweet.[616]

Strictly speaking, we're getting very little, and some might say nothing at all. The NFT of the tweet doesn't come with any rights the buyer can exercise—the buyer may not put it on a T-shirt and sell it. The copyright remains with Dorsey as the author of the tweet. Nor can the buyer order Twitter to take down the newly purchased tweet; Twitter's terms of use with the tweeter remain in full force. Asset-wise, the buyer's ownership amounts to bragging rights. To the skeptic, this vastly overpriced "nothingness" is the definitive evidence of a speculative asset bubble.

Yet there's more here than meets the eye. Joe Pine, co-author of the international best seller *The Experience Economy,* tweeted, "NFTs are digital memorabilia (a former oxymoron) of experiences, that in essence become experiences unto themselves."[617] That's the difference between an autographed baseball and one we can buy off the shelf. Physically, they're pretty much the same. Yet if it's a home-run baseball signed by the game-winning batter, the difference pricewise can be millions. The autographed baseball can be part of history, like Jack Dorsey's tweet.

Wladawsky-Berger concurred, suggesting that NFTs have similarities with autographed books, with the added benefits of proof of authenticity and ownership: "Dorsey's first ever tweet—I mean, it's historical, it's a collectible."[618] The same goes for a bottle of 46-year-old single malt scotch whiskey aged in Armagnac barrels. The legendary brand Glenfiddich partnered with BlockBar, an NFT marketplace for luxury spirits, to issue 15 NFTs of limited-edition liquor, where each NFT links to a specific bottle of Glenfiddich.[619]

That social experience is what's on offer. Whoever buys it buys something that connects people. It defines the owner as a collector, or it brings a fan closer to the all-star athlete. Someone may have a Picasso over the mantelpiece as a talking point, a chance to discuss art or impress others. Hejazi of Cent sees these assets as extensions of our identities and the relationships we have with others:

We have people reclaiming ownership of their data and what they create. ... You can put any type of arbitrary data into an NFT. The thing that makes an NFT an NFT is that it is unique. I

> would venture to say that the conversation that we're having right now is a one of one. There won't be another one. So, this container that captures this data is very generic and very flexible. What you build by putting it on a blockchain is this open graph of relationship data between people. That's the real value long term. It's not the fact that some high name celebrity is coming in and doing a drop.[620]

Today, the interactions among people are temporary. They're data exhaust. Yet, as customers and employees spend more time in digital spaces, organizations have opportunities to capture those data and preserve those relationships and interactions in a way that's meaningful to all parties. Said Hejazi, "The faster we can get to the point of making that data very available, produced at a very high rate on the public blockchain, the more that we can really start to understand the value that tokenization provides, which is immortalized interoperable relationships between people."[621] It's an amplifier of the social graph, of gaming activities, of the relationships and behaviors in online communities.

Canadian science fiction writer and futurist Karl Schroeder said objects on the blockchain are social constructs.[622] He illustrated using an example of the president of the United States. The president isn't a physical designation, said Schroeder. "There's no physics that could allow you to find the president of the United States."[623] Yet the designation is just as real. "The president of the United States still has an effect on the world regardless of whether you believe in him," he explained. [624] The presidential role is a purely social construct, and collective beliefs about that role give it its clout. It's no different for NFTs and cryptocurrencies. Said Schroeder:

> They are just as real and just as unreal as those social constructs. That could be read as disappointing in that there's something

evanescent, something fragile, about NFTs. They could go away at any minute, because we just have to decide that they go away. So if the social value collapses, then they collapse, too. On the other hand, while they are accepted, they are as real as you want them to be.[625]

Asking whether NFTs are real assets is the wrong question. Assets like money are social constructs, and in that way, they're not any different from NFTs or any less real. In an email to Satoshi Nakamoto regarding his work on Bitcoin, Dustin D. Trammell wrote, "The real trick will be to get people to actually value the Bitcoins so that they become currency," to which Satoshi responded, "If enough people think the same way, that becomes a self-fulfilling prophecy."[626]

With blockchain technologies, we can embed these social constructs in tangibles and intangibles and then manage them. In his short story, "The Suicide of Our Troubles," Schroeder illustrated how a blockchain-based pointer could personify mercury contamination in groundwater.[627] What does it mean? For starters, NFTs are not solely speculative assets but instruments for representing the value all around us, in every interaction—but not as Facebook does, trading in and profiting from our transactional data.

As Pine noted, NFTs are digital means to preserve experiences as we do when we take and share digital photographs. NFTs are a cryptographically secure means of customizing and personalizing consumer experiences with brands online and with merchandise—putting them in a social context or situating them in time and place—and a means of showing an affinity or preference to others in digital spaces. NFTs can represent anything that a society, a community, or a culture deems socially important. These are unmet needs and opportunities for entrepreneurs, franchises, artists, universities, clubs, governments, and consumer and business brands to connect with and mobilize fans, audiences, stakeholders, and each other through NFTs.

HOW NFTS ENGAGE COMMUNITIES

NFTs and other assets appear to play a catalytic role in many blockchain communities. They encourage economies of participation and help users engage with a community while giving the community's users a stake in its success. Actively harnessed, NFTs can form part of a positive feedback loop critical to the success of a community or even an entire ecosystem.

NFTS AS SELF-FULFILLING PROPHECIES

In many economic and social circumstances, beliefs alone may alter the course of events. For example, in complex social systems, merely believing in something (like prices of X will rise) can cause it to transpire if people are motivated to buy X as a result of that belief. Beeple is clearly familiar with the practice: "My work is going to be super f------ valuable in the future. I could be wrong. But right now, mathematically, it is stupid not to buy my artwork because all of it has gone up at least 300 percent or 400 percent immediately."[628]

As Satoshi Nakamoto recognized, a belief can serve as a *self-fulfilling prophecy*, which sociologist Robert K. Merton described as a belief about the future that alters the course of human conduct.[629] Others have called it *reflexivity*, defined as a circular relationship between cause and effect.[630] It's common in game theory, too, such as the prisoner's dilemma—where a player's beliefs and resulting choices affect the outcome of the game. NFTs play this role in many blockchain-related communities. It offers users skin in the game and a stake in a community's success. Actively harnessed as feedback loops, NFTs can help a community, or entire ecosystem, to succeed.

Hejazi explained how this process works between a fan and a creator when a fan purchases a piece of a creator's work (and NFTs can play similar roles in the purchase of land and other community assets):

The value might go up as the creator gets more reputable and that is indirectly an opportunity to invest in the creator. Now it's not a pure investment, because the first reason you're doing this is to support the creators and to support their work. But it's that indirect opportunity where you get recognition as a fan economically, and in the form of status later, once they become something bigger than they are today.[631]

NFTS AS MODELS OF ENGAGEMENT

For some, owning NFTs is about speculative possibilities and profits; for others, an NFT is a close personal connection to something or someone of interest (like a baseball card for a collector); or it can be about belonging, reputation, or a rite of passage. NFTs can reinforce all these motives, orchestrating community functioning and engagement and addressing, for example, the United Nations sustainable development goals such as climate action.[632]

For example, Coca-Cola partnered with the blockchain start-up OpenSea to create "Friendship NFTs to commemorate National Friendship Day and raise funds for the Special Olympics International. Josh Schwarber, global digital design senior director for Coca-Cola, said NFTs give the storied brand a new way to connect with consumers in the metaverse. Coca-Cola wanted to "bring people together through unique, surprise-and-delight moments" in the virtual world, not just the real world.[633] In an online auction, the winning bid was $575,883.[634]

Similarly, the Campbell Soup Company commissioned street artist Sophia Chang to create 100 pieces of art codified in an NFT collection titled *AmeriCANa — SOPHIA CHANG X CAMPBELL'S*.[635] Dole teamed up with artist David Datuna to create an NFT collection raising awareness of food insecurity, with proceeds going to the Boys & Girls Clubs of America.[636] Sunbeam Products spun up an NFT on OpenSea to commemorate the 50th anniversary of its

Crockpot brand.[637] Taco Bell's taco NFTs sold out in 30 minutes, generating extra revenue for the fast food chain; Microsoft rewarded players of its Azure Space Mystery game with NFTs that unlocked collectibles within the Minecraft gaming experience; and Nike paired physical shoes with digital versions in NFTs after acquiring the patent for the blockchain-based sneakers, CryptoKicks.[638]

Healthy communities may have aspects of investment and speculative behavior, but that shouldn't drive them. Taken to an extreme, such behavior can be toxic—ultimately hindering true community building. Hejazi said NFTs are best suited to "creator led communities, where it's not just a group of people trying to make money; rather, there's a clear goal, which is to fund the creator, and community members are gathered around in helping to support creators is a very natural place for NFTs to fit in and unlock that monetization potential."[639] It's a natural fit in these cases because, as Hejazi said, "The fans already love the work that the creators are doing; and a lot of times, it's happening for free."[640]

It's also intimately tied to social capital. Just as ownership of an NFT or participating in a creator's work serves a social function in creator-led communities, NFTs may be interesting to consider in other circumstances, too: employee engagement, for example. Corporations already make considerable use of these social cues today—whether it's by sharing the employee of the month, an elite sales achievement, or a luxury watch given out at retirement. NFTs could serve some of these same purposes and are well-suited for visibility within digital and collaborative tools.

NFTS FOR COMMODITIES

The gains from mass-produced commodities have been astounding. Costs of production plummeted while speed increased. Most importantly, production moved out of the minds of skilled craftsmen and into the system itself, allowing unskilled workers to produce complex products on the other side of the planet. Today, our supply chains and manufacturing systems have evolved to produce items of such complexity that no skilled worker could easily build, say, an iPhone from scratch (unless the worker had a pile of old iPhones for parts).[641]

Mass manufactured goods and the systems that produced them resulted from a series of complementary innovations over time: a division of labor; preassembly of parts; machine gauged and inter-changeable parts; a continuous flow of work over rail systems, through assembly lines, and by conveyor belt; flexible manufacturing; and three-dimensional printing with minimal waste.[642] "If you can digi-tize it, then you can customize it," wrote management author Joe Pine in his book, *Mass Customization*.[643]

THE MYTH OF MASS COMMODIFICATION

The truth is that no two physical items are identical. The makers of most of what we own have a degree of manufacturing *tolerance*—which is a defined range of measurements in which a part must fall for it to function properly—and their products and product parts are interchangeable.[644] We can quickly establish this fact by measur-ing identical valves by the same manufacturer. They appear the same, but when we weigh them with a precision jeweler's scale, the differ-ences become apparent.

Other categories of commodities have such variations. In agricul-ture, for example, one farmer may use chemical fertilizers, pesticides, and herbicides to protect plant growth, whereas another farmer uses compost and manure to fertilize the soil, birds and insects to gobble up pests, and crop rotation to manage weeds.[645] The latter method is organic: it increases nutrients in the food and decreases human expo-sure to toxins in the environment.

Emma Weston, CEO of AgriDigital, explained that the global supply chain for grain strips away these valuable differences for expe-diency: if the grain is the same grade, then it is completely fungible.

Weston said, "There's a trend to a level of decommodification, and NFTs potentially support that."[646]

For example, we could assign an NFT to a batch of grain that captures unique and valuable properties. Weston explained, "If you have an NFT representing a non-fungible asset in the real or the digital world, you can actually fractionalize that NFT, and the fractions can then be exchanged for each other. It becomes fungible." We could also aggregate and fractionalize NFTs. That's possible within the ERC-1155 specification since it "can represent any number of fungible and non-fungible token types."[647] NFTs can help digitize supply chains and aggregate data across many fragmented systems because the relevant asset data reside within the tokens, not in data silos.

FROM GLOBAL SUPPLY CHAINS TO LOCAL MAKERSPACES

Imagine if designers could have direct relationships with the buyers of the products they designed, from automobiles and home furnishings to toys, footwear, and fashion, whether those are virtual or physical objects (Table 8-3).[648] Designer Misha Kahn, best known for his bold and imaginative furniture, issued his own series of NFTs auctioned by Christie's in August 2021. Each lot represented an individual frame of one of Kahn's 13-second video animations in which characters morph into furniture. Each NFT came with an additive-manufactured version of the piece and a 3D design file for printing additional copies locally.

"My biggest guilt in making objects is the globalized supply chain and heavy shipping ecosystem," said Kahn. "You become part of this insane carbon footprint."[649] In his view, the process is impersonal—buyers have no relationship with the objects they buy and are therefore more likely to discard them, contributing to the global waste problem.[650] "The idea is that the NFT is a contract and that the owner can make copies of it without ever affecting the actual work," said Kahn. "With the NFT, you get this asset that you could put in a digital landscape. It could be incorporated into a video game, movie or any place an avatar lives, or it could be fully printed and functional."[651] If the NFT owner prints a copy through Kahn's studio, then Kahn will authorize it as an authentic Kahn. The point is, the owner plays an active role in creation, usage, and transfer.

TABLE 8-3
ADDITIONAL NFT USE CASES

CATEGORY	USE CASE DESCRIPTION
Apparel/fashion	Nike acquired a patent for this use case to tokenize footwear.[652] The associated token CryptoKick appears to be part collectible/part title and hints at a genetics-like system to generate shoe offspring.[653]
Automobile	Barrett-Jackson auctioned off four NFTs paired to vehicles (including video footage, images, and illustrations) that it had sold in charity auctions.[654] The automotive sector may consider NFTs for title, provenance, maintenance records, vehicle ID numbers (VINs), awards, and features-as-a-service.[655]
Credentials	NFTs can confer status or credentials and represent memberships, IDs, tickets, or other certifications.[656]
Decentralized finance (DeFi)	The finance sector is well known for securitizing assets and creating derivatives such as mortgage-backed securities and collateralized debt obligations.[657] NFTs expand the range of assets to securitize, customize, and derive additional value peer to peer, as allowable under the law and regulations.[658]
Intellectual property (conventional)	Trademarks, copyright, and patents are well-established forms of IP ownership. NFTs could potentially confer licenses or titles not just of copyrighted works but also trademarks and patents as with 3D printing design files.[659] For example, IPwe is working with IBM to create an NFT market for patents.[660]
Intellectual property (new applications)	Some forms of IP (e.g., traditional knowledge or trade secrets) are unrecognized or difficult to protect under current IP law.[661] Enterprise could use NFTs to represent and confer customized bundles of these rights or licenses.
Natural assets/physical commodities	Examples like AgriDigital show how agriculture and natural asset sectors could represent commodities like grain and timber via NFTs for use in finance and insurance contracts.
Real estate	While some businesses have used NFTs to represent title over digital real estate such as Mars House, enterprise could use NFTs to represent other legal elements tied to real estate such as liens, titles, and easements.[662]

Weston asked whether NFTs were true titles and fully negotiable instruments like drafts, checks, promissory notes, or certificates of deposit—or representations of those instruments held elsewhere in print or as a digital record.[663] The former opens up interesting opportunities, as it becomes a negotiable asset class for financing via secondary markets as well as new kinds of derivatives.

Kia Mosayeri, product manager at the digital currency payment processor BitGo, told *American Banker*, "If the NFT is something of value, it can be borrowed against or used as a way to pay someone as part of a fraction of a collective."[664] Grain could become a value-creating negotiable instrument, meaning that farmers could use it in multiple supply chains and secondary markets along with other financial instruments. The International Insurance Society sees NFTs as a means of creating parametric insurance contracts (where specific events trigger pre-specified insurance payouts) and increasing data transparency among small and medium-sized enterprises transacting in global supply chains.[665]

IMPLEMENTATION CHALLENGES OF NFTS

As with many new technologies, NFTs raise a great many new questions for their early adopters. Nevertheless, who's selling which bundle of rights with an NFT? What sorts of legal and regulatory unknowns do issuers and buyers face in marketplaces for NFTs? What promises does a creator make in issuing an NFT, and who or what enforces those promises? Who exactly owns these assets, how does the law treat them, and how should buyers and sellers account for them?

LEGAL AND REGULATORY UNKNOWNS

Today, crypto itself involves many legal and regulatory unknowns. Brian Armstrong, the founder of Coinbase, discussed these issues on

Twitter: "There is not a ton of regulatory clarity today in the [United States] because crypto is not just one thing. Some cryptos might be securities (SEC), some are commodities (CFTC), some are currencies/property (Treasury/IRS), and some are none of the above."[666] These uncertainties affect NFTs as well.

Even whether NFTs are securities is not entirely clear. Dapper Labs, inventor of CryptoKitties and NBA Top Shot, recently contended with that question when one customer filed a class action lawsuit against the company. The suit alleged that the company's NFTs were securities because they constituted "an investment of money in a common enterprise with a reasonable expectation of profit to be derived from the efforts of others."[667]

Individual issuers have come under fire as well. Toronto artist Krista Kim sold an NFT titled *Mars House* for $500,000 on the SuperRare marketplace.[668] The house is an attractive, modern-looking 3D design that the contracted 3D modeler Mateo Sanz Pedemonte described as meditative. IP rights to the work, however, are under dispute. Pedemonte claimed that, though he was a freelancer, his modeling was not work for hire that would have given Krista Kim full copyright and design file ownership.[669]

So which IP rights must proprietors or enterprises hold that would entitle them to issue and sell an NFT of a work? When do these rights accrue to consumers? Consider the publishing industry. Buyers of digital music or e-book files cannot resell these digital assets as they could physical copies such as bound books or vinyl records because the first-sale doctrine applies only to physical forms of copyrighted works.[670] But what if the publishing upgraded all its digital files to NFTs, where the terms of resale provide some percentage of the funds received to those who would typically get a share of royalty revenue? It's a situation that may need some complex legal untangling and that highlights the importance of due diligence when it comes to the minting of NFTs.[671]

TAX AND ACCOUNTING UNKNOWNS

While speculating on tax and accounting implications goes beyond the expertise of this author (and it's always best to consult a professional), it's useful to point out some existing practices that may help ground the answers. First, NFTs *are* assets, and therefore, we treat them as property for tax purposes.[672] The most difficult question remains, though: who owns the rights to minting a particular NFT? The publishing industry has experienced disruptive new changes before, so ascertaining new categories of rights and opportunities is something publishers and artists alike are already familiar with.

For example, *merchandising* has become an important (and extremely profitable) part of the film industry. As a result, many contractual agreements have clauses that allocate those merchandising rights. Same with the ownership of new kinds of digital ownership rights and channels. Often, contracts may contain information about subsidiary rights.[673] While every contract is different, a frequent default appears to be for these rights to accrue to the publisher. Creators will want to take a closer look at the language in their publishing agreements and see whether subsidiary rights are addressed, and whether NFTs might fit in under existing definitions of merchandising or other relevant categories. Many creators may decide not to license such rights, particularly if they have plans regarding NFTs. As one article states, "There's no legal obligation for authors to license merchandising rights to the publisher at all," and default arrangements are often a windfall for publishers.[674]

LACK OF DIGITAL TECHNOLOGY EXPERTISE

With great power comes great responsibility, and that's particularly true when it comes to both crypto and NFTs. Technology expertise matters. The power of immutability means that once a key is lost it's gone forever, so even the basics of key management are important considerations. Institutions and companies are vulnerable, too. The MakerDAO (designed to support stablecoins, which are cryptocurrencies designed to hold a stable value) is only one example where a complex written-in-stone smart contract created unforeseen circumstances and a significant loss (in this case, a sharp market drop followed by traffic congestion, which prevented oracles from providing accurate contract pricing that led to millions in losses).[675] And then there's downright theft, like the example at popular NFT seller Nifty Gateway where people lost access to their credentials following a hack.[676]

Last, it's not just familiarity with NFTs and smart contracts, but technical expertise regarding digital assets themselves. When Christie's announced an NFT auction of Andy Warhol's digital work created on a Commodore Amiga and "restored … in a digital format that can be accessed with today's technology," some critics complained that the digital copies were no longer the low-resolution originals but versions upscaled to a higher resolution.[677] Still, they sold for $3.37 million.[678] In cases where the stakes are high, attention to detail matters: would-be bidders must have some means of verifying that the parties involved are authorized to mint an NFT for an original work and that the digital version embedded in the NFT correctly represents that work. At these early formative stages for NFTs, avoiding unnecessary missteps is key.

CONCLUSIONS AND RECOMMENDATIONS

Since the Blockchain Research Institute's first publication on NFTs in 2019, the market for these digital assets has changed dramatically. Popularity of NFTs has soared, but with more mature tools, infrastructure, and use cases. This maturity has catalyzed the interest of mainstream players and incumbents seeking to understand the enterprise value of NFTs and how it might intersect with industry applications. The good news is that we are beginning to see serious enterprise use cases; no industry or sector has fallen behind this opportunity. So, what can entrepreneurs, corporations, and government agencies take away from this fledgling industry and the areas in which it's generating value today? Here are some takeaways.

Enterprise can use NFTs to monetize former digital wastelands. Many copyright holders (even famous ones) related how they struggled to make a living from digital work, and how NFTs were able to change that. The same is true in every digital space. NFTs can breathe life into new monetization opportunities that simply could not exist without NFTs. Individuals and organizations have an opportunity to tokenize tangible and intangible assets such as customized products, specially grown crops, limited editions, IP, reputation, conversations, and more.

Variation creates value. The last 100 years have been about commodities and mass manufacturing. NFTs are helping to reverse those trends, moving to a future where variation is more common and even desirable. By reversing many of the ownership and information management practices that supported commoditization and mass manufacturing, NFTs may inspire us to develop new ways of organizing work, managing people, and creating value.

Tokenization can help with fractionalization and securitization. Developing more granular specifications of assets—tangible assets such as grains or lumber and intangible assets such as patents—as well as the portfolio of rights associated with them (e.g., leasing or licensing over time) can help with P2P transactions and collaboration. Think "peer-to-peer Bowie Bond."[679] With fractionalization, community members can each own a portion of a shared resource and can participate in its governance. With securitization, we can derive other financial instruments from these assets, and those derivatives can generate untapped value.

Today, NFT rights are better, but they're still a mess. The explosion of NFT issuance and the speculative hype around them are raising important questions about ownership and rights. Both buyers and sellers must think more systematically about NFTs and the bundle of rights they want to transfer or acquire. Lack of specificity around these rights harms all parties to NFT transactions, and developing expertise and marketplace best practices will help NFT adoption in general. Those seeking to enter the NFT market as intermediaries will find ample opportunities to differentiate themselves through greater transparency and participation in governance such as standards development and policy setting.

NFTs are tools for community building. Brands, platforms, and companies have an extraordinary opportunity to benefit from the engagement and community patterns that exist in NFT communities. The catalytic nature of NFTs helps produce deeper levels of engagement and helps reinforce communities and ecosystems. It's a tremendous unmet need, and an opportunity for franchises, publishers, and brands to use NFTs as a vehicle for connecting to existing fans and audiences.

Early days means it's still a land grab. Today, most digital brands and assets are not effectively monetized. In the same way that Valuables/Cent is monetizing the formerly unexplored landscape of tweets, a large number of domains and areas of application still warrant further exploration. From social media and online gaming to enterprise software and physical goods, there are many use cases to explore.

ACRONYMS AND ABBREVIATIONS

AAVE, native token of Aave's pooled lending protocols

AI, artificial intelligence

aka, also known as

AML, anti-money laundering

AMM, automated market maker

API, application programming interface

ASIC, application-specific integrated circuit

ASX, Australian Securities Exchange

ATM, automated teller machine

ATOM, native token of Cosmos Network

AVAX, native token of Avalanche

B2B, business-to-business

BBVA, formerly a subsidiary of Banco Bilbao Vizcaya Argentaria

BFT, Byzantine-fault tolerant consensus engine

BNB, Binance Coin, a crypto-exchange token

BPaaS, blockchain platform-as-a-service

BTC, bitcoin

CAPP, Canadian Association of Petroleum Producers

CBDC, central bank digital currency

Cboe, Chicago Board Options Exchange

CCP, central counterparty clearings

CDM, Common Domain Model

CDP, collateralized debt position

CEO, chief executive officer

CFD, contract for difference

CFTC, US Commodity Futures Trading Commission

CHF, Swiss Franc

COMP, native token of Compound's pooled lending protocols

COVID-19, coronavirus disease 2019, short for the severe acute respiratory syndrome coronavirus 2 (SARS-CoV-2) discovered in 2019

CSA, Canadian Securities Administrators

DAC, decentralized autonomous corporation

DAI, MakerDAO's stablecoin, pegged to USD

DAML, digital asset modeling language

DAO, decentralized autonomous organization

dapp, decentralized application

d/b/a, doing business as

DCEP, digital currency electronic payment in China

DEEP Centre, Centre for Digital Entrepreneurship and Economic Performance

DeFi, decentralized finance

Deloitte, Deloitte Touche Tohmatsu

DEX, decentralized exchange

DINO, decentralized in name only

DLT, distributed ledger technology

DNA, deoxyribonucleic acid

DOT, native token of Polkadot Network

DTCC, Depository Trust & Clearing Corporation

DYDX, native token of dYdX, meaning "the derivative of y with respect to x" in mathematical terms

E&P, exploration and production companies

EMD, exempt market dealer

ERC-20, Ethereum request for comment 20, a fungible token standard

ETF, exchange traded fund

ETH, ether, native token of Ethereum

EY, Ernst & Young

FCA, UK Financial Conduct Authority

fintech, financial technology

FpML, financial products markup language

FSB, Financial Stability Board

FTT, FTX Token, a crypto-exchange token

GAN, Generative Adversarial Network

GBP, British pound sterling

GDP, gross domestic product

GDPR, General Data Protection Regulation

GSC, global stablecoin

GUSD, Gemini Dollar

HTTP, hypertext transfer protocol

IBC, inter-blockchain communication

ICF, Interchain Foundation

ID, identity

IETF, Internet Engineering Task Force

Inria, French National Institute for Research in Computer Science and Automation

IoT, Internet of Things

IP, intellectual property

IPO, initial public offering

IRS, Internal Revenue Service

ISDA, International Swaps and Derivatives Association

JSON file, JavaScript Object Notation file

KPI, key performance indicator

KPMG, Klynveld Peat Marwick Goerdeler

KRW, Korean Republic won (₩)

kWh, kilowatt-hours

KYC, know-your-customer

MANA, Decentraland's native cryptocurrency

MATIC, Polygon's native token

mGOOGL, Mirrored Google, a synthetic security

mTSLA, Mirrored Tesla, a synthetic security

multisig, multisignature

Nasdaq, once an acronym for National Association of Securities Dealers Automated Quotations, developed by NASD, National Association of Securities Dealers

NAST, natural asset security tokens

NAT, natural asset token

NBA, National Basketball Association

NFL, National Football League

NFT, non-fungible token

NRT, natural resource token

NYDFS, New York State Department of Financial Services

NYSE, New York Stock Exchange

OCC, US Office of the Comptroller of the Currency

OGBiF, oil and gas blockchain-integrated framework

OTC, over-the-counter

P2P, peer-to-peer

PERP, native token of Perpetual Protocol

Perps, perpetual futures contracts

POC, proof of concept

PoS, proof of stake

PoW, proof of work

PPA, power purchase agreement

PPE, personal protective equipment

prop, proprietary, as in prop trading desk

PTAC, Petroleum Technology Alliance Canada

PwC, PricewaterhouseCoopers

QE, quantitative easing

QUICK, token for QuickSwap decentralized exchange

RARI, token for Rarible investment aggregator

RINO, Republican in name only

ROI, return on investment

SDK, software development kit

SDR, special drawing rights

SEC, US Securities and Exchange Commission

SME, small and medium-sized enterprise

SMTP, simple mail transfer protocol

SOTA, smart offtake agreements

SUSHI, token for SushiSwap decentralized exchange

SWIFT, Society for Worldwide Interbank Financial Telecommunications

SX, native token of SX Network

TARP, Troubled Asset Relief Program

T-bills, Treasury bills

TCP/IP, transmission control protocol/Internet protocol

TradFi, traditional finance

TVL, total value locked

tWh, terawatt-hours

UNI, token for Uniswap decentralized exchange

USDC, Centre Consortium's stablecoin, USD Coin

USDP, Paxos Trust Company's US dollar–backed stablecoin

USDT, Tether's stablecoin

UST, TerraUSD, Terra Luna's stablecoin

UX, user experiences

WBG, World Bank Group

XCHF, Blockimmo's stablecoin

YFI, pronounced "Wi-Fi," token for Yearn Finance investment aggregator

ZEC, Zcash token

ABOUT THE BLOCKCHAIN RESEARCH INSTITUTE

Co-founded in 2017 by Don and Alex Tapscott, the Blockchain Research Institute is an independent, global think tank established to help realize the new promise of the digital economy. For five years now, we have been investigating the transformative and disruptive potential of distributed ledger technologies on business, government, and society.

Our syndicated research program, funded by major corporations, government agencies, and blockchain innovators, aims to fill a large gap in the global understanding of blockchain protocols, applications, and ecosystems. We look at their strategic and operational implications for enterprise executives, supply chains, and industry verticals—including financial services, manufacturing, retail, energy and the climate crisis, technology, media and education, telecommunications, healthcare and the pandemic, public services and the institutions of democracy.

Our global team of blockchain experts focus on informing leaders of the economic opportunities and challenges of this nascent technology. Research areas include the transformation of industries, the enterprise, and government; the regulation of innovation and the use of data, digital currencies, and self-sovereign identities; and the trivergence of blockchain, AI, and IoT.

Deliverables include lighthouse cases, big idea white papers, research briefs, roundtable reports, infographics, videos, and webinars. Our findings are initially proprietary to our members, then released under a Creative Commons license to help achieve our mission. To find out more, please visit

blockchainresearchinstitute.org

ABOUT THE CONTRIBUTORS

MOHAMED EL-MASRI

Mohamed El-Masri is the founder and CEO of PermianChain Technologies Inc. His expertise is in corporate finance, alternative investments, tokenization, and blockchain. In early 2018, El-Masri embarked on a journey to change the dynamics of wealth creation, generation, and preservation. "I am proposing a radical change to the global socioeconomic construct, but not without serious considerations toward global energy sustainability. That's why I found bitcoin to be the purest form of treasury that contributes to global energy sustainability."

El-Masri is also the director and CEO of Brox Equity Ltd., a new-era energy company investing in wasted/stranded energy for low-cost power and carbon-neutral bitcoin mining. El-Masri earned a diploma in sociology from Vanier College. He attended numerous political science and economics courses at Concordia University before continuing to receive Canadian securities qualifications from the Canadian Securities Institute. He holds a general securities qualification certificate with the Capital Market Authority of Riyadh, KSA. He is certified in corporate finance regulations with the UK Chartered Institute for Securities and Investments.

J. CHRISTOPHER GIANCARLO

Dubbed "CryptoDad" for his celebrated call on the US Congress to respect a new generation's interest in cryptocurrency, the Honorable J. Christopher Giancarlo served as thirteenth chairman of the US Commodity Futures Trading Commission. Considered one of "the most influential individuals in financial regulation," Giancarlo also served as a member of the US Financial Stability Oversight Committee, the President's Working Group on Financial Markets, and the Executive Board of the International Organization of Securities Commissions.

Giancarlo is the author of *CryptoDad: The Fight for the Future of Money*, an account of his oversight of the world's first regulated market for bitcoin derivatives and the coming transformation of financial services, including the most valuable thing of all: money. Giancarlo is senior counsel to the international law firm, Willkie Farr & Gallagher. He is also a board director, advisor, and angel investor in numerous technology and financial services companies. In addition, Giancarlo is a co-founder of the Digital Dollar Project, a not-for-profit initiative to advance exploration of a US central bank digital currency. Twitter: @GiancarloMKTS.

ALAN MAJER

Alan Majer is the founder of Good Robot. For the first half of his career, Majer worked as a technology researcher and writer, helping to identify cutting-edge technology and business innovations. Today, he also works with technology hands on, exploring the potential of AI, robotics, blockchain, and the metaverse. The result is exciting new opportunities to innovate and transform client experiences, and the ability to combine strategy and research activities with a real-world approach to their implementation. Majer is an active member of the local "maker" scene, frequenting spaces like HackLab.TO and InterAccess. He holds an MBA from McGill University.

MASSIMO MORINI

Massimo Morini is chief economist of the Algorand Foundation. His role involves the design and evolution of blockchain network incentives and community distribution frameworks, and the analysis, research, and development of the decentralized Algorand market and resources. Before that, he was head of rates and credit modeling at Intesa, Italy's largest bank. He is a professor of fixed income at

Bocconi University and teaches blockchain and financial markets at universities in Italy, Switzerland, and the United Kingdom.

In the blockchain space, Morini was a board member of R3, where he headed valuation, collateral, and risk management, and co-authored the R3 report on "Implementing Derivatives Clearing on Distributed Ledger Technology Platforms" with Colin Platt and Peter Csoka. Later, he co-developed smart contracts for collateralized derivatives with provably honest computation on Ethereum. His papers on smart contracts have been reported in *CoinDesk* and cited in official government proceedings.

ALYZE SAM

Alyze Sam is a blockchain strategist, a novel educator, an award-winning author, and a vehemently driven advocate. She is founder and chief executive officer of Tech & Authors, a collective of technology and manuscript experts, and co-founder of GIVE Nation, a children's financial literacy protocol that rewards altruism. Sam has remained passionate about her director roles at several blockchain companies, including Constellation, Lattice Exchange, NewLife.ai, and PAC Global. She is a current stakeholder and former director of the World Ethical Data Forum, and she serves as a social impact advisor to the nonprofits Women in Blockchain International, Blockchance.eu, and the Liberland Foundation Aide. Sam writes for over a dozen tech magazines, and she is author of the *Complete Stablecoin Guide* (2020), *Stablecoin Economy: Ultimate Guide to Secure Digital Finance* (2020), and *Stablecoin Evolution: The Overall Unbiased History and Projected Future of Financial Technology* (2022).

ALEX TAPSCOTT

Alex Tapscott is an entrepreneur, author, and seasoned capital markets professional focused on the impact of the emerging technologies (such as blockchain and cryptocurrencies) on business, government, and society. He is managing director of the Digital Asset Group, a division of Ninepoint Partners LP, an investment firm with $8 billion in assets under management and institutional contract. Ninepoint's Bitcoin ETF (BITC-TSX) is the first carbon-neutral spot Bitcoin ETF in the world. Tapscott also chairs the advisory council of Prophecy DeFi (PDFI-CSE). He is co-author (with Don Tapscott) of the critically acclaimed nonfiction best seller *Blockchain Revolution* (New York: Penguin Portfolio, 2016 and 2018), which has been translated into more than 15 languages and has sold more than 500,000 copies worldwide.[680] He also edited and wrote a preface to *Financial Services Revolution* on how DeFi is transforming the financial industry.[681]

Tapscott is sought after worldwide for his expertise by business and government audiences. He has delivered over 200 lectures and executive briefings at such firms as Goldman Sachs (*Talks at GS*), Google, Allianz, IBM, Microsoft, and Accenture.[682] His TEDx talk, "Blockchain is Eating Wall Street" has been viewed over 808,000 times. Tapscott has also written for the *New York Times*, *Harvard Business Review*, *Globe and Mail*, *National Post*, and many other publications. In 2017, Tapscott co-founded the Blockchain Research Institute, a global think tank investigating blockchain strategies, opportunities, and use cases.[683] Previously, Tapscott was director of institutional equity sales at Canaccord Genuity. Tapscott is a graduate of Amherst College (Cum Laude) and a CFA charter holder. He lives in Toronto.

DON TAPSCOTT

Don Tapscott is CEO of the Tapscott Group, executive chairman of the Blockchain Research Institute, and one of the world's leading authorities on the impact of technology on business and society. He has authored more than 16 books, including *Wikinomics: How Mass Collaboration Changes Everything* (with Anthony Williams), which has been translated into over 25 languages. He coined the term, "The Digital Economy," in his 1994 book of that title, and many of his big ideas are part of the business vernacular today.

In 2016, he co-authored *Blockchain Revolution: How the Technology Behind Bitcoin and Other Cryptocurrencies Is Changing the World* with Alex Tapscott. His new book, *Supply Chain Revolution: How Blockchain Technology Is Transforming the Digital Flow of Assets*, debuted as the "#1 New Release" in the commerce category on Amazon.com (June 2020); and *Platform Revolution: Blockchain Technology as the Operating System of the Digital Age* launched as the "#1 New Release" in management science (Nov. 2021). In 2019, then-ranked as the #2 living business thinker, Don was inducted into the Thinkers50 Hall of Fame. He is an adjunct professor at INSEAD and former two-term chancellor of Trent University in Ontario.

ANTHONY D. WILLIAMS

Anthony D. Williams is co-founder and president of the Digital Entrepreneurship and Economic Performance (DEEP) Centre and an internationally recognized authority on the digital revolution, innovation, and creativity in business and society. He is co-author (with Don Tapscott) of the groundbreaking best seller, *Wikinomics: How Mass Collaboration Changes Everything*, and its sequel, *Macrowikinomics: New Solutions for a Connected Planet*. Among other appointments, Williams has served as an expert adviser to the Markle Foundation's Initiative for America's Economic Future, a senior fellow with the Lisbon Council in Brussels and the Institute on Governance in Ottawa, and chief adviser to Brazil's Free Education Project, a national strategy to equip two million young Brazilians with the skills required for a twenty-first-century workforce. His work on technology and innovation has been featured in such publications as the *Huffington Post, Harvard Business Review*, and the *Globe and Mail*.

ANDREW FENNELL YOUNG

Andrew F. Young is CEO of Layer2 Blockchain and a co-founder of SX Network (SportX), a DeFi prediction market and blockchain. Young has been working full time in the crypto space since 2017. He specializes in the analysis of economic incentives and tokenomics of new DeFi projects. Young engages regularly in DeFi-related podcasts and interviews and often publishes research reports examining the crypto space.

ACKNOWLEDGMENTS

Special thanks to Galia Benartzi, Ethan Buchman, Charlie Morris, Do Kwon, Sandeep Nailwal, Andrew Young, and Peng Zhong for their insights into digital assets; to tech investor Kevin Rooke for his initial research on Cosmos and Polkadot, to those Kevin interviewed (Ethan Buchman and Jack Zampolin), and to Michael Perklin for his feedback; to Chris Giancarlo for a riveting conversation on CBDCs; to Koosha Azim and Adam Alonzi for their editorial and design expertise, and to Patrick Devereaux, Jean-Phillippe Beaudet, and Tommy Austin for their contributions to the chapter on stablecoins; to Lee Braine of Barclays, the Nivaura Team (Dr. Avtar Singh Sehra, Dr. Vic Arulchandran), and the MakerDAO team on financial derivatives; to Cameron Hejazi, Witek Radomski, Christian S., Karl Schroeder, Emma Weston, Irving Wladawsky-Berger, and Gauthier Zuppinger for their insights into NFTs and the NFT market; and to BRI editor-in-chief Kirsten Sandberg for pulling all the pieces together.

We thank the Blockchain Research Institute's members for their engagement in our programs: Accenture, Aon, Bank of Canada, Bell Canada, BPC Banking Technologies, Brightline (a Project Management Institute initiative), Canada Health Infoway, Canadian Imperial Bank of Commerce, Capgemini, Catallaxy/ Raymond Chabot Grant Thornton, Centrica, Cimcorp, Cisco Systems Inc., City of Toronto, the Coca-Cola Company, Deloitte, Delta Air Lines Inc., Depository Trust & Clearing Corporation, ExxonMobil Global Service Company, FedEx Corporate Services, Fidelity Investments, Government of Ontario, Gowling WLG, IBM, ICICI Bank, INSEAD, Interac, Intuit, IOHK, ISED Canada, JumpStart, KPMG, Loblaw Companies, Manulife, Microsoft, MKS (Switzerland) SA, Moog, Nasdaq, Navigator, Ontario Ministry of Health and Long-Term Care, Orange, Pfizer, Philip Morris International Management, PepsiCo, PNC Bank,

Procter & Gamble, Reliance Industries, Revenu Québec, Salesforce, SAP SE, Standard Bank, Sun Life Financial, Tata Consultancy Services, Teck Resources, TELUS, Tencent, Thomson Reuters, TMX Group, University Health Network, University of Arkansas, University of Texas-Dallas, and WISeKey.

We are grateful for our pioneer members: Access Copyright, Artlery, Attest, Ava Labs, Blockchain Guru, Blockchain Technology Partners, Bloq, CarbonX, Cityzeen, Collider-X, Cosmos, Decentral Inc., EVRYTHNG, GuildOne, Hedera Hashgraph, Huobi, Icon, Jumpstart, Liechtenstein Cryptoassets Exchange, LongHash, Matic, Medicalchain, Navigator Ltd., NEM Foundation, Numeracle, Orion, Ownum, Paycase Financial, PermianChain Technologies Inc., Polymath, Prophecy DeFi, SGInnovate, Shyft, Slant AG, Solve.Care, Sovereign Wallet Network and MetaMUI, SpaceChain, Stride Africa, Sweetbridge, Telos Foundation, Tendermint, Veriphi, and YouBase.

Thanks, too, to our affiliate organizations and global partners: Alastria, BeInCrypto, Blockchain For Energy, Blockchain in Transport Alliance, Blockchain Industry Group, Blockchain Research Institute Nanjing, Blockwall Management (BRI Europe), BOSAGORA Foundation (BRI Korea), BRI Brazil, Chamber of Digital Commerce, Coalition of Automated Legal Applications, Enterprise Ethereum Alliance, Government Blockchain Association, Healthcare Information and Management Systems Society, Hyperledger hosted by The Linux Foundation, Institute for Austrian and International Law, the InterWork Alliance, Konnect & Co. (BRI Middle East), Liechtenstein Bankers Association, Loudhailer, South African National Blockchain Alliance, and the Standard Bank Group (BRI Africa).

NOTES

1. Nick Szabo, "Smart Contracts: Building Blocks for Digital Markets," 1996. Rob van Son, University of Amsterdam, tinyurl.com/y79krqzl, accessed 2 June 2020.

2. Satoshi Nakamoto to Hal Finney, "Re: Bitcoin P2P E-cash Paper," *Cryptography Mailing List*, Metzger, Dowdeswell & Co. LLC, 14 Nov. 2008 (14:29:22). www.mail-archive.com/cryptography%40metzdowd. com/msg10001.html, accessed 16 Oct. 2021.

3. Satoshi Nakamoto, "Bitcoin: A Peer-to-Peer Electronic Cash System," White Paper, *Bitcoin.org*, 1 Nov. 2008. www.bitcoin.org/bitcoin.pdf.

4. Matthew Martin, "Difference between Website and Web Application (Web App)," *Guru99.com*, Guru99 Tech Pvt. Ltd., updated 7 Oct. 2021. www.guru99.com/difference-web-application-website.html, accessed 16 Oct. 2021.

5. "The Top 10 Most Significant Data Breaches of 2020," *Aria Cybersecurity Solutions Blog*, 29 April 2021. blog.ariacybersecurity.com/blog/the-top-10-most-significant-data-breaches-of-2020, accessed 15 Oct. 2021.

6. Chris Dixon (@cdixon), Twitter post, 20 Sept. 2021 (2:55 pm). twitter. com/cdixon/status/1440026971979800579, accessed 16 Oct. 2021.

7. Chris Dixon (@cdixon), Twitter post, 20 Sept. 2021 (2:56 pm). twitter. com/cdixon/status/1440026974903230464, and Chris Dixon (@ cdixon), Twitter post, 20 Sept. 2021 (2:56 pm). twitter.com/cdixon/ status/1440026978048958467, accessed 16 Oct. 2021.

8. DeFi Pulse, n.d. defipulse.com, accessed 16 Oct. 2021.

9. "Top 100 DeFi Coins by Market Capitalization," *CoinGecko.com*, Gecko Labs Pte. Ltd., as of 30 Sept. 2021. www.coingecko.com/en/defi.

10. Sandeep Nailwal, email exchange with Alex Tapscott, 2 Oct. 2021.

11. Ben Davenport, "What Is Multisig and What Can It Do?" Coin Center, 1 Jan. 2015. www.coincenter.org/education/advanced-topics/multi-sig, accessed 15 Oct. 2021.

12. When the NASDAQ exchange began operations in 1971, the name was an acronym for the National Association of Securities Dealers Automated Quotations. Adam Hayes, "Nasdaq," Investopedia.com, Dotdash Meredith, InterActiveCorp., last updated 6 Nov. 2021. www. investopedia.com/terms/n/nasdaq.asp, accessed 6 Nov. 2021.

13. In mathematical terms, dYdX means "the derivative of y with respect to x." Mathematics Stack Exchange, math.stackexchange.com/questions/340744/what-do-the-symbols-d-dx-and-dy-dx-mean, accessed 15 Oct. 2021.

14. "Big Four Accounting Firms," *CorporateFinanceInstitute.com*, CFI Education Inc., n.d. corporatefinanceinstitute.com/resources/careers/companies/big-four-accounting-firms-services-overview, accessed 6 Nov. 2021.

15. For in-depth research, see our recommended readings in Brian Behlendorf, Stephen Curran, and Nathan George, "Blockchain and the Future of Digital Identity," panel moderated by Don Tapscott, *New Directions for Government* webinar series, Blockchain Research Institute and Hyperledger, 11 May 2021. www.dropbox.com/s/5lwwjh470vg4o46/Tapscott_Blockchain%20and%20the%20Future%20of%20Digital%20Identity_Blockchain%20Research%20Institute_Hyperledger.pdf?dl=0.

16. For more information on how public key infrastructure (PKI) establishes identity, please see "Introduction to PKI," www.ncsc.gov.uk/collection/in-house-public-key-infrastructure/introduction-to-public-key-infrastructure, accessed 15 Oct. 2021.

17. Messari (@MessariCrypto), Twitter post, 21 Sept. 2021 (10:32 am). twitter.com/MessariCrypto/status/1440322964390486024, accessed 4 Oct. 2021.

18. We introduced this concept in the paperback edition of *Blockchain Revolution*.

19. "DAOs Are the New Companies. What's on Their Balance Sheets?" *Open-Orgs.info*, created by David Mihal, n.d. open-orgs.info, accessed 4 Nov. 2021.

20. Benjamin Sutton, "What You Need to Know from the Art Market 2020 Report," *Artsy.net*, Art.sy Inc., 5 March 2020. www.artsy.net/article/artsy-editorial-art-market-2020-report, accessed 4 Nov. 2021.

21. BNB and FTT values, *CoinMarketCap.com*, CoinMarketCap OpCo LLC, as of 7 Nov. 2021. coinmarketcap.com.

22. See Mirror Finance's documentation here: docs.mirror.finance.

23. Stablecoin asset values, *CoinMarketCap.com*, CoinMarketCap OpCo LLC, as of 4 Oct. 2021. coinmarketcap.com.

24. "Central Bank Digital Currency Tracker," GeoEconomics Center, Atlantic Council, as of 30 Sept. 2021. www.atlanticcouncil.org/cbdctracker, accessed 4 Nov. 2021.

25. "Uniswap vs. Coinbase and Binance Trade Volume," *TheBlockCrypto. com*, Block Crypto Inc., as of 30 Sept. 2021. www.theblockcrypto.com/ data/decentralized-finance/dex-non-custodial/uniswap-vs-coinbase-and-binance-trade-volume-7dma.

26. Chayanika Deka, "Yearn Finance TVL across All Products Hits New Record of $5 Billion," *Tron Weekly*, 17 June 2021. www.tronweekly.com/ yearn-finance-tvl-5-billion, accessed 4 Nov. 2021.

27. Clare O'Hara and Sean Silcoff, "Wealthsimple Announces $750-Million Financing Investor Group, Including Drake, Ryan Reynolds," *The Globe and Mail*, Globe and Mail Inc., 3 May 2021. www.theglobeandmail. com/business/article-wealthsimple-announces-landmark-750-million-financing-from-investor, accessed 30 Sept. 2021.

28. Ryan Watkins and Roberto Talamas, "Q2'21 DeFi Review," *Messario.io*, Messari Inc., 13 July 2021. messari.io/article/q2-21-defi-review, accessed 4 Oct. 2021.

29. Ryan Watkins and Roberto Talamas, "Q2'21 DeFi Review"

30. Marshall Hargrave, "Bulge Bracket," *Investopedia.com*, Dotdash Meredith, InterActiveCorp., 8 Nov. 2020. www.investopedia.com/terms/b/ bulgebracket.asp, accessed 4 Oct. 2021.

31. Ethan Buchman, interviewed by Alex Tapscott, 10 July 2019.

32. Peng Zhong, email exchange with Alex Tapscott, 30 Sept. 2021.

33. Cuy Sheffield, "Crypto Is Going Mainstream: What You Need to Know," *Visa Navigate*, Visa USA Inc., April 2021. navigate.visa.com/na/money-movement/crypto-currency-the-real-opportunity, accessed 4 Oct. 2021.

34. Tim Fries, "Interview: Terra CEO Discusses Luna, Mirror, Chair Terraswap, More," *The Tokenist*, The Tokenist Media LLC, 20 March 2021. tokenist.com/interview-terra-ceo-discusses-luna-mirror-chai-terraswap-more, accessed 4 Oct. 2021.

35. Chainalysis Team, "The 2021 Global Crypto Adoption Index: Worldwide Adoption Jumps over 880% with P2P Platforms Driving Cryptocurrency Usage in Emerging Markets," *Chainalysis Blog*, Chainalysis Insights, 18 Aug. 2021. blog.chainalysis.com/reports/2021-global-crypto-adoption-index, accessed 4 Oct. 2021.

36. Chainalysis Team, "The 2021 Global Crypto Adoption Index."

37. Nelson Renteria, Tom Wilson, and Karin Strohecker, "In a World First, El Salvador Makes Bitcoin Legal Tender," *Reuters.com*, Thomson Reuters, 9 June 2021. www.reuters.com/world/americas/el-salvador-approves-first-law-bitcoin-legal-tender-2021-06-09, accessed 15 Oct. 2021.

38. Luke Conway, "All the Countries Where Bitcoin Adoption Is Being Considered," *The Street Crypto*, Arena Group, 8 June 2021. www. thestreet.com/crypto/bitcoin/politicians-from-these-countries-have-called-for-bitcoin-adoption, accessed 15 Oct. 2021.

39. "GDP (current US$)," *World Bank Data*, World Bank Group, as of 15 Oct. 2021. data.worldbank.org/indicator/NY.GDP.MKTP.CD, accessed 15 Oct. 2021.

40. "The World's Unbanked Population," *Acuant Blog*, Acuant Inc., 25 Nov. 2020. www.acuant.com/blog/the-worlds-unbanked-population, accessed 15 Oct. 2021.

41. "Bitcoin Avg. Transaction Fee Historical Chart," *BitInfoCharts.com*, as of 30 Sept. 2021. bitinfocharts.com/comparison/bitcoin-transactionfees. html#3m, accessed 4 Nov. 2021.

42. Joseph Poon and Thaddeus Dryja, "The Bitcoin Lightning Network: Scalable Off-Chain Instant Payments," White Paper V0.5.9.2, *Lightning Network*, 14 Jan. 2016. lightning.network/lightning-network-paper.pdf, accessed 16 Oct. 2021.

43. Yogita Khatri, "Bitcoin's Lightning Network Capacity Reaches an All-Time High," *TheBlockCrypto.com*, Block Crypto Inc., 29 Sept. 2021, updated 16 Oct. 2021. www.theblockcrypto.com/linked/119025/bitcoin-lightning-network-capacity-reaches-all-time-high.

44. Remi Lederman, "Strike Launches Its API Platform for Businesses and Partners with Twitter to Power Instant Global Payments Using Bitcoin," *BusinessWire.com*, Business Wire Inc., 23 Sept. 2021. www.businesswire. com/news/home/20210923005851/en/Strike-Launches-Its-API-Platform-for-Businesses-and-Partners-With-Twitter-to-Power-Instant-Global-Payments-Using-Bitcoin, accessed 15 Oct. 2021.

45. Yogita Khatri, "Bitcoin's Lightning Network Capacity Reaches an All-Time High"

46. Do Kwon, email exchange with Alex Tapscott, 27 Sept. 2021.

47. Martin Baumann and Charlie Morris, "The Emerging Terra Ecosystem," *CMCC.vc Insights*, CMCC Global Asset Management Ltd., June 2021. www.cmcc.vc/insights/the-emerging-terra-ecosystem, accessed 4 Oct. 2021.

48. "Crypto Asset Custody for Institutions," Coinbase.com, Coinbase Inc., n.d. custody.coinbase.com; and "Gemini Custody," *Gemini.com*, Gemini Trust Co. LLC, n.d. www.gemini.com/custody, accessed 4 Oct. 2021.

49. "MetaMask Surpasses 10 Million [Monthly Active Users], Making It the World's Leading Noncustodial Crypto Wallet," *ConsenSys.net Blog*, ConsenSys Software Inc., 31 Aug. 2021. consensys.net/blog/press-release/metamask-surpasses-10-million-maus-making-it-the-worlds-leading-non-custodial-crypto-wallet, accessed 4 Oct. 2021

50. "Comparison Chart: Bitski vs. MetaMask vs. TokenPocket vs. Trust Wallet," *SourceForge.net*, Slashdot Media LLC, n.d. sourceforge.net/software/compare/Bitski-vs-MetaMask-vs-TokenPocket-vs-Trust-Wallet; and "Comparison Chart: Ledger vs. Rainbow Wallet vs. TokenPocket vs. Trezor," *SourceForge.net*, Slashdot Media LLC, n.d. sourceforge.net/software/compare/Ledger-vs-Rainbow-Wallet-vs-TokenPocket-vs-Trezor, accessed 15 Oct. 2021.

51. Phantom (@Phantom), Twitter Post, 29 Sept. 2021 (12:49 pm). twitter.com/phantom/status/1443256406673485830, accessed 15 Oct. 2021.

52. Eric Winer, "Cold Storage, Keys & Crypto: How Gemini Keeps Assets Safe," *Product Blog*, Gemini Trust Co. LLC, 12 Feb. 2019. www.gemini.com/blog/cold-storage-keys-crypto-how-gemini-keeps-assets-safe, accessed 15 Oct. 2021.

53. "Gemini Surpasses $30 Billion in Crypto under Custody," *Product Blog*, Gemini Trust Co. LLC, 11 May 2021. www.gemini.com/blog/gemini-crypto-under-custody, accessed 15 Oct. 2021.

54. Coinbase Global Inc. Form S-1 Registration Statement under the Securities Act of 1933, as filed with the SEC on 25 Feb. 2021. www.sec.gov/Archives/edgar/data/1679788/000162828021003168/coinbaseglobalincs-1.htm, accessed 15 Oct. 2021.

55. Bilal Jafar, "Coinbase Custody Accounted for 11% of All Cryptocurrency Assets in 2020," *FinanceMagnates.com*, Finance Magnates Ltd., 3 Feb. 2021. www.financemagnates.com/cryptocurrency/news/coinbase-custody-accounted-for-11-of-all-cryptocurrency-assets-in-2020, accessed 15 Oct. 2021.

56. Hugh Son, "US Bank Launches Bitcoin Custody Service as Institutions Race to Cater to Crypto Demand," *CNBC.com*, NBC Universal Media LLC, 5 Oct. 2021. www.cnbc.com/2021/10/05/bitcoin-custody-us-bank-launches-service-as-institutions-race-to-cater-to-crypto-demand.html, accessed 15 Oct. 2021.

57. "Federally Chartered Banks and Thrifts May Provide Custody Services for Crypto Assets," News Release 2020-98, Office of the Comptroller of the Currency, US Dept. of Treasury, 22 July 2020. www.occ.gov/news-issuances/news-releases/2020/nr-occ-2020-98.html, accessed 15 Oct. 2021.

58. "Your Swiss Cryptocurrency Investment Partner," *BitcoinSuisse.com*, Bitcoin Suisse AG, as of 11 Nov. 2021. www.bitcoinsuisse.com.

59. Vildana Hajric, "Novogratz's Galaxy Buys BitGo in $1.2 Billion Crypto Deal," *Bloomberg News*, Bloomberg LP, updated 5 May 2021. www.bloomberg.com/news/articles/2021-05-05/novogratz-s-galaxy-buys-crypto-custodian-bitgo-for-1-2-billion, accessed 4 Oct. 2021.

60. "BNY Mellon Forms New Digital Assets Unit to Build Industry's First Multi-Asset Digital Platform," Newsroom, Bank of New York Mellon Corp., 11 Feb. 2021. www.bnymellon.com/us/en/about-us/newsroom/press-release/bny-mellon-forms-new-digital-assets-unit-to-build-industrypercent27s-first-multi-asset-digital-platform-130169.html, accessed 4 Oct. 2021.

61. "About Coinbase," *Coinbase.com*, Coinbase Inc., as of 11 Nov. 2021. www.coinbase.com/about.

62. "BNY Mellon Picks Digital Asset Custody Firm Fireblocks Which Raises $133 Million," *Ledger Insights*, Ledger Insights Ltd., 18 March 2021. www.ledgerinsights.com/bny-mellon-picks-digital-asset-custody-firm-fireblocks-which-raises-133-million, accessed 4 Oct. 2021.

63. Gemini Trust Co. LLC, "Gemini Acquires Leading Crypto Custody Technology," Press Release, PRNewswire.com, Cision US Inc., 9 June 2021. www.prnewswire.com/news-releases/gemini-acquires-leading-crypto-custody-technology-301308519.html, accessed 11 Nov. 2021.

64. "Choice," *ChoiceApp.io*, Kingdom Trust Co., as of 11 Nov. 2021. www.choiceapp.io/kingdomtrust.

65. "New Cryptocurrency Custody Services for Institutional Investment Managers," Press Release, *USBank.com*, US Bancorp, 5 Oct. 2021. www.usbank.com/about-us-bank/company-blog/article-library/cryptocurrency-custody-services.html, accessed 6 Oct. 2021.

66. "US Bank Acquires Debt Servicing and Securities Custody Services Client Portfolio of MUFG Bank," *US Bancorp Investor Relations*, US Bancorp, 6 Jan. 2021. ir.usbank.com/news-releases/news-release-details/us-bank-acquires-debt-servicing-and-securities-custody-services, accessed 15 Oct. 2021.

67. Andrew Young, email exchange with Alex Tapscott, 1 Oct. 2021.

68. "DAOs Are the New Companies. What's on Their Balance Sheets?" *Open-Orgs.info*, n.d. open-orgs.info; and Ty Haqqi, "15 Companies with the Most Cash Reserves in America," *Yahoo Finance*, Apollo Global Management Inc., 22 May 2021. finance.yahoo.com/news/15-companies-most-cash-reserves-182708211.html, accessed 15 Oct. 2021.

69. Coinbase SEC Filings, investor.coinbase.com/financials/sec-filings/default.aspx, accessed 15 Oct. 2021.

70. Cointelegraph Consulting, "Aave's Avenue to over $11 Billion in TVL," *Cointelegraph.com*, 12 May 2021. cointelegraph.com/news/cointelegraph-consulting-aave-s-avenue-to-over-11-billion-in-tvl, accessed 15 Oct. 2021.

71. Adriana Hamacher, "What Are Flash Loans? The DeFi Lending Phenomenon Explained," *Decrypt Learn*, Decrypt Media Inc., 28 June 2021. decrypt.co/resources/what-are-flash-loans-the-defi-lending-phenomenon-explained, accessed 15 Oct. 2021.

72. Peng Zhong, email exchange with Alex Tapscott, 30 Sept. 2021.

73. Galia Benartzi, email exchange with Alex Tapscott, 1 Oct. 2021.

74. "Bancor Network Token," *CoinGecko.com*, as of 30 Sept. 2021. www.coingecko.com/en/coins/bancor-network.

75. Naval (@Naval), Twitter Post, 3 Oct. 2021 (3:09 pm). twitter.com/naval/status/1444741381579177984, accessed 15 Oct. 2021.

76. Galia Benartzi, email exchange with Alex Tapscott, 1 Oct. 2021.

77. "Coins: Osmosis," *CoinGecko.com*, Gecko Labs Pte. Ltd., as of 30 Sept. 2021. www.coingecko.com/en/coins/osmosis.

78. Ryan Watkins (@RyanWatkins_), Twitter Post, 20 July 2021 (7:44 pm). twitter.com/RyanWatkins_/status/1417631595742236675, accessed 15 Oct. 2021.

79. Adam Hayes, "Event Risk," *Investopedia.com*, Dotdash Meredith, InterActiveCorp., 15 July 2020. www.investopedia.com/terms/e/eventrisk.asp, accessed 17 Oct. 2021.

80. J.B. Maverick, "How Big Is the Derivatives Market?" *Investopedia.com*, Dotdash Meredith, InterActiveCorp., 28 April 2020. www.investopedia.com/ask/answers/052715/how-big-derivatives-market.asp, accessed 17 Oct. 2021.

81. "Top Derivatives Tokens by Market Capitalization," *CoinMarketCap.com*, CoinMarketCap OpCo LLC, as of 17 Oct. 2021. coinmarketcap.com/view/derivatives.

82. "dYdX," *CoinMarketCap.com*, CoinMarketCap OpCo LLC, as of 17 Oct. 2021. coinmarketcap.com/currencies/dydx.

83. See "SportX," *CoinMarketCap.com*, CoinMarketCap OpCo LLC, coinmarketcap.com/currencies/sportx for data.

84. Andrew Young, email exchange with Alex Tapscott, 1 Oct. 2021.

85. "CNBC Excerpts: Billionaire Investor Warren Buffett on CNBC's *Squawk Box* Today," CNBC.com, NBC Universal Media LLC, 2 March 2015. www.cnbc.com/2015/03/02/cnbc-excerpts-billionaire-investor-warren-buffett-on-cnbcs-squawk-box-today.html, accessed 17 Oct. 2021.

86. Tim Harford, "Is This the Most Influential Work in the History of Capitalism?" *50 Things That Made the Modern Economy*, BBC World Service, 23 Oct. 2017. www.bbc.com/news/business-41582244, accessed 15 Oct. 2021.

87. Tim Harford, "Is This the Most Influential Work in the History of Capitalism?" See also *The Origins of Accounting Culture: The Venetian Connection*, eds. Chiara Mio, Massimo Sargiacomo, Roberto Di Pietra, Stefano Coronella, and Ugo Sostero (New York: Taylor & Francis, 2018). www.google.com/books/edition/The_Origins_of_Accounting_Culture, accessed 15 Oct. 2021.

88. Tim Harford, "Is This the Most Influential Work in the History of Capitalism?" See also Luca Pacioli, *Su[m]ma de Arithmetica Geometria Proportioni [et] Proportionalita* (Venice: Paganinus de Paganinis, 1494). Internet Archive, archive.org/details/summadearithmeti00paci/page/n171/mode/2up, accessed 15 Oct. 2021.

89. *The Origins of Accounting Culture: The Venetian Connection*, eds. Chiara Mio, Massimo Sargiacomo, Roberto Di Pietra, Stefano Coronella, and Ugo Sostero (New York: Taylor & Francis, 2018). www.google.com/books/edition/The_Origins_of_Accounting_Culture, accessed 15 Oct. 2021.

90. Don Tapscott and Alex Tapscott, *Blockchain Revolution* (New York: Penguin Portfolio, 2016): 77–79. www.google.com/books/edition/Blockchain_Revolution/NqBiCgAAQBAJ.

91. "Yearn Quarterly Finance Report: Q2-2021," *GitHub.com*, GitHub Inc., 10 Sept. 2021. github.com/yearn/yearn-pm/blob/master/financials/reports/2021Q2-yearn-quarterly-report.pdf, accessed 15 Oct. 2021.

92. Chris Dixon (@cdixon), Twitter Post, 26 Sept. 2021 (2:57 pm). twitter.com/cdixon/status/1442201639994068997, accessed 15 Oct. 2021.

93. Ian Allison, "Shyft Debuts 'Decentralized Version of SWIFT' for FATF 'Travel Rule,'" *CoinDesk*, Digital Currency Group, 14 July 2020, updated 14 Sept. 2021. www.coindesk.com/business/2020/07/14/shyft-debuts-decentralized-version-of-swift-for-fatf-travel-rule, accessed 15 Oct. 2021.

94. "FedEx Marks 40th Anniversary with Community Service, Eye to the Future," Press Release, FedEx Corp., 17 April 2013. newsroom.fedex.com/newsroom/fedex-marks-40th-anniversary-with-community-service-eye-to-the-future, accessed 15 Oct. 2021.

95. "Virtual Assets," Financial Action Task Force–General Authority for Investment and Free Zones, *FATF-GAFI.org*, n.d. www.fatf-gafi.org/publications/virtualassets/documents/virtual-assets-fatf-standards.html, accessed 16 Oct. 2021.

96. Note that some projects on this site such as uPort may have changed or are no longer active. defiprime.com/decentralized_kyc_identity, accessed 15 Oct. 2021. See also Lukas Stockburger, Georgios Kokosioulis, Alivelu Mukkamala, Raghava Rao Mukkamala, and Michel Avital, "Blockchain-Enabled Decentralized Identity Management: The Case of Self-Sovereign Identity in Public Transportation," *Blockchain: Research and Applications*, Elsevier, 26 May 2021. Science Direct, www.sciencedirect.com/science/article/pii/S2096720921000099.

97. Jesse Leingruber, Alain Meier, and John Backus, "Bloom Protocol," Early Community Draft Version 3, Bloom.co, 27 Jan. 2018. bloom.co/whitepaper.pdf, accessed 16 Oct. 2021.

98. Blockpass UK Ltd., n.d. www.blockpass.org, accessed 15 Oct. 2021.

99. Marco Iansiti and Karim R. Lakhani, "The Truth about Blockchain," *Harvard Business Review* 95, no. 1 (Jan.–Feb. 2017): 118–127. hbr.org/2017/01/the-truth-about-blockchain, accessed 30 Sept. 2021.

100. Dan Jewell, Angus Eames, and James Carter, "The Law Commission's Review of the Law on Digital Assets and Smart Contracts," *DLAPiper.com*, DLA Piper LLP, 9 Nov. 2020. www.dlapiper.com/en/us/insights/publications/2020/11/the-law-commissions-review-of-the-law-on-digital-assets-and-smart-contracts, accessed 30 Oct. 2021.

101. John Baldwin, "In Digital We Trust: Bitcoin Discourse, Digital Currencies, and Decentralized Network Fetishism," *Nature.com*, Springer Nature Ltd., 13 Feb. 2018. www.nature.com/articles/s41599-018-0065-0, accessed 15 Oct. 2021.

102. Billy Bambrough, "Visa, Mastercard and PayPal Are Changing Their Tune on Bitcoin and Crypto," *Forbes.com*, Forbes Media LLC, 24 July 2020. www.forbes.com/sites/billybambrough/2020/07/24/visa-mastercard-and-paypal-are-changing-their-tune-on-bitcoin-and-crypto.

103. Shawn Tully, "Elon Musk May Be Betting on Bitcoin—But Here's What 50 Other CFOs Really Think about It," *Fortune Rankings*, Fortune Media Group Holdings Ltd., 17 Feb. 2021. fortune.com/2021/02/17/bitcoin-elon-musk-tesla-tsla-btc-investment-cfos-experts, accessed 5 Nov. 2021.

104. Portions of this section first appeared in Alex Tapscott, "Bitcoin Offers Freedom from Political Repression—and That's a Key to Its Future," *Fortune.com*, Fortune Media Group Holdings Ltd., 18 Feb. 2021. fortune.com/2021/02/18/bitcoin-censorship-political-repression-deplatforming-china-belarus-russia-nigeria-crypto, accessed 4 Oct. 2021.

105. Sandila Handagama, "Nigeria Protest Show Bitcoin Adoption Is Not Coming: It's Here," *CoinDesk*, Digital Currency Group, 21 Oct. 2020. www.coindesk.com/nigeria-bitcoin-adoption, accessed 15 Oct. 2021.

106. "Nigeria NG: Average Transaction Cost of Sending Remittances to a Specific Country," *CEIC Data*, ISI Emerging Markets Group Co., 1 Dec. 2011–1 Dec. 2017. www.ceicdata.com/en/nigeria/payment-system/ng-average-transaction-cost-of-sending-remittances-to-a-specific-country, accessed 15 Oct. 2021.

107. "Nigeria: Punitive Financial Moves against Protesters," *HRW.org*, Human Rights Watch, 13 Nov. 2020. www.hrw.org/news/2020/11/13/nigeria-punitive-financial-moves-against-protesters#, accessed 6 Oct. 2021.

108. "Gas and Fees," *Ethereum.org*, last updated by @minimalsm, 29 Sept. 2021. ethereum.org/en/developers/docs/gas, accessed 15 Oct. 2021.

109. Ethereum (ETH), *CoinMarketCap.com*, CoinMarketCap OpCo LLC, as of 17 Oct. 2021. coinmarketcap.com/currencies/ethereum, accessed 15 Oct. 2021.

110. "Total Value Locked All Chains," *DeFi Llama*, DeFiLlama.com, as of 30 Sept. 2021. defillama.com/chains, accessed 15 Oct. 2021.

111. Joel Monegro, "Fat Protocols," Blog, Union Square Ventures, 8 Aug. 2016. Wayback Machine, web.archive.org/web/20191026011419/https://www.usv.com/writing/2016/08/fat-protocols, accessed 15 Oct. 2021.

112. Peng Zhong, email exchange with Alex Tapscott, 30 Sept. 2021.

113. Do Kwon, email exchange with Alex Tapscott, 27 Sept. 2021.

114. Charlie Wells and Olga Kharif, "What the Solana Blackout Reveals about the Fragility of Crypto," *Bloomberg News*, Bloomberg LP, 18 Sept. 2021. www.bloomberg.com/news/articles/2021-09-18/solana-trading-how-outage-reveals-vulnerability-of-crypto-blockchains, accessed 4 Oct. 2021.

115. Joanna Ossinger, "Solana Promises 'Detailed Post-Mortem' after 17-Hour Outage," *Bloomberg News*, Bloomberg LP, 15 Sept. 2021, updated 16 Sept. 2021. www.bloomberg.com/news/articles/2021-09-16/solana-network-of-top-10-sol-token-applies-fixes-after-outage, accessed 4 Oct. 2021.

116. Sandeep Nailwal, email exchange with Alex Tapscott, 2 Oct. 2021.

117. Sandeep Nailwal, email exchange with Alex Tapscott, 2 Oct. 2021.

118. Peng Zhong, email exchange with Alex Tapscott, 30 Sept. 2021.

119. "About Project," *Cosmos.Network Jobs*, Interchain Foundation, n.d. jobs. cosmos.network/project/tendermint, accessed 7 Nov. 2021.

120. Elizabeth Schulze, "Cryptocurrencies Are 'Clearly Shaking the System,' IMF's Lagarde Says," *CNBC.com*, NBC Universal Media LLC, 10 April 2019. www.cnbc.com/2019/04/11/cryptocurrencies-fintech-clearly-shaking-the-system-imfs-lagarde.html, accessed 11 Sept. 2019.

121. Adam Hayes, "Decentralized Banking: Monetary Technocracy in the Digital Age," *MCIS 2016 Proceedings*, Association for Information Systems, 26 Oct. 2016. AIS e-library, aisel.aisnet.org/mcis2016/3, accessed 15 Oct. 2021.

122. "China Aims to Launch the World's First Official Digital Currency," *Economist.com*, Economist Newspaper Ltd., 25 April 2020. www. economist.com/finance-and-economics/2020/04/23/china-aims-to-launch-the-worlds-first-official-digital-currency, accessed 15 Oct. 2021.

123. Global Legal Research Directorate, *Regulation of Cryptocurrency in Selected Jurisdictions* (Washington, DC: Law Library of Congress, June 2018). www.loc.gov/item/2018298388; and Scott Nover, "China's Latest Crypto Crackdown Is Its Toughest Yet," *QZ.com*, Quartz Media Inc., 26 Sept. 2021. qz.com/2065015/how-chinas-new-ban-on-crypto-breaks-from-the-past, accessed 15 Oct. 2021.

124. Portions of this section appeared in Alex Tapscott, "Bitcoin Offers Freedom from Political Repression—and That's a Key to Its Future," *Fortune Commentary*, Fortune Media Group Holdings Ltd., 18 Feb. 2021. fortune. com/2021/02/18/bitcoin-censorship-political-repression-deplatforming-china-belarus-russia-nigeria-crypto, accessed 16 Oct. 2021.

125. Marshall McLuhan, *Understanding Media: The Extensions of Man*, intro. by Lewis H. Lapham (Cambridge: MIT Press, Oct. 1994), reissued ed. mitpress.mit.edu/books/understanding-media.

126. Some of this material first appeared in Alex Tapscott, "With NFTs, the Digital Medium Is the Message," *Fortune.com*, Fortune Media Group Holdings Ltd., 4 Oct. 2021. fortune.com/2021/10/04/nfts-art-collectibles-medium-is-the-message, accessed 15 Oct. 2021.

127. Caroline Goldstein, "Damien Hirst's New NFT Project Forces Buyers to Choose between Owning a Digital Token or a Work on Paper," *ArtNet News*, Artnet Worldwide Corp., 13 July 2021. news.artnet.com/art-world/damien-hirst-the-currency-1988535, accessed 4 Oct. 2021.

128. Caroline Goldstein, "Damien Hirst's NFT Initiative, Which Asks Buyers to Choose between a Digital Token and IRL Art, Has Already Generated $25 Million," *ArtNet News*, Artnet Worldwide Corp.,

25 Aug. 2021. news.artnet.com/market/damien-hirst-nft-update-2002582, accessed 4 Oct. 2021.

129. Frank Chaparro, "Axie Infinity Is Launching a Decentralized Chain," *TheBlockCrypto.com*, Block Crypto Inc., 1 Oct. 2021. www.theblockcrypto.com/linked/119283/axie-infinity-is-launching-a-decentralized-exchange, accessed 4 Oct. 2021.

130. Frank Chaparro, "A Conversation with Jeff Zirlin," *The Scoop*, Ep. 61, Season 3, Block Crypto Inc. and Bakkt, 22 Sept. 2021. www.theblockcrypto.com/linked/119283/axie-infinity-is-launching-a-decentralized-exchange, accessed 4 Oct. 2021.

131. Vittoria Elliott, "Workers in the Global South Are Making a Living Playing the Blockchain Game Axie Infinity," Report, *Rest of World*, Rest of World Media Inc., 19 Aug. 2021. restofworld.org/2021/axie-infinity, accessed 15 Oct. 2021.

132. Vittoria Elliott, "Some Axie Infinity Players Amassed Fortunes—Now the Philippine Government Wants Its Cut," News, *Rest of World*, Rest of World Media Inc., 30 Sept. 2021 restofworld.org/2021/axie-players-are-facing-taxes, accessed 15 Oct. 2021.

133. "Axie Infinity," *CoinGecko Coins*, Gecko Labs Pte. Ltd., as of 1 Oct. 2021. www.coingecko.com/en/coins/axie-infinity.

134. Ryan Watkins (@ryanwatkins_), Twitter Post, 1 Oct. 2021 (5:25 pm). twitter.com/RyanWatkins_/status/1444050982946672647, accessed 4 Oct. 2021.

135. Chris Dixon (@cdixon), Twitter Post, 26 Sept. 2021 (2:57 pm). twitter.com/cdixon/status/1442201638895177729, accessed 4 Oct. 2021.

136. Stablecoins, *TheBlockCrypto.com*, Block Crypto Inc., as of 22 Sept. 2021. www.theblockcrypto.com/data/decentralized-finance/stablecoins.

137. CENTRE Consortium, "USDC Crosses 30 Billion in Circulation," *Centre Blog*, 23 Sept. 2021. www.centre.io/blog/usdc-crosses-30-billion-in-circulation, accessed 4 Oct. 2021. Find Grant Thornton's audit reports here: www.centre.io/usdc-transparency.

138. Imani Moise and Siddharth Venkataramakrishnan, "Facebook Promotes Paxos in Stablecoin Race," *Financial Times*, Financial Times Ltd., 25 Oct. 2021. www.ft.com/content/22670cf1-d957-48b4-89fd-3307cd6aa752; and Nikhilesh De, "Facebook's Novi Taps Paxos, Coinbase Ahead of Diem Rollout," *CoinDesk*, Digital Currency Group, 19 Oct. 2021. www.coindesk.com/business/2021/10/19/facebooks-novi-taps-paxos-coinbase-ahead-of-diem-rollout, accessed 25 Oct. 2021.

139. Walter Hessert, "USDP Chosen for Novi Pilot," *Paxos Blog*, Paxos Trust Co. LLC, 19 Oct. 2021. paxos.com/2021/10/19/usdp-chosen-for-novi-pilot, accessed 20 Oct. 2021.

140. Elizabeth Dwoskin, "Facebook Is Changing Its Name to Meta as It Focuses on the Virtual World," *Washington Post*, WP Co. LLC, 28 Oct. 2021. www.washingtonpost.com/technology/2021/10/28/facebook-meta-name-change, accessed 4 Nov. 2021.

141. "DAI," *CoinGecko Coins*, Gecko Labs Pte. Ltd., as of 30 Sept. 2021. www.coingecko.com/en/coins/dai; and David Curry, "Venmo Revenue and Usage Statistics (2021)," *Business of Apps*, Soko Media Ltd., 6 May 2021. www.businessofapps.com/data/venmo-statistics, accessed 4 Oct. 2021.

142. Do Kwon, email exchange with Alex Tapscott, 27 Sept. 2021.

143. Do Kwon, email exchange with Alex Tapscott, 27 Sept. 2021.

144. "President's Working Group on Financial Markets Releases Report and Recommendations on Stablecoins," Press Release, US Department of Treasury, 1 Nov. 2021. home.treasury.gov/news/press-releases/jy0454, accessed 4 Nov. 2021.

145. "President's Working Group on Financial Markets (PWG), the Federal Deposit Insurance Corp., and the Office of the Comptroller of the Currency," Fact Sheet, US Department of Treasury, 1 Nov. 2021. home.treasury.gov/news/press-releases/jy0456, accessed 4 Nov. 2021.

146. Chair Gary Gensler, "President's Working Group Report on Stablecoins," Statement, *SEC.org*, US Securities and Exchange Commission, 1 Nov. 2021. www.sec.gov/news/statement/gensler-statement-presidents-working-group-report-stablecoins-110121, accessed 4 Nov. 2021.

147. Pippa Stephens and Jordan Smith, "SEC Chair Gary Gensler Wants to Crack Down on the 'Wild West' of Crypto," *NBC After Hours*, CNBC.com, NBC Universal Media LLC, 14 Sept. 2021. www.cnbc.com/2021/09/14/sec-chair-gary-gensler-wants-to-crack-down-on-the-wild-west-of-crypto.html, accessed 15 Oct. 2021.

148. Lael Brainard, "Private Money and Central Bank Money as Payments Go Digital: An Update on CBDCs," Speech (via webcast), Consensus by *CoinDesk* 2021 Conference, Washington, DC, 24 May 2021. Federal Reserve, www.federalreserve.gov/newsevents/speech/brainard20210524a.htm, accessed 4 Oct. 2021.

149. Randal K. Quarles, "Parachute Pants and Central Bank Money," Speech, 113th Annual Utah Bankers Association Convention, Sun Valley, ID, 28 June 2021. Federal Reserve, www.federalreserve.gov/newsevents/speech/quarles20210628a.htm, accessed 4 Oct. 2021.

150. Randal K. Quarles, "Parachute Pants and Central Bank Money," Speech, 113th Annual Utah Bankers Association Convention, Sun Valley, ID, 28 June 2021.

151. Statista Research Department, "Development of Assets of Global Exchange Traded Funds (EFTs) from 2003 to 2020," *Statista.com*, Ströer SE & Co. KGaA, 18 Feb. 2021. www.statista.com/statistics/224579/worldwide-etf-assets-under-management-since-1997, accessed 4 Oct. 2021.

152. Do Kwon, email exchange with Alex Tapscott, 27 Sept. 2021.

153. Cheang Ming, "The World Bank Is Preparing for the World's First Blockchain Bond," *CNBC.com*, NBC Universal Media LLC, 10 Aug. 2018. www.cnbc.com/2018/08/10/world-bank-picks-commonwealth-bank-for-worlds-first-blockchain-bond.html; Wolfie Zhao, "Auction of a Bond Worth around $1.3 Billion," *CoinDesk*, Digital Currency Group, 25 Sept. 2018, updated 13 Sept. 2021. www.coindesk.com/markets/2018/09/27/austrian-government-to-notarize-13-billion-bond-auction-using-ethereum; and "New FinTech Applications in Bond Markets," *ICMAGroup.org*, International Capital Market Assoc., 2021. www.icmagroup.org/Regulatory-Policy-and-Market-Practice/fintech/new-fintech-applications-in-bond-markets.

154. Francois-Xavier Lord, "MakerDAO Valuation," *Messario.io*, Messari Inc., 5 Aug. 2021. messari.io/article/makerdao-valuation, accessed 15 Oct. 2021.

155. Marc Andreessen, "Why Software Is Eating the World," *Wall Street Journal*, Dow Jones & Co. Inc., 20 Aug. 2011. www.wsj.com/articles/SB10001424053111903480904576512250915629460, accessed 15 Oct. 2021.

156. Binance Coin (BNB), *CoinMarketCap.com*, CoinMarketCap OpCo LLC, as of 4 Oct. 2021. coinmarketcap.com/currencies/binance-coin.

157. "Nasdaq Inc.," *Google Finance*, Google LLC, as of 4 Oct. 2021. www.google.com/finance/quote/NDAQ:NASDAQ.

158. Binance CEO CZ, "15th BNB Burn: Quarterly Highlights and Insights from CZ," *Binance Blog*, Binance Holdings Ltd., 15 April 2021. www.binance.com/en/blog/421499824684901944/15th-bnb-burn-%7C-quarterly-highlights-and-insights-from-cz, accessed 4 Oct. 2021.

159. OKB, *CoinMarketCap.com*, CoinMarketCap OpCo LLC, as of 4 Oct. 2021. coinmarketcap.com/currencies/okb.

160. Huobi Token, *CoinMarketCap.com*, CoinMarketCap OpCo LLC, as of 4 Oct. 2021. coinmarketcap.com/currencies/huobi-token.

161. KuCoin Token, *CoinMarketCap.com*, CoinMarketCap OpCo LLC, as of 4 Oct. 2021. coinmarketcap.com/currencies/kucoin-token.

162. Mike Butcher, "Single.Earth to Link Carbon Credits to Crypto Token Market, Raises $7.9M from EQT Ventures," *TechCrunch.com*, Apollo Global Management Inc., 6 July 2021. techcrunch.com/2021/07/06/single-earth-to-link-carbon-credits-to-crypto-token-market-raises-7-9m-from-eqt-ventures, accessed 16 Oct. 2021.

163. Here we shortened the original list from ten to eight by removing "Distributed Autonomous Agents Will Form Skynet" and "Big Brother Is Still Watching You" as we cover it under "Governments Will Stifle or Twist It."

164. Tobixen, "A Brief History of the Bitcoin Block Size War," *Steemit.com*, Steemit Inc., ~7 Nov. 2017. steemit.com/bitcoin/@tobixen/a-brief-history-of-the-bitcoin-block-size-war, accessed 15 Oct. 2021.

165. Portions of this section appeared in Alex Tapscott, "Busting Bitcoin Myths: 7 Misconceptions about the Currency," *Fortune Commentary*, Fortune Media Group Holdings Ltd., 17 March 2021. fortune.com/2021/03/17/bitcoin-myths-bubble-miners-energy-waste-stablecoin, accessed 4 Oct. 2021.

166. "Bitcoin Energy Consumption Index," *Digiconomist.net*, as of 6 Nov. 2021. digiconomist.net/bitcoin-energy-consumption.

167. Shawn Tully, "Famed Economist Jeffrey Sachs Rails against Bitcoin: Highly Polluting and 'Almost Like Counterfeiting,'" *Fortune Finance*, Fortune Media Group Holdings Ltd., 16 March 2021. fortune.com/2021/03/16/bitcoin-jeffrey-sachs-critiques-btc, accessed 15 Oct. 2021.

168. Will Daniel, "Bitcoin's Energy Consumption Has Jumped 80% since the Beginning of 2020, According to a Study from Cambridge," *Business Insider: Markets Insider*, Insider Inc. and Finanzen.net GmbH, 12 March 2021. markets.businessinsider.com/news/currencies/bitcoin-energy-consumption-cambridge-study-cryptocurrencies-bitcoin-mining-climate-change-2021-3, accessed 15 Oct. 2021.

169. "Ninepoint Bitcoin ETF," *Ninepoint Partners*, n.d. gogreenbitcoin.com, accessed 5 Nov. 2021.

170. "Introducing CarbonX: Personal Carbon Trading," CarbonX Personal Carbon Trading Inc., n.d. www.carbonx.ca and www.carbon-ratings.com, accessed 4 Nov. 2021.

171. Adam Cochran (@adamscochran), Twitter Post, 16 Sept. 2021 (9:19 am). twitter.com/adamscochran/status/1438492766154240012.

172. Tom Emmer (@RepTomEmmer), Twitter Post, 5 Oct. 2021 (2:51 pm). twitter.com/RepTomEmmer/status/1445461701567160320, accessed 15 Oct. 2021.

173. Angel List (@angellist), Twitter Post, 28 Sept. 2021 (1:17 pm). twitter.com/AngelList/status/1442901252552101888, accessed 15 Oct. 2021.

174. Raj Dhamodharan, "Why Mastercard Is Bringing Crypto onto Its Network," *Mastercard newsroom: Innovation,*" *Mastercard Newsroom,* Mastercard International Inc., 10 Feb. 2021. www.mastercard.com/news/perspectives/2021/why-mastercard-is-bringing-crypto-onto-our-network, accessed 15 Oct. 2021.

175. "Digital Currency Comes," *VISA Everywhere Blog,* Visa USA Inc., 26 March 2021. usa.visa.com/visa-everywhere/blog/bdp/2021/03/26/digital-currency-comes-1616782388876.html, accessed 15 Oct. 2021.

176. Ryan Weeks, "PayPal Has Held Exploratory Talks about Launching a Stablecoin: Sources," *TheBlockCrypto.com,* Block Crypto Inc., 3 May 2021. www.theblockcrypto.com/post/103617/paypal-has-held-exploratory-talks-about-launching-a-stablecoin-sources, accessed 15 Oct. 2021.

177. Jeff John Roberts, "Visa Unveils 'Layer 2' Network for Stablecoins, Central Bank Currencies," *Decrypt News: Business,* Decrypt Media Inc., 30 Sept. 2021. https://decrypt.co/82233/visa-universal-payment-channel-stablecoin-cbdc, accessed 15 Oct. 2021.

178. Hugh Son, "US Bank Launches Bitcoin Custody Service as Institutions Race to Cater to Crypto Demand," *CNBC.com,* NBC Universal Media LLC, 5 Oct. 2021. www.cnbc.com/2021/10/05/bitcoin-custody-us-bank-launches-service-as-institutions-race-to-cater-to-crypto-demand.html, accessed 15 Oct. 2021.

179. Chris Dixon (@cdixon), Twitter Post, 1 Oct. 2021 (6:50 pm). twitter.com/cdixon/status/1444072368859533316, accessed 15 Oct. 2021.

180. Chris Dixon (@cdixon), Twitter Post, 1 Oct. 2021 (6:50 pm). twitter.com/cdixon/status/1444072370788978691, and twitter.com/cdixon/status/1444072374798675970, accessed 15 Oct. 2021.

181. For one visualization of bootstrapping, see Chris Dixon's blog post, "Crypto Tokens: A Breakthrough in Open Network Design," 27 May 2017. cdixon.org/2017/05/27/crypto-tokens-a-breakthrough-in-open-network-design.

182. "DAO Jobs: Find Great Crypto Jobs at a DAO," Cryptocurrency Jobs, as of 5 Nov. 2021. cryptocurrencyjobs.co/dao.

183. AnnElizabeth Konkel, "Job Seeker Interest Spikes in Crypto and Blockchain," *Indeed Hiring Lab*, Indeed Inc., 3 Aug. 2021. www.hiringlab. org/2021/08/03/job-seeker-interest-spikes-crypto-and-blockchain, accessed 15 Oct. 2021.

184. Mengqi Sun, "Crypto Firms Beef Up Compliance Hiring as Regulatory Scrutiny Mounts," *Wall Street Journal*, Dow Jones & Co. Inc., 30 Sept. 2021. www.wsj.com/articles/crypto-firms-beef-up-compliance-hiring-as-regulatory-scrutiny-mounts-11632994202, accessed 15 Oct. 2021.

185. Kyung Taeck Minn, "Towards Enhanced Oversight of 'Self-Governing' Decentralized Autonomous Organizations: Case Study of the DAO and Its Shortcomings," *NYU Journal of Intellectual Property and Entertainment Law 9*, No. 1, 24 Jan. 2020. jipel.law.nyu.edu/vol-9-no-1-5-minn, accessed 15 Oct. 2021.

186. Roy Learner, "Blockchain Voter Apathy," *Wave Financial Blog*, Wave Financial Group, 29 March 2019. medium.com/wave-financial/blockchain-voter-apathy-69a1570e2af3. See also Nic Carter, "A Cross-Sectional Overview of Cryptoasset Governance and Implications for Investors," Dissertation, University of Edinburgh Business School, 2016/2017. niccarter.info/papers, accessed 15 Oct. 2021.

187. "SX Network: The Blockchain for Prediction Markets," *SportX Bet Blog*, SX Network, 22 Sept. 2021. medium.com/sportx-bet/sx-network-the-blockchain-for-prediction-markets-603badcdad3b, accessed 15 Oct. 2021.

188. Chainalysis Team, "Crypto Crime Summarized: Scams and Darknet Markets Dominated 2020 by Revenue, But Ransomware Is the Bigger Story," *Chainalysis Blog*, Chainalysis Inc., 19 Jan. 2021. blog.chainalysis.com/reports/2021-crypto-crime-report-intro-ransomware-scams-darknet-markets; and Michael J. Morell, "Report: An Analysis of Bitcoin's Use in Illicit Finance," *Cipher Brief*, Cipher Online Media Inc., 13 April 2021. www.thecipherbrief.com/report-an-analysis-of-bitcoins-use-in-illicit-finance, accessed 15 Oct. 2021.

189. David Herman, "The Silences of Eric Hobsbawm," *Salmagundi* No. 204–205, Fall 2019. salmagundi.skidmore.edu/articles/184-the-silences-of-eric-hobsbawm, accessed 15 Oct. 2021.

190. Win McCormack, "Fukuyama's Inner Civic Republicanism (Part 1): The End of History, 30 Years on," *The New Republic*, 17 Oct. 2019. newrepublic.com/article/155260/francis-fukuyama-anniversary-end-history-inner-civic-republicanism, accessed 15 Oct. 2021.

191. Timothy Leary (1920-1996), "The Effects of Psychotropic Drugs," Department of Psychology, President and Fellows of Harvard College, n.d. psychology.fas.harvard.edu/people/timothy-leary, accessed 15 Oct. 2021.

192. Cory Doctorow, "Adversarial Interoperability," *EFF.org*, Electronic Frontier Foundation, 2 Oct. 2019. www.eff.org/deeplinks/2019/10/ adversarial-interoperability, accessed 21 June 2021.

193. For email, see Jonathan B. Postel, "Simple Mail Transfer Protocol," RFC 821, *Network Working Group*, Internet Engineering Task Force (IETF), Aug. 1982. datatracker.ietf.org/doc/html/rfc821; J. K. Reynolds, "Post Office Protocol," RFC 918, *Network Working Group*, IETF, Oct. 1984. datatracker.ietf.org/doc/html/rfc918; and M. Crispin, "Interactive Mail Access Protocol—Version 2," RFC 1064, *Network Working Group*, RFC Editor, July 1988. www.rfc-editor.org/rfc/rfc1064.html. For the Internet, see "Transmission Control Protocol," RFC 793, IETF, Sept. 1981. datatracker.ietf.org/doc/html/rfc793; "Internet Protocol," RFC 791, Jon Postel, preface, DARPA Internet Program Protocol Specification, IETF, Sept. 1981. datatracker.ietf.org/doc/html/rfc791; Tim Berners-Lee, R. Fielding, and H. Frystyk, "Hypertext Transfer Protocol—HTTP/1.0," RFC 1945, DOI 10.17487/RFC1945, IETF, May 1996. www.rfc-editor. org/info/rfc1945; and Tim Berners-Lee, Larry Masinter, and Mark McCahill, "Uniform Resource Locators," RFC 1738, IETF, Dec. 1994. datatracker.ietf.org/doc/rfc1738, accessed 18 June 2021.

194. Jonathan Masters, "What Is Internet Governance?" *CFR.org*, Council on Foreign Relations, 23 April 2014. www.cfr.org/backgrounder/what-internet-governance, accessed 7 July 2021.

195. Michael Zochowski, "Why Proof-of-Work Is Not Viable in the Long-Term," *Logos Network Blog*, A Medium Corp., 19 Feb. 2019. medium. com/logos-network/why-proof-of-work-is-not-viable-in-the-long-term-dd96d2775e99, accessed 7 July 2021.

196. A consensus mechanism enables a distributed computer network to reach a sufficient consensus despite malicious components (nodes) failing or propagating incorrect information to other peers. By achieving Byzantine-fault tolerance, blockchain networks can defend against catastrophic system failures by mitigating the influence of malicious nodes on the capacity of the honest nodes in the system to reach the right consensus. For more, see Jae Kwon, "Tendermint: Consensus Without Mining," Draft v.0.6, *Tendermint.com*, Tendermint Inc., 2014. tendermint.com/static/ docs/tendermint.pdf; and Miguel Castro and Barbara Liskov, "Practical Byzantine Fault Tolerance," *Proceedings of the Third Symposium on Operating Systems Design and Implementation* (New Orleans, Feb. 1999): 173–186. pmg.csail.mit.edu/papers/osdi99.pdf, accessed 14 July 2020.

197. Robert Devoe, "The Problems with Cryptocurrency Mining: Energy Use and Centralization," *Blockonomi.com*, Kooc Media Ltd., 8 March 2018. blockonomi.com/mining-problems; and "Bitcoin Energy Consumption

Index," *Digiconomist.net*, as of 11 July 2021. digiconomist.net/bitcoin-energy-consumption, accessed 23 June 2021.

198. Mateusz Raczy ski, "What Is the Fastest Blockchain and Why? Analysis of 43 Blockchains," Aleph Zero Blog, Aleph Zero Foundation, 4 Jan. 2021. alephzero.org/blog/what-is-the-fastest-blockchain-and-why-analysis-of-43-blockchains, accessed 7 July 2021. See also Adam G gol, Damian Le niak, Damian Straszak, and Michał wi tek, "Aleph: Efficient Atomic Broadcast in Asynchronous Networks with Byzantine Nodes," White Paper, Aleph Zero Foundation, 29 Aug. 2019. arXiv.org, arxiv.org/pdf/1908.05156.pdf, accessed 11 July 2021.

199. Jae Kwon and Ethan Buchman, "Cosmos: A Network of Distributed Ledgers," White Paper v1.0, *Cosmos Network*, Tendermint Inc., 2016. v1.cosmos.network/resources/whitepaper, accessed 21 June 2021.

200. "What Is Cosmos—the Vision of Cosmos (Blockchain 3.0)," *Cosmos Network*, Tendermint Inc., n.d. v1.cosmos.network/intro, accessed 8 July 2021.

201. Ana Berman, "Cross-Platform Blockchain Project Cosmos Launches First Hub after $17 Million ICO," *Cointelegraph*, 14 March 2019. cointelegraph.com/news/cross-platform-blockchain-project-cosmos-launches-first-hub-after-17-million-ico, accessed 7 July 2021.

202. Leigh Cuen, "How to Turn a $17 Million ICO into $104 Million: The Cosmos Story," *CoinDesk*, Digital Currency Group, 11 Nov. 2019. www.coindesk.com/how-to-turn-a-17-million-ico-into-104-million-the-cosmos-story, accessed 8 July 2021.

203. "What Is the Utility of ATOM?" *Cosmos Network*, Tendermint Inc., n.d. v1.cosmos.network/resources/faq, accessed 23 June 2021.

204. "Cosmos [Software Development Kit]," *Cosmos Network*, Tendermint Inc., n.d. v1.cosmos.network/sdk, accessed 8 July 2021.

205. "Application-Specific Blockchains: What Are Application-Specific Blockchains?" Introduction, *Cosmos Network*, Tendermint Inc., n.d. docs.cosmos.network/master/intro/why-app-specific.html; and Christine Kim, "Cosmos Will Have Three Coding Languages—Here's Why That Matters," *CoinDesk*, Digital Currency Group, 6 Aug. 2019. www.coindesk.com/cosmos-will-have-3-coding-languages-heres-why-that-matters-for-ethereum, accessed 23 June 2021.

206. Ori Pomerantz, "Programming Languages," *Ethereum.org*, Ethereum Foundation, 31 May 2021. ethereum.org/en/developers/docs/programming-languages, accessed 23 June 2021.

207. "Starport," *Cosmos SDK Tutorials*, Tendermint Inc., n.d. tutorials.cosmos. network/scavenge/tutorial/03-starport-scaffolding.html, accessed 8 July 2021.

208. Daniel Kuhn, "The Myths and Realities of 'Green Bitcoin,'" *CoinDesk*, Digital Currency Group, 1 April 2021. www.coindesk.com/the-myths-and-realities-of-green-bitcoin, accessed 23 June 2021.

209. Paradigm, "Interview with Peng Zhong—CEO and President at Tendermint," *Paradigm Fund Blog*, A Medium Corp., 22 Oct. 2020. medium.com/paradigm-fund/interview-with-peng-zhong-ceo-president-at-tendermint-fa10607d0e55, accessed 8 July 2021.

210. "Acknowledgment," *Binance Chain Docs*, Binance Holdings Ltd., n.d. docs.binance.org/acknowledgement.html; and "The Cryptocurrency Exchange with the Most Options," OKEx.com, Aux Cayes FinTech Co. Ltd., n.d. www.okex.com, accessed 23 June 2021.

211. "Acknowledgment," *Binance Chain Docs*, Binance Holdings Ltd., n.d. docs.binance.org/acknowledgement.html, accessed 8 July 2021.

212. "What Is IBC?" *IBC Protocol.org*, n.d. ibcprotocol.org/faq, accessed 23 June 2021.

213. Ethan Buchman, interviewed by Kevin Rooke, 25 Jan. 2021.

214. Walmertt, "Polkadot—the Cryptocurrency You Need to Be Buying and Why It's Going to Make You Rich," *Walmertt Blog*, A Medium Corp., 12 March 2021. marwolwarl.medium.com/polkadot-the-cryptocurrency-you-need-to-be-buying-and-why-its-going-to-make-you-rich-3126a83e87d6, accessed 23 June 2021.

215. Jae Kwon and Ethan Buchman, "Cosmos White Paper: A Network of Distributed Ledgers," *Cosmos Network*, Tendermint Inc., n.d. v1.cosmos. network/resources/whitepaper, accessed 8 July 2021.

216. iqlusion, "Enable IBC Transfers," Proposal 41, *Big Dipper Cosmos Hub*, as of 29 March 2021. cosmos.bigdipper.live/proposals/41, accessed 8 July 2021.

217. Brady Dale and Jamie Crowley, "Cosmos Investors to Approve InterBlockchain Communication," *CoinDesk*, Digital Currency Group, 29 March 2021. www.coindesk.com/cosmos-vote-approve-inter-blockchain-communication, accessed 8 July 2021.

218. Paradigm, "Interview with Peng Zhong—CEO and President at Tendermint," *Paradigm Fund Blog*, A Medium Corp., 22 Oct. 2020. medium.com/paradigm-fund/interview-with-peng-zhong-ceo-president-at-tendermint-fa10607d0e55, accessed 8 July 2021.

219. On 12 July 2021, ATOM's price was $13.56, and its market cap was $3.24 billion. "Cosmos (ATOM) Price," *CoinRanking.com*, 12 July 2021. coinranking.com/coin/Knsels4_Ol-Ny+cosmos-atom. On 15 Jan. 2022, ATOM's price was $39.83, and its market cap was $9.049 billion. "Cosmos .ATOM," *CoinMarketCap.com*. coinmarketcap.com/currencies/cosmos.

220. "Cosmos Market Capitalization," *Cosmos Network*, Tendermint Inc., n.d. cosmos.network/ecosystem/tokens, updated 15 Jan. 2022.

221. Ethan Buchman, interviewed by Kevin Rooke, 25 Jan. 2021.

222. "262 Apps and Services Built on Cosmos," *Cosmos Network*, Tendermint Inc., n.d. cosmos.network/ecosystem/apps, accessed 15 Jan. 2022.

223. Deborah Simpier, "NetEquity and Althea Announce Strategic Partnership to Build Broadband Networks by Using Smart Contracts," *Althea Blog*, Althea.net, 1 June 2021. blog.althea.net/netequity-and-althea; as of 15 Jan. 2022, BLZ price was $.1881, and its market cap was $60.85 million. "Bluzelle (BLZ) price," *CoinMarketCap.com*. coinmarketcap.com/currencies/bluzelle; Ryan John King, "FOAM 2020 Summer Updates," *FOAM Blog*, A Medium Corp., 25 Aug. 2020. blog. foam.space/foam-2020-summer-updates-7c78cbd5fdca; Staff, "Regen Network Sells Out $10.5M Round, Launches Regen Ledger," *Bankless Times*, 16 April 2021. www.banklesstimes.com/2021/04/16/regen-network-sells-out-10-5m-round-launches-regen-ledger; and Mike Butcher, "In the Race toward Web3 Financial Privacy, Secret Network Attracts Backing from Key Players," *TechCrunch*, Verizon Media, 3 May 2021. techcrunch.com/2021/05/03/in-the-race-towards-web-3-financial-privacy-secret-network-attracts-backing-from-key-players, most accessed 8 July 2021.

224. "Platform for a Thriving Planet," *Regen Network*, Regen Network Development Inc., n.d. www.regen.network, accessed 8 July 2021.

225. Noah Miller, "She(256) Wants to Disrupt the Male Dominated Field of Blockchain," *Newsweek*, Newsweek Digital LLC, 21 Feb 2019. www. newsweek.com/2019/03/08/she256-disrupt-male-dominated-tech-blockchain-1339553.html, accessed 8 July 2021.

226. "An Introduction to Polkadot," Light Paper, *Polkadot Network*, Web3 Foundation, p. 3. polkadot.network/Polkadot-lightpaper.pdf, accessed 23 June 2021.

227. "An Introduction to Polkadot," Light Paper, *Polkadot Network*, Web3 Foundation, p. 3.

228. "Blockchain Infrastructure for the Decentralised Web," *Parity.io*, Parity Technologies, n.d. www.parity.io, accessed 8 July 2021.

229. "Inria, an Ecosystem," French National Institute for Research in Digital Science and Technology, Inria Foundation, n.d. www.inria.fr/en/inria-ecosystem, accessed 8 July 2021.

230. "About," Web3 Foundation, n.d. web3.foundation/about, accessed 8 July 2021.

231. Mike Butcher, "Polkadot Passes the $140M Mark for Its Fundraise to Link Private and Public Blockchains," *TechCrunch*, Verizon Media, 17 Oct. 2017. techcrunch.com/2017/10/17/polkadot-passes-the-140m-mark-for-its-fund-raise-to-link-private-and-public-blockchains, accessed 8 July 2021.

232. "Bridges," *Polkadot Network*, Web3 Foundation, n.d. wiki.polkadot.network/docs/en/learn-bridges, accessed 8 July 2021.

233. Moonbeam Team, "Moonbeam Network Completes TestNet Integration of Chainbridge, the Network's First Bridge to Ethereum," Announcements, *Moonbeam Network*, PureStake Inc., 27 Jan. 2021. moonbeam.network/announcements/chainbridge-testnet-integration-first-ethereum-bridge, accessed 9 July 2021.

234. Nikolai Kuznetsov, "Ethereum 2.0 and Polkadot Offer Alternative Solutions to Scaling Issue," *Cointelegraph*, 18 July 2020. cointelegraph.com/news/ethereum-20-and-polkadot-offer-alternative-solutions-to-scaling-issue, accessed 9 July 2021.

235. Lucas Mearian, "Sharding: What It Is and Why Many Blockchain Protocols Rely on It," *ComputerWorld*, IDG Communications, 28 Jan. 2019. www.computerworld.com/article/3336187/sharding-what-it-is-and-why-so-many-blockchain-protocols-rely-on-it.html, accessed 23 June 2021.

236. Laura Shin, "How Polkadot Hopes to Help Blockchains Scale," *Forbes.com*, Forbes Media LLC, 14 May 2019. www.forbes.com/sites/laurashin/2019/05/14/how-polkadot-hopes-to-help-blockchains-scale/?sh=6f258d0d13b3, accessed 9 July 2021.

237. "Teams Building on Substrate," *Substrate.io*, Parity Technologies, n.d. www.substrate.io/substrate-users, accessed 9 July 2021.

238. "Polkadot (DOT) ICO," *CoinCodex*, n.d. coincodex.com/ico/polkadot, accessed 9 July 2021.

239. Jordan Lyanchev, "The Story of Polkadot Starts with the 2017 ICO: 2,000% ROI for Early Investors," *CryptoPotato*, CT POTATO, 30 Aug. 2020. cryptopotato.com/the-story-of-polkadot-starts-with-the-2017-ico-2000-roi-for-early-investors, accessed 9 July 2021.

240. Jordan Lyanchev, "The Story of Polkadot Starts with the 2017 ICO: 2,000% ROI for Early Investors."

241. "Mission," *Edgewa.re*, Commonwealth Labs, n.d. edgewa. re; "ExeedMe Launches the First-Ever Blockchain CS:GO Live Tournament," *Hacker Noon*, Artmap Inc., 24 Feb. 2021. hackernoon. com/announcement-exeedme-launches-the-first-ever-blockchain-csgo-live-tournament-v33t33yo; "Edgeware: An Adaptive Smart Contract Blockchain," White Paper Draft v1.02, Commonwealth Labs Inc., 16 July 2019. arena-attachments.s3.amazonaws.com/4643268/c8d128724f36b716660e4bf21823e760.pdf; "Organizations We're Proud to Collaborate With," *OceanProtocol.com*, Ocean Protocol Foundation Ltd., n.d. oceanprotocol.com/collaborators; Polkastarter, "DeFi Startup Polkastarter Raises $875,000 to Launch Polkadot-Based DEX for Cross-Chain Token Pools," *GlobeNewswire*, Intrado Corp., 17 Sept. 2020. www.globenewswire.com/news-release/2020/09/17/2095399/0/en/DeFi-Startup-Polkastarter-Raises-875-000-to-Launch-Polkadot-Based-DEX-for-Cross-Chain-Token-Pools.html; Adam Dossa, Graeme Moore, Jesse Lancaster, Michael Buchanan, and Pablo Ruiz, "Polymesh," White Paper, *Polymath*, 29 Jan. 2020. uploads-ssl.webflow. com/5d2ccf16358ee969a317e33d/5e3205edf287300611a1bf33 Polymesh%20Whitepaper.pdf; Polymath, "Polymath Adds Tokenise and Saxon Advisors as Node Operators on Institutional-Grade Polymesh Blockchain," *PR Newswire*, Cision US Inc., 11 May 2021. www.prnewswire.com/news-releases/polymath-adds-tokenise-and-saxon-advisors-as-node-operators-on-institutional-grade-polymesh-blockchain-301288368.html; "Polymath," *CoinDesk*, Digital Currency Group, n.d. www.coindesk.com/company/polymath; and Ki Chong Tran, "What Is a Lockdrop?" *Decrypt.co*, Decrypt Media Inc., 27 Sept. 2019. decrypt.co/resources/what-is-a-lockdrop, accessed 23 June 2021.

242. "Parachain Slots Auction," *Polkadot Network*, Web3 Foundation, n.d. wiki.polkadot.network/docs/en/learn-auction, accessed 9 July 2021.

243. "Parachain Slots Auction," *Polkadot Network*, Web3 Foundation, n.d.

244. Osprey Funds, "Osprey Funds Launches Osprey Polkadot Trust," *BusinessWire*, Business Wire Inc., 28 April 2021. www.businesswire.com/news/home/20210428005241/en/Osprey-Funds-Launches-Osprey-Polkadot-Trust, accessed 9 July 2021.

245. 21Shares, "21Shares Launches the First Polka ETP," *GlobeNewswire*, Intrado Corp., 2 Feb. 2021. www.globenewswire.com/news-release/2021/02/02/2167832/0/en/21Shares-Launches-The-World-s-First-Polkadot-ETP.html, accessed 9 July 2021.

246. Web3 Foundation Team, "What Is Polkadot? A Brief Introduction," *Polkadot Network Blog*, A Medium Corp., 14 May 2020. medium.com/polkadot-network/what-is-polkadot-a-brief-introduction-ca3eac9ddca5, accessed 9 July 2021.

247. "Introduction," *IRISnet.org*, IRIS Foundation Ltd., n.d. www.irisnet.org, accessed 9 July 2021.

248. michalisFr, "Voting for Councillors," *Polkadot Wiki*, Web3 Foundation, last updated 10 July 2021. wiki.polkadot.network/docs/maintain-guides-how-to-vote-councillor, accessed 23 June 2021.

249. Ethan Buchman, interviewed by Kevin Rooke, 25 Jan. 2021.

250. Ethan Buchman, interviewed by Kevin Rooke, 25 Jan. 2021.

251. Jack Zampolin, interviewed by Kevin Rooke, 18 Feb. 2021.

252. Rafael Belchior, André Vasconcelos, Sérgio Guerreiro, and Miguel Correia, "A Survey on Blockchain Interoperability: Past, Present, and Future Trends," *arXiv.org*, Cornell Univ., 22 March 2021. arxiv.org/pdf/2005.14282.pdf, accessed 23 June 2021.

253. Rafael Belchior et al., "A Survey on Blockchain Interoperability: Past, Present, and Future Trends."

254. Cory Doctorow, "Adversarial Interoperability," *EFF.org*, Electronic Frontier Foundation, 2 Oct. 2019. www.eff.org/deeplinks/2019/10/adversarial-interoperability, accessed 21 June 2021.

255. Adam Hayes, "Facebook's Most Important Acquisitions," *Investopedia.com*, About Inc., 6 Feb. 2020. www.investopedia.com/articles/investing/021115/facebooks-most-important-acquisitions.asp, accessed 9 July 2021.

256. Information Technology Solutions Technology and Innovation Lab, "Blockchain Interoperability," *WorldBank.org*, World Bank Group, 22 March 2021. documents1.worldbank.org/curated/en/373781615365676101/pdf/Blockchain-Interoperability.pdf, accessed 23 June 2021.

257. The idea is to leverage the wisdom of the crowd. Iowa Electronic Markets, Henry B. Tippie College of Business, University of Iowa, 2021. iemweb.biz.uiowa.edu; Hollywood Stock Exchange, HSX LLC, n.d. www.hsx.com; and Daniel E. O'Leary, "Prediction Markets as a Forecasting Tool," *Advances in Business and Management Forecasting* 8 (2011): 169–184. www.marshall.usc.edu/sites/default/files/oleary/intellcont/Prediction_Markets-1.pdf, accessed 20 Nov. 2021.

258. "The Ultimate Guide to Decentralized Prediction Markets," *Augur*, PM Research Ltd., 2018. www.augur.net/blog/prediction-markets, accessed 8 Nov. 2021.

259. Daniel E. O'Leary, "Prediction Markets as a Forecasting Tool," *Advances in Business and Management Forecasting* 8 (2011): 172–174. www.marshall. usc.edu/sites/default/files/oleary/intellcont/Prediction_Markets-1.pdf, accessed 20 Nov. 2021.

260. Troy Lennon, "Death Followed Glory for Chariot Champions," *Daily Telegraph* (Sydney), Business: Feature (27 Oct. 2004): 52. EBSCO Newspaper Source, search-ebscohost-com, accessed 20 Nov. 2021.

261. Elizabeth A. Killick and Mark D. Griffiths, "Why Do Individuals Engage in In-Play Sports Betting? A Qualitative Interview Study," *Journal of Gambling Studies* 37 (13 Aug. 2020): 221–240. Springer, link.springer.com/ article/10.1007/s10899-020-09968-9, accessed 20 Nov. 2021.

262. Paul Crosby and Jordi McKenzie, "The Economics of Ticket Scalping," *The Conversation*, Conversation US Inc., 10 Sept. 2017. theconversation. com/the-economics-of-ticket-scalping-83434, accessed 20 Nov. 2021.

263. Chris Shelton, "Mattress Mack Continues His Tradition with $20M Astros World Series Bet, Promotion," *Houston Chronicle*, Hearst Communications Inc., 8 Oct. 2021. www.houstonchronicle.com/texas-sports-nation/astros/article/Mattress-Mack-continues-his-postseason-tradition-16519303.php, accessed 15 Nov. 2021.

264. Alper Ozgit, "The Bookie Puzzle: Auction Versus Dealer Markets in Online Sports Betting," Working Paper, Department of Economics, University of California at Los Angeles, 29 Sept. 2005. ResearchGate, www.researchgate.net/publication/228864766_The_bookie_puzzle_auction_versus_dealer_markets_in_online_sports_betting; and Steven D. Levitt, "Why Are Gambling Markets Organized So Differently from Financial Markets?" *Economic Journal* 114 (April 2004): 223–246. Royal Economic Society and Blackwell Publishing, economics.yale.edu/ sites/default/files/files/Workshops-Seminars/Industrial-Organization/ levitt-040304.pdf, accessed 3 Nov. 2021.

265. Steve Petrella, "What Is a Betting Exchange and Why Are There None in the United States Yet?" *Action Network*, Action Network Group Inc., 24 Nov. 2021. www.actionnetwork.com/education/betting-exchange, accessed 24 Nov. 2021.

266. Chris Yuscavage, "How Do Sportsbooks Make Money," *Complex.com*, Complex Media Inc., 30 Jan. 2015. www.complex.com/sports/2015/01/ how-betting-lines-work/how-do-sportsbooks-make-money, accessed 3 Nov. 2021.

267. Jean-Charles Rochet and Jean Tirole, "Platform Competition in Two-Sided Markets," *Journal of the European Economic Association* 1, no. 4 (Feb. 2003): 990–1029. Oxford UP, academic.oup.com/jeea/article/1/4/990/2280902, accessed 3 Nov. 2021.

268. Chris Dixon, "Why Decentralization Matters," *One Zero Blog*, Medium Corp., 18 Feb. 2018. onezero.medium.com/why-decentralization-matters-5e3f79f7638e, accessed 3 Nov. 2021.

269. OnlyFoolsAndHorsesWork, "The Betfair Monopoly," *Chit Chat Forum*, Betfair Community, 17 July 2019. community.betfair.com/chit_chat/go/thread/view/94038/31544641/the-betfair-monopoly, accessed 3 Nov. 2021.

270. The author has adapted some of the material in this section from "Crypto Network Fundamentals," *Andrew Young Blog*, Medium.com, 19 Dec. 2017. medium.com/@andrew_young/crypto-network-fundamentals-dfa11f15d026, accessed 3 Nov. 2021.

271. John Authers, "Don't Call Bitcoin a Bubble. It's an Epidemic," *Bloomberg Opinion*, Bloomberg LP, 9 June 2021. www.bloomberg.com/opinion/articles/2021-06-09/don-t-call-bitcoin-a-bubble-it-s-an-epidemic, accessed 3 Nov. 2021.

272. Jon Swartz, "What Is a Platform, and What Should One Do? The Answer Could Determine the Future of Apple and the Rest of Big Tech," *MarketWatch.com*, MarketWatch Inc., 31 Aug. 2021, last updated 3 Sept. 2021. www.marketwatch.com/story/what-is-a-platform-and-what-should-one-do-the-answer-could-determine-the-future-of-apple-and-the-rest-of-big-tech-1163042462, accessed 3 Nov. 2021.

273. Marco Iansiti, "Assessing the Strength of Network Effects in Social Network Platforms," Harvard Business School Working Paper, No. 21-086, Harvard University, Feb. 2021. www.hbs.edu/faculty/Pages/item.aspx?num=59714, accessed 3 Nov. 2021.

274. See Sangeet Paul Choudary, "Why Business Models Fail: Pipes vs. Platforms," *WIRED.com*, Condé Nast, Oct. 2013. www.wired.com/insights/2013/10/why-business-models-fail-pipes-vs-platforms; Barry Libert, Yoram (Jerry) Wind, and Megan Beck, "What Airbnb, Uber, and Alibaba Have in Common," *Harvard Business Review*, Harvard Business Publishing Corp., 20 Nov. 2014. hbr.org/2014/11/what-airbnb-uber-and-alibaba-have-in-common; and Omar Hoda, Joseph Vitale Jr., and Craig A. Giffi, "The Revenue Multiplier Effect: How Enabling Technology Drives Company Value," *Deloitte Insights*, Deloitte Touche Tohmatsu Ltd. (DTTL), 2018, referenced in Anne Kwan, Maximilian Schroeck, Venki Seshaadri, and Deepak Sharma, "Digital Platform as a

Growth Lever," *Deloitte Insights*, DTTL, 29 July 2020. www2.deloitte. com/us/en/insights/focus/industry-4-0/digital-platform-strategy.html, accessed 3 Nov. 2021.

275. Cathy Barrera, "Blockchain Incentive Structures: What They Are and Why They Matter," *PrysmEconomics Blog*, Prysm Group, 22 Aug. 2018. medium.com/prysmeconomics/blockchain-incentives-101-what-they-are-and-why-they-matter-5127afb56aeb, accessed 3 Nov. 2021.

276. Ian Carlos Campbell and Julia Alexander, "A Guide to Platform Fees," *The Verge*, Vox Media LLC, last updated 24 Aug. 2021. www.theverge. com/21445923/platform-fees-apps-games-business-marketplace-apple-google, accessed 3 Nov. 2021.

277. "Decentralized Prediction Markets," *DeFiPrime.com*, Nick Sawinyh, n.d. defiprime.com/prediction-markets; and Alyssa Hertig, "How Crypto Transforms Prediction Markets," *CoinDesk*, Digital Currency Group, 18 Feb. 2021, updated 14 Sept. 2021. www.coindesk.com/tech/2021/02 /18/how-crypto-transforms-prediction-markets, accessed 3 Nov. 2021.

278. Note, these rates may vary depending on jurisdiction and other factors. "SportX Fees," SX Network, updated ~2 Jan. 2022. help.sportx.bet/en/ articles/2798017-sportx-fees; and "Exchange: What Is the Market Base Rate?" *Betfair Support*, Flutter Entertainment PLC, n.d. support.betfair. com/app/answers/detail/a_id/412, accessed 8 Jan. 2022.

279. Dan Reiter and Allan C. Stam III, "Democracy and Battlefield Military Effectiveness," *Journal of Conflict Resolution* 42, no. 3 (June 1998): 259–277. Sage Publications Inc., web.stanford.edu/class/polisci211z/2.7/ Reiter&Stam%20JCR%201998.pdf, accessed 3 Nov. 2021.

280. The author has adapted this material from "Crypto Network Fundamentals," *Andrew Young Blog*, Medium.com, 19 Dec. 2017. medium.com/@andrew_young/crypto-network-fundamentals-dfa11f15d026, accessed 3 Nov. 2021.

281. A whale is an individual or entity that holds such a large amount of token or cryptocurrency that its market activity could affect the token's or cryptocurrency's value. Caroline Banton, "Bitcoin Whale," *Investopedia. com*, About Inc., updated 8 Feb. 2021. www.investopedia.com/terms/b/ bitcoin-whale.asp, accessed 18 March 2021.

282. Robin D. Hanson, "Futarchy: Vote Values, But Bet Beliefs," Department of Economics, George Mason University, 2013. mason.gmu. edu/~rhanson/futarchy2013.pdf; and "Shall We Vote on Value, But Bet on Beliefs?" Department of Economics, George Mason University, Feb. 2003, updated 14 Jan. 2013. mason.gmu.edu/~rhanson/futarchy.pdf, accessed 3 Nov. 2021.

283. This is an edited transcript of the webinar. To view the complete session, see "Going Cashless: The Digital Dollar in the Face of COVID-19," Webinar, *YouTube.com*, Blockchain Research Institute, 28 April 2020. www.youtube.com/watch?v=ZEgfFCBTTuQ, accessed 30 April 2020.

284. Don Tapscott, Alex Tapscott, et al., "Blockchain Solutions in Pandemics: A Call for Innovation and Transformation in Public Health," Blockchain Research Institute, 7 April 2020. www.blockchainresearchinstitute.org/blockchain-and-pandemics, accessed 2 June 2020.

285. Victor Hugo, speech at a banquet in his honor, Hotel Continental (now a Westin), Paris, 1883. It is said that the phrase is an adaptation of "More powerful than an invading army is an idea whose time has come."

286. Satoshi Nakamoto, "Bitcoin: A Peer-to-Peer Electronic Cash System," Bitcoin Project, 31 Oct. 2009. bitcoin.org/bitcoin.pdf, accessed 6 April 2020.

287. Nick Statt, "The Libra Project Will Now Support Existing Currencies in Addition to the Proposed Libra Token," *The Verge*, Vox Media LLC, 3 March 2020. www.theverge.com/2020/3/3/21163658/facebook-libra-cryptocurrency-token-ditching-plans-calibra-wallet-delay, accessed 6 April 2020.

288. "Statement of CFTC Commissioner Sharon Y. Bowen on the Launch of LabCFTC," News Release, US Commodity Futures Trading Commission, 17 May 2017. www.cftc.gov/PressRoom/SpeechesTestimony/bowenstatement051717, accessed 2 June 2020.

289. "The Digital Dollar Project: A Multi-Stakeholder Initiative to Develop Options for a Digital Dollar," Press Release, The Digital Dollar Foundation, Jan. 2020. www.digitaldollarproject.org/issue-briefing, accessed 2 June 2020.

290. Don Tapscott and Alex Tapscott, *Blockchain Revolution: How the Technology Behind Bitcoin and Other Cryptocurrencies Is Change the World* (New York: Penguin Portfolio, 2018). www.amazon.com/Blockchain-Revolution-Technology-Cryptocurrencies-Changing-dp-1101980141/dp/1101980141, accessed 2 June 2020.

291. *Financial Services Revolution: How Blockchain Is Transforming Money, Markets, and Banking*, edited with foreword by Alex Tapscott (Toronto: Blockchain Research Institute/Barlow Book Publishing, 5 Feb. 2020). www.amazon.com/Financial-Services-Revolution-Blockchain-Transforming/dp/1988025494, accessed 2 June 2020.

292. "The Futures of Capitalism; CME Group," *The Economist* 407, no. 8835, The Economist Newspaper Ltd., 11 May 2013: 77. www.economist.com/finance-and-economics/2013/05/11/the-futures-of-capitalism, accessed 2 June 2020.

293. The organization was the GFI Group Inc., www.gfigroup.com. Here is a page from its archive during Chris' tenure, 22 Feb. 2008. web.archive. org/web/20080222095043/http://www.gfigroup.com/portal/index. jsp?pageID=def_aboutgfi_structm, accessed 2 June 2020.

294. "Credit Default Swaps," CFA Institute, 2020 Curriculum, n.d. www. cfainstitute.org/en/membership/professional-development/refresher-readings/2020/credit-default-swaps, accessed 2 June 2020.

295. "Treasuries," *InvestingAnswers.com*, Investing Answers Inc., 18 Sept. 2019. investinganswers.com/dictionary/t/treasuries, accessed 2 June 2020.

296. Bryan Cave Leighton Paisner, "10 Years of Troubled Asset Relief Program," *JD Supra*, JD Supra LLC, 3 Oct. 2018. www.jdsupra.com/ legalnews/10-years-of-troubled-asset-relief-73818, accessed 2 June 2020.

297. "Wholesale Markets Brokers' Association, Americas Commends Historic US Financial Legislation," Press Release, Wholesale Markets Brokers Association (Americas), 21 July 2010. www.wmbaa.com/wp-content/ uploads/2012/01/WMBAA-Dodd-Frank-Law-press-release-final123. pdf, accessed 2 June 2020.

298. Weizhen Tan, "Cryptocurrency Regulation Requires a 'Do No Harm' Approach, US Regulator Says," *CNBC.com*, NBC Universal, 14 Sept. 2018. www.cnbc.com/2018/09/14/do-no-harm-in-regulating-cryptocurrencies-but-be-vigilant-cftc.html, accessed 2 June 2020.

299. Office of Public Affairs, "CFTC Backgrounder on Self-Certified Contracts for Bitcoin Products," US Commodity Futures Trading Commission, 1 Dec. 2017. www.cftc.gov/sites/default/files/idc/groups/ public/@newsroom/documents/file/bitcoin_factsheet120117.pdf, accessed 2 June 2020.

300. For additional analysis, see Steven P. Goldberg and John Cooney, "OTC Derivatives: Their Role in the Financial Crisis, the Impact of Financial Reform, and the Outlook for the Future," *Journal of Taxation and Regulation of Financial Institutions* 24, 13 (Sept./Oct. 2010); Matthew F. Kluchenek and Nicole M. Kuchera, "A Credit Default Swaps Primer: Uses, Mechanics, Benefits, Risks, Regulation, and Developments," *Journal of Taxation of Investments* 27, 3 (Fall 2009); and John F. Rosato, "Note and Commentaries: Down the Road to Perdition: How the Flaws of Basel II Led to the Collapse of Bear Stearns and Lehman Brothers," *Connecticut Insurance Law Journal* 17, 475 (2010/2011).

301. Marco Di Maggio and Nicholas Platias, "Is Stablecoin the Next Big Thing in E-Commerce?" *Harvard Business Review*, Harvard Business School Publishing Corp., 21 May 2020. hbr.org/2020/05/is-stablecoin-the-next-big-thing-in-e-commerce, accessed 3 June 2020.

302. "Why Are T-Bills Used When Determining Risk-Free Rates?" *Investopedia.com*, Dotdash Publishing, About Inc., updated 7 Nov. 2018. www.investopedia.com/ask/answers/040915/how-riskfree-rate-determined-when-calculating-market-risk-premium.asp#, accessed 3 June 2020.

303. For additional analysis, see Joel S. Telpner, "The Lion, the Unicorn, and the Crown: Striking a Balance between Regulation and Blockchain Innovation," foreword by Don Tapscott, Blockchain Research Institute, 10 May 2018. www.blockchainresearchinstitute.org/7914-2.

304. For actual text, see Cong. Research Serv., "Fourth Amendment: Historical Background," *Constitution of the United States: Analysis and Interpretation*, US Library of Congress, n.d. constitution.congress.gov/browse/essay/amdt4_1/ALDE_00000774, accessed 3 June 2020.

305. "Economic Impact Payments," *Coronavirus Tax Relief*, Internal Revenue Service, US Department of the Treasury, updated 2 June 2020. www.irs.gov/coronavirus/economic-impact-payments, accessed 2 June 2020.

306. Jake Frankenfield, "Cryptocurrency Airdrop," *Investopedia.com*, Dotdash Publishing Co., About Inc., 12 Nov. 2019. www.investopedia.com/terms/a/airdrop-cryptocurrency.asp, accessed 2 June 2020.

307. For more detail, see "Distribution of Currency and Coins," US Department of the Treasury, last updated 13 Nov. 2014. www.treasury.gov/about/education/Pages/distribution.aspx, accessed 2 June 2020.

308. Carolyn Sofman et al., *Infrastructure Report Card 2017: A Comprehensive Assessment of America's Infrastructure*, foreword by Norma Jean Mattei, American Society of Civil Engineers, 21 Feb. 2019. www.infrastructurereportcard.org/wp-content/uploads/2019/02/Full-2017-Report-Card-FINAL.pdf, accessed 2 June 2020.

309. Mark Carney, "The Growing Challenges for Monetary Policy in the Current International Monetary and Financial System," Speech, Bank of England, Jackson Hole Symposium, Kansas City, MO, 23 Aug. 2019. www.bankofengland.co.uk/-/media/boe/files/speech/2019/the-growing-challenges-for-monetary-policy-speech-by-mark-carney.pdf, accessed 8 Sept. 2019.

310. *World Health Statistics 2019: Monitoring Health for the SDGs*, foreword by Tedros Adhanom Ghebreyesus, World Health Organization, 30 Oct. 2019, modified 7 Jan. 2020. apps.who.int/iris/bitstream/handle/10665/324835/9789241565707-eng.pdf, accessed 2 June 2020.

311. See also "Organisational Structure and Governance," Financial Stability Board, n.d. www.fsb.org/organisation-and-governance, accessed 2 June 2020.

312. "Coinage of the British East India Company," Colonial India, The Fitzwilliam Museum, University of Cambridge, n.d. www.fitzmuseum. cam.ac.uk/gallery/East-West/India 1.html.

313. Sewall Hamm Menzel, *Cobs, Pieces of Eight, and Treasure Coins: The Early Spanish-American Mints and Their Coinages 1536–1773* (New York: American Numismatic Society, 2004).

314. "Cryptocurrency Part II: Hester Peirce on the SEC's Role in Crypto," hosted by Dori Goldstein and Meg McEvoy, *Law X.0 Podcast*, Prod. RJ Jewell, Bloomberg Law Analysis, 20 Nov. 2019. news.bloomberglaw. com/bloomberg-law-analysis/analysis-hester-peirce-on-the-secs-role-in-crypto-podcast, accessed 3 June 2020.

315. Jim Seymour, "Do Graphical Results Require a Graphical Interface?" *PC Magazine*, Ziff-Davis Publishing Co., 15 Jan. 1991, p. 87. books.google. com/books?id=WwMCsPuGSLEC, accessed 3 June 2020.

316. Nathan Heller, "Estonia, the Digital Republic," *New Yorker*, Condé Nast, 11 Dec. 2017. www.newyorker.com/magazine/2017/12/18/estonia-the-digital-republic, accessed 3 June 2020.

317. Libra Association, "An Introduction to Libra," White Paper V2.0, 10 April 2020. libra.org/en-US/white-paper, accessed 2 June 2020.

318. Libra Association, "An Introduction to Libra," White Paper V1.0, 14 June 2019. libra.org/en-US/wp-content/uploads/sites/23/2019/06/LibraWhitePaper en US.pdf, accessed 2 June 2020.

319. For examples, look for the following case studies in the BRI public research hub: Massimo Morini, "Utility Settlement Coin: The Need for Digital Currencies in the Banking Industry," foreword by Don Tapscott, Blockchain Research Institute, 25 May 2018. Alan Majer, "Non-Fungible Tokens: Transforming the Worlds of Assets, Gaming, and Collectibles," foreword by Alex Tapscott, Blockchain Research Institute, 30 Aug. 2019. Massimo Morini, "Financial Derivatives with Blockchain and Smart Contracts," foreword by Alex Tapscott, Blockchain Research Institute, 16 Jan. 2020. Anthony D. Williams, "Nivaura's Blockchain-Based Securities: How a Start-up Worked with a UK Regulator," foreword by Alex Tapscott, Blockchain Research Institute, 5 May 2020.

320. Alex Tapscott, "The Coming Cataclysm: Blockchain and Financial Services," foreword by Don Tapscott, Blockchain Research Institute, 30 Sept. 2019.

321. Sid Coelho-Prabhu, "A Beginner's Guide to Decentralized Finance (DeFi)," *The Coinbase Blog*, Coinbase, 6 Jan. 2020. blog. coinbase.com/a-beginners-guide-to-decentralized-finance-defi-574c68ff43c4?gi=1c54b5f62592, accessed 2 June 2020.

322. Charles H. Giancarlo, J. Christopher Giancarlo, Daniel Gorfine, and David B. Treat, "The Digital Dollar Project: Exploring a US CBDC," White Paper, The Digital Dollar Foundation and Accenture, 29 May 2020. tinyurl.com/ya8bzc6v, accessed 2 June 2020.

323. David R. Williams, "Chronology of US Astronaut Missions (1961–1972)," NASA Space Science Data Coordinated Archive, National Aeronautics and Space Administration, last updated 12 April 2016. nssdc. gsfc.nasa.gov/planetary/chrono astronaut.html, accessed 2 June 2020.

324. Satoshi Nakamoto, "Bitcoin: A Peer-to-Peer Electronic Cash System," White Paper, *Bitcoin.org*, 1 Nov. 2008. bitcoin.org/bitcoin.pdf, accessed 29 Oct. 2020.

325. Vitalik Buterin, "The Search for a Stable Cryptocurrency," *Ethereum Blog*, Ethereum Foundation, 11 Nov. 2014. blog.ethereum.org/2014/11/11/search-stable-cryptocurrency, accessed 29 Oct. 2020.

326. Vitalik Buterin, "The Search for a Stable Cryptocurrency."

327. For the original paper, see J. R. Willett, "The Second Bitcoin Whitepaper," Version 0.5, n.d. drive.google.com/file/d/18iRKDmZy44 YDd3jyEtafouT1PA7dEi5e/view; for commentary on the original paper, see Dominik Zynis, "A Brief History of Mastercoin," *Omni Blog*, Omni Foundation, 29 Nov. 2013. blog.omni.foundation/2013/11/29/a-brief-history-of-mastercoin, both accessed 29 Oct. 2020.

328. Daniel Larimer, Charles Hoskinson, and Stan Larimer, "BitShares—A Peer-to-Peer Polymorphic Digital Asset Exchange (P2P-PDAE)," *BitMEX.com*, HDR Global Trading Ltd., uploaded June 2018. blog. bitmex.com/wp-content/uploads/2018/06/173481633-BitShares-White-Paper.pdf, accessed 29 Oct. 2020. Originally published by authors on *BitcoinTalk.org*, 19 Oct. 2013. bitcointalk.org/index.php?topic=313873.0.

329. Daniel Larimer, Charles Hoskinson, and Stan Larimer, "BitShares."

330. Daniel Larimer, Charles Hoskinson, and Stan Larimer, "BitShares."

331. Adam Hayes, "Fiat Money vs. Commodity Money: Which Is More Prone to Inflation?" *Investopedia*, Dotcash, 15 July 2020. www. investopedia.com/ask/answers/041515/fiat-money-more-prone-inflation-commodity-money.asp, accessed 29 Oct. 2020.

332. "Top 10 Use Cases and Benefits of the Dai Stablecoin," *Maker Blog*, Maker Foundation, 8 April 2020. blog.makerdao.com/top-10-use-cases-and-benefits-of-the-dai-stablecoin, accessed 29 Oct. 2020.

333. Lucas Mearian, "For Real Estate, Blockchain Could Unshackle Investment," *Computerworld*, IDG Communication Inc., 24 May 2019. www.computerworld.com/article/3396627/for-real-estate-blockchain-could-unshackle-investment.html, accessed 29 Oct. 2020.

334. Jeff John Roberts, "Winklevoss Twins: Bitcoin Can Overtake Gold with the Right Rules," *Fortune.com*, Fortune Media IP Ltd., 13 Jan. 2019. fortune.com/2019/01/13/winklevoss-gemini, accessed 29 Oct. 2020.

335. Ameer Rosic, "Smart Contracts: The Blockchain Technology that Will Replace Lawyers," *Blockgeeks.com*, Blockgeeks, n.d. blockgeeks.com/guides/smart-contracts, accessed 29 Oct. 2020.

336. Thomas M. Humphrey, "The Quantity Theory of Money: Its Historical Evolution and Role in Policy Debates," *Economic Review*, Federal Reserve Bank of Richmond, May/June 1974. www.richmondfed.org/~/media/richmondfedorg/publications/research/economic_review/1974/pdf/er600301.pdf, accessed 2 Nov. 2020.

337. Thomas M. Humphrey, "The Quantity Theory of Money."

338. Koshy Mathai, "Monetary Policy: Stabilizing Prices and Output," International Monetary Fund, last updated 24 Feb. 2020. www.imf.org/external/pubs/ft/fandd/basics/monpol.htm, accessed 1 Nov. 2020.

339. Taegun Charles Kim, "[ENG] The World of Stablecoin: Mapping Stablecoin (Part 1)," *Decon*, Medium.com, 12 Oct. 2018. medium.com/decon-lab/the-world-of-stablecoin-mapping-stablecoin-1-84970903cb0d, accessed 1 Nov. 2020.

340. Jackie Lohrey, "Fisher Effect Formula," *Zacks.com*, Zacks Investment Research, last updated 5 Feb. 2019. finance.zacks.com/fisher-effect-formula-9023.html, accessed 30 Oct. 2020.

341. Daniel Larimer, "Overpaying for Security: The Hidden Costs of Bitcoin," *Let's Talk Bitcoin!*, BTC Media LLC, 7 Sept. 2013. letstalkbitcoin.com/is-bitcoin-overpaying-for-false-security, accessed 30 Oct. 2020.

342. Daniel Larimer, "Overpaying for Security: The Hidden Costs of Bitcoin."

343. Daniel Larimer, "Overpaying for Security: The Hidden Costs of Bitcoin."

344. BitMEX Research, "A Brief History of Stablecoins," *BitMEX.com*, HDR Global Trading Ltd., 2 July 2018. blog.bitmex.com/a-brief-history-of-stablecoins-part-1, accessed 29 Oct. 2020.

345. Preston Byrne, "Basecoin (aka the Basis Protocol): The Worst Idea in Cryptocurrency, Reborn," *The Back of the Envelope Blog*, PrestonBryne.com, 13 Oct. 2017. prestonbyrne.com/2017/10/13/basecoin-bitshares-2-electric-boogaloo, accessed 29 Oct. 2020.

346. Preston Byrne, "The Cryptopocalypse," *The Back of the Envelope Blog*, PrestonBryne.com, 16 Jan. 2018. prestonbyrne.com/2018/01/16/on-the-investors-field-guide, accessed 29 Oct. 2020.

347. Mike Orcutt, "'Stablecoins' Are Trending, But They May Ignore Basic Economics," *MIT Technology Review*, Massachusetts Institute of Technology, 7 June 2018. www.technologyreview. com/2018/06/07/240613/stablecoins-are-trending-but-they-may-ignore-basic-economics, accessed 1 Nov. 2020.

348. For more on Hashcash, see Adam Back, "The Hashcash Proof-of-Work Function," Network Working Group Draft, The Internet Society, June 2003. www.hashcash.org/papers/draft-hashcash.txt, accessed 30 Oct. 2020.

349. Cassio Gusson, "Exclusive: 'Nothing Is above Bitcoin, No CBDC, No Stablecoins,' Says Blockstream CEO Adam Back," *Cointelegraph.com*, 25 Nov. 2019. cointelegraph.com/news/exclusive-nothing-is-above-bitcoin-no-cbdc-no-stablecoins-says-blockstream-ceo-adam-back, accessed 30 Oct. 2020.

350. John Shipman and George Samman, "Stable Coin Evolution and Market Trends: Key Observations," *PwC.com.au*, PricewaterhouseCoopers International Ltd., Oct. 2018. www.pwc.com.au/pdf/stable-coin-evolution-and-market-trends.pdf, accessed 29 Oct. 2020.

351. BitMEX Research, "A Brief History of Stablecoins," *BitMEX.com*, HDR Global Trading Ltd., 2 July 2018. blog.bitmex.com/a-brief-history-of-stablecoins-part-1, accessed 29 Oct. 2020.

352. Steven Ehrlich, "After an $850 Million Controversy, What Everyone Should Know about Bitfinex, Tether and Stablecoins," *Forbes.com*, Forbes Media LLC, 2 May 2019. www.forbes.com/sites/stevenehrlich/2019/05/02/after-an-850-million-controversy-what-everyone-should-know-about-bitfinex-tether-and-stablecoins; and Cali Haan, "Bitfinex Starts Buying Back LEO Tokens Issued to Cover Funds Seized by Law Enforcement," *CrowdFundInsider.com*, Crowded Media Group, LLC, 15 June 2016. www.crowdfundinsider.com/2019/06/148443-bitfinex-starts-buying-back-leo-tokens-issued-to-cover-funds-seized-by-law-enforcement, both accessed 1 Nov. 2020.

353. "H.R.5197—Managed Stablecoins Are Securities Act of 2019," 116th Congress, *Congress.gov*, Library of Congress, United States Copyright Office, 20 Nov. 2019. www.congress.gov/bill/116th-congress/house-bill/5197, accessed 30 Oct. 2020.

354. "Rep. Sylvia Garcia and Rep. Lance Gooden Introduce the 'Managed Stablecoins Are Securities Act of 2019,'" Press Release, *SylviaGarcia.House.gov*, US House of Representatives, 21 Nov. 2019. sylviagarcia.house.gov/media/press-releases/rep-sylvia-garcia-and-rep-lance-gooden-introduce-managed-stablecoins-are, accessed 30 Oct. 2020.

355. "Rep. Sylvia Garcia and Rep. Lance Gooden Introduce the 'Managed Stablecoins Are Securities Act of 2019.'"

356. Nick Lioudis, "What Is the Gold Standard?" *Investopedia*, Dotdash, last updated 24 Sept. 2020. www.investopedia.com/ask/answers/09/gold-standard.asp, accessed 2 Nov. 2020.

357. The United States hung onto some version of the gold standard until the early 1970s. See Nick Lioudis, "What Is the Gold Standard?"

358. Carla Tardi, "Why Has Gold Always Been Valuable?" *Investopedia*, Dotdash, last updated 14 Sept. 2020. www.investopedia.com/articles/investing/071114/why-gold-has-always-had-value.asp, accessed 30 Oct. 2020.

359. Mark Cartwright, "Mansa Musa I," *Ancient History Encyclopedia*, Ancient History Encyclopedia Foundation, 26 Feb. 2019. www.ancient.eu/Mansa_Musa_I, accessed 30 Oct. 2020.

360. Clem Chambers, "Bitcoin Is Better than Gold for One Simple Reason," *Forbes.com*, Fortune Media IP Ltd., 4 Nov. 2019. www.forbes.com/sites/investor/2019/11/04/bitcoin-is-better-than-gold-for-one-simple-reason, accessed 3 Nov. 2020.

361. Marie Huillet, "Crypto Trailblazer Nick Szabo: Central Banks Could Turn to Crypto to Support Reserves," *Cointelegraph.com*, 9 Jan. 2019. cointelegraph.com/news/crypto-trailblazer-nick-szabo-central-banks-could-turn-to-crypto-to-support-reserves, accessed 2 Nov. 2020.

362. Georgi Georgiev, "'Uncanny': Historic Gold & Bitcoin Price Charts Almost Identical," *Bitcoinist.com*, 8 Sept. 2018. bitcoinist.com/gold-bitcoin-history-identical, accessed 30 Oct. 2020.

363. Alyze Sam, "BITCOIN vs GOLD: What's Valuable & What's Not," *The Capital*, Medium.com, 26 April 2019. medium.com/the-capital/bitcoin-vs-gold-whats-valuable-what-s-not-db117c40ad0d, accessed 30 Oct. 2020.

364. "Fiat," *Merriam-Webster.com Dictionary*, Merriam-Webster Inc., last updated 25 Oct. 2020. www.merriam-webster.com/dictionary/fiat, accessed 3 Nov. 2020.

365. The Editors of Encyclopaedia Britannica, "Gold Standard," ed. Brian Duignan, *Encyclopaedia Britannica*, Encyclopædia Britannica Inc., n.d. www.britannica.com/topic/gold-standard; "What Is Fiat Money?" *CorporateFinanceInstitute.com*, CFI Education Inc., n.d. corporatefinanceinstitute.com/resources/knowledge/economics/fiat-money-currency, accessed 30 Oct. 2020.

366. John Maxfield, "JPMorgan Chase Is 10 Times Bigger than You Think It Is," *The Motley Fool*, The Motley Fool, 24 Aug. 2016, last updated 9 Oct. 2018. www.fool.com/investing/2016/08/24/jpmorgan-chase-is-10-times-bigger-than-you-think-i.aspx, accessed 30 Oct. 2020.

367. Stan Higgins, "JPMorgan Launches Interbank Payments Platform on Quorum Blockchain," *CoinDesk*, Digital Currency Group, 16 Oct. 2017. www.coindesk.com/jpmorgan-launches-interbank-payments-platform-quorum-blockchain; Daniel Palmer, "JPMorgan Expanding Blockchain Project with 220 Banks to Include Payments," *CoinDesk*, Digital Currency Group, 22 April 2019. www.coindesk.com/jpmorgan-expanding-blockchain-project-with-220-banks-to-include-payments, accessed 31 Oct. 2020.

368. "Liink by J.P.Morgan: Transforming How Information Moves," *J.P.Morgan*, JPMorgan Chase & Co., n.d. www.jpmorgan.com/onyx/liink, accessed 1 Nov. 2020.

369. Ian Allison, "ConsenSys Acquires JPMorgan's Quorum Blockchain," *CoinDesk*, Digital Currency Group, 25 Aug 2020. www.coindesk.com/consensys-acquires-jp-morgan-quorum-blockchain, accessed 1 Nov. 2020.

370. Ian Allison, "JPMorgan Adds Privacy Features to Ethereum-Based Quorum Blockchain," *CoinDesk*, Digital Currency Group, 28 May 2019. www.coindesk.com/jpmorgan-adds-new-privacy-features-to-its-ethereum-based-quorum-blockchain, accessed 30 Oct. 2020.

371. "J.P.Morgan Creates Digital Coin for Payments," Press Release, *JPMorgan.com*, JPMorgan Chase & Co., 14 Feb. 2019. www.jpmorgan.com/solutions/cib/news/digital-coin-payments, accessed 1 Nov. 2020.

372. Saumya Vaishampayan, "J.P. Morgan's Jamie Dimon Says Bitcoin Is a 'Terrible Store of Value,'" *Thetell Blog*, MarketWatch Inc., 23 Jan. 2014. www.marketwatch.com/story/jp-morganaposs-jamie-dimon-says-bitcoin-is-a-aposterrible-store-of-valueapos-1390498669, accessed 1 Nov. 2020.

373. Yessi Bello Perez, "Jamie Dimon: Bitcoin Will Not Survive," *CoinDesk*, Digital Currency Group, 5 Nov. 2015, last updated 19 May 2017. www.coindesk.com/jamie-dimon-bitcoin-will-not-survive, accessed 1 Nov. 2020.

374. Aaron Hankin, "Jamie Dimon: 'I Don't Really Give a Shit about Bitcoin,'" *MarketWatch*, MarketWatch Inc., 31 Oct. 2018. www.marketwatch.com/story/jamie-dimon-i-dont-really-give-a-shit-about-bitcoin-2018-10-31, accessed 1 Nov. 2020.

375. Alyze Sam, "The J.P.Morgan Cryptocurrency Criticisms and Their Cryptocurrency … ," *The Capital*, Medium.com, 3 Oct. 2019. medium.com/the-capital/the-j-p-morgan-cryptocurrency-criticisms-and-their-cryptocurrency-49bef4ec4fbeJ, accessed 21 Nov. 2020.

376. "J.P.Morgan Creates Digital Coin for Payments," *JPMorgan.com*, JPMorgan Chase & Co., 14 Feb. 2019. www.jpmorgan.com/global/news/digital-coin-payments; Daniel Palmer, "JPMorgan's 'JPM Coin' Is

Live, Execs Say," *CoinDesk*, Digital Currency Group, 27 Oct. 2020. www. coindesk.com/jpmorgans-jpm-coin-is-live-exec-says, both accessed 1 Nov. 2020.

377. Hugh Son, "JPMorgan Is Rolling Out the First US Bank-Backed Cryptocurrency to Transform Payments Business," *CNBC.com*, CNBC LLC, 14 Feb. 2019. www.cnbc.com/2019/02/13/jp-morgan-is-rolling-out-the-first-us-bank-backed-cryptocurrency-to-transform-payments--. html, accessed 1 Nov. 2020.

378. Ian Allison, "JPMorgan Adds Privacy Features to Ethereum-Based Quorum Blockchain"; "GoQuorum Projects," *GoQuorum*, ConsenSys, n.d. docs.goquorum.consensys.net/en/stable/Reference/GoQuorum-Projects; and Benedikt Bünz, Shashank Agrawal, Mahdi Zamani, and Dan Boneh, "Zether: Towards Privacy in a Smart Contract World," *Crypto.stanford. edu.*, Applied Cryptography Group, Stanford University, Feb. 2020. crypto.stanford.edu/~buenz/papers/zether.pdf, all accessed 1 Nov. 2020.

379. Ian Allison, "JPMorgan Adds Privacy Features to Ethereum-Based Quorum Blockchain."

380. Hugh Son, "JPMorgan Creates New Unit for Blockchain Projects, Says the Technology Is Close to Making Money," *CNBC.com*, CNBC LLC, 27 Oct. 2020. www.cnbc.com/2020/10/27/jpmorgan-creates-new-unit-for-blockchain-projects-as-it-says-the-technology-is-close-to-making-money.html, accessed 31 Oct. 2020.

381. "Signet," *Signature*, Signature Bank, 4 Dec. 2018. www.signatureny. com/business/signet, accessed 21 Nov. 2020; and Benjamin Pirus, "Signature Bank Beats JPMorgan to Ethereum-Based Token Services," *Forbes.com*, Forbes Media LLC, 22 Feb. 2019. www.forbes.com/sites/ benjaminpirus/2019/02/22/signature-bank-already-has-hundreds-of-clients-using-private-ethereum-jpm-coin-still-in-testing, accessed 1 Nov. 2020.

382. Andrew Singer, "WisdomTree Grows a Stablecoin Today to Nurture a Crypto ETF Tomorrow," *Cointelegraph*, 18 Jan. 2020. cointelegraph.com/ news/wisdomtree-grows-a-stablecoin-today-to-nurture-a-crypto-etf-tomorrow, accessed 1 Nov. 2020.

383. Haseeb Qureshi, "Stablecoins: Designing a Price-Stable Cryptocurrency," *HaseebQ.com*, 19 Feb. 2018. haseebq.com/stablecoins-designing-a-price-stable-cryptocurrency, accessed 1 Nov. 2020.

384. James Chen, "Commodity," *Investopedia*, Dotdash, last updated 14 Feb. 2020. www.investopedia.com/terms/c/commodity.asp, accessed 1 Nov. 2020.

385. Anthem Blanchard, message to authors, n.d. See also Anthem Gold, AnthemGold Inc., n.d. anthemgold.com; Patrick Donohoe, "Financial Structures: A New Gold Standard with Anthem Blanchard," Podcast, *TheWealthStandard.com*, 16 April 2020. thewealthstandard.com/financial-structures-a-new-gold-standard-with-anthem-blanchard, accessed 16 Oct. 2020.

386. Julia Kagan, "Fractional Reserve Banking," *Investopedia*, Dotdash, last updated 4 May 2020. www.investopedia.com/terms/f/fractionalreservebanking.asp, accessed 31 Oct. 2020.

387. John M. Griffin and Amin Shams, "Is Bitcoin Really Un-Tethered?" *SSRN.com*, Elsevier, 28 Oct. 2019, last updated 5 Nov. 2019. ssrn.com/abstract=3195066, accessed 1 Nov. 2020.

388. "United States District Court Southern District of New York," Case 1:20-cv-00169, *CourtHouseNews.com*, 8 Jan. 2020. www.courthousenews.com/wp-content/uploads/2020/01/Bitcoin.pdf; Michael del Castillo, "New York Court Approves Investigation into $10 Billion Cryptocurrency Created by a Presidential Candidate," *Forbes.com*, Forbes Media LLC, 9 July 2020. www.forbes.com/sites/michaeldelcastillo/2020/07/09/ny-supreme-court-approves-investigation-into-10-billion-cryptocurrency-created-by-a-presidential-candidate/?sh=66446fc3783b, both accessed 1 Nov. 2020.

389. Nikhilesh De, "Tether Lawyer Admits Stablecoin Now 74% Backed by Cash and Equivalents," *CoinDesk*, Digital Currency Group, 30 April 2019, last updated 1 May 2019. www.coindesk.com/tether-lawyer-confirms-stablecoin-74-percent-backed-by-cash-and-equivalents, accessed 2 Nov. 2020.

390. "Risk Disclosure Statement," *Tether*, Tether Operations Ltd., last updated 12 May 2020. tether.to/legal, accessed 2 Nov. 2020.

391. Robert Sams, "A Note on Cryptocurrency Stabilisation: Seigniorage Shares," *GitHub.com*, GitHub Inc., 24 Oct. 2014, last revised 28 April 2015. github.com/rmsams/stablecoins/blob/master/paper.pdf; Ferdinando M. Ametrano, "Hayek Money: The Cryptocurrency Price Stability Solution," *SSRN.com*, Elsevier, 17 April 2014, last revised 13 Aug. 2016. ssrn.com/abstract=2425270, both accessed 1 Nov. 2020.

392. Vitalik Buterin, "The Search for a Stable Cryptocurrency," *Ethereum Blog*, Ethereum Foundation, 11 Nov. 2014. blog.ethereum.org/2014/11/11/search-stable-cryptocurrency, accessed 31 Oct. 2020.

393. Richard Senner and Didier Sornette, "The 'New Normal' of the Swiss Balance of Payments in a Global Perspective: Central Bank Intervention, Global Imbalances and the Rise of Sovereign Wealth Funds," Swiss

Finance Institute Research Paper No. 17-22, *SSRN.com*, Elsevier, 1 June 2017. ssrn.com/abstract=2990512, accessed 31 Oct. 2020.

394. Neil Irwin, "Quantitative Easing Is Ending. Here's What It Did, in Charts," *New York Times*, New York Times Company. 29 Oct. 2014. www. nytimes.com/2014/10/30/upshot/quantitative-easing-is-about-to-end-heres-what-it-did-in-seven-charts.html, accessed 31 Oct. 2020.

395. Richard Senner and Didier Sornette, "The 'New Normal' of the Swiss Balance of Payments in a Global Perspective."

396. Preston Byrne, "Basecoin (aka the Basis Protocol): The Worst Idea in Cryptocurrency, Reborn," *The Back of the Envelope Blog*, PrestonByrne. com, 13 Oct. 2017. prestonbyrne.com/2017/10/13/basecoin-bitshares-2-electric-boogaloo, accessed 31 Oct. 2020.

397. Patrick Devereaux, CEO of Aperum, contributed this quote to the manuscript.

398. Nat Wittayatanaseth, "Stablecoins: De-Risking Non-Collateralized Stablecoins," Medium.com, 27 April 2018. medium.com/@ natwittayatanaseth/https-medium-com-fintech-kellogg-de-risking-non-collateralized-stablecoins-40e832562090, accessed 31 Oct. 2020.

399. Evan Kuo, Brandon Iles, and Manny Rincon Cruz, "Ampleforth: A New Synthetic Commodity," Ampleforth, 12 July 2019. drive.google.com/file/ d/1I-NmSnQ6E7wY1nyouuf-GuDdJWNCnJWl/view; Connie Loizos, "Basis, Backed with $133 Million from Top VCs to Build a Price-Stable Cryptocurrency, Says It's Shutting Down and Returning the Money," *TechCrunch*, Verizon Media, 13 Dec. 2018. techcrunch.com/2018/12/13/ basis-backed-with-133-million-from-top-vcs-to-build-a-price-stable-cryptocurrency-says-its-shutting-down-and-returning-the-money, both accessed 31 Oct. 2020.

400. Sam Trautwein, "Why Hybrid?" *LinkedIn*, LinkedIn Corp., 20 Sept. 2018. www.linkedin.com/pulse/why-hybrid-sam-trautwein, accessed 31 Oct. 2020.

401. Yogita Khatri, "Carbon's Stablecoin Can Now Be Swapped between EOS and Ethereum," *CoinDesk*, Digital Currency Group, 9 Nov. 2018, last updated 12 Nov. 2018. www.coindesk.com/carbons-stablecoin-can-now-be-swapped-between-eos-and-ethereum-blockchains, accessed 31 Oct. 2020.

402. Frax, "Trump and Reagan Advisors Join Frax to Launch World's First Fully Decentralized Global Currency," *Cision PR Newswire*, Newswire Association LLC, 22 Oct. 2019. www.prnewswire.com/news-releases/ trump-and-reagan-advisors-join-frax-to-launch-worlds-first-fully-decentralized-global-currency-300943571.html, accessed 31 Oct. 2020.

403. Jeff John Roberts, "Trump's Former Fed Pick Stephen Moore Announces Cryptocurrency to Compete with Central Banks," *Fortune.com*, Fortune Media IP Ltd., 21 Oct. 2019. fortune.com/2019/10/21/stephen-moore-trump-fed-nomination-cryptocurrency-stablecoin-frax, accessed 31 Oct. 2020.

404. Not to be confused with the Fracture Risk Assessment Tool. See the Frax white paper here: Sam Kazemian and Jason Huan, "Introduction," *Frax. Finance*, ~8 Nov. 2020. docs.frax.finance/overview, accessed 1 Dec. 2020.

405. Bogdan Ulm, "Brock Pierce Unveils Realcoin to Fix Bitcoin's Volatility Concerns," *Cointelegraph.com*, 9 July 2014. cointelegraph.com/news/brock-pierce-unveils-realcoin-to-fix-bitcoins-volatility-concerns, accessed 1 Nov. 2020.

406. Pete Rizzo, "Realcoin Rebrands as 'Tether' to Avoid Altcoin Association," *CoinDesk*, Digital Currency Group, 20 Nov. 2014. www.coindesk.com/realcoin-relaunches-tether-avoid-altcoin-association, accessed 1 Nov. 2020.

407. Stan Higgins, "Million in US Dollar Token Stolen," *CoinDesk*, Digital Currency Group, 20 Nov. 2017. www.coindesk.com/tether-claims-30-million-stable-token-stolen-attacker, accessed 2 Nov. 2020.

408. Gareth Jenkinson, "Untethered: The History of Stablecoin Tether and How It Has Lost Its $1 Peg," *Cointelegraph.com*, 17 Oct. 2018. cointelegraph.com/news/untethered-the-history-of-stablecoin-tether-and-how-it-has-lost-its-1-peg, accessed 1 Nov. 2020.

409. Paul Vigna and Steven Russolillo, "The Mystery behind Tether, the Crypto World's Digital Dollar," *Wall Street Journal*, Dow Jones & Co. Inc., 12 Aug. 2018. www.wsj.com/articles/the-mystery-behind-tether-the-crypto-worlds-digital-dollar-1534089601, accessed 1 Nov. 2020.

410. Paul Vigna and Steven Russolillo, "The Mystery Behind Tether, the Crypto World's Digital Dollar."

411. Richard K. Lyons and Ganesh Viswanath-Natraj, "What Keeps Stablecoins Stable?" Working Paper 27136, *NBER Working Paper Series*, National Bureau of Economic Research, May 2020, p. 43. www.nber.org/system/files/working_papers/w27136/w27136.pdf, accessed 1 Nov. 2020.

412. Jemima Kelly, "Tether Slammed as 'Part-Fraud, Part-Pump-and-Dump, and Part-Money Laundering,'" FT Alphaville, *Financial Times*, Financial Times Ltd., 7 Oct. 2019. www.ft.com/content/eb5cf045-1ea1-3b54-80cd-e9f8c8287f08, accessed 2 Nov. 2020.

413. John M. Griffin and Amin Shams, "Is Bitcoin Really Untethered?" *Journal of Finance* 75 (Aug. 2020): 1913–1964. onlinelibrary.wiley.com/doi/full/10.1111/jofi.12903, accessed 2 Nov. 2020.

414. "Attorney General James Announces Court Order against 'Crypto' Currency Company under Investigation for Fraud," Press Release, *AG.NY. Gov*, New York State Attorney General, 25 April 2019. ag.ny.gov/press-release/2019/attorney-general-james-announces-court-order-against-crypto-currency-company, accessed 1 Nov. 2020.

415. "Bitfinex Responds to New York Attorney General's Actions," *Bitfinex*, iFinex Inc., 26 April 2019. www.bitfinex.com/posts/356, accessed 1 Nov. 2020.

416. "Legal," *Tether.io*, Tether Operations Ltd., last updated 12 May 2020. tether.to/legal, accessed 2 Nov. 2020.

417. "Why Use Tether?" *Tether.io*, Tether Operations Ltd., n.d. tether.to/why-use-tether, accessed 1 Nov. 2020.

418. "Circle Internet Financial Closes $17 Million Series B Financing," Press Release, Business Wire Inc., 26 March 2014. www.businesswire.com/news/home/20140326005423/en/Circle-Internet-Financial-Closes-17-Million-Series-B-Financing, accessed 29 Nov. 2020.

419. Jeremy Allaire, Testimony, Hearing on "Beyond Silk Road: Potential Risks, Threats and Promises of Virtual Currencies," US Senate Committee on Homeland Security and Governmental Affairs Hearing, 18 Nov. 2013. www.hsgac.senate.gov/imo/media/doc/Testimony-Allaire-2013-11-18.pdf, accessed 29 Nov. 2020.

420. Dean Starkman, "Goldman Sachs Invests in Bitcoin Start-Up Circle Internet Financial," *Los Angeles Times*, Los Angeles Times Communications LLC, 30 April 2015. www.latimes.com/business/la-fi-goldman-sachs-bitcoin-20150430-story.html, accessed 29 Nov. 2020.

421. Dean Starkman, "Goldman Sachs Invests in Bitcoin Start-Up Circle Internet Financial."

422. Sarah Hansen, "Circle Launches USD-Backed Stablecoin," *Forbes.com*, Forbes Media LLC, 26 Sept. 2018. www.forbes.com/sites/sarahhansen/2018/09/26/circle-launches-usd-backed-stablecoin/?sh=4fb9a8125d3f, accessed 29 Nov. 2020.

423. Sarah Hansen, "Circle Launches USD-Backed Stablecoin."

424. CENTRE Consortium, "CENTRE White Paper," version 2.0, *CENTRE.io*, 15 May 2018. www.centre.io/index.html, accessed 29 Nov. 2020.

425. "USDC: The Fastest Growing, Fully Reserved Digital Dollar Stablecoin," *Circle.com*, Circle Internet Financial Inc., n.d. www.circle.com/en/usdc, accessed 29 Nov. 2020.

426. CENTRE Consortium, "USDC: Celebrating the First Anniversary of the Fastest Growing Stablecoin," *Centre Blog*, Medium.com, 25 Sept. 2019. medium.com/centre-blog/usdc-celebrating-the-1st-anniversary-of-the-fastest-growing-stablecoin-4a05dc3784b8, accessed 31 Oct. 2020.

427. "Circle USDC User Agreement," *About Circle USDC: Legal*, Circle Internet Financial Inc., last updated 12 May 2020. support.usdc.circle.com/hc/en-us/articles/360001233386-Circle-USDC-User-Agreement, accessed 14 Dec. 2020.

428. Mark DuBose and Amy Luo, "Re: Addressing the Regulatory, Supervisory, and Oversight Challenges Raise by 'Global Stablecoin' Arrangements," Memorandum to the Financial Stability Board Bank for International Settlements, *FSB.org*, Circle and Coinbase, 15 July 2020. www.fsb.org/wp-content/uploads/CircleCoinbase.pdf, accessed 29 Nov. 2020.

429. Mark DuBose and Amy Luo, "Re: Addressing the Regulatory, Supervisory, and Oversight Challenges Raise by 'Global Stablecoin' Arrangements."

430. Circle Internet Financial Inc., "Circle Announces Partnership with Visa to Bring the Benefits of Stablecoins to Businesses Worldwide," Press Release, *Cision PR Newswire*, Newswire Association LLC, 3 Dec. 2020. www.prnewswire.com/news-releases/circle-announces-partnership-with-visa-to-bring-the-benefits-of-stablecoins-to-businesses-worldwide-301185942.html, accessed 14 Dec. 2020.

431. Binance Research, "Binance GBP (BGBP): A GBP Collateralized Stablecoin Backed by Fiat Reserves," *Binance.com*, 21 May 2020. research.binance.com/en/projects/binance-gbp, accessed 6 Dec. 2020.

432. Christina Comben, "How Could a GBP-Pegged Stablecoin Threaten UK Banks?" *Coin Rivet*, Yahoo Finance UK, 14 June 2019. uk.finance.yahoo.com/news/could-gbp-pegged-stablecoin-threaten-080019270.html, accessed 6 Dec. 2020.

433. Arnab Shome, "Binance Jersey Expands Trading Options with BGBP Listing," *FinanceMagnates.com*, Finance Magnates Ltd., 19 July 2019. www.financemagnates.com/cryptocurrency/news/binance-jersey-expands-trading-options-with-bgbp-listing; and "Binance Weekly Report: Oops, We Staked It Again (WINk, WINk)," *Binance Blog*, Binance.com, 22 July 2019. www.binance.com/en/blog, both accessed 6 Dec. 2020.

434. Nikhilesh De, "Binance Launches Dollar-Backed Crypto Stablecoin with NYDFS Blessing," *CoinDesk*, Digital Currency Group, 5 Sept. 2019. www.coindesk.com/binance-launches-dollar-backed-stablecoin-with-nydfs-blessing, accessed 10 Dec. 2020.

435. Binance Jersey Team, "Closure of Binance Jersey," *Binance.je*, ~15 Oct. 2020. support.binance.je/hc/en-us/articles/360051246251-Closure-of-Binance-Jersey, accessed 6 Dec. 2020.

436. Maker (MKR), *CoinMarketCap.com*, as of 29 Nov. 2020. coinmarketcap.com/currencies/maker.

437. "Maker Sells $12M of MKR to Partners, Led by Andreessen Horowitz and Polychain Capital," *Maker Blog*, MakerDAO.com, 16 Dec. 2017. blog.makerdao.com/maker-sells-12m-of-mkr-to-partners-led-by-andreessen-horowitz-and-polychain-capital, accessed 31 Oct. 2020.

438. "The Maker Protocol: MakerDAO's Multi-Collateral Dai (MCD) System," *MakerDAO.com*, n.d. makerdao.com/en/whitepaper#abstract, accessed 31 Oct. 2020.

439. Dai (DAI), *CoinMarketCap.com*, as of 29 Nov. 2020. coinmarketcap.com/currencies/multi-collateral-dai.

440. "The Maker Protocol: MakerDAO's Multi-Collateral Dai (MCD) System."

441. "Multi-Collateral Dai: Collateral Types," *Maker Blog*, MakerDAO, 27 June 2019. blog.makerdao.com/multi-collateral-dai-collateral-types, accessed 31 Oct. 2020.

442. "The Maker Protocol: MakerDAO's Multi-Collateral Dai (MCD) System."

443. "The Maker Protocol: MakerDAO's Multi-Collateral Dai (MCD) System."

444. Søren Peter Nielsen, "Announcing the Dai Foundation," MakerDAO Forum, 31 Dec. 2019. forum.makerdao.com/t/announcing-the-dai-foundation/1046, accessed 29 Nov. 2020.

445. "Multi-Collateral Dai: Milestones Road Map," *Maker Blog*, MakerDAO. com, 27 June 2019. blog.makerdao.com/multi-collateral-dai-milestones-roadmap, accessed 29 Nov. 2020.

446. See Everipedia.org and Genius Media Group Inc., genius.com.

447. Sam Kazemian and Jason Huan, "Frax: Fractional-Algorithmic Stablecoin Protocol," *Frax.Finance*, ~1 Nov. 2020. docs.frax.finance, accessed 1 Dec. 2020.

448. Jeff John Roberts, "Trump's Former Fed Pick Stephen Moore Announces Cryptocurrency to Compete with Central Banks." See also "Frax Bonds (FXB)," *Frax.Finance*, ~1 Nov. 2020. docs.frax.finance/frax-bonds-fxb, accessed 1 Dec. 2020.

449. Jeff John Roberts, "Trump's Former Fed Pick Stephen Moore Announces Cryptocurrency to Compete with Central Banks."

450. EazyC (Sam Kazemian), "DeFi Algorithmic Stablecoin: FRAX (feedback wanted)," *ETHresearch*, Sept. 2019. ethresear.ch/t/defi-algorithmic-stablecoin-frax-feedback-wanted/6169, accessed 1 Nov. 2020.

451. TrustToken, "TrueCurrency Attestation Reports," *TrustToken Blog*, A Medium Corp., 23 May 2018, updated 31 May 2020. blog.trusttoken. com/trueusd-attestation-reports-86f693b90a4, accessed 29 Nov. 2020.

452. "Independent Accountants' Report: Escrow Holdings Report to the Members and TrueUSD Token Holders, TrueCoin LLC," Cohen & Company Ltd., 1 March 2018. drive.google.com/file/d/1okXidblukRNH s6RgPLJVjMOIOJAVIfuH/view, accessed 29 Nov. 2020.

453. TrustToken, "TrueCurrency Attestation Reports."

454. Armanino, "Real-Time Attest Reporting," White Paper, Armanino LLP, 30 Oct. 2019, p. 3. www.armaninollp.com/-/media/pdf/white-papers/ whitepaper-trustexplorer-real-time-audit.pdf, accessed 29 Nov. 2020.

455. "Concepts Common to All Attestation Engagements," AT-C § 105. A76, *Statement on Standards for Attestation Engagements (SSAE)* No. 18, American Institute of Certified Public Accountants (AICPA) Auditing Standards Board, 2020. www.aicpa.org/Research/Standards/ AuditAttest/DownloadableDocuments/AT-C-00105.pdf; "Examination Engagements," AT-C § 205.04, SSAE No. 19, AICPA Auditing Standards Board, 2020. www.aicpa.org/Research/Standards/AuditAttest/ DownloadableDocuments/AT-C-00205.pdf, accessed 29 Nov. 2020.

456. Armanino, "Real-Time Attest Reporting," p. 9.

457. Armanino, "Real-Time Attest Reporting," p. 9.

458. Armanino, "Real-Time Attest Reporting," pp. 9–10.

459. TrustToken, "TrustToken Introduces Proof of Reserve for TUSD Stablecoin in Collaboration with Chainlink and Armanino," *TrustToken Blog*, A Medium Corp., 11 Nov. 2020. blog.trusttoken.com/trusttoken-introduces-proof-of-reserve-for-tusd-stablecoin-in-collaboration-with-chainlink-and-584b3674b89f; and Armanino, "Real-Time Attest," TrustExplorer.io, Armanino LLP, n.d. real-time-attest.trustexplorer.io/ trusttoken, both accessed 29 Nov. 2020.

460. "Paxos Launches New Stablecoin, Paxos Standard," Press Release, *Cision PR Newswire*, Newswire Association LLC, 10 Sept. 2018. www. prnewswire.com/news-releases/paxos--launches-new-stablecoin-paxos-standard-300709434.html, accessed 30 Nov. 2020.

461. "Paxos Launches New Stablecoin, Paxos Standard."

462. "Paxos Standard (PAX) Audit Report," *Nomic Labs Blog*, Medium.com, 10 Sept. 2018. medium.com/nomic-labs-blog/paxos-standard-pax-audit-report-ca743c9575dc, both accessed 1 Nov. 2020.

463. "Paxos Launches New Stablecoin, Paxos Standard."

464. "Paxos Launches New Stablecoin, Paxos Standard."

465. Kabompo Holdings Ltd., "Notice of Exempt Offering of Securities," OMB Number: 3235-0076, Form D, US Securities and Exchange Commission, SEC.gov, 6 Nov. 2017. www.sec.gov/Archives/edgar/data/1587702/000158770217000002/xslFormDX01/primary_doc.xml; and Aequi Acquisition Corp., "Amendment No. 2 to Form S-1, Registration Statement under the Securities Act of 1933," Registration No. 333-249337, US SEC, *SEC.gov*, 16 Nov. 2020. www.sec.gov/Archives/edgar/data/1823826/000121390020037147/fs12020a2_aequiacqcorp.htm, both accessed 30 Nov. 2020.

466. WithumSmith+Brown PC, "Paxos Trust Company LLC, Examination of Management Assertions Reserve Accounts Report – PAX Standard Token, 30 Oct. 2020 – with Independent Accountant's Report," *Paxos.com*, Paxos Trust Co. LLC, 30 Oct. 2020. www.paxos.com/attestations, accessed 30 Nov. 2020.

467. WithumSmith+Brown PC, "Paxos Trust Company LLC, Examination of Management Assertions Reserve Accounts Report – BUSD Token 30 Oct. 2020 – with Independent Accountant's Report," *Paxos.com*, Paxos Trust Co. LLC, 30 Oct. 2020. www.paxos.com/attestations, accessed 30 Nov. 2020.

468. WithumSmith+Brown PC, "Paxos Trust Company LLC, Examination of Management Assertions Reserve Accounts Report – PAX Gold Token, 30 Oct. 2020 – with Independent Accountant's Report," *Paxos.com*, Paxos Trust Co. LLC, 30 Oct. 2020. www.paxos.com/wp-content/uploads/2020/11/PAX-Gold-Report-October-2020.pdf, accessed 30 Nov. 2020.

469. "About Gemini," Gemini Trust Company LLC, n.d. gemini.com/about, accessed 30 Nov. 2020.

470. "Governor Cuomo Announces Approval of First US-Based Ethereum Exchange, Created and Operated In New York," Press Release, Office of the Governor of New York State Andrew M. Cuomo, 5 May 2016. www.governor.ny.gov/news/governor-cuomo-announces-approval-first-us-based-ethereum-exchange-created-and-operated-new, accessed 30 Nov. 2020.

471. Andrew Lowenthal, "Re: Cboe Futures Exchange LLC, Product Certification for Bitcoin Futures, Submission Number CFE-2017-018," submitted to Christopher J. Kirkpatrick, Commodity Futures Trading Commission, *CFE.Cboe.com*, 1 Dec. 2017. cfe.cboe.com/publish/CFErulefilings/SR-CFE-2017-018.pdf, accessed 30 Nov. 2020.

472. Andrew Lowenthal, "Re: Cboe Futures Exchange LLC."

473. Team Gemini, "Introducing Gemini Block Trading," *Cameron Winklevoss Blog*, Medium.com, 8 April 2018. medium.com/@winklevoss/introducing-gemini-block-trading-ac80bdaa6320, accessed 30 Nov. 2020.

474. "Gemini to Launch Market Surveillance Technology in Collaboration with Nasdaq," Press Release, Nasdaq Inc., 25 April 2018. ir.nasdaq.com/news-releases/news-release-details/gemini-launch-market-surveillance-technology-collaboration, accessed 30 Nov. 2020.

475. "DFS Authorizes Gemini Trust Company to Provide Additional Virtual Currency Products and Services: Gemini Is the First Qualified Custodian and Exchange to Receive DFS Approval to Offer Trading of Emerging Digital Currency Zcash in New York," Press Release, New York State Department of Financial Services, *DFS.NY.gov*, 14 May 2018. www.dfs.ny.gov/reports_and_publications/press_releases/pr1805141, accessed 30 Nov. 2020.

476. "DFS Authorizes Gemini Trust Company to Provide Additional Virtual Currency Products and Services."

477. Robert Hackett, "Winklevoss Twins Win Regulatory Approval for State Street-Backed, Dollar-Pegged Cryptocurrency," *Fortune.com*, Fortune Media IP Ltd., 10 Sept. 2018. fortune.com/2018/09/10/cryptocurrency-state-street-winklevoss-gemini-dollar-regulator-nydfs; and "Gemini dollar," Gemini.com, Gemini Trust Company LLC, n.d. gemini.com/static/dollar/gemini-dollar-whitepaper.pdf, accessed 31 Oct. 2020.

478. *CoinMarketCap.com* started reporting on Gemini's price on 6 Oct. 2018. See Gemini Dollar Charts, coinmarketcap.com/currencies/gemini-dollar.

479. "The Gemini Dollar: A Regulated Stable Value Coin," White Paper, Gemini Trust Company LLC, 10 Sept. 2018. gemini.com/static/dollar/gemini-dollar-whitepaper.pdf, accessed 30 Nov. 2020.

480. "The Gemini Dollar: A Regulated Stable Value Coin."

481. "The Gemini Dollar: A Regulated Stable Value Coin."

482. "The Gemini Dollar: A Regulated Stable Value Coin."

483. "Gemini Obtains Digital Asset Insurance via Aon: Digital Asset Insurance Coverage Adds to Gemini's Existing FDIC Insurance for Fiat Funds," Press Release, Business Wire Inc., 3 Oct. 2018. www.businesswire.com/news/home/20181003005283/en/Gemini-Obtains-Digital-Asset-Insurance-Aon, accessed 30 Nov. 2020.

484. For more on BPM LLP, see www.bpmcpa.com/Industries/Blockchain-and-Digital-Assets, accessed 30 Nov. 2020. Gemini explains "proof of solvency" further in its white paper.

485. For all reports to date, see gemini.com/dollar#reports. For the latest, see "Independent Accountants' Report: Gemini Dollar and Cash Balances as of 30 Nov. 2020," BPM CPA (NY) LLP, 30 Nov. 2020. assets.ctfassets.net/ jg6lo9a2ukvr/4BkDN9UnhB3dR0nsmdFrl8/6bd8079e5c3caad17aa 61d536ff38bd9/Gemini_Dollar_Examination_Report_11-30-20.pdf, accessed 6 Dec. 2020.

486. Muhammad Tahir-ul-Qadri, *Mawlid Al-nabi: Celebration and Permissibility* (United Kingdom: Minhaj-ul-Quran Publications, 2014).

487. John Berthoud, "Milton Friedman Full Interview on Anti-Trust and Tech," Video Interview, National Taxpayers Union, 1 March 1999, uploaded to *YouTube.com* 9 Aug. 2012. youtu.be/mlwxdyLnMXM, accessed 1 Nov. 2020.

488. Jason Chen, "Hedge," *Investopedia.com*, Dotdash, last updated 20 Aug. 2018. www.investopedia.com/terms/d/de-hedge.asp, accessed 6 Dec. 2020.

489. Will Kenton, "Harvest Strategy," *Investopedia.com*, Dotdash, last updated 6 Aug. 2020. www.investopedia.com/terms/h/harvest-strategy.asp, accessed 29 Oct. 2020.

490. "Section 26 U.S. Code § 1031–Exchange of Real Property Held for Productive Use or Investment," Legal Information Institute, Cornell Law School, n.d. www.law.cornell.edu/uscode/text/26/1031, accessed 29 Oct. 2020.

491. "Notice 2014-21," *IRS.gov*, Internal Revenue Service, 2014. www.irs.gov/ pub/irs-drop/n-14-21.pdf; and "Frequently Asked Questions on Virtual Currency Transactions," *IRS.gov*, Internal Revenue Service, last updated 8 Oct. 2020. www.irs.gov/individuals/international-taxpayers/frequently-asked-questions-on-virtual-currency-transactions, accessed 29 Oct. 2020.

492. "Wash Sale: Avoid this Tax Pitfall," *Fidelity.com*, FMR LLC, 26 March 2020. www.fidelity.com/learning-center/personal-finance/wash-sales-rules-tax, accessed 29 Oct. 2020.

493. BitMEX Research, "A Brief History of Stablecoins," *BitMEX.com*, HDR Global Trading Ltd., 2 July 2018. blog.bitmex.com/a-brief-history-of-stablecoins-part-1, accessed 29 Oct. 2020.

494. Marie Huillet, "Crypto Trailblazer Nick Szabo: Central Banks Could Turn to Crypto to Support Reserves," *Cointelegraph.com*, 9 Jan. 2019. cointelegraph.com/news/crypto-trailblazer-nick-szabo-central-banks-could-turn-to-crypto-to-support-reserves, accessed 31 Oct. 2020.

495. BitMEX Research, "A Brief History of Stablecoins," *BitMEX.com*, HDR Global Trading Ltd., 2 July 2018. blog.bitmex.com/a-brief-history-of-stablecoins-part-1, accessed 29 Oct. 2020.

496. Lael Brainard, "Digital Currencies, Stablecoins, and the Evolving Payments Landscape," Speech, *The Future of Money in the Digital Age*, Peterson Institute for International Economics and Princeton University's Bendheim Center for Finance, Washington DC, 16 Oct. 2019. www.federalreserve.gov/newsevents/speech/brainard20191016a.htm, accessed 29 Oct. 2020.

497. LedgerX, "What We Do," *LedgerX.com*, Ledger Holdings Inc., n.d. www.ledgerx.com/company, accessed 10 Jan. 2020.

498. BitMEX, "About Us," *BitMEX.com*, HDR Global Trading Ltd., n.d. www.bitmex.com/app/aboutUs; and Deribit, "General," *Deribit.com*, Deribit BV, n.d. www.deribit.com/pages/docs/general, both accessed 10 Jan. 2020.

499. Nandini Sukumar, Siobhan Cleary, Matthias Voelkel, Markus Röhrig, Roger Rouhana, and Christian Schaette, "Fintech Decoded: Capturing the Opportunity in Capital Markets Infrastructure," McKinsey & Company and World Federation of Exchanges, March 2018. www.world-exchanges.org/storage/app/media/research/Studies_Reports/wfe-amp-mckinsey-fintech-decoded-report.pdf, accessed 14 Nov. 2019.

500. "OTC Derivatives Statistics at End-June 2019," *BIS.org*, Bank of International Settlement, 8 Nov. 2019. www.bis.org/publ/otc_hy1911.htm, accessed 6 Dec. 2019.

501. J. Christopher Giancarlo, "Introduction: Virtual Currency," Written Testimony before the Senate Banking Committee, Washington DC, 6 Feb. 2018. US Commodity Futures Trading Commission, www.cftc.gov/PressRoom/SpeechesTestimony/opagiancarlo37, accessed 6 Dec. 2019.

502. Massimo Morini and Robert Sams, "'Smart' Derivatives Can Cure XVA Headaches," *Risk.net*, Infopro Digital Risk (IP) Ltd., 27 Aug. 2015. www.risk.net/derivatives/2422606/smart-derivatives-can-cure-xva-headaches, accessed 14 Nov. 2019.

503. Malgorzata Osiewicz, Linda Fache-Rousova, and Kirsi-Maria Kulmala, "Reporting of Derivatives Transactions in Europe: Exploring the Potential of EMIR Micro Data against the Challenges of Aggregation across Six Trade Repositories," Irving Fisher Committee on Central Bank Statistics, Bank for International Settlement, Warsaw, Poland, 14–15 Dec. 2015. www.bis.org/ifc/publ/ifcb41zd.pdf, accessed 14 Nov. 2019. The authors stated:

> *Around 85 data fields are to be reported for each transaction ... . Such a wide-scaled and detailed reporting implies huge data volumes. Over*

the first year of reporting, almost 10 billion of records were received and processed by the six TRs [trade repositories] in Europe ... the heterogeneous landscape in TR data provision and non-standardised data collection pose significant challenges for regulators accessing and analysing the data ... any meaningful data aggregation requires the reconciliation of the information between the duplicated trades ... the other data fields submitted by the two counterparties very often do not match, which raises the question which of the two to keep in the final database with de-duplicated trades. Even for trades reported to the same TR, there can be significant discrepancies for variables such as execution timestamp, price per contract or notional value.

504. Scott O'Malia, "ISDA Common Domain Model," *ISDA.org*, International Swaps and Derivatives Association Inc., 26 Nov. 2019. www.isda.org/2019/10/14/isda-common-domain-model, accessed 6 Dec. 2019.

505. For more information about *financial products markup language*, see International Swaps and Derivatives Association's site dedicated to FpML, www.fpml.org/about.

506. ISDA Market Infrastructure and Technology, "What Is the ISDA CDM?" *ISDA.org*, International Swaps and Derivatives Association Inc., 22 Nov. 2018. www.isda.org/a/z8AEE/ISDA-CDM-Factsheet.pdf, accessed 6 Dec. 2019.

507. ISDA Market Infrastructure and Technology, "What Is the ISDA CDM?" See also "New Concept Paper Aims to Realize Technology Potential," *ISDA Quarterly* 3, No. 3 (International Swaps and Derivatives Association Inc., Nov. 2017): 8, 30–33. www.isda.org/a/0IKEE/IQ-ISDA-Quarterly-November-2017.pdf, accessed 6 Dec. 2019.

508. Dr. Lee Braine, interviewed in person by Massimo Morini, 16 Oct. 2019.

509. "DTCC Enters Test Phase on Distributed Ledger Project for Credit Derivatives with MarkitSERV and 15 Leading Global Banks," *DTCC.com*, Depository Trust and Clearing Corporation, 6 Nov. 2018. www.dtcc.com/news/2018/november/06/dtcc-enters-test-phase-on-distributed-ledger-project-for-credit-derivatives-with-markitserv, accessed 10 Jan. 2020.

510. Its website is variabl.io.

511. Hadrien Charlanes, "StabL Bringing Stable Tokens and Derivative Products to the Ethereum Blockchain," *VariabL Blog*, Medium.com, 14 March 2018. blog.variabl.io/stabl-bringing-stable-tokens-and-derivative-products-to-the-ethereum-blockchain-df4d5eba89d9, accessed 10 Jan. 2020.

512. Vincent Eli, "VariabL Products: ETH/USD Derivatives and Stable Tokens," *VariabL Blog*, Medium.com, 9 Oct. 2017. blog.variabl.io/

variabl-eth-usd-derivatives-and-stable-tokens-529839a91ba4, accessed 10 Jan. 2020.

513. Zhuoxun Yin, "Utilizing Margin and Leverage on DYdX," *dYdXProtocol Blog*, Medium.com, 10 July 2019. medium.com/dydxderivatives/utilizing-margin-and-leverage-on-dydx-60b34ca8f3cb, accessed 10 Jan. 2020.

514. Josh Constine, "Andreessen-Funded DYdX Plans 'Short Ethereum' Token for Haters," *TechCrunch*, Verizon Media, 3 Aug. 2018. techcrunch.com/2018/08/03/short-ethereum, accessed 10 Jan. 2020.

515. Diar, *State of the Digital Assets Industry*, Report, Vol. 2, No. 33/34 (20/27 Aug. 2018). diar.co/volume-2-issue-33-34, accessed 10 Jan. 2020.

516. Maker Team, "The Dai Stablecoin System," White Paper, *MakerDAO.com*, Dec. 2017. makerdao.com/whitepaper/Dai-Whitepaper-Dec17-en.pdf, accessed 10 Jan. 2020. For an analysis of this white paper, see Bennett Tomlin, "A Deep Look at MakerDAO and Dai and MKR," Bennett's Blog, Bennett F. Tomlin, 6 May 2019. bennettftomlin.com/2019/05/05/a-deep-look-at-makerdao-and-dai-and-mkr.

517. Conversation with MakerDAO team.

518. Conversation with MakerDAO team.

519. Richard Cohen, Philip Smith, Vic Arulchandran, and Avtar Sehra, "Automation and Blockchain in Securities Issuances," *Butterworths Journal of International Banking and Financial Law* 35 (March 2018): 144–150. docs.wixstatic.com/ugd/66eaa6_c8b6d7a1d63b4be083e5bafd6ab4185d.pdf, accessed 14 Nov. 2019.

520. Conversation with Nivaura team.

521. Richard Cohen, Philip Smith, Vic Arulchandran, and Avtar Sehra, "Automation and Blockchain in Securities Issuances," *Butterworths Journal of International Banking and Financial Law* 35 (March 2018): 144–150. docs.wixstatic.com/ugd/66eaa6_c8b6d7a1d63b4be083e5bafd6ab4185d.pdf, accessed 29 Aug. 2019.

522. Richard Cohen, Philip Smith, Vic Arulchandran, and Avtar Sehra, "Automation and Blockchain in Securities Issuances," *Butterworths Journal of International Banking and Financial Law* 35 (March 2018): 144–150. docs.wixstatic.com/ugd/66eaa6_c8b6d7a1d63b4be083e5bafd6ab4185d.pdf, accessed 22 July 2019.

523. Richard Cohen et al., "Automation and Blockchain in Securities Issuances."

524. Richard Cohen et al., "Automation and Blockchain in Securities Issuances."

525. Richard Cohen et al., "Automation and Blockchain in Securities Issuances."

526. Richard Cohen et al., "Automation and Blockchain in Securities Issuances."

527. Steven Globerman and Joel Emes, "Investment in the Canadian and US Oil and Gas Sectors: A Tale of Diverging Fortunes," Summary, Fraser Institute, 7 May 2019. www.fraserinstitute.org/studies/investment-in-the-canadian-and-us-oil-and-gas-sectors-a-tale-of-diverging-fortunes; and Geoffrey Morgan, "'Borderline Treasonous': Oil Executives Sound Alarm as Foreign Investors Flee," *Financial Post*, Postmedia Network Inc., 15 Nov. 2018. business.financialpost.com/commodities/energy/borderline-treasonous-oil-executives-sound-alarm-as-foreign-investors-flee, both accessed 2 June 2020.

528. "The World Factbook," Central Intelligence Agency, last updated 14 May 2020. www.cia.gov/library/publications/the-world-factbook/geos/xx.html, accessed 2 June 2020.

529. Steven Globerman and Joel Emes, "Investment in the Canadian and US Oil and Gas Sectors: A Tale of Diverging Fortunes," Report, Frasier Institute, 29 April 2019. www.fraserinstitute.org/sites/default/files/investment-in-canadian-and-us-oil-and-gas-sector.pdf, accessed 11 June 2020.

530. Steven Globerman and Joel Emes, "Investment in the Canadian and US Oil and Gas Sectors," Report.

531. Daniel Fisher and Martin J. Wooster, "Multi-Decade Global Gas Flaring Change Inventoried Using the ATSR-1, ATSR-2, AATSR and SLSTR Data Records," *Remote Sensing of Environment*, No. 232 (Oct. 2019). ScienceDirect, Elsevier BV, www.sciencedirect.com/science/article/pii/S0034425719303177, accessed 2 June 2020.

532. George Kamiya, "Data Centres and Data Transmission Networks," Tracking Report, International Energy Agency, June 2020. www.iea.org/reports/data-centres-and-data-transmission-networks, accessed 10 June 2020.

533. Xiaojing Zhang et al., "Data Center Energy and Cost Saving Evaluation," *Energy Procedia* 75 (28 Aug. 2015): 1255–1260. Elsevier, ScienceDirect, doi.org/10.1016/j.egypro.2015.07.178, accessed 6 June 2020.

534. Fred Pearce, "Energy Hogs: Can World's Huge Data Centers Be Made More Efficient?" Yale School of Forestry and Environmental Studies, 3 April 2018. e360.yale.edu/features/energy-hogs-can-huge-data-centers-be-made-more-efficient, accessed 10 Nov. 2019; and Peter Judge, "Global Forecast Bright for the Data Center Construction Market," Data Centre Dynamics Ltd., 7 Jan. 2015. www.datacenterdynamics.com/en/news/global-forecast-bright-for-the-data-center-construction-market, accessed 10 June 2020.

535. Brad Smith, "Microsoft Pledges to Cut Carbon Emissions by 75 Percent by 2030," *Microsoft on the Issues Blog*, Microsoft Corp., 14 Nov. 2017. blogs.microsoft.com/on-the-issues/2017/11/14/microsoft-pledges-cut-carbon-emissions-75-percent-2030, accessed 6 June 2020.

536. Maggie McGrath and Alex Konrad, "A Surprising Push by the Invisible Hand: Why More Companies Are Doing Better by Being Good," *Forbes.com*, Forbes Media LLC, 10 Dec. 2018. www.forbes.com/sites/maggiemcgrath/2018/12/10/wealth-of-the-nation-why-americas-most-valuable-companies-are-also-its-most-ethical/#68e407527bb9, accessed 2 June 2020.

537. Yevgeniy Sverdlik, "Microsoft Launches Pilot Natural Gas-Powered Data Center in Seattle," *Data Center Knowledge*, Informa USA Inc., 27 Sept. 2017. www.datacenterknowledge.com/design/microsoft-launches-pilot-natural-gas-powered-data-center-seattle, accessed 2 June 2020.

538. Max J. Krause and Thabet Tolaymat, "Quantification of Energy and Carbon Costs for Mining Cryptocurrencies," *Nature Sustainability* 1 (Nov. 2018): 771–718. Springer Nature Ltd., www.nature.com/articles/s41893-018-0152-7.epdf, accessed 12 June 2020.

539. George Kamiya, "Bitcoin Energy Use: Mined the Gap," Commentary, International Energy Agency, 5 July 2019. www.iea.org/commentaries/bitcoin-energy-use-mined-the-gap, accessed 6 June 2020.

540. IEA, "The Future of Cooling," Tracking Report, International Energy Agency, Paris, May 2018. www.iea.org/reports/the-future-of-cooling, accessed 6 June 2020.

541. Bill Kosik, "Data Centers Used for Bitcoin Mining," *Consulting-Specifying Engineer*, CFE Media and Technology, 27 June 2018. www.csemag.com/articles/data-centers-used-for-bitcoin-mining, accessed 2 June 2020.

542. Peter Judge, "Global Forecast bright for the Data Center Construction Market," Data Centre Dynamics Ltd., 7 Jan. 2015. www.datacenterdynamics.com/en/news/global-forecast-bright-for-the-data-center-construction-market, accessed 10 June 2020.

543. George Kamiya, "Data Centres and Data Transmission Networks," Tracking Report, International Energy Agency, June 2020. www.iea.org/reports/data-centres-and-data-transmission-networks, accessed 10 June 2020. According to the International Energy Agency, if current trends in the efficiency of hardware and data center infrastructure hold steady, then the energy consumed by data centers will also hold steady through 2022, despite a 60 percent increase in the demand for their services.

544. "Brox Equity Ltd. Token," *StoMarket.com*, Security Token Market LLC, last updated 29 Aug. 2021. stomarket.com/sto/brox-equity-ltd.-brox, accessed 1 Sept. 2021.

545. Aman Verma, "Global Oil and Gas Investment Outlook," Canadian Energy Research Institute, Jan. 2020. ceri.ca/assets/files/CERI%20 Crude%20Oil%20Report%20%20-%20January%202020.pdf, accessed 2 June 2020.

546. Laurent Martin, interviewed via telephone by Mohamed El-Masri, 16 April 2020.

547. Envion AG (Rogal), "Swiss Law Prospectus for the Issue of 150,000,000 Tokens Representing Subordinated Unsecuritized Profit Participation Rights ... under German Law in the Maximum Amount of $150,000,000," 15 Dec. 2017, rev. 12 Jan. 2018, p. 8. envion-founders. org/documents, accessed 4 June 2020.

548. Envion AG, "Swiss Law Prospectus," rev. 12 Jan. 2018, p. 8.

549. Laurent Martin, interviewed via telephone by Mohamed El-Masri, 16 April 2020.

550. "Founders Sue Envion CEO Matthias Woestmann's Corp. for World's First Analogue ICO Hacking," *Envion Founders Blog*, Trado GmbH, 17 May 2018. envion-founders.org/founders-sue-envion-ceo-matthias-woestmanns-corp-for-worlds-first-analogue-ico-hacking, accessed 2 June 2020.

551. Uwe Wolff, NAÏMA Strategic Legal Services GmbH, "Envion AG Founders to Donate Millions to Crypto Community after Favorable Ruling against Ex-CEO Mattias Woestmann, Co-Conspirators in Berlin's High Court," Press Release, *Realwire.com*, Realwire Ltd., 30 Sept. 2019. www.realwire.com/releases/Envion-AG-founders-to-donate-millions-to-crypto-community, accessed 2 June 2020.

552. Kris Jones, email message to Mohamed El-Masri, 29 Aug. 2019.

553. CSA Regulatory Sandbox, Canadian Securities Administrators, n.d. www.securities-administrators.ca/industry_resources.aspx?id=1588, accessed 10 June 2020.

554. Forester Yang, interviewed via telephone by Mohamed El-Masri, 2 May 2020.

555. S&P Global Platts, "Blockchain for Commodities, Trading Opportunities for a Digital Age," foreword by Martin Fraenkel, S&P Global Inc., Sept. 2018. s3-ap-southeast-1.amazonaws.com/sp-platts/ Blockchain.pdf, accessed 2 June 2020.

556. Alibaba Cloud, "Promoting Innovations and Digitization in the Commodity Industry with Blockchain," *Alibaba Cloud Blog*, Medium.com, 3 Feb. 2020. medium.com/@Alibaba_Cloud/promoting-innovations-and-digitization-in-the-commodity-industry-with-blockchain-b92975459a78, accessed 2 June 2020.

557. "PTAC Event: PermianChain Technologies Inc. Webinar," Petroleum Technology Alliance Canada, 21 April 2020. www.ptac.org/events/ptac-event-permianchain-technologies-inc-webinar, accessed 25 April 2020.

558. Philip Collins, email message to Mohamed El-Masri, 18 Dec. 2019.

559. "Gartner Unveils Top Predictions for IT Organizations and Users in 2022 and Beyond," *Express Computer*, India Express Ltd., 22 Oct. 2021. www.expresscomputer.in/news/gartner-unveils-top-predictions-for-it-organizations-and-users-in-2022-and-beyond/80453, accessed 24 Oct. 2021.

560. "Non-Fungible Tokens Yearly Report," *NonFungible.com*, NonFungible Corp., 2019. nonfungible.com/static/nft-report-2019.pdf. Overall crypto market cap fell from a peak of $831 billion in 2018 to $370 billion in 2019. "Global Cryptocurrency Charts," *CoinMarketCap.com*, CoinMarketCap OpCo LLC, Binance Holdings Ltd., as of 7 Oct. 2021. coinmarketcap.com/charts.

561. Dan Kelly and Gauthier Zuppinger, "Non-Fungible Tokens Quarterly Report: Q1 – 2021," *NonFungible.com*, NonFungible Corp., n.d. nonfungible.com/blog/nft-yearly-report-2020, accessed 7 Oct. 2021.

562. Gauthier Zuppinger, interviewed via telephone by Alan Majer, 24 May 2021.

563. Aaron Mak, "How Much Money People Have Made—or Lost—Selling Farts, Blog Posts, and Cat Tweets as NFTs," *Slate.com*, Slate Group LLC, 23 March 2021, slate.com/technology/2021/03/nfts-fees-rarible-opensea-auction-profit.html, accessed 7 Oct. 2021.

564. On 24 May 2021, an ether transfer could cost 21,000 gas at 144 gwei (~.003 ether) or $7.67 at ether/gas prices. "CryptoKitties Birthing Fees Increases in Order to Accommodate Demand," *CryptoKitties Blog*, Medium.com, 4 Dec. 2017. medium.com/cryptokitties/cryptokitties-birthing-fees-increases-in-order-to-accommodate-demand-acc314fcadf5, accessed 7 Oct. 2021. Calculation: $7.668864=(144*21000)/1,000,000,000)*2536.

565. Jonathan Mann, "NFTs Are Dead | Song A Day #4538," *SuperRare.com*, SuperRare Labs Inc., n.d. superrare.com/artwork-v2/nfts-are-dead-%7C-song-a-day-4538-25134, accessed 20 Sept. 2021.

566. Sebastian Smee, "The Louvre Wants This $450 Million 'Leonardo' in Its Big Show. But Its Mystery Owner Appears to Be Balking," *WashingtonPost.com*, WP Company LLC, 15 Oct. 2019. washingtonpost. com/entertainment/museums/the-louvre-wants-this-450-million-leonardo-in-its-big-show-but-its-mystery-owner-appears-to-be-balking/2019/10/15/85bc5094-eec2-11e9-b648-76bcf86eb67e_story. html, accessed 19 Sept. 2021.

567. Christie's, "Leonardo's *Salvator Mundi* Restored—Time-lapse Video," *TheGuardian.com*, Guardian News & Media Ltd., 16 Nov. 2017, last modified 22 Feb. 2018. www.theguardian.com/artanddesign/video/2017/ nov/16/leonardos-salvator-mundi-restored-timelapse-video, accessed 19 Sept. 2021.

568. Sarah Cascone, "The Saudi Crown Prince Refused to Lend *Salvator Mundi* to the Louvre Because the Museum Disputed Its Authenticity, a New Film Says," *Artnet.com*, Artnet Worldwide Corp., 7 April 2021. news.artnet.com/art-world/the-louvre-salvator-mundi-attribution-1957477, accessed 20 Sept. 2021.

569. Suzanne Rowan Kelleher, "Saudi Crown Prince MBS Pressed the Louvre to Lie about His Fake Leonardo Da Vinci, per New Documentary," *Forbes.com*, Forbes Media LLC, 9 April 2021. www.forbes.com/ sites/suzannerowankelleher/2021/04/09/saudi-crown-prince-mbs-pressed-the-louvre-to-lie-about-his-fake-leonardo-da-vinci-per-new-documentary, accessed 19 Sept. 2021.

570. Mike Masnick, "Can You Infringe on da Vinci? Judge Seems to Think So," *TechDirt.com*, Floor64 Inc., 7 Oct. 2011. techdirt.com/ articles/20111007/03455916248/can-you-infringe-da-vinci-judge-seems-to-think-so.shtml, accessed 19 Sept. 2021.

571. Ben Lewis (@theuniversalben), *Twitter.com*, Twitter Inc., 7 April 2021 (9:11 AM). twitter.com/theuniversalben/status/1379783776901926912, accessed 18 Sept. 2021.

572. CRL, "Salvator Metaversi," *OpenSea.io*, Ozone Networks Inc., n.d. opensea.io/assets/0x495f947276749ce646f68ac8c248420045cb7b5e/645 99744694261334350686477227640403997547294842323217985851030 55188683256758273; CS (mooncat mints 16, 18 (33%), 41, 59), *Twitter. com*, Twitter Inc., 9 April 2021 (10:53 PM). twitter.com/Investmentshark/ status/1380715621407543300?s=20, accessed 20 Sept. 2021.

573. Alan Majer, communication with Christian S. via Twitter, 20 May 2021.

574. Alan Majer, communication with Christian S. via Twitter, 20 May 2021.

575. "The Met 360° Project," dir. Nina Diamond, *MetMuseum.org*, Metropolitan Museum of Art, 2017. www.metmuseum.org/art/online-features/met-360-project, accessed 19 Sept. 2021.

576. Tom Arnstein, "Beijing's UCCA to Hold the World's First-Ever Crypto Art Exhibition. But What the Hell Is Crypto Art?" *TheBeijinger. com*, True Run Media, 12 March 2021. www.thebeijinger.com/blog/2021/03/12/beijing-ucca-host-worlds-first-crypto-art-exhibition, accessed 19 Sept. 2021.

577. "NFT Marketplaces," *DappRadar.com*, DappRadar UAB, as of 26 May 2021. dappradar.com/nft/marketplaces.

578. "NFT Marketplaces," *DappRadar.com*, DappRadar UAB, as of 24 Oct. 2021. dappradar.com/nft/marketplaces.

579. Cryptorigami, "Introducing ERC 420[1]—The Dank Standard," PepeDapp Blog, Medium, 27 May 2018. medium.com/pepedapp/erc-420%C2%B9-the-dank-standard-83d7bb5fe18e; and Eugene Mishura and Seb Mondet, "FA2–Multi-Asset Interface, 012," *GitLab.com*, Software Freedom Conservancy, 24 Jan. 2020. gitlab.com/tezos/tzip/-/blob/master/proposals/tzip-12/tzip-12.md, accessed 7 Oct. 2021.

580. For the current NFT specification on the Flow Blockchain, see "Onflow/flow-nft," *GitHub.com*, GitHub Inc., n.d. github.com/onflow/flow-nft, accessed 7 Oct. 2021.

581. Help, "Frequently Asked Questions," *Cent Help Center*, Cent, last updated 2021. intercom.help/cent/en/articles/5221758-frequently-asked-questions#h_8ec1119d56, accessed 20 Sept. 2021.

582. Besancia, "From Pixel to Block: Nine Chronicles," *NonFungible.com*, NonFungible Corp., 2 March 2021. nonfungible.com/blog/from-pixel-to-block-nine-chronicles, accessed 20 Sept. 2021.

583. "Frequently Asked Questions," *Cent Help Center*, Cent, last updated 2021. intercom.help/cent/en/articles/5221758-frequently-asked-questions#h_8ec1119d56, accessed 20 Sept. 2021.

584. "Primer," OnFlow.org, Dapper Labs Inc., n.d. www.onflow.org/primer; Ilija Rolovic, "Introducing Efinity: NFT Blockchain on Polkadot," *Enjin Blog*, Enjin Pte. Ltd., 31 March 2021. enjin.io/blog/efinity, accessed 18 Sept. 2021.

585. Witek Radomski, interviewed via mobile/video call by Alan Majer, 21 May 2021.

586. Witek Radomski, interviewed via mobile/video call by Alan Majer, 21 May 2021.

587. "NFT v. Non-Fungible Token: A Twelve-Month Timeline," *Google Trends*, Google LLC, as of 25 Sept. 2021. trends.google.com/trends/explore?geo=US&q=NFT,%2Fg%2F11g0g4sbp3.

588. Gauthier Zuppinger, "The 2020 Non-fungible Tokens Report Is Online!" *NonFungible France Blog*, Medium.com, 16 Feb. 2021. medium.com/nonfungible-france/le-rapport-2020-sur-les-tokens-non-fongibles-est-en-ligne-c9c9df18aa26, accessed 27 Oct. 2021.

589. "About NBA Top Shots," *NBATopShot.com*, Dapper Labs Inc., NBA Properties Inc., and the National Basketball Players Assoc., 2021. nbatopshot.com/about, accessed 24 Oct. 2021.

590. Gautam Bhattacharyya, "Cricket Fans Set to Enter Blockchain Era to 'Own' Golden Moments of Stars," *Gulf News (United Arab Emirates)*, Al Nisr Publishing LLC, 29 Sept. 2021. gulfnews.com/sport/cricket/icc/cricket-fans-set-to-enter-blockchain-era-to-own-golden-moments-of-stars-1.82583202, accessed 27 Oct. 2021.

591. "Is Artificial Intelligence Set to Become Art's Next Medium?" *Christies.com*, Christie's International PLC, Groupe Artémis SA, 12 Dec. 2018. www.christies.com/features/A-collaboration-between-two-artists-one-human-one-a-machine-9332-1.aspx, accessed 20 Sept. 2021.

592. Andres Guadamuz, "Can the Monkey Selfie Case Teach Us Anything about Copyright Law?" *WIPO Magazine*, World Intellectual Property Organization, Feb. 2018. www.wipo.int/wipo_magazine/en/2018/01/article_0007.html; Dorothy R. Auth and Howard Wizenfeld, "Can Computer Systems Using Artificial Intelligence Patent Their Own Inventions?" *National Law Review*, National Law Forum LLC, 9 Oct. 2021. www.natlawreview.com/article/can-computer-systems-using-artificial-intelligence-patent-their-own-inventions, accessed 24 Oct. 2021.

593. William K. Kane, Zachary Golda, and William De Sierra-Pambley, "Wyoming Takes the Lead with Decentralized Autonomous Organizations," *Law of the Ledger Blog*, Sheppard, Mullin, Richter, and Hampton LLP, 25 May 2021. www.lawoftheledger.com/2021/05/articles/dao/wyoming-decentralized-autonomous-organizations, accessed 24 Oct. 2021.

594. Katelyn Kraunelis, "Major Collection of the Fall Auction Season to be Recorded with Blockchain Technology," Press Release, *Christies.com*, Christie's International PLC, Groupe Artémis SA, 11 Oct. 2018. www.christies.com/about-us/press-archive/details?PressReleaseID=9160&lid=1; Henri Neuendorf, "Christie's Will Become the First Major Auction House to Use Blockchain in a Sale," *ArtNet.com*, ArtNet Worldwide Corp., 12 Oct. 2018. news.artnet.com/market/christies-artory-blockchain-pilot-1370788; and Artory

Inc., "Engineering Lead / VP of Engineering job," *Lensa.com*, Lensa Inc., 14 July 2021. lensa.com/engineering-lead--vp-of-engineering-jobs/new-york/jd/393af05e327b4ea8471f435dcc9b14ee, accessed 25 Sept. 2021. According to Artory's engineering job description, Artory offers an "Ethereum-backed Registry, private registrations on a permissioned blockchain, and next tokenization of physical assets."

595.　Christie's, "Art+Tech Summit: Exploring Blockchain—Is the Art World Ready for Consensus?" *Christies.com*, Christie's International PLC, Groupe Artémis SA, 17 July 2018. www.christies.com/exhibitions/2018/art-and-tech-summit-exploring-blockchain, accessed 20 Sept. 2021.

596.　Robert Alice, *Block 21* (42.36433° N, -71.26189° E), Lot 433, *Christies.com*, Christie's International PLC, Groupe Artémis SA, closed 6 Oct. 2020. www.christies.com/en/lot/lot-6283759; Avi Salzman, "NFTs Are the Hot Craze in the Art World. Why Auction House Christie's Jumped into This Wild Market," *Barrons.com*, Dow Jones & Company Inc., 21 March 2021. www.barrons.com./articles/nfts-are-the-hot-craze-in-the-art-world-why-auction-house-christies-jumped-into-this-wild-market-51616189052, accessed 20 Sept. 2021.

597.　"Beeple's Opus," *Christies.com*, Christie's International PLC, Groupe Artémis SA, n.d. www.christies.com/features/Monumental-collage-by-Beeple-is-first-purely-digital-artwork-NFT-to-come-to-auction-11510-7.aspx, accessed 20 Sept. 2021.

598.　Helen Holmes, "Net Artist Beeple Just Set a Nifty Gateway Auction Record with Sales of $3.5 Million," *Observer.com*, Observer Holdings LLC, 15 Dec. 2020. observer.com/2020/12/net-artist-beeple-nifty-gateway-auction-record/J, accessed 7 Oct. 2021.

599.　Robert Frank, "Beeple NFT Becomes Most Expensive Ever Sold at Auction after Fetching over $60 Million," *CNBC.com*, NBCUniversal, 11 March 2021. www.cnbc.com/2021/03/11/most-expensive-nft-ever-sold-auctions-for-over-60-million.html; Statista Research Department, "Bidders of the Christie's Auction of *The First 5000 Days* by Beeple 2021, by Region," *Statista.com*, Statista GmbH, 11 May 2021. www.statista.com/statistics/1221556/regional-breakdown-of-bidders-at-christie-s-beeple-auction, accessed 20 Sept. 2021.

600.　Angelica Villa, "Crypto Investor Justin Sun Revealed as Buyer of $20 M. Picasso," *ARTnews.com*, Penske Business Media LLC, 1 April 2021. www.artnews.com/art-news/market/justin-sun-picasso-warhol-christies-buyer-1234588521, accessed 20 Sept. 2021.

601.　"Larva Labs (EST. 2005): Nine CryptoPunks: 2, 532, 58, 30, 635, 602, 768, 603, and 757," *Christies.com*, Christie's International PLC, Groupe

Artémis SA, closed 10 May 2021. www.christies.com/lot/lot-6316969; and Emily Ratajkowski, *Buying Myself Back: A Model for Redistribution*, Lot 213, *Christies.com*, Christie's International PLC, Groupe Artémis SA, closed 13 May 2021. www.christies.com/lot/lot--6317722, accessed 25 Sept. 2021.

602. Elizabeth Howcroft, "'CryptoPunk' NFT Sells for $11.8 Million at Sotheby's," *Reuters.com*, Thomson Reuters, 10 June 2021. www.reuters.com/technology/cryptopunk-nft-sells-118-million-sothebys-2021-06-10; Angelica Villa, "World Wide Web Code NFT Sells for $5.4 M. at Sotheby's Auction," *ARTnews.com*, Penske Business Media LLC, 30 June 2021. www.artnews.com/art-news/market/world-wide-web-code-nft-sale-sothebys-1234597406; and Tommy Beer, "NFTs of Cartoon Apes Sell for over $24 Million in Sotheby's Auction," *Forbes.com*, Forbes Media LLC, last updated 9 Sept. 2021. www.forbes.com/sites/tommybeer/2021/09/09/nfts-of-cartoon-apes-sell-for-over-24-million-in-sothebys-auction/?sh=291d2d9913f9, accessed 19 Sept. 2021.

603. Avi Salzman, "NFTs Are the Hot Craze in the Art World. Why Auction House Christie's Jumped into This Wild Market," *Barrons.com*, Dow Jones & Co. Inc., 21 March 2021. www.barrons.com./articles/nfts-are-the-hot-craze-in-the-art-world-why-auction-house-christies-jumped-into-this-wild-market-51616189052, accessed 20 Sept. 2021.

604. Georgina Adam, "But Is It Legal? The Baffling World of NFT Copyright and Ownership Issues," *TheArtNewpaper.com*, The Art Newspaper Ltd., 6 April 2021. www.theartnewspaper.com/analysis/but-is-it-legal-the-baffling-world-of-nft-copyright-and-ownership-questions, accessed 4 Oct. 2021.

605. Jim Dumont, "First Nations Regional Longitudinal Health Survey (RHS) Cultural Framework," Feb 2005. uploads-ssl.webflow.com/5b786757ee914c5f85ba8959/5b7f15660151a07eacefd2b6_5_developing-a-cultural-framework.pdf, accessed 4 Oct. 2021.

606. "Corporations," *Legal Information Institute*, Cornell Law School, n.d. www.law.cornell.edu/wex/corporations, accessed 26 Sept. 2021.

607. Elinor Ostrom and Charlotte Hess, "Private and Common Property Rights," Bloomington: Indiana Univ. School of Public and Environmental Affairs Research Paper No. 2008-11-01. ssrn.com/abstract=1304699; Maxwell Briskman Stanfield and Michael G. Monyok, "A Primer on NFTs: What Do You Really Own?" *The Legal Intelligencer*, Law.com, ALM Media Properties LLC, 26 May 2021. www.law.com/thelegalintelligencer/2021/05/26/a-primer-on-nfts-what-do-you-really-own/?slreturn=20210925161700; and Bruce Yandle and Andrew P. Morriss, "The Technologies of Property Rights: Choice among Alternative Solutions to Tragedies of the Commons,"

Ecology Law Quarterly, No. 1 (2001): 123–168. JSTOR, www.jstor.org/stable/24114041, accessed 15 Oct. 2021.

608. Emily Ratajkowski, "Buying Myself Back, When Does a Model Own Her Own Image?" *TheCut.com*, Vox Media LLC., 15 Sept. 2020. www.thecut.com/article/emily-ratajkowski-owning-my-image-essay.html, accessed 14 Oct. 2021.

609. Emily Ratajkowski, "Buying Myself Back, When Does a Model Own Her Own Image?"

610. "What Is IPFS?" *IPFS.io*, InterPlanetary File System, Protocol Labs Inc., last updated 22 June 2021. docs.ipfs.io/concepts/what-is-ipfs, accessed 5 Oct. 2021.

611. Cameron Hejazi, interviewed via mobile/video call by Alan Majer, 4 May 2021.

612. Irving Wladawsky-Berger, interviewed via mobile/video call by Alan Majer, 15 April 2021.

613. Mike Winkelmann, "Beeple on How and Why He Raked in $3.5 Million," interview by Laura Shin, Ep.156, *Unchained Podcast*, YouTube.com, 32:05, 18 Dec. 2020. www.youtube.com/watch?v=3DM3o5GJ3EI, accessed 18 Oct. 2021.

614. Mike Winkelmann, "Beeple on How and Why He Raked in $3.5 Million."

615. Taylor Locke, "Jack Dorsey Sells His First Tweet Ever as an NFT for over $2.9 Million," *Make It CNBC.com*, NBC Universal, 22 March 2021, last updated 24 March 2021. www.cnbc.com/2021/03/22/jack-dorsey-sells-his-first-tweet-ever-as-an-nft-for-over-2point9-million.html; Jack Dorsey (@Jack), *Twitter.com*, Twitter Inc., 21 March 2006 (3:50 PM). Valuables by Cent, v.cent.co/tweet/20, accessed 4 Oct. 2021.

616. Cameron Hejazi, interviewed via mobile/video call by Alan Majer, 4 May 2021.

617. B. Joseph Pine II (@joepine), *Twitter.com*, Twitter Inc., 9 July 2021 (11:53 AM). twitter.com/joepine/status/1413526791902441472; and B. Joseph Pine II and James H. Gilmore, "Welcome to the Experience Economy," *Harvard Business Review* (July–Aug. 1998). Harvard Business School Publishing Corp., hbr.org/1998/07/welcome-to-the-experience-economy, accessed 4 Oct. 2021.

618. Irving Wladawsky-Berger, interviewed via mobile/video call by Alan Majer, 15 April 2021.

619. Bharggavi Ssayee, "Glenfiddich to Launch Rare Whiskey NFT at $18,000," *International Business Times Australia*, IBTimes LLC, 18 Oct. 2021. www.ibtimes.com/glenfiddich-launch-rare-whiskey-nft-18000-3318621, accessed 27 Oct. 2021.

620. Cameron Hejazi, interviewed via mobile/video call by Alan Majer, 4 May 2021.

621. Cameron Hejazi, interviewed via mobile/video call by Alan Majer, 4 May 2021.

622. Karl Schroeder, interviewed via mobile/video call by Alan Majer, 27 May 2021.

623. Karl Schroeder, interviewed via mobile/video call by Alan Majer, 27 May 2021.

624. Karl Schroeder, interviewed via mobile/video call by Alan Majer, 27 May 2021.

625. Karl Schroeder, interviewed via mobile/video call by Alan Majer, 27 May 2021.

626. Satoshi Nakamoto, "Re: Bitcoin v0.1 Released," *Mail-Archive.com*, The Mail Archive, 11 Jan. 2009. www.mail-archive.com/cryptography@metzdowd.com/msg10162.html, accessed 4 Oct. 2021.

627. Karl Schroeder, "The Suicide of Our Troubles," *Slate.com*, Slate Group LLC, 28 Nov. 2020. slate.com/technology/2020/11/karl-schroeder-suicide-of-our-troubles.html, accessed 20 Sept. 2021.

628. Andrew Goldman, "A Man Known as Beeple Made $3.5 Million Selling His Digital Art in a Weekend," *Wealthsimple Magazine*, Wealthsimple Technologies Inc., 26 Jan. 2021. www.wealthsimple.com/en-ca/magazine/beeple, accessed 24 Oct. 2021.

629. Robert K. Merton, "The Unanticipated Consequences of Purposive Social Action," *American Sociological Review* 1, No. 6 (Dec. 1936): 894–904. www.suz.uzh.ch/dam/jcr:00000000-7fb2-5367-0000-0000522e4c47/03.14_merton_unanticipated_consequences.pdf, accessed 4 Oct. 2021.

630. Eva R. Porras, *Bubbles and Contagion in Financial Markets: An Integrative View*, vol. 1 (Palgrave Macmillan, Springer Nature, 20 April 2016): 61–63. Google Books, books.google.com/books?id=snyQDAAAQBAJ, accessed 22 Oct. 2021.

631. Cameron Hejazi, interviewed via mobile/video call by Alan Majer, 4 May 2021.

632. See, for example, Selva Ozelli, "Charitable Sustainable NFTs for the United Nations' 17 SDGs," *Cointelegraph.com*, 25 Sept. 2021.

cointelegraph.com/news/charitable-sustainable-nfts-for-the-united-nations-17-sdgs; and Unique Network Ltd., "Unique Network Chosen as Exclusive Blockchain Partner for United Nations Associated NFT Climate Initiative," Press Release, *GlobeNewswire.com*, Intrado Corp., 3 Aug. 2021. www.globenewswire.com/en/news-release/2021/08/03/2273966/0/en/Unique-Network-Chosen-As-Exclusive-Blockchain-Partner-for-United-Nations-Associated-NFT-Climate-Initiative.html, accessed 24 Oct. 2021.

633. "Coca-Cola to Offer First-Ever NFT Collectibles in International Friendship Day Charity Auction," News, Coca-Cola Company, 28 July 2021. www.coca-colacompany.com/news/coca-cola-to-offer-first-ever-nft-collectibles, accessed 18 Oct. 2021.

634. "Coca-Cola NFT Auction Fetches More than $575,000," News, Coca-Cola Company, 5 Aug. 2021. www.coca-colacompany.com/news/coca-cola-nft-auction-fetches-more-than-575000, accessed 18 Oct. 2021.

635. "Campbell's Commissions First Official NFT Collection by Artist Sophia Chang to Celebrate Changes to Its Iconic Soup Can Labels," Press Release, Campbell Soup Co., 27 July 2021. www.campbellsoupcompany.com/newsroom/press-releases/campbells-commissions-first-official-nft-collection-by-artist-sophia-chang-to-celebrate-changes-to-its-iconic-soup-can-labels, accessed 27 Oct. 2021.

636. Marty Swant, "World's Most Influential CMOs 2021," *Forbes.com*, Forbes Media LLC, 29 Sept. 2021. www.forbes.com/sites/martyswant/2021/09/29/worlds-most-influential-cmos-2021, accessed 27 Oct. 2021.

637. "The Crockpot Brand Auctioning First-ever NFT to Celebrate its 50th Anniversary," *Contify Retail News*, 14 Oct. 2021. www.prnewswire.com/news-releases/the-crockpot-brand-auctioning-first-ever-nft-to-celebrate-its-50th-anniversary-301399827.html, accessed 27 Oct. 2021.

638. Carly McCrory, "Everything Marketers Need to Know about NFTs," *Newstex Blogs*, Business2Community.com, 4 Oct. 2021. www.business2community.com/marketing/everything-marketers-need-to-know-about-nfts-02434331, accessed 27 Oct. 2021.

639. Cameron Hejazi, interviewed via mobile/video call by Alan Majer, 4 May 2021.

640. Cameron Hejazi, interviewed via mobile/video call by Alan Majer, 4 May 2021.

641. Eric Limer, "Is It Possible to Build Your Own iPhone from Spare Parts?" *Popular Mechanics*, Hearst Magazine Media Inc., 13 April 2017. www.popularmechanics.com/technology/gadgets/a26047/build-iphone-spare-parts, accessed 4 Oct. 2021.

642. For more on each of these innovations, please see "The Factory," Eli
Whitney Museum, n.d. www.eliwhitney.org/7/museum/about-eli-
whitney/factory; Steve C. Gordon, "From Slaughterhouse to Soap-Boiler:
Cincinnati's Meat Packing Industry, Changing Technologies, and the
Rise of Mass Production, 1825–1870," *Journal of the Society for Industrial
Archeology* 16, no. 1 (1990): 55–67. www.jstor.org/stable/40968184; Phil
Ament, "Assembly Line," *Great Idea Finder*, 16 May 2005. Wayback
Machine, web.archive.org/web/20190913080810/http://www.ideafinder.
com/history/inventions/assbline.htm; "Ford Installs First Moving
Assembly Line, 1913," People and Discoveries Databank, *WGBH.
org*, WGBH Educational Foundation, archived 14 Sept. 2019. www.
pbs.org/wgbh/aso/databank/entries/dt13as.html; Erick Schonfeld,
"The Customized, Digitized, Have-It-Your-Way Economy: Mass
Customization Will Change the Way Products Are Made—Forever,"
Fortune Magazine, CNN Money, Cable News Network, 28 Sept. 1998.
money.cnn.com/magazines/fortune/fortune_archive/1998/09/28/248738;
B. Joseph Pine II, Bart Victor, and Andrew C. Boynton, "Making Mass
Customization Work," *Harvard Business Review* (Sept.–Oct. 1993).
HBS Publishing Corp., hbr.org/1993/09/making-mass-customization-
work; James H. Gilmore and B. Joseph Pine II, "The Four Faces of
Mass Customization," *Harvard Business Review* (Jan.–Feb. 1997).
HBS Publishing Corp., hbr.org/1997/01/the-four-faces-of-mass-
customization; and Terry Wohlers and Tim Gornet, "History of Additive
Manufacturing," *Wohlers Report 2014*, Wohler Associates Inc., last
modified 1 May 2014. www.wohlersassociates.com/history2014.pdf, all
accessed 18 Sept. 2021.

643. B. Joseph Pine II, *Mass Customization: The New Frontier in Business
Competition*, foreword by Stan Davis (Cambridge, MA: HBR Press,
1992): frontmatter. www.amazon.com/Mass-Customization-Frontier-
Business-Competition/dp/0875843727, accessed 22 Oct. 2021.

644. Engineering Department, "Why Are Tolerances Important in
Manufacturing?" *Manufacturing Blog*, Pacific Research Labs Inc.,
n.d. www.pacific-research.com/why-are-tolerances-important-in-
manufacturing-prl; PCB Design Solutions, "How Do Manufacturing
Tolerances Work?" *OrCAD Blog*, Cadence Design Systems Inc., 7 May
2018. resources.orcad.com/orcad-blog/how-do-manufacturing-
tolerances-work, accessed 24 Oct. 2021.

645. "Organic vs. Conventional Farming," Rodale Institute, n.d.
rodaleinstitute.org/why-organic/organic-basics/organic-vs-conventional,
accessed 26 Sept. 2021.

646. Emma Weston, interviewed via mobile/video call by Alan Majer,
13 April 2021.

647. Witek Radomski et al., "EIP-1155: Multi Token Standard," Ethereum Improvement Proposals, no. 1155, June 2018. eips.ethereum.org/EIPS/eip-1155, accessed 4 Oct. 2021.

648. "Five Things: Additive Manufacturing," *Assembly Magazine*, BNP Media Inc., 5 Aug. 2021. www.assemblymag.com/articles/96533-five-things-additive-manufacturing; Little You by Sheloo Inc., n.d. www.littleyou.ca; and "The Future of Fashion: From Design to Merchandising, How Tech Is Reshaping the Industry," *CBInsights.com*, CB Information Services Inc., 11 May 2021. www.cbinsights.com/research/fashion-tech-future-trends, accessed 24 Oct. 2021.

649. Misha Kahn, "'I Wanted to Push the Idea of Furniture'—Misha Kahn on Creating the First Design NFT," interviewed by Nick Haramis, *Christies.com*, Christie's International PLC, Groupe Artémis SA, 14 Aug. 2021. www.christies.com/features/Misha-kahn-on-the-first-design-nft-11795-1.aspx, accessed 25 Oct. 2021.

650. Mike Ives, "The COVID Crisis Is Now a Garbage Crisis, Too," *NYTimes.com*, New York Times Co., 18 Sept. 2021, updated 24 Sept. 2021. www.nytimes.com/2021/09/18/world/covid-trash-recycling.html, accessed 25 Oct. 2021.

651. Misha Kahn, "'I Wanted to Push the Idea of Furniture'—Misha Kahn on Creating the First Design NFT."

652. Witek Radomski et al., "EIP-1155: Multi Token Standard," Ethereum Improvement Proposals, no. 1155, June 2018. eips.ethereum.org/EIPS/eip-1155, accessed 4 Oct. 2021.

653. John Adams, "Visa, Mastercard, and Ripple Plant Flags in the NFT Market," *American Banker* 186, No. 196, SourceMedia LLC, 13 Oct. 2021. www.americanbanker.com/payments/news/visa-mastercard-and-ripple-plant-flags-in-the-nft-market, accessed 27 Oct. 2021.

654. David Piesse, "De-Risking the Supply Chain with Blockchain Technology and Data Integrity," *IIS Executive Insights Blog*, International Insurance Society, 10 June 2021. www.internationalinsurance.org/de-risking-supply-chain-blockchaintechnology-and-data-integrity, accessed 24 Oct. 2021.

655. "System and Method for Providing Cryptographically Secured Digital Assets," US10505726B1, *Google Patents*, Google.com, n.d. patents.google.com/patent/US10505726B1, accessed 10 Oct. 2021.

656. David Boag and Jodee Rich, "Nike's Dec 2019 Patent Reveals Revolutionary NFT Use," *NFT.NYC*, PeopleBrowsr.com Inc., 9 Feb. 2020. nftnyc.medium.com/nikes-dec-2019-patent-reveals-revolutionary-nft-use-a74c115bd0c, accessed 4 Oct. 2021.

657. Jim Motavalli, "NFTs Are Popping Up in the Automotive Space—and Why This Is Exciting," *Autoweek.com*, Hearst Autos Inc., 15 June 2021. www.autoweek.com/news/a36730311/barrett-jackson-nft-auction, accessed 4 Oct. 2021.

658. Mo Al-Bodour, "Can Automakers Use NFTs to Create Their Own Ecosystems?" *LinkedIn.com*, Microsoft Corp., 12 March 2021. www. linkedin.com/pulse/can-automakers-use-nfts-create-own-ecosystems-mo-al-bodour.

659. Phil Windley, "NFTs, Verifiable Credentials, and Picos," *Technometria Blog*, PJW LC, 11 Oct. 2021. www.windley.com/archives/2021/10/nfts verifiable credentials and picos.shtml, accessed 24 Oct. 2021.

660. David Gogel, "DeFi Beyond the Hype: The Emerging World of Decentralized Finance," Wharton Blockchain and Digital Asset Project, Univ. of Pennsylvania, and World Economic Forum, May 2021. wifpr. wharton.upenn.edu/wp-content/uploads/2021/05/DeFi-Beyond-the-Hype.pdf, accessed 24 Oct. 2021.

661. Kevin Werbach, "DeFi Is the Next Frontier for Fintech Regulation," *The Regulatory Review*, Penn Program on Regulation, University of Pennsylvania Law School, 28 April 2021. www.theregreview.org/2021/04 /28/werbach-defi-next-frontier-fintech-regulation, accessed 24 Oct. 2021.

662. See Jeremy Goldman, "A Primer on NFTs and Intellectual Property," *IP and Media Law Updates*, Frankfurt Kurnit Klein & Selz PC, 11 March 2021. ipandmedialaw.fkks.com/post/102gt4b/a-primer-on-nfts-and-intellectual-property.

663. Veronica Combs, "IBM and IPwe Want to Issue Patents as NFTs and Make Them Easier to Monetize," *TechRepublic.com*, TechnologyAdvice LLC, 21 April 2021. www.techrepublic.com/article/ibm-and-ipwe-want-to-issue-patents-as-nfts-and-make-them-easier-to-monetize, accessed 24 Oct. 2021.

664. "Traditional Knowledge," *WIPO.int*, World Intellectual Property Organization, 5 Nov. 2021. www.wipo.int/tk/en/tk; see also WIPO Secretariat, "List and Brief Technical Explanation of Various Forms in Which Traditional Knowledge May Be Found," WIPO/GRTKF/IC/17/ INF/9, Intergovernmental Committee on Intellectual Property and Genetic Resources, Traditional Knowledge, and Folklore, 17th Session, 6–10 Dec. 2010. www.wipo.int/edocs/mdocs/tk/en/wipo grtkf ic 17/ wipo grtkf ic 17 inf 9.pdf, accessed 24 Oct. 2021.

665. Natalia Karayaneva, "NFTs Work for Digital Art. They Also Work Perfectly for Real Estate," *Forbes.com*, Forbes Media LLC, 8 April 2021. www.forbes.com/sites/nataliakarayaneva/2021/04/08/nfts-work-for-digital-art-they-also-work-perfectly-for-real-estate, accessed 4 Oct. 2021.

666. SEC = Securities and Exchange Commission, CFTC = Commodity Futures Trading Commission, and IRS = Internal Revenue Service. Brian Armstrong (@brian_armstrong), *Twitter.com*, Twitter Inc., 14 May 2021 (10:06 PM). twitter.com/brian_armstrong/status/1393387280337801216, accessed 4 Oct. 2021.

667. Courtney Rogers Perrin, "We Knew It Was Coming: The First NFT Lawsuit Is Here," *Blockchain and Banking Blog*, Frost Brown Todd LLC, 9 June 2021. frostbrowntodd.com/we-knew-it-was-coming-the-first-nft-lawsuit-is-here, accessed 24 Oct. 2021. See also *Friel et al. v. Dapper Labs Inc. and Gharegozlou*, New York County Clerk Index No. 653134/2021, 13 May 2021. iapps.courts.state.ny.us/fbem//DocumentDisplayServlet ?documentId=0gfOgjsIUYbTc7Cxd2cGCw==&system=prod, accessed 24 Oct. 2021.

668. Krista Kim, "Mars House," *SuperRare.com*, SuperRare Labs Inc., last updated 13 Sept. 2021. superrare.com/artwork-v2/mars-house-21383, accessed 4 Oct. 2021.

669. Tom Ravenscroft, "Dispute Breaks Out Over Ownership of World's First NFT House," *Deezen.com*, Dezeen Ltd., 26 March 2021. www.dezeen.com /2021/03/26/mars-house-fraud-3d-visualiser-nft, accessed 24 Oct. 2021.

670. Katya Fisher, "Once Upon a Time in NFT: Blockchain, Copyright and the Right of First Sale Doctrine," *Cardozo Arts and Entertainment Law Journal*, Yeshiva University, March 2019. www.cardozoaelj.com/ wp-content/uploads/2019/03/Fisher-Once-Upon-a-Time-in-NFT.pdf, accessed 4 Oct. 2021.

671. Jennifer English, Toby Futter, David Grable, Emily Kapur, Luke Nikas, and Robert Schwartz, "NFTs: Legal Risks from 'Minting' Art and Collectibles on Blockchain," *JDSupra.com*, JD Supra LLC, 25 March 2021. www.jdsupra.com/legalnews/nfts-legal-risks-from-minting-art-and-4997056, accessed 4 Oct. 2021.

672. Andrew James Lom, Rachael Browndorf, and James Larkin Smith, "Anatomy of an NFT," *Norton Rose Fulbright*, Norton Rose Fulbright Verein, April 2021. www.nortonrosefulbright.com/en-us/knowledge/ publications/5995f99d/anatomy-of-an-nft, accessed 7 Oct. 2021.

673. See this excellent overview of subsidiary rights: Brandon J. Huffman, "What Are Subsidiary Rights in a Literary Publishing Agreement?" *OdinLaw.com*, Odin Law and Media, 30 Nov. 2017. odinlaw.com/ subsidiary-rights-literary-publishing-agreement; and Mindy Klasky, "A Contract Primer: Subsidiary Rights," *MindyKlasky.com*, Jan. 2011. www. mindyklasky.com/index.php/for-writers/writing-toolkit/a-contract-primer-subsidiary-rights, accessed 7 Oct. 2021.

674. Susan Spann, "Merchandising Rights in Publishing Deals," *Writers in the Storm Blog*, 8 April 2016. writersinthestormblog.com/2016/04/merchandising-rights-in-publishing-deals, accessed 24 Oct. 2021.

675. Osato Avan-Nomayo, "MakerDAO Takes New Measures to Prevent Another 'Black Swan' Collapse," *Cointelegraph.com*, 4 May 2020. cointelegraph.com/news/makerdao-takes-new-measures-to-prevent-another-black-swan-collapse, accessed 24 Oct. 2021.

676. Benjamin Powers, "Lessons from the Nifty Gateway NFT Heist: Not Your Keys, Not Your Art," *CoinDesk*, Digital Currency Group, 17 March 2021, last updated 24 Sept. 2021. www.coindesk.com/nifty-gateway-nft-hack-lessons, accessed 24 Oct. 2021.

677. Overview, "Andy Warhol: Machine Made," *Christies.com*, Christie's International PLC, Groupe Artémis SA, 27 May 2021. onlineonly.christies.com/s/andy-warhol-machine-made/overview/2051; and Angelica Villa, "Christie's Auction of Warhol NFTs Raises Questions of Authenticity among Experts," *ARTnews.com*, Penske Business Media LLC, 21 May 2021. www.artnews.com/art-news/market/christies-warhol-nfts-1980s-amiga-sale-1234593542, accessed 24 Oct. 2021.

678. Overview, "Andy Warhol: Machine Made," *Christies.com*, Christie's International PLC, Groupe Artémis SA, 27 May 2021. onlineonly.christies.com/s/andy-warhol-machine-made/overview/2051, accessed 24 Oct. 2021.

679. Scott Galloway, "What Might Bowie Have Done with Crypto?" *Medium.com*, 30 April 2021. marker.medium.com/what-might-bowie-have-done-with-crypto-b529758a89bf, accessed 26 Oct. 2021.

680. Don Tapscott and Alex Tapscott, *Blockchain Revolution: How the Technology Behind Bitcoin and Other Cryptocurrencies Is Changing the World* (New York: Penguin Portfolio, 2018). www.amazon.com/Blockchain-Revolution-Technology-Cryptocurrencies-Changing-dp-1101980141/dp/1101980141, accessed 6 Sept. 2020.

681. *Financial Services Revolution: How Blockchain Is Transforming Money, Markets, and Banking*, edited with preface by Alex Tapscott (Toronto: Blockchain Research Institute/Barlow Book Publishing, 5 Feb. 2020). www.amazon.com/Financial-Services-Revolution-Blockchain-Transforming/dp/1988025494, accessed 2 June 2020.

682. Alex Tapscott, "The Blockchain Revolution," *Talks at GS*, inter. Tom Jessop, Goldman Sachs, New York, 12 July 2016 (00:07:47). www.goldmansachs.com/insights/talks-at-gs/alex-tapscott.html, accessed 6 Nov. 2021.

683. The Tapscott Group d/b/a Blockchain Research Institute, n.d. www.blockchainresearchinstitute.org.

INDEX